CAPITAL PUNISHMENT
CRUEL AND UNUSUAL?

ISSN 1538-6678

CAPITAL PUNISHMENT
CRUEL AND UNUSUAL?

Kim Masters Evans

INFORMATION PLUS® REFERENCE SERIES
Formerly Published by Information Plus, Wylie, Texas

GALE
CENGAGE Learning·

Detroit • New York • San Francisco • New Haven, Conn • Waterville, Maine • London

GALE
CENGAGE Learning®

Capital Punishment: Cruel and Unusual?

Kim Masters Evans

Kepos Media, Inc.: Paula Kepos and Janice Jorgensen, Series Editors

Project Editors: Elizabeth Manar, Kathleen J. Edgar, Kimberley McGrath

Rights Acquisition and Management: Leitha Etheridge-Sims, Jackie Jones, Kimberly Potvin

Composition: Evi Abou-El-Seoud, Mary Beth Trimper

Manufacturing: Cynde Lentz

Cover photograph: Image copyright Kim Seidl, 2011. Used under license from Shutterstock.com.

While every effort has been made to ensure the reliability of the information presented in this publication, Gale, a part of Cengage Learning, does not guarantee the accuracy of the data contained herein. Gale accepts no payment for listing; and inclusion in the publication of any organization, agency, institution, publication, service, or individual does not imply endorsement of the editors or publisher. Errors brought to the attention of the publisher and verified to the satisfaction of the publisher will be corrected in future editions.

Gale
27500 Drake Rd.
Farmington Hills, MI 48331-3535

ISBN-13: 978-0-7876-5103-9 (set)   ISBN-10: 0-7876-5103-6 (set)
ISBN-13: 978-1-4144-8134-0   ISBN-10: 1-4144-8134-9

ISSN 1538-6678

This title is also available as an e-book.
ISBN-13: 978-1-4144-9632-0 (set)
ISBN-10: 1-4144-9632-X (set)
Contact your Gale sales representative for ordering information.

Printed in the United States of America
1 2 3 4 5 6 7 16 15 14 13 12

TABLE OF CONTENTS

opposing the death penalty, the rate of imposition, fairness of the death penalty, the death penalty as a deterrent, and the likelihood that an innocent person has been convicted of murder or executed.

CHAPTER 10

An international consideration of the death penalty is offered in this chapter. Information includes United Nations resolutions regarding capital punishment, statistics on countries that have retained capital punishment and those that have abolished it, rulings on U.S. death penalty cases by the International Court of Justice, and international public opinion polls on the death penalty.

CHAPTER 11

This chapter contains statements that have been made in support of capital punishment by Anne Rossi (the wife of a murder victim), State Representative Steven T. Mikutel of the Connecticut House of Representatives, Robert Blecker (a law professor), John C. Kissinger Jr. (a member of the Commission to Study the Death Penalty in New Hampshire), and Justice Clarence Thomas of the U.S. Supreme Court.

CHAPTER 12

This chapter contains statements that have been made in favor of abolishing capital punishment by Ray Krone (a former death row inmate exonerated of murder), State Senator Martin M. Looney of the Connecticut Senate, the Yale University Chapter of Amnesty International, Renny Cushing (the son of a murder victim), and former Justice John Paul Stevens of the U.S. Supreme Court.

PREFACE

Capital Punishment: Cruel and Unusual? is part of the *Information Plus Reference Series*. The purpose of each volume of the series is to present the latest facts on a topic of pressing concern in modern American life. These topics include the most controversial and studied social issues of the 21st century: abortion, care for senior citizens, crime, education, the environment, health care, immigration, minorities, national security, social welfare, sports, women, youth, and many more. Even though this series is written especially for high school and undergraduate students, it is an excellent resource for anyone in need of factual information on current affairs.

By presenting the facts, it is the intention of Gale, Cengage Learning to provide its readers with everything they need to reach an informed opinion on current issues. To that end, there is a particular emphasis in this series on the presentation of scientific studies, surveys, and statistics. These data are generally presented in the form of tables, charts, and other graphics placed within the text of each book. Every graphic is directly referred to and carefully explained in the text. The source of each graphic is presented within the graphic itself. The data used in these graphics are drawn from the most reputable and reliable sources, such as from the various branches of the U.S. government and from private organizations and associations. Every effort has been made to secure the most recent information available. Readers should bear in mind that many major studies take years to conduct and that additional years often pass before the data from these studies are made available to the public. Therefore, in many cases the most recent information available in 2012 is dated from 2009 or 2010. Older statistics are sometimes presented as well if they are landmark studies or of particular interest and no more-recent information exists.

Even though statistics are a major focus of the *Information Plus Reference Series*, they are by no means its only content. Each book also presents the widely held positions and important ideas that shape how the book's subject is discussed in the United States. These positions are explained in detail and, where possible, in the words of their proponents. Some of the other material to be found in these books includes historical background, descriptions of major events related to the subject, relevant laws and court cases, and examples of how these issues play out in American life. Some books also feature primary documents or have pro and con debate sections that provide the words and opinions of prominent Americans on both sides of a controversial topic. All material is presented in an evenhanded and unbiased manner; readers will never be encouraged to accept one view of an issue over another.

HOW TO USE THIS BOOK

Few topics are as controversial as capital punishment. Capital punishment has been debated in the United States since the colonial period and is currently a worldwide issue. This book includes the history of capital punishment plus discussions of numerous court cases, legal decisions, and historical statistics. Also included is information about execution methods, minors and the death penalty, public attitudes, and capital punishment around the world.

Capital Punishment: Cruel and Unusual? consists of 12 chapters and three appendixes. Each chapter is devoted to a particular aspect of capital punishment. For a summary of the information that is covered in each chapter, please see the synopses provided in the Table of Contents. Chapters generally begin with an overview of the basic facts and background information on the chapter's topic, then proceed to examine subtopics of particular interest. For example, Chapter 7: Issues of Fairness discusses issues that death penalty opponents commonly raise as evidence that the death penalty is applied unfairly. These issues include geographic disparities, racial bias, and the quality of legal representation. There are certainly geographic differences—both between death penalty states and within these states—in how often the death penalty is prescribed. Analysts, however, attribute these differences to varying death penalty laws between states and to variations in local attitudes regarding crime and punishment. This chapter also describes numerous studies that indicate a race-of-victim bias in death penalty cases, chiefly that the murderers of white victims are more likely to receive the death penalty than the murderers of African-American victims. Death penalty advocates argue that if such an imbalance does exist it should be remedied by applying capital punishment more often in cases involving African-American victims. Lastly, this chapter examines claims that indigent (poor) defendants receive poor legal representation during death penalty trials. Readers can find their way through a chapter by looking for the section and subsection headings, which are clearly set off from the text. They can also refer to the book's extensive Index if they already know what they are looking for.

Statistical Information

The tables and figures featured throughout *Capital Punishment: Cruel and Unusual?* will be of particular use to readers in learning about this issue. The tables and figures represent an extensive collection of the most recent and important statistics on capital punishment and related issues—for example, graphics cover jurisdictions with and without the death penalty; public opinion concerning capital punishment; capital offenses by state; federal laws that provide for the death penalty; demographic characteristics of prisoners under the sentence of death; and the number of executions and the methods of execution used by each state. Gale, Cengage Learning believes that making this information available to readers is the most important way to fulfill the goal of this book: to help readers understand the issues and controversies surrounding capital punishment in the United States and to reach their own conclusions about them.

Each table or figure has a unique identifier appearing above it for ease of identification and reference. Titles for the tables and figures explain their purpose. At the end of each table or figure, the original source of the data is provided.

To help readers understand these often complicated statistics, all tables and figures are explained in the text. References in the text direct readers to the relevant statistics. Furthermore, the contents of all tables and figures are fully indexed. Please see the opening section of the Index at the back of this volume for a description of how to find tables and figures within it.

Appendixes

Besides the main body text and images, *Capital Punishment: Cruel and Unusual?* has three appendixes. The first is the Important Names and Addresses directory. Here, readers will find contact information for a number of government and private organizations that can provide further information on aspects of capital punishment. The second appendix is the Resources section, which can also assist readers in conducting their own research. In this section the author and editors of *Capital Punishment: Cruel and Unusual?* describe some of the sources that were most useful during the compilation of this book. The final appendix is the detailed Index. It has been greatly expanded from previous editions and should make it even easier to find specific topics in this book.

ADVISORY BOARD CONTRIBUTIONS

The staff of Information Plus would like to extend its heartfelt appreciation to the Information Plus Advisory Board. This dedicated group of media professionals provides feedback on the series on an ongoing basis. Their comments allow the editorial staff who work on the project to continually make the series better and more user-friendly. The staff's top priority is to produce the highest-quality and most useful books possible, and the Information Plus Advisory Board's contributions to this process are invaluable.

The members of the Information Plus Advisory Board are:

- Kathleen R. Bonn, Librarian, Newbury Park High School, Newbury Park, California

- Madelyn Garner, Librarian, San Jacinto College, North Campus, Houston, Texas

- Anne Oxenrider, Media Specialist, Dundee High School, Dundee, Michigan

- Charles R. Rodgers, Director of Libraries, Pasco-Hernando Community College, Dade City, Florida

- James N. Zitzelsberger, Library Media Department Chairman, Oshkosh West High School, Oshkosh, Wisconsin

COMMENTS AND SUGGESTIONS

The editors of the *Information Plus Reference Series* welcome your feedback on *Capital Punishment: Cruel and Unusual?* Please direct all correspondence to:

Editors
Information Plus Reference Series
27500 Drake Rd.
Farmington Hills, MI 48331-3535

CHAPTER 1

A CONTINUING CONFLICT: A HISTORY OF CAPITAL PUNISHMENT IN THE UNITED STATES

Capital punishment is the ultimate punishment—death—administered by the government for the commission of serious crimes. The word *capital* comes from the Latin word *capitalis*, meaning "of the head." Throughout history societies have considered some crimes so appalling that the death penalty has been prescribed for them. Over time, changing moral values and ideas about government power have limited the number and types of offenses deemed worthy of death. Many countries have eliminated capital punishment completely, dismissing it as an inhumane response to criminal behavior. The United States is one of only a handful of modern societies that still administers the death penalty. This distinction from the United States' peers is not easily explainable. It arises from a complicated mix of social, legal, and political factors that shape American ideas about justice and the role of government in matters of law and order. Figure 1.1 shows the number of inmates under sentence of death in the United States between 1953 and 2009. The number skyrocketed during the 1980s and 1990s before leveling off around the turn of the 21st century and then declining over the following decade. Just over 3,000 inmates were under sentence of death at the end of 2009.

Capital punishment enjoys popular support in the United States. Figure 1.2 shows the results of a poll that was conducted in October 2010 by the Gallup Organization. Nearly two-thirds (64%) of respondents at that time favored the death penalty for a person convicted of murder, compared with 29% who opposed it. In spite of the overwhelming support, the topic is rife with controversy. Proponents and opponents of the death penalty are passionate in their beliefs. People on both sides of the debate often use philosophical, moral, and religious reasoning to justify their positions. This makes capital punishment a highly charged issue in which emotional opinions can outweigh all other arguments.

The U.S. system of governance is based on the separation of federal and state powers. This means that individual states decide for themselves if they want to practice capital punishment. As of July 2011, the death penalty was approved by the statutes of the federal government (including the U.S. military) and 34 states. (See Table 1.1.) The other 16 states (plus the District of Columbia) that did not have the death penalty are listed in Table 1.2. The legality of capital punishment has historically hinged on the interpretation of the short, but monumental, statement that composes the Eighth Amendment to the U.S. Constitution: "Excessive bail shall not be required, nor excessive fines imposed, nor cruel and unusual punishments inflicted." Is capital punishment cruel and unusual or not? American society has struggled with this question since the founding of the nation and continues to do so in the 21st century.

THE COLONIAL PERIOD

Since the first European settlers arrived in North America, the death penalty has been accepted as just punishment for a variety of offenses. In fact, the earliest recorded execution occurred in 1608, only a year after the English constructed their first settlement in Jamestown, Virginia. Captain George Kendall, one of the original leaders of the Virginia colony, was convicted of mutiny by a jury of his peers and sentenced to death by shooting in Jamestown. In 1632 Jane Champion, a slave, became the first woman to be put to death in the new colonies. She was hanged in James City, Virginia, for the murders of her master's children.

According to *Society's Final Solution: A History and Discussion of the Death Penalty* (Laura E. Randa, ed., 1997), capital law in the early colonies was based on English law, which prescribed the death penalty for hundreds of crimes by the 1700s. Actual practice, however, varied from colony to colony. The Quakers, who settled in the mid-Atlantic region, initially adopted much milder laws than those who settled in the Massachusetts, New York, and Virginia colonies.

FIGURE 1.1

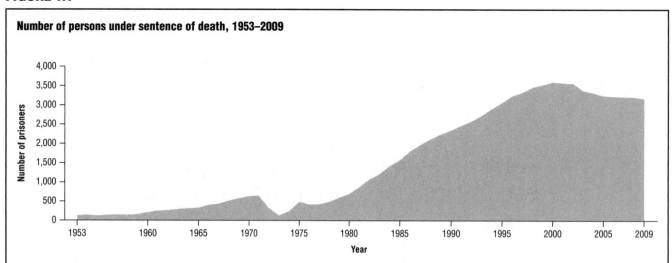

Number of persons under sentence of death, 1953–2009

SOURCE: Tracy L. Snell, "Figure 1. Number of Persons under Sentence of Death in the United States, 1953–2009," in *Capital Punishment, 2009—Statistical Tables*, U.S. Department of Justice, Office of Justice Programs, Bureau of Justice Statistics, December 2010, http://bjs.ojp.usdoj.gov/content/pub/pdf/cp09st.pdf (accessed July 5, 2011)

FIGURE 1.2

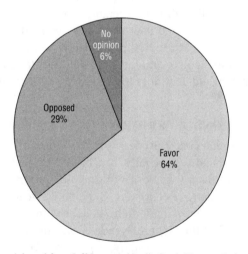

Public opinion poll on the death penalty, October 2010

ARE YOU IN FAVOR OF THE DEATH PENALTY FOR A PERSON CONVICTED OF MURDER?

SOURCE: Adapted from Jeff Jones and Lydia Saad, "Are you in favor of the death penalty for a person convicted of murder?" in *Gallup Poll Social Series: Crime—Final Topline*, The Gallup Organization, October 7–10, 2010, http://www.gallup.com/poll/File/144278/Death_Penalty_Nov_8_2010.pdf (accessed July 4, 2011). Copyright © 2011 by the Gallup Organization. Reproduced by permission of The Gallup Organization.

TABLE 1.1

States with the death penalty, July 2011

Alabama	Maryland	Tennessee
Arizona	Mississippi	Texas
Arkansas	Missouri	Utah
California	Montana	Virginia
Colorado	Nebraska	Washington
Connecticut	Nevada	Wyoming
Delaware	New Hampshire	
Florida	North Carolina	-plus
Georgia	Ohio	U.S. Gov't
Idaho	Oklahoma	U.S. Military
Indiana	Oregon	
Kansas	Pennsylvania	
Kentucky	South Carolina	
Louisiana	South Dakota	

SOURCE: "States with the Death Penalty," in *Facts about the Death Penalty*, Death Penalty Information Center, July 19, 2011, http://www.deathpenaltyinfo.org/documents/FactSheet.pdf (accessed July 21, 2011)

"breaking at the wheel," wherein the executioner would snap all the offender's arm and leg joints with a chisel and then weave the extremities through the spokes of a large wheel like meaty ribbons. The prisoner would then be left outside to die of blood loss and exposure.

These executions were held in public as a warning to others, and often a festival atmosphere prevailed. Crowds of onlookers gathered near the gallows, and merchants sold souvenirs. Some spectators got drunk, turning unruly and sometimes violent. After the execution, the body of the convict was sometimes left hanging above the square in a metal cage.

David G. Chardavoyne describes a typical 19th-century execution scene in *A Hanging in Detroit: Stephen Gifford Simmons and the Last Execution under Michigan Law*

The methods of execution in the fledgling North American colonies could be especially brutal. M. Watt Espy and John Ortiz Smykla note in *Executions in the United States, 1608–2002: The ESPY File* (2005) that even though hanging was the preferred method, some criminals were burned alive or pressed to death by heavy stones. Probably the cruelest punishment was known as

TABLE 1.2

States without the death penalty, July 2011

Alaska	Minnesota	West Virginia
Hawaii	New Jersey	Wisconsin
Illinois	New Mexico*	
Iowa	New York	-plus
Maine	North Dakota	District of Columbia
Massachusetts	Rhode Island	
Michigan	Vermont	

*Two inmates remain on death row in New Mexico.

SOURCE: "States without the Death Penalty," in *Facts about the Death Penalty*, Death Penalty Information Center, July 19, 2011, http://www.deathpenaltyinfo.org/documents/FactSheet.pdf (accessed July 21, 2011)

(2003). One of only two executions in Michigan before the death penalty was outlawed there in 1846, Simmons was hanged in September 1830 for murdering his pregnant wife. Chardavoyne explains that at the time, "public executions owed much of their continuing legitimacy to the use of ritual." The associated rituals could last for hours and included parading the condemned prisoner through the crowd with a coffin by his side and a noose around his neck, speeches by public officials and religious leaders denouncing the crime, and in some cases a repentance speech by the prisoner.

Over time, the colonies phased out the crueler methods of execution, and almost all death sentences were carried out by hanging. The colonies also rewrote their death penalty statutes to cover only serious crimes involving willful acts of violence or thievery. By the late 1700s typical death penalty crimes included arson, piracy, treason, murder, and horse stealing. Southern colonies executed people for slave stealing or aiding in a slave revolt. After the American Revolution (1775–1783), some states went further by adopting death penalty statutes similar to those of Pennsylvania, which in 1682 had limited its death penalty to treason and murder. New York built its first penitentiary in 1796. With a place to house burglars and nonviolent criminals, the state reduced its capital offenses from 13 to two. Other states followed suit by constructing large jails and cutting their capital offenses to just a few of the worst crimes.

THE DEATH PENALTY ABOLITION MOVEMENT

Even though the founders of the United States generally accepted the death penalty, many early Americans did oppose capital punishment. During the late 18th century Benjamin Rush (1746–1813), a physician who helped establish the slavery abolition movement, decried capital punishment. He attracted the support of Benjamin Franklin (1706–1790), and it was at Franklin's home in Philadelphia, Pennsylvania, that Rush became one of the first Americans to propose a "House of Reform," a prison where criminals could be detained until they changed their antisocial behavior. Consequently, in 1790 the Walnut

Street Jail, the primitive seed from which the U.S. penal system grew, was built in Philadelphia.

Rush published many pamphlets, the most notable of which was *Considerations on the Justice and Policy of Punishing Murder by Death* (1792). He argued that the biblical support given to capital punishment was questionable and that the threat of hanging did not deter crime. Influenced by the philosophy of the Enlightenment (an intellectual movement during the 17th and 18th centuries), Rush believed the state exceeded its granted powers when it executed a citizen. Besides Franklin, Rush attracted many other Pennsylvanians to his cause, including William Bradford (1755–1795), the attorney general of Pennsylvania. Bradford suggested the idea of different degrees of murder, some of which did not warrant the death penalty. As a result, in 1794 Pennsylvania repealed the death penalty for all crimes except for first-degree murder, which was defined as "willful, deliberate, and premeditated killing or murder committed during arson, rape, robbery, or burglary."

The 19th Century

Rush's proposals attracted many followers, and petitions aiming to abolish all capital punishment were presented in New Jersey, New York, Massachusetts, and Ohio. No state reversed its laws, but the number of crimes punishable by death was often reduced.

The second quarter of the 19th century was a time of reform in the United States. Capital punishment opponents rode the tide of righteousness and indignation created by antisaloon and antislavery advocates. Abolitionist societies (organizations against the death penalty) sprang up, especially along the East Coast. In 1845 the American Society for the Abolition of Capital Punishment was founded.

PUBLIC EXECUTIONS ARE PHASED OUT. Prior to the 1830s, executions were mostly public (and festive) events that attracted large and sometimes unruly crowds. Maine outlawed public executions and in 1835 put into effect a temporary moratorium (suspension) of executions after one public execution brought in 10,000 people, many of whom became violent after the execution and had to be restrained by the police. Other states followed suit. According to *Society's Final Solution: A History and Discussion of the Death Penalty*, many capital punishment abolitionists were opposed to these measures. They believed that executions conducted in public would eventually arouse the revulsion of American society against capital punishment.

During the late 1840s Horace Greeley (1811–1872), the founder and editor of the *New York Tribune* and a leading advocate of most abolitionist causes, led the crusade against the death penalty. In 1846 Michigan became the first state to abolish the death penalty for all crimes except treason (until 1963), making it the first English-speaking jurisdiction in the world to abolish the death penalty for common crimes.

Common crimes, also called ordinary crimes, are crimes committed during peacetime. Ordinary crimes that could lead to the death penalty include murder, rape, and, in some countries, robbery or embezzlement of large sums of money. In comparison, exceptional crimes are military crimes committed during exceptional times, mainly wartime. Examples are treason, spying, or desertion (leaving the armed services without permission). The Michigan law took effect in March 1847. In 1852 and 1853 Rhode Island and Wisconsin, respectively, became the first two states to outlaw the death penalty for all crimes. Most states began limiting the number of capital crimes. Outside the South, murder and treason became the only acts punishable by death.

As the Civil War (1861–1865) neared, concern about the death penalty was lost amid the growing antislavery movement. It was not until after the Civil War that Maine and Iowa abolished the death penalty. Almost immediately, however, their legislatures reversed themselves and reinstated the death penalty. In 1887 Maine again reversed itself and abolished capital punishment. It has remained an abolitionist state ever since. Colorado abolished capital punishment in 1897, a decision that was apparently against the will of many of its citizens. In 1901 the state restored the death penalty. Meanwhile, the federal government, following considerable debate in Congress, reduced the number of federal crimes punishable by death to treason, murder, and rape.

INTRODUCTION OF ELECTROCUTION AS A METHOD OF EXECUTION. Around the end of the 19th century the use of electricity came into favor as a new means of execution. According to *Society's Final Solution: A History and Discussion of the Death Penalty*, the Edison Company electrocuted animals in public demonstrations. In 1888 New York became the first state to tear down its gallows and erect an electric chair. Two years later the chair was first used on a convict named William Kemmler. Even though electrocution was described as "clumsy, at best," other states quickly embraced the electric chair for carrying out capital punishment.

THE ANTI–DEATH PENALTY MOVEMENT

At the start of the 20th century, death penalty abolitionists again benefited from American reformism as the Progressives (liberal reformers) worked to correct perceived problems in the U.S. legal system. *Society's Final Solution: A History and Discussion of the Death Penalty* reports that by 1917 capital punishment had been abolished or limited to only a handful of serious crimes in nine states. However, many of these states reversed their decisions in the following decades. The Prohibition era (1920–1933), which was characterized by frequent disdain for law and order, almost destroyed the abolitionist movement, as many Americans began to believe that the

death penalty was the only proper punishment for gangsters who committed murder.

The movement's complete collapse was prevented by the determined efforts of Clarence Seward Darrow (1857–1938), the "attorney for the damned"; Lewis Edward Lawes (1883–1947), the abolitionist warden of Sing Sing Prison in New York; and the American League to Abolish Capital Punishment (founded in 1927). Nonetheless, between 1917 and 1957 no state abolished the death penalty.

Society's Final Solution: A History and Discussion of the Death Penalty reports that the abolitionist movement made a mild comeback during the mid-1950s. In 1957 the U.S. territories of Alaska and Hawaii abolished the death penalty. In the states, however, the movement's singular success in Delaware (1958) was reversed three years later (1961), a major disappointment for death penalty opponents. In 1963 Michigan, which in 1847 had abolished capital punishment for all crimes except treason, finally outlawed the death penalty for that crime as well. Oregon (1964), Iowa (1965), New York (1965), Vermont (1965), West Virginia (1965), and New Mexico (1969) all abolished capital punishment, whereas many other states sharply reduced the number of crimes punishable by death.

RESOLVING THE CONSTITUTIONAL ISSUES

Until the mid-20th century there was legally no question that the death penalty was acceptable under the U.S. Constitution. In 1958, however, the U.S. Supreme Court opened up the death penalty for reinterpretation when it ruled in *Trop v. Dulles* (356 U.S. 86) that the language of the Eighth Amendment (which states that criminals cannot be subjected to a cruel and unusual punishment) held the "evolving standards of decency that mark the progress of a maturing society." Opponents of capital punishment believed the death penalty should be declared unconstitutional in light of the *Trop* decision (which did not specifically address capital punishment). The abolitionists claimed that society had evolved to a point where the death penalty was cruel and unusual by the established "standards of decency." As such, the death penalty violated the Eighth Amendment of the Constitution.

In 1963 Justice Arthur J. Goldberg (1908–1990) dissented in *Rudolph v. Alabama* (375 U.S. 889), a rape case in which the defendant had been sentenced to death. Joined by Justices William O. Douglas (1898–1980) and William J. Brennan (1906–1997), Justice Goldberg raised the question of the legality of the death penalty. The filing of many lawsuits during the late 1960s led to an implied moratorium on executions until the court could decide whether the death penalty was constitutional.

In 1972 the high court finally handed down a landmark decision in *Furman v. Georgia* (408 U.S. 238), when it ruled that the death penalty violated the Eighth and 14th Amendments (the right to due process) because of the arbitrary nature with which the death penalty was administered across the United States. The court also laid down some guidelines for states to follow, declaring that a punishment was cruel and unusual if it was too severe, arbitrary, or offended society's sense of justice.

Before the late 1960s U.S. death penalty laws varied considerably from state to state and from region to region. Few national standards existed on how a murder trial should be conducted or which types of crimes deserved the death penalty. Specifically, *Furman* brought into question the laws of Georgia and a number of other states that allowed juries complete discretion in delivering a sentence. Critics feared the punishments such juries meted out were arbitrary and discriminatory against minorities.

CREATING A UNIFORM DEATH PENALTY SYSTEM ACROSS THE UNITED STATES

Within a year of the Supreme Court's ruling in *Furman*, most states had updated their laws regarding the death penalty. Many of these new statutes were brought before the high court during the mid-1970s. By issuing rulings on the constitutionality of these state statutes, the court created a uniform death penalty system for the United States. Table 1.3 provides a summary of the major cases decided by the court dealing with the death penalty between 1972 and 2008.

States amended their laws once again after the Supreme Court issued the new rulings. Every state switched to a bifurcated (two-part) trial system, where the first trial is used to determine a defendant's guilt, and the second trial determines the sentence of a guilty defendant. Generally, only those convicted of first-degree murder were eligible for the death penalty. Most states also required the jury or judge in the sentencing phase of the trial to identify one or more aggravating factors (circumstances that may increase responsibility for a crime) beyond a reasonable doubt before they could sentence a person to death. State legislatures drafted lists of aggravating factors that could result in a penalty of death. Typical aggravating factors included murders committed during robberies, the murder of a pregnant woman, murder committed after a rape, and the murder of an on-duty firefighter or police officer. The long appeals process for capital cases was also established during the mid-1970s.

THE END OF THE NATIONWIDE MORATORIUM

With the Supreme Court–approved laws in place, the states resumed executions. In January 1977 the nationwide moratorium ended when the state of Utah executed

TABLE 1.3

Major U.S. Supreme Court decisions involving the death penalty, selected years 1972–2008

Case	Year decided	Decision	Major effect
Furman v. Georgia	1972	5 to 4	The death penalty as administered by states at the time was deemed cruel and unusual punishment in violation of the Eighth and Fourteenth Amendments.
Gregg v. Georgia *Proffit v. Florida* *Jurek v. Texas*	1976	7 to 2	New death penalty statutes in Georgia, Florida, and Texas ruled constitutional.
Woodson v. North Carolina	1976	5 to 4	Mandatory death sentences ruled unconstitutional.
Coker v. Georgia	1977	5 to 4	The death penalty may not be imposed for raping an adult woman if the victim does not die.
Godfrey v. Georgia	1980	6 to 3	State statutes must clearly define the circumstances that qualify a crime as a capital crime.
Spaziano v. Florida	1984	5 to 3	Upheld as constitutional a judge's decision to impose a death sentence despite jury's recommendation of life in prison.
Ford v. Wainwright	1986	5 to 4	Inflicting the death penalty upon the insane ruled unconstitutional.
Murray v. Giarratamo	1989	5 to 4	Defendants under sentence of death do not have a constitutional right to counsel during postconviction proceedings.
Ring v. Arizona	2002	7 to 2	Only juries, not judges, can determine the presence of aggravating circumstances that warrant a death sentence.
Atkins v. Virginia	2002	6 to 3	Inflicting the death penalty upon the mentally retarded ruled unconstitutional.
Roper v. Simmons	2005	5 to 4	Death sentences imposed against minors (i.e., those less than 18 years of age when crime committed) ruled unconstitutional.
Baze and Bowling v. Rees	2008	7 to 2	Found that Kentucky's lethal injection "cocktail" (which was widely used in other death penalty states) did not violate the Eighth Amendment.
Kennedy v. Louisiana	2008	5 to 4	The death penalty may not be imposed for raping a child if the crime was not intended to cause, nor resulted in, the child's death.

SOURCE: Created by Kim Masters Evans for Gale, 2011

Gary Gilmore (1940–1977). Gilmore had been convicted of killing Ben Bushnell, a motel manager in Provo, Utah, on July 20, 1976. Authorities had also charged him with the July 19 murder of Max Jensen, a gas station attendant, in Orem, Utah. Gilmore received the death penalty for the Bushnell murder. He refused to appeal his case, demanding that his sentence be carried out swiftly. Gilmore requested the state supreme court to grant his wish because he did not want to spend his life on death row. The court granted his wish, but interventions by Gilmore's mother, as well as by anti–death penalty organizations, resulted in several stays (postponement) of execution. These organizations were concerned that the defendant's refusal to appeal his case and the court's agreement to carry out his wish might establish a precedent that would hurt the causes of other inmates. After several suicide attempts, Gilmore was finally executed by firing squad in January 1977.

Several other states reinstated the death penalty after the Supreme Court declared it constitutional. Oregon brought back the death penalty in 1978. In 1995 New York became the 38th state to reinstate the death penalty, ending its 30-year ban on capital punishment.

After the nationwide moratorium ended in 1977, the number of executions began to rise. (See Figure 1.3.) As shown in Table 1.4, executions hit the double digits in 1984, when 21 inmates were put to death in the United States, and peaked in 1999, when 98 inmates were executed. The number of inmates put to death then dipped to 37 in 2008—the lowest level in about a decade and a half, before rising to 52 in 2009 and 46 in 2010. Of course, these numbers were much smaller than the number of

TABLE 1.4

Number of persons executed, by year, 1977–2010

Year	Number
1977	1
1978	0
1979	2
1980	0
1981	1
1982	2
1983	5
1984	21
1985	18
1986	18
1987	25
1988	11
1989	16
1990	23
1991	14
1992	31
1993	38
1994	31
1995	56
1996	45
1997	74
1998	68
1999	98
2000	85
2001	66
2002	71
2003	65
2004	59
2005	60
2006	53
2007	42
2008	37
2009	52
2010	46

SOURCE: Adapted from "Number of Persons Executed in the United States, 1930–2010," in *Key Facts at a Glance*, U.S. Department of Justice, Office of Justice Programs, Bureau of Justice Statistics, January 20, 2011, http://bjs.ojp.usdoj.gov/content/glance/sheets/exe.csv (accessed July 5, 2011)

FIGURE 1.3

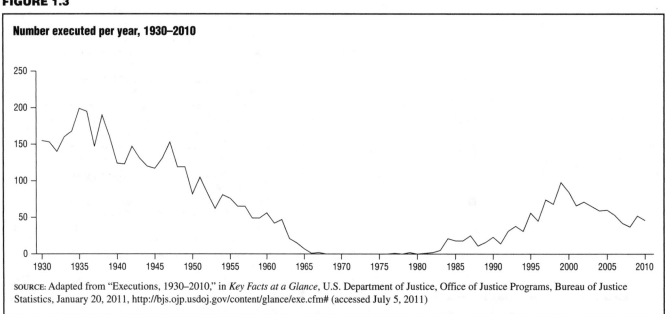

Number executed per year, 1930–2010

SOURCE: Adapted from "Executions, 1930–2010," in *Key Facts at a Glance*, U.S. Department of Justice, Office of Justice Programs, Bureau of Justice Statistics, January 20, 2011, http://bjs.ojp.usdoj.gov/content/glance/exe.cfm# (accessed July 5, 2011)

FIGURE 1.4

Number of prisoners under sentence of death and number of executions, 1953–2009

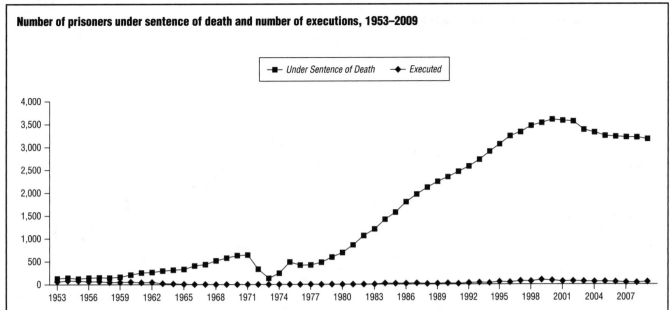

SOURCE: Adapted from "Number of Persons under Sentence of Death, 1953–2009," in *Key Facts at a Glance*, U.S. Department of Justice, Office of Justice Programs, Bureau of Justice Statistics, November 5, 2010, http://bjs.ojp.usdoj.gov/content/glance/sheets/dr.csv (accessed July 5, 2011) and "Number of Persons Executed in the United States, 1930–2010," in *Key Facts at a Glance*, U.S. Department of Justice, Office of Justice Programs, Bureau of Justice Statistics, January 20, 2011, http://bjs.ojp.usdoj.gov/content/glance/sheets/exe.csv (accessed July 5, 2011)

executions that occurred during the early part of the 20th century. In 1938 alone, for instance, 190 people were executed. Overall, between 1977 and 2010, 1,234 people were put to death.

As shown in Figure 1.4, more than 400 people were on death row in 1977. The number climbed dramatically over the following decades, peaking at just over 3,600 in 2000. It then began a downward trend, dropping to 3,173 in 2009. Figure 1.4 clearly shows the rarity with which executions are carried out in the United States, compared with the large number of people under the sentence of death. Between 2000 and 2009 the United States executed an average of 59 people per year, whereas the number on death row averaged around 3,350 per year. This constitutes an execution rate of less than 2% per year.

THE HOMICIDE RATE CONNECTION

Figure 1.5 compares the homicide (murder) rate and the number of executions that were conducted each year between 1960 and 2009. The increasing usage of capital punishment during the 1980s and early 1990s was a response to rising homicide rates in the country. Between 1960 and 1980 the homicide rate doubled from 5.1 cases per 100,000 population to 10.2 cases per 100,000 population. After falling slightly during the early 1980s, it surged again, reaching its penultimate (second-highest) level in 1991, when 9.8 homicides occurred for every 100,000 people. Since that time the rate has generally declined. By 2000 it was 5.5 cases per 100,000 population. It remained

around that level through 2007 and then declined in 2008 and 2009.

The country also experienced a surge of homicides in the early 1930s, during the Prohibition era. As mentioned earlier, this was a time when support for the death penalty strengthened around the country. As shown in Figure 1.3, the execution rate was historically high at that time.

NEW RULES IN THE MODERN DEATH PENALTY ERA

U.S. Supreme Court decisions continued to redefine state death penalty laws well after the *Furman* opinion. In particular, the court has ruled the death penalty to be unconstitutional for three groups of defendants: the insane, the mentally retarded, and juveniles.

Executing the Insane

In *Ford v. Wainwright* (477 U.S. 399 [1986]), the U.S. Supreme Court ruled that executing an insane person constituted a cruel and unusual punishment and was thus in violation of the Eighth Amendment. Because a precedent did not exist in U.S. legal history about executing the insane, the justices looked to English common law to make this ruling. English law expressly forbade the execution of insane people. The English jurist Sir Edward Coke (1552–1634) observed that even though the execution of a criminal was to serve as an example, the execution of a madman was considered "of extream inhumanity and cruelty, and can be no example to others."

FIGURE 1.5

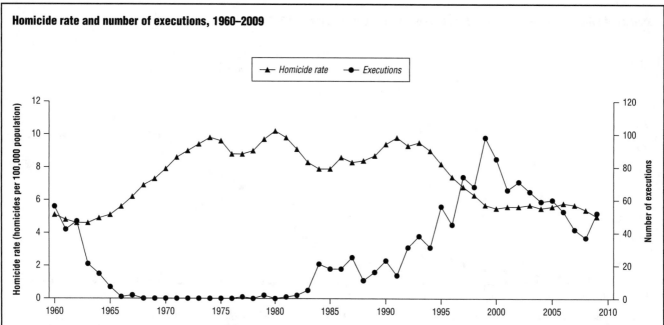

Homicide rate and number of executions, 1960–2009

SOURCE: Adapted from "Homicide Victimization, 1950–2005," in *Homicide Trends in the U.S.*, U.S. Department of Justice, Office of Justice Programs, July 23, 2011, http://bjs.ojp.usdoj.gov/content/homicide/tables/totalstab.cfm (accessed July 23, 2011); "Table 1. Crime in the United States, by Volume and Rate per 100,000 Inhabitants, 1990–2009," in *Crime in the United States*, U.S. Department of Justice, Office of Justice Programs, September 2010, http://www2.fbi.gov/ucr/cius2009/data/table_01.html (accessed July 23, 2011); and "Executions, 1930–2010," in *Key Facts at a Glance*, U.S. Department of Justice, Office of Justice Programs, Bureau of Justice Statistics, January 20, 2011, http://bjs.ojp.usdoj.gov/content/glance/exe.cfm# (accessed July 5, 2011)

Executing Mentally Retarded People

In 1989 the Supreme Court held in *Penry v. Lynaugh* (492 U.S. 302) that it was not unconstitutional to execute a mentally retarded person found guilty of a capital crime. According to the court, there was no emerging national consensus against such execution. Just two death penalty states—Georgia and Maryland—banned putting mentally retarded people to death. In 1988 Georgia became the first state to prohibit the execution of murderers found "guilty but mentally retarded." The legislation resulted from the 1986 execution of Jerome Bowden, who had an intelligence quotient (IQ) of 65. It is generally accepted that an IQ below 70 is evidence of mental retardation. (Normal IQ is considered 90 and above.) In 1988 Maryland passed similar legislation, which took effect in July 1989.

Between 1989 and 2001, 18 states outlawed the execution of offenders with mental retardation. The federal government also forbids the execution of mentally retarded inmates. In the Anti-Drug Abuse Act of 1988 the government permits the death penalty for any person working "in furtherance of a continuing criminal enterprise or any person engaging in a drug-related felony offense, who intentionally kills or counsels, commands, or causes the intentional killing of an individual," but forbids the imposition of the death penalty against anyone who is mentally retarded who commits such a crime. In 1994, when Congress enacted the Federal Death Penalty Act, which added more than 50 crimes punishable by death, it also exempted people with mental retardation from the death sentence.

Even though the Supreme Court had agreed to review the case of the North Carolina death row inmate Ernest McCarver in 2001 to consider whether it is unconstitutional to execute inmates with mental retardation, the case was rendered moot when a state bill was passed that banned such executions. In June 2002 the Supreme Court finally ruled on a case involving the execution of mentally retarded convicts. In *Atkins v. Virginia* (536 U.S. 304), the court ruled 6–3 that executing the mentally retarded violates the Eighth Amendment ban against a cruel and unusual punishment. The court did not say what mental retardation consists of, leaving it to the states to set their own definitions.

Juveniles

The term *juvenile* varies under state criminal statutes. For example, some states consider people aged 17 years and younger to be juveniles, whereas other states define juveniles as those aged 16 years and younger. Literature on the death penalty typically considers "juvenile offenders" as people who were under the age of 18 years when they committed their crimes. According to Victor L. Streib of Ohio Northern University, in *The Juvenile Death Penalty Today: Death Sentences and Executions for Juvenile Crimes, January 1, 1973–February 28, 2005* (2005, http://www.deathpenaltyinfo.org/juvdeathstreib.pdf), the first

TABLE 1.5

Juveniles executed in the United States in the modern era since January 1, 1973

Name	Date of execution	Place of execution	Race	Age at crime	Age at execution
Charles Rumbaugh	9/11/85	Texas	White	17	28
J. Terry Roach	1/10/86	South Carolina	White	17	25
Jay Pinkerton	5/15/86	Texas	White	17	24
Dalton Prejean	5/18/90	Louisiana	Black	17	30
Johnny Garrett	2/11/92	Texas	White	17	28
Curtis Harris	7/1/93	Texas	Black	17	31
Frederick Lashley	7/28/93	Missouri	Black	17	29
Ruben Cantu	8/24/93	Texas	Latino	17	26
Chris Burger	12/7/93	Georgia	White	17	33
Joseph Cannon	4/22/98	Texas	White	17	38
Robert Carter	5/18/98	Texas	Black	17	34
Dwayne Allen Wright	10/14/98	Virginia	Black	17	24
Sean Sellers	2/4/99	Oklahoma	White	16	29
Douglas Christopher Thomas	1/10/00	Virginia	White	17	26
Steven Roach	1/13/00	Virginia	White	17	23
Glen McGinnis	1/25/00	Texas	Black	17	27
Shaka Sankofa (Gary Graham)	6/22/00	Texas	Black	17	36
Gerald Mitchell	10/22/01	Texas	Black	17	33
Napoleon Beazley	5/28/02	Texas	Black	17	25
T.J. Jones	8/8/02	Texas	Black	17	25
Toronto Patterson	8/28/02	Texas	Black	17	24
Scott Allen Hain	4/3/03	Oklahoma	White	17	32

Note: No juveniles were executed between January 1, 1973 and September 10, 1985.

SOURCE: "Juveniles Executed in the United States in the Modern Era (since January 1, 1973)," in *Execution of Juveniles in the U.S. and Other Countries*, Death Penalty Information Center, February 23, 2011, http://www.deathpenaltyinfo.org/execution-juveniles-us-and-other-countries (accessed July 24, 2011)

execution of a juvenile in the United States took place in Plymouth Colony, Massachusetts, in 1642. Streib estimates that between 1642 and 2003, 366 inmates who were juveniles during the commission of their crimes were executed in the United States. In "Executing Female Juveniles" (*Connecticut Law Review*, vol. 22, no. 1, Fall 1989), Victor L. Streib and Lynn Sametz note that only 10 of the executed juveniles were females.

According to the Death Penalty Information Center (DPIC), 22 inmates who were juveniles at the time of their crimes were executed between 1973 and 2003, that is, within the modern death penalty era. (See Table 1.5.) Texas implemented the death penalty of 13 juvenile offenders, followed by Virginia (3) and Oklahoma (2). Georgia, Louisiana, Missouri, and South Carolina each executed one juvenile offender. Note that one of the executed juveniles was 16 years old when he committed a capital crime; the other 21 juveniles were aged 17 years when they committed capital crimes.

In *Roper v. Simmons* (543 U.S. 551 [2005]), the court decided that executing Donald Roper was cruel and unusual based on the fact that Roper was younger than 18 when he committed murder. The majority reasoned that adolescents do not have the emotional maturity or understanding of lasting consequences that adults have and therefore should not be held to an adult standard or punished with a sentence of death. All states with the death penalty subsequently changed their laws to prohibit death sentences for people under the age of 18 years.

DNA TAKES THE STAND

During the 1980s and 1990s deoxyribonucleic acid (DNA) testing procedures advanced to the point where such evidence could be used in criminal cases. Across the United States, police suddenly had the ability to identify a suspect and place him or her squarely at the scene of a crime with a small sample of hair, blood, or other biological material. Because of the accuracy of DNA testing, DNA evidence could hold as much sway in a courtroom as an eyewitness or camera footage. States started collecting biological samples, such as blood and saliva, from criminal offenders and storing these DNA profiles in databases.

In 1994 Virginia became the first state to execute a person who was convicted as a result of DNA evidence. The defendant, Timothy Spencer, was convicted in 1988 for several rapes and murders he committed starting in 1984. Virginia also became the first state to execute someone based on a DNA "cold hit" when it executed James Earl Patterson in March 2002. (A cold hit is when DNA evidence collected at a crime scene matches a DNA sample already in a database.) In 1999 Patterson was in prison on a rape conviction when DNA from the 1987 rape and murder of Joyce Aldridge was found to match his DNA in the database. He confessed to the Aldridge crime in 2000 and was sentenced to death. Patterson waived his appeals to let his execution proceed as scheduled.

First Death Row Inmate Is Freed by DNA Testing

Not only has DNA evidence been useful in convicting felons but also it has been crucial in proving the innocence of falsely convicted criminals. Kirk Bloodsworth of Maryland was the nation's first death row inmate to be exonerated (cleared) based on postconviction DNA testing. Bloodsworth was convicted for the rape and murder of a nine-year-old girl in 1984. He was sentenced to death in 1985. On retrial, Bloodsworth received two life terms. DNA testing in 1992 excluded him from the crime. In 1993 Bloodsworth was released from prison. In 1999 the state paid Bloodsworth $300,000 for wrongful conviction and imprisonment, including time on death row.

State and Federal Legislatures Enact Laws to Expand DNA Testing

The Innocence Protection Act became law in October 2004. The law laid down the conditions with which a federal prisoner who pleaded not guilty could receive postconviction DNA testing. If a trial defendant faced conviction, the act called for the preservation of the defendant's biological evidence. A five-year, $25 million grant program was also established to help eligible states pay for postconviction testing.

Many state legislatures have passed similar DNA testing legislation. The American Society of Law, Medicine, and Ethics (2011, http://www.aslme.org/DNA_ELSI _Grant) maintains databases that list the relevant statutes and testing protocols on a state-by-state basis.

CAPITAL PUNISHMENT RECONSIDERED

During the 1980s and early 1990s public opinion polls showed strong support for capital punishment. According to the Gallup Organization (2011, http://www.gallup.com/poll/1606/Death-Penalty.aspx), this support reached its highest level in 1994, when 80% of Americans favored use of the death penalty for murderers.

Beginning in the mid-1990s support for capital punishment decreased for a variety of reasons. The advent of DNA testing resulted in highly publicized cases of inmates being released from prison, and even from death row. Abolitionists seized on these opportunities as proof that the U.S. capital punishment system was flawed. In addition, studies were released indicating that racial biases were occurring in death penalty cases and raising questions about the fairness of the system. Many states added life without parole sentences to their justice systems. According to the DPIC, in "Year That States Adopted Life without Parole (LWOP) Sentencing" (2011, http://www.deathpenaltyinfo.org/year-states-adopted-life-without-parole-lwop-sentencing), 18 states practicing the death penalty adopted life without parole sentences during the 1990s:

- Arizona (1993)
- Florida (1994)
- Georgia (1993)
- Indiana (1994)
- Kentucky (1998)
- Louisiana (1994)
- Montana (1995)
- New Jersey (1995)
- New Mexico (1997)
- New York (1995)
- North Carolina (1994)
- North Dakota (1997)
- Ohio (1995)
- South Carolina (1995)
- Tennessee (1995)
- Utah (1992)
- Virginia (1994)
- Washington (1993)

They were joined during the first decade of the 21st century by Colorado (2002), Delaware (2003), Idaho (2004), Kansas (2004), Nebraska (2002), and Texas (2005).

By the turn of the 21st century capital punishment had been abolished in Canada and in nearly all of Europe, which led to intense criticism in the international press of the United States' reliance on the death penalty. Pope John Paul II (1920–2005) also condemned capital punishment. Two popular movies—*Dead Man Walking* (1995) and *The Green Mile* (1999)—raised questions about the morality of the death penalty.

Two particular death penalty cases also aroused passion about the morality of capital punishment. Karla Faye Tucker became a born-again Christian while on death row in Texas for the brutal 1984 slayings of two people. In the months leading up to her execution in 1998, she received widespread media attention and garnered support nationally and internationally for commutation of her sentence to life in prison. Her supporters included some unlikely allies: a handful of conservative-minded religious and political figures who believed that Tucker's religious conversion merited clemency (an act of leniency by a convening authority to reduce a sentence). Nevertheless, George W. Bush (1946–), the Texas governor, signed her death warrant.

In 2005 the execution of Stanley "Tookie" Williams also garnered considerable public attention. Williams received a death sentence for killing three people in 1981. At the time, he was a leading figure in the notorious and violent Crips gang in Los Angeles, California. During his decades on death row Williams became an outspoken critic of gangs and wrote books encouraging children to avoid gangs and violence. For his work he received nominations for the Nobel Peace Prize. His supporters included Hollywood celebrities who lobbied the California governor

Arnold Schwarzenegger (1947–) for clemency, arguing that Williams had redeemed himself while in prison. The governor refused, noting that Williams had never expressed remorse for his crimes.

The onset of the economic recession (which lasted from late 2007 to mid-2009) spurred some states to reconsider the financial costs that are associated with administering the death penalty, as will be described in Chapter 6. In general, capital cases are more costly than noncapital homicide cases because they take much longer to proceed through the court system. Legal safeguards, such as automatic appeals, mean that judges, prosecutors, and defense attorneys spend more time on capital cases. These litigation costs are largely paid through tax dollars. In addition, there are extra expenses associated with housing death row inmates, because they are kept in specially designed facilities and receive much more intense supervision than non–death row inmates.

In March 2009 New Mexico eliminated the death penalty for new capital crimes. As of September 2011, two previously convicted death row inmates remained under sentence of death. New Mexico's governor abolished capital punishment due to concerns about racial bias in its administration and the growing number of exonerations. In March 2011 Illinois abandoned the death penalty and resentenced all death row inmates to life in prison without the possibility of parole. Again, concerns about capital punishment's fairness and accuracy were driving factors.

From the 1990s through 2011 a number of factors combined to lessen application of the death penalty.

These include lower homicide rates (see Figure 1.5), growing numbers of death row inmates exonerated due to DNA evidence and other factors, and the increasing availability in state statutes of life prison sentences with no chance of parole. As shown in Figure 1.6, the annual number of death sentences issued nationwide decreased by more than half, from just over 300 sentences per year during the mid-1990s to 114 sentences in 2010. Texas, the nation's most active death penalty state, also witnessed a decrease, from a high of 48 sentences in 1999 to eight in 2010.

The 2011 execution of Troy Davis, a Georgia death row inmate, captured widespread public attention and spurred anti–death penalty demonstrations around the world. Davis was convicted for the 1989 murder of Mark MacPhail, an off-duty police officer. Davis's conviction was based almost entirely on the testimony of seven eyewitnesses to the crime and two people who claimed that Davis confessed to them afterward. However, over subsequent years seven of these individuals issued recantations (official denials) of portions or all of their original statements. The details of this case are examined in Chapter 8.

Human rights groups and prominent public figures, including former president Jimmy Carter (1924–), advocated for Davis to receive a new trial. In 2009 the U.S. Supreme Court ordered a U.S. district court to hold an evidentiary hearing on the case. At the 2010 hearing the district court discounted the authenticity and evidentiary importance of the recantations and allowed the death sentence to stand. Davis exhausted his remaining appeals.

FIGURE 1.6

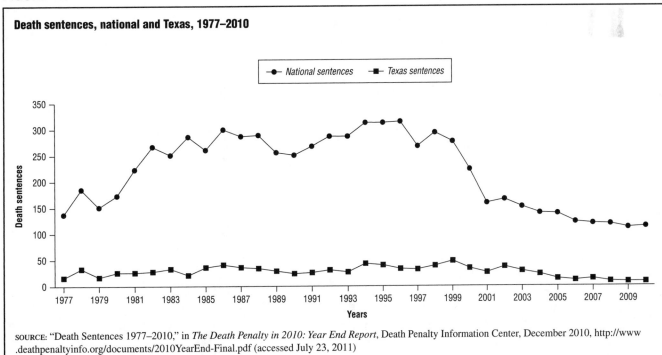

Death sentences, national and Texas, 1977–2010

SOURCE: "Death Sentences 1977–2010," in *The Death Penalty in 2010: Year End Report*, Death Penalty Information Center, December 2010, http://www.deathpenaltyinfo.org/documents/2010YearEnd-Final.pdf (accessed July 23, 2011)

As his execution date approached, hundreds of thousands of people signed petitions calling for him to be pardoned, but the request was denied by the Georgia State Board of Pardons and Paroles. Davis was executed in September 2011.

Davis's supporters believe that he was innocent or that sufficient doubt existed to justify overturning his death sentence. To them the case epitomizes the tragic shortcomings and irreversible nature of capital punishment. Death penalty advocates argue that Davis's claims of innocence were carefully considered by the legal system and ultimately rejected for lack of merit. They believe that his execution was just punishment for the horrific crime for which he was convicted.

WORLDWIDE TREND

The moratorium on the death penalty in the United States between 1967 and 1976 paralleled a general worldwide movement, especially among Western nations, toward the abolition of capital punishment. Even though the United States resumed executions in 1977, most of the Western world either formally or informally abolished capital punishment.

As of September 2011, among the Western democratic nations (with which the United States traditionally compares itself), only the United States imposed the death penalty. There are technical exceptions: for example, Israel maintains the death penalty in its statute books for "crimes against mankind" but has executed only Adolf Eichmann (1906–1962). As a Schutzstaffel (SS) officer, Eichmann was responsible for the murder of millions of Jews in Nazi-occupied Europe during the Holocaust and World War II (1939–1945). Some countries still maintain the death penalty for treason—although no Western democracy has actually imposed it. One of the first acts of the parliaments of many of the east European countries after the fall of communism was to abolish capital punishment.

According to Amnesty International, in "Abolitionist and Retentionist Countries" (http://www.amnesty.org/en/death-penalty/abolitionist-and-retentionist-countries), 58 countries and territories around the world continued to maintain and use the death penalty for ordinary crimes in 2011. However, some of these countries had not actually implemented a death sentence for many years. Amnesty International reports in *Death Sentences and Executions, 2010* (March 2011, http://www.amnesty.org/en/library/asset/ACT50/001/2011/en/ea1b6b25-a62a-4074-927d-ba51e88df2e9/act500012011en.pdf) that there were at least 527 executions (excluding China) carried out in 23 countries in 2010. China is believed to have conducted thousands of executions, but the exact number is a state secret. According to Amnesty International, the six countries with the highest number of executions in 2010 were China (1,000s), Iran (252+), North Korea (60+), Yemen (53+), the United States (46), and Saudi Arabia (27+). In addition, the organization estimates that 2,024 death sentences were issued in 67 countries in 2010.

CHAPTER 2
SUPREME COURT RULINGS I: CONSTITUTIONALITY OF THE DEATH PENALTY, GUIDELINES FOR JUDGES AND JURIES, JURY SELECTION, AND SENTENCING PROCEDURES

In 1967 a coalition of anti–death penalty groups sued Florida and California, the states with the most inmates on death row at that time, challenging the constitutionality of state capital punishment laws. An unofficial moratorium (temporary suspension) of executions resulted, pending U.S. Supreme Court decisions on several cases on appeal. The defendants in these cases claimed that the death penalty is a cruel and unusual punishment in violation of the Eighth Amendment to the U.S. Constitution. Moreover, they alleged that the death penalty also violates the 14th Amendment, which prevents states from denying anyone equal protection of the laws. This moratorium lasted until January 17, 1977, when the convicted murderer Gary Gilmore (1940–1977) was executed by the state of Utah.

IS THE DEATH PENALTY CONSTITUTIONAL?

On June 29, 1972, a split 5–4 Supreme Court reached a landmark decision in *Furman v. Georgia* (408 U.S. 238, which included *Jackson v. Georgia* and *Branch v. Texas*), holding that "as the statutes before us are now administered . . . [the] imposition and carrying out of [the] death penalty in these cases [is] held to constitute cruel and unusual punishment in violation of [the] Eighth and Fourteenth Amendments." In other words, the justices did not address whether capital punishment as a whole is unconstitutional. Rather, they considered capital punishment in the context of its application in state statutes (laws created by state legislatures). The justices, whether they were of the majority opinion or of the dissenting opinion, could not agree on the arguments explaining why they opposed or supported the death penalty. As a result, the decision consisted of nine separate opinions, the longest ruling in court history as of September 2011.

Majority Opinions in *Furman*

Justice William O. Douglas (1898–1980), in his concurring majority opinion, quoted the observation of the former U.S. attorney general Ramsey Clark (1927–) in his book

Crime in America: Observations on Its Nature, Causes, Prevention, and Control (1970): "It is the poor, the sick, the ignorant, the powerless and the hated who are executed." Douglas added, "We deal with a system of law and of justice that leaves to the uncontrolled discretion of judges or juries the determination whether defendants committing these crimes should die or be imprisoned. Under these laws no standards govern the selection of the penalty. People live or die, dependent on the whim of one man or of 12. . . . Thus, these discretionary statutes are unconstitutional in their operation. They are pregnant with discrimination and discrimination is an ingredient not compatible with the idea of equal protection of the laws that is implicit in the ban on 'cruel and unusual' punishments."

Justice William J. Brennan (1906–1997) stated, "At bottom, then, the Cruel and Unusual Punishments Clause prohibits the infliction of uncivilized and inhuman punishments. The State, even as it punishes, must treat its members with respect for their intrinsic worth as human beings. A punishment is 'cruel and unusual,' therefore, if it does not comport with human dignity."

Justice Potter J. Stewart (1915–1985) stressed another point, saying, "These death sentences are cruel and unusual in the same way that being struck by lightning is cruel and unusual. For, of all the people convicted of rapes and murders in 1967 and 1968, many just as reprehensible as these, the petitioners are among a capriciously selected random handful upon whom the sentence of death has in fact been imposed."

This did not mean that Justice Stewart would rule out the death penalty. He believed that the death penalty was justified, but he wanted to see a more equitable system of determining who should be executed. He explained, "I cannot agree that retribution is a constitutionally impermissible ingredient in the imposition of punishment. The instinct for retribution is part of the nature of man, and channeling that instinct in the administration of criminal justice serves an important purpose in promoting the stability of a society governed by law. When people begin to believe that organized society is unwilling or unable to impose upon criminal offenders the punishment they 'deserve,' then there are sown the seeds of anarchy—of self-help, vigilante justice, and lynch law."

Justice Byron R. White (1917–2002), believing that the death penalty was so seldom imposed that executions were ineffective deterrents to crime, chose instead to address the role of juries and judges in imposing the death penalty. He concluded that the cases before the courts violated the Eighth Amendment because the state legislatures, having authorized the application of the death penalty, left it to the discretion of juries and judges whether or not to impose the punishment.

Justice Thurgood Marshall (1908–1993) thought that "the death penalty is an excessive and unnecessary punishment that violates the Eighth Amendment." He added that "even if capital punishment is not excessive, it nonetheless violates the Eighth Amendment because it is morally unacceptable to the people of the United States at this time in their history." Justice Marshall also noted that the death penalty was applied with discrimination against certain classes of people (the poor, the uneducated, and members of minority groups) and that innocent people had been executed before they could prove their innocence. He also believed that it hindered the reform of the treatment of criminals and that it promoted sensationalism during trials.

Dissenting Opinions

Chief Justice Warren Burger (1907–1995), disagreeing with the majority, observed that "the constitutional prohibition against 'cruel and unusual punishments' cannot be construed to bar the imposition of the punishment of death." Justice Harry A. Blackmun (1908–1999) was disturbed by Justices Stewart's and White's remarks that as long as capital punishment was mandated for specific crimes, it could not be considered unconstitutional. He feared "that statutes struck down today will be re-enacted by state legislatures to prescribe the death penalty for specified crimes without any alternative for the imposition of a lesser punishment in the discretion of the judge or jury, as the case may be."

Justice Lewis F. Powell Jr. (1907–1998) declared, "I find no support—in the language of the Constitution, in its history, or in the cases arising under it—for the view that this Court may invalidate a category of penalties because we deem less severe penalties adequate to serve the ends of penology.... This Court has long held that legislative decisions in this area, which lie within the special competency of that branch, are entitled to a presumption of validity." In other words, he believed that the court would not question the validity of a government entity properly doing its job unless its actions were way out of line.

Justice William H. Rehnquist (1924–2005) agreed with Justice Powell, adding, "How can government by the elected representatives of the people co-exist with the power of the federal judiciary, whose members are constitutionally insulated from responsiveness to the popular will, to declare invalid laws duly enacted by the popular branches of government?"

Summary of Court Decision

Only Justices Brennan and Marshall concluded that the Eighth Amendment prohibited the death penalty for all crimes and under all circumstances. Justice Douglas, while ruling that the death penalty statutes reviewed by the high court were unconstitutional, did not necessarily require the final abolition of the death penalty. Justices Stewart and White also did not rule on the validity of the death penalty, noting instead that, because of the capricious (unpredictable) imposition of the sentence, the death penalty violated the Eighth Amendment. However, Justices Rehnquist, Burger, Powell, and Blackmun concluded that the Constitution allows capital punishment.

Consequently, most state legislatures went to work to revise their capital punishment laws. They strove to make these laws more equitable to swing the votes of Justices Stewart and White (and later that of Justice John Paul Stevens [1920–], who replaced the retired Justice Douglas).

PROPER IMPOSITION OF THE DEATH PENALTY

Four years later, on July 2, 1976, the Supreme Court ruled decisively on a series of cases. In *Gregg v. Georgia* (428 U.S. 153), perhaps the most significant of these cases, the justices concluded 7–2 that the death penalty was, indeed, constitutional as presented in some new state laws. With Justices Brennan and Marshall dissenting, the court stressed (just in case *Furman* had been misunderstood) that "the death penalty is not a form of punishment that may never be imposed, regardless of the circumstances of the offense, regardless of the character of the offender, and regardless of the procedure followed in reaching the decision to impose it." Furthermore, "the infliction of death as a punishment for murder is not without justification and thus is not unconstitutionally severe."

The court upheld death penalty statutes in Georgia (*Gregg v. Georgia*), Florida (*Proffitt v. Florida*, 428 U.S. 242 [1976]), and Texas (*Jurek v. Texas*, 428 U.S. 262 [1976]), but struck down laws in North Carolina (*Woodson v. North Carolina*, 428 U.S. 280 [1976]) and Louisiana (*Roberts v. Louisiana*, 428 U.S. 325 [1976]). It ruled that laws in the latter two states were too rigid in imposing mandatory death sentences for certain types of murder.

Citing the new Georgia laws in *Gregg*, Justice Stewart supported the bifurcated (two-part) trial system, in which the accused is first tried to determine his or her guilt. Then, in a separate trial, the jury considers whether the convicted person deserves the death penalty or whether mitigating factors (circumstances that may lessen responsibility for a crime) warrant a lesser sentence, usually life imprisonment without parole. He believed that this system meets the requirements demanded by *Furman*. Noting how the Georgia statutes fulfilled these demands, Justice Stewart observed:

> These procedures require the jury to consider the circumstances of the crime and the criminal before it recommends sentence. No longer can a Georgia jury do as Furman's jury did: reach a finding of the defendant's guilt and then, without guidance or direction, decide whether he should live or die. Instead, the jury's attention is directed to the specific circumstances of the crime: Was it committed in the course of another capital felony? Was it committed for money? Was it committed upon a peace officer or judicial officer? Was it committed in a particularly heinous way or in a manner that endangered the lives of many persons? In addition, the jury's attention is focused on the characteristics of the person who committed the crime: Does he have a record of prior convictions for capital offenses? Are there any special facts about this defendant that mitigate against imposing capital punishment (e. g., his youth, the extent of his cooperation with the police, his emotional state at the time of the crime). As a result, while some jury discretion still exists, "the discretion to be exercised is controlled by clear and objective standards so as to produce non-discriminatory application."

In addition, the Georgia law required that all death sentences be automatically appealed to the state supreme court, an "important additional safeguard against arbitrariness and caprice." The bifurcated trial system has since been adopted in the trials of all capital murder cases.

In *Proffitt v. Florida*, the high court upheld Florida's death penalty laws that had a bifurcated trial system similar to Georgia's. In Florida, however, the sentence was determined by the trial judge rather than by the jury, who assumed an advisory role during the sentencing phase. (This is often referred to as a trifurcated trial system, because there are three levels of decision-making involved.) The court found Florida's sentencing guidelines adequate in preventing unfair imposition of the death sentence.

Predictability of Future Criminal Activity

In *Jurek v. Texas*, the issue centered on whether a jury can satisfactorily determine the future actions of a convicted murderer. The Texas statute required that during the sentencing phase of a trial, after the defendant had been found guilty, the jury would determine whether it is probable the defendant would commit future criminal acts of violence that would threaten society. Even though agreeing with Jerry Lane Jurek's attorneys that predicting future behavior is not easy, Justice Stewart noted:

> The fact that such a determination is difficult, however, does not mean that it cannot be made. Indeed, prediction of future criminal conduct is an essential element in many

of the decisions rendered throughout our criminal justice system. The decision whether to admit a defendant to bail, for instance, must often turn on a judge's prediction of the defendant's future conduct. And any sentencing authority must predict a convicted person's probable future conduct when it engages in the process of determining what punishment to impose. For those sentenced to prison, these same predictions must be made by parole authorities. The task that a Texas jury must perform in answering the statutory question in issue is thus basically no different from the task performed countless times each day throughout the American system of criminal justice.

Flexible Guidelines for Judges and Jurors Are Required

In *Woodson v. North Carolina*, the Supreme Court addressed for the first time the question of whether the jury's handing down of a death sentence under North Carolina's mandatory death penalty for all first-degree murders constituted a cruel and unusual punishment within the meaning of the Eighth and 14th Amendments. If a person was convicted of first-degree murder in North Carolina, he or she was automatically sentenced to death. The justices held that as a whole the American public rejected the idea of mandatory death sentences long ago. In addition, North Carolina's new statute provided "no standards to guide the jury in its inevitable exercise of the power to determine which first-degree murderers shall live and which shall die." Furthermore, the North Carolina law did not let the jury consider the convicted defendant's character, criminal record, or the circumstances of the crime before the imposition of the death sentence.

The Louisiana mandatory death sentence for first-degree murder suffered from similar inadequacies. It did, however, permit the jury to consider lesser offenses such as second-degree murder. In *Roberts v. Louisiana*, the Supreme Court rejected the Louisiana law because it forced the jury to find the defendant guilty of a lesser crime to avoid imposing the death penalty. In other words, if the crime was not heinous enough to warrant the death penalty, then the jury was forced to convict the defendant of second-degree murder or a lesser charge. The jury did not have the option of first determining if the accused was indeed guilty of first-degree murder for the crime he or she had actually committed and then recommending a lesser sentence if there were mitigating circumstances to support it.

As a result of either *Furman* or *Gregg* or both, virtually every state's capital punishment statute had to be rewritten. These statutes would provide flexible guidelines for judges and juries so that they might fairly decide capital cases and consider, then impose, if necessary, the death penalty.

JURY MAY CONSIDER A LESSER CHARGE

In 1977 Gilbert Beck was convicted of robbing and murdering 80-year-old Roy Malone. According to Beck, he and an accomplice entered Malone's home and were tying up the victim to rob him when Beck's accomplice unexpectedly struck and killed Malone. Beck admitted to the robbery but claimed the murder was not part of the plan. Beck was tried under an Alabama statute for "robbery or attempts thereof when the victim is intentionally killed by the defendant."

Under Alabama law the judge was specifically prohibited from giving the jury the option of convicting the defendant of a lesser, included offense. Instead, the jury was given the choice of either convicting the defendant of the capital crime, in which case he possibly faced the death penalty, or acquitting him, thus allowing him to escape all penalties for his alleged participation in the crime. The judge could not have offered the jury the lesser alternative of felony murder, which did not deal with the accused's intentions at the time of the crime.

Beck appealed, claiming this law created a situation in which the jury was more likely to convict. The Supreme Court, in *Beck v. Alabama* (447 U.S. 625 [1980]), agreed and reversed the lower court's ruling, thus vacating (annulling) his death sentence. The high court observed that, while not a matter of due process, it was virtually universally accepted in lesser offenses that a third alternative be offered. The court noted, "That safeguard would seem to be especially important in a case such as this. For when the evidence unquestionably establishes that the defendant is guilty of a serious, violent offense—but leaves some doubt with respect to an element that would justify conviction of a capital offense—the failure to give the jury the 'third option' of convicting on a lesser included offense would seem inevitably to enhance the risk of an unwarranted conviction."

According to the ruling, such a risk could not be tolerated in a case where the defendant's life was at stake. *Beck*, however, did not require a jury to consider a lesser charge in every case, but only where the consideration would be justified.

EXCLUSION FROM JURIES OF THOSE AGAINST CAPITAL PUNISHMENT

In *Witherspoon v. Illinois* (391 U.S. 510 [1968]), the Supreme Court held that a death sentence cannot be carried out if the jury that imposed or recommended such punishment was selected by excluding prospective jurors simply because they have qualms against the death penalty or reservations against its infliction. The court found that the prosecution excluded those who opposed the death penalty without determining whether their beliefs would compel them to reject capital punishment out of hand. The defendant argued that this selective process had resulted in a jury that was not representative of the community.

The justices could not definitively conclude that the exclusion of jurors opposed to the death penalty results in an unrepresentative jury. However, they believed that a person who opposes the death penalty can still abide by his or her duty as a juror and consider the facts presented at trial before making his or her decision about the defendant's punishment. The court observed, "If the State had excluded only those prospective jurors who stated in advance of trial that they would not even consider returning a verdict of death, it could argue that the resulting jury was simply 'neutral' with respect to penalty. But when it swept from the jury all who expressed conscientious or religious scruples against capital punishment and all who opposed it in principle, the State crossed the line of neutrality. In its quest for a jury capable of imposing the death penalty, the State produced a jury uncommonly willing to condemn a man to die."

The court specifically noted that its findings in *Witherspoon* did not prevent the infliction of the death sentence when the prospective jurors excluded had made it "unmistakably clear" that they would automatically vote against the death sentence without considering the evidence presented during the trial or that their attitudes toward capital punishment would keep them from making a fair decision about the defendant's guilt. Consequently, based on *Witherspoon*, it has become the practice in most states to exclude prospective jurors who indicate that they could not possibly in good conscience return a death penalty.

This ruling was reinforced in *Lockett v. Ohio* (438 U.S. 586 [1978]). The defendant in *Lockett* contended, among several things, that the exclusion of four prospective jurors violated her Sixth Amendment right to trial by an impartial jury and 14th Amendment right under the principles established in *Witherspoon*. The Supreme Court upheld *Witherspoon* in this case because the prospective jurors told the prosecutor that they were so against the death penalty they could not be impartial about the case. They had also admitted that they would not take an oath saying they would consider the evidence before making a judgment of innocence or guilt.

A Special Selection Process Is Not Required When Selecting Jurors in Capital Cases

In *Wainwright v. Witt* (469 U.S. 412 [1985]), a 7–2 Supreme Court decision eased the strict requirements of *Witherspoon*. Writing for the majority, Justice Rehnquist declared that the new capital punishment procedures left less discretion to jurors. Rehnquist indicated that potential jurors in capital cases should be excluded from jury duty in a manner similar to how they were excluded in noncapital cases. (In a noncapital case, the prospective jurors typically go through a selection process in which the prosecution and the defense question them about their attitudes toward the crime and the people and issues related to it to determine if they are too biased to be fair.)

No longer would a juror's "automatic" bias against imposing the death penalty have to be proved with "unmistakable clarity." A prosecutor could not be expected to ask all the questions necessary to determine if a juror would automatically rule against the death penalty or fail to convict a defendant if he or she were likely to face execution. Fundamentally, the question of exclusion from a jury should be determined by the interplay of the prosecutor and the defense lawyer and by the decision of the judge based on his or her initial observations of the prospective juror. Judges can see firsthand whether prospective jurors' beliefs would bias their ability to impose the death penalty.

In his dissent, Justice Brennan claimed that making it easier to eliminate those who opposed capital punishment from the jury created a jury not only more likely to impose the death sentence but also more likely to convict. He also attacked the majority interpretation that now treated exclusion from a capital case as being similar to exclusion from any other case.

It Does Not Matter if "Death-Qualified" Juries Are More Likely to Convict

In *Lockhart v. McCree* (476 U.S. 162 [1986]), the Supreme Court firmly resolved the issue presented in *Witherspoon* regarding a fair trial with a death-qualified jury. (A death-qualified jury is another name for a jury that is willing to sentence a person to death after hearing the evidence of the case.)

Ardia McCree was convicted of murdering Evelyn Boughton while robbing her gift shop and service station in Camden, Arkansas, in February 1978. In accordance with Arkansas law, the trial judge removed eight prospective jurors because they indicated they could not, under any circumstances, vote for the imposition of the death sentence. The resulting jury then convicted McCree and, even though the state sought the death penalty, sentenced the defendant to life imprisonment without parole.

McCree appealed, claiming that the removal of the so-called *Witherspoon* excludables violated his right to a fair trial under the Sixth and 14th Amendments. These amendments guaranteed that his innocence or guilt would be determined by an impartial jury selected from a representative cross-section of the community, which would include people strongly opposed to the death penalty. McCree cited several studies, revealing that death-qualified juries were more likely to convict. Both the federal district court and the federal court of appeals agreed with McCree, but in a 6–3 decision, the Supreme Court disagreed.

The high court majority did not accept the validity of the studies. Speaking for the majority, Justice Rehnquist argued that, even if the justices did accept the validity of these studies, "the Constitution does not prohibit the States from 'death qualifying' juries in capital cases." Justice Rehnquist further observed:

The exclusion from jury service of large groups of individuals not on the basis of their inability to serve as jurors, but on the basis of some immutable characteristic such as race, gender, or ethnic background, undeniably gave rise to an "appearance of unfairness."

[Nevertheless], unlike blacks, women, and Mexican-Americans, "*Witherspoon*-excludables" are singled out for exclusion in capital cases on the basis of an attribute that is within the individual's control. It is important to remember that not all who oppose the death penalty are subject to removal for cause in capital cases; those who firmly believe that the death penalty is unjust may nevertheless serve as jurors in capital cases so long as they state clearly that they are willing to temporarily set aside their own beliefs in deference to the rule of law. Because the group of "*Witherspoon*-excludables" includes only those who cannot and will not conscientiously obey the law with respect to one of the issues in a capital case, "death qualification" hardly can be said to create an "appearance of unfairness."

Writing in dissent, Justice Marshall observed that if the high court thought in *Witherspoon* that excluding those who opposed the death penalty meant that a convicted murderer would not get a fair hearing during the sentencing part of the trial, it would also logically mean that he or she would not get a fair hearing during the initial trial part. The court minority generally accepted the studies showing "that 'death qualification' in fact produces juries somewhat more 'conviction-prone' than 'non-death-qualified' juries."

DOES THE BUCK STOP WITH THE JURY?

During the course of a robbery in October 1980 Bobby Caldwell shot and killed the owner of a Mississippi grocery store. He was tried and found guilty. In the sentencing phase of the trial Caldwell's attorney pleaded for mercy, concluding his summation by emphasizing to the jury, "I implore you to think deeply about this matter.... You are the judges and you will have to decide his fate. It is an awesome responsibility, I know—an awesome responsibility."

Responding to the defense attorney's plea, the prosecutor played down the responsibility of the jury, stressing that a life sentence would be reviewed by a higher court: "[The defense] would have you believe that you're going to kill this man and they know—they know that your decision is not the final decision.... Your job is reviewable.... They know, as I know, and as Judge Baker has told you, that the decision you render is automatically reviewable by the Supreme Court."

The jury sentenced Caldwell to death, and the case was automatically appealed. The Mississippi Supreme Court upheld the conviction, but split 4–4 on the validity of the death sentence, thereby upholding the death sentence by an equally divided court. Caldwell appealed to the U.S. Supreme Court.

In a 5–3 decision (Justice Powell took no part in the decision), the Supreme Court, in *Caldwell v. Mississippi* (472 U.S. 320 [1985]), vacated (annulled) the death sentence. Writing for the majority, Justice Marshall noted, "It is constitutionally impermissible to rest a death sentence on a determination made by a sentencer who has been led to believe, as the jury was in this case, that the responsibility for determining the appropriateness of the defendant's death rests elsewhere.... [This Court] has taken as a given that capital sentencers would view their task as the serious one of determining whether a specific human being should die at the hands of the State."

Furthermore, the high court pointed out that the appeals court was not the place to make this life-or-death decision. Most appellate courts would presume that the sentencing was correctly done, which would leave the defendant at a distinct disadvantage. The jurors, expecting to be reversed by an appeals court, might choose to "send a message" of extreme disapproval of the defendant's acts and sentence him or her to death to show they will not tolerate such actions. Should the appeals court fail to reverse the decision, the defendant might be executed when the jury only intended to "send a message."

The three dissenting judges believed "the Court has overstated the seriousness of the prosecutor's comments" and that it was "highly unlikely that the jury's sense of responsibility was diminished."

KEEPING PAROLE INFORMATION FROM THE JURY

In 1990 Jonathan Dale Simmons beat an elderly woman to death in her home in Columbia, South Carolina. The week before his capital murder trial began, he pleaded guilty to first-degree burglary and two counts of criminal sexual conduct in connection with two prior assaults on elderly women. These guilty pleas resulted in convictions for violent offenses, which made him ineligible for parole if convicted of any other violent crime.

At the capital murder trial, over the defense counsel's objection, the court did not allow the defense to ask prospective jurors if they understood the meaning of a "life" sentence as it applied to the defendant. Under South Carolina law a defendant who was deemed a future threat to society and receiving a life sentence was ineligible for parole. The prosecution also asked the judge not to mention parole.

During deliberation, the jurors asked the judge if the imposition of a life sentence carried with it the possibility of parole. The judge told the jury, "You are instructed not to consider parole or parole eligibility in reaching your verdict.... The terms life imprisonment and death sentence are to be understood in their plan [*sic*] and ordinary meaning."

The jury convicted Simmons of murder, sentencing him to death. On appeal the South Carolina Supreme Court upheld the sentence. The case was brought before the U.S. Supreme Court. In *Simmons v. South Carolina* (512 U.S. 154 [1994]), the high court overruled the South Carolina Supreme Court in a 6–2 decision, concluding:

> Where a defendant's future dangerousness is at issue, and state law prohibits his release on parole, due process requires that the sentencing jury be informed that the defendant is parole ineligible. An individual cannot be executed on the basis of information which he had no opportunity to deny or explain. Petitioner's jury reasonably may have believed that he could be released on parole if he were not executed. To the extent that this misunderstanding pervaded [the jury's] deliberations, it had the effect of creating a false choice between sentencing him to death and sentencing him to a limited period of incarceration. The trial court's refusal to apprise the jury of information so crucial to its determination, particularly when the State alluded to the defendant's future dangerousness in its argument, cannot be reconciled with this Court's well established precedents interpreting the Due Process Clause.

JUDGE SENTENCING

As will be explained in Chapter 5, as of September 2011 three states—Alabama, Delaware, and Florida—allowed trial judges to override jury-imposed sentences in capital cases. The constitutionality of the Alabama and Florida laws has been considered by the U.S. Supreme Court.

Florida

Under Florida's trifurcated trial system for capital cases, the jury decides the innocence or guilt of the accused. If the jury finds the defendant guilty, it recommends an advisory sentence of either life imprisonment or death. The trial judge considers mitigating and aggravating circumstances, weighs them against the jury recommendation, and then sentences the convicted murderer to either life or death. (Mitigating circumstances may lessen the responsibility for a crime, whereas aggravating circumstances may increase the responsibility for a crime.)

In 1975 a Florida jury convicted Joseph Spaziano of torturing and murdering two women. The jury recommended that Spaziano be sentenced to life imprisonment, but the trial judge, after considering the mitigating and aggravating circumstances, sentenced the defendant to death. In his appeal, Spaziano claimed the judge's overriding of the jury's recommendation of life imprisonment violated the Eighth Amendment's prohibition against a cruel and unusual punishment. The Supreme Court, in a 5–3 decision in *Spaziano v. Florida* (468 U.S. 447 [1984]), did not agree.

Spaziano's lawyers claimed juries, not judges, were better equipped to make reliable capital-sentencing decisions and that a jury's decision of life imprisonment should not be superseded. They reasoned that the death penalty was unlike any other sentence and required that the jury have the ultimate word. This belief had been upheld, Spaziano claimed, because 30 out of 37 states with capital punishment had the jury decide the prisoner's fate. Furthermore, the primary justification for the death penalty was retribution and an expression of community outrage. The jury served as the voice of the community and knew best whether a particular crime was so terrible that the community's response must be the death sentence.

The high court indicated that even though Spaziano's argument had some appeal, it contained two fundamental flaws. First, retribution played a role in all sentences, not just death sentences. Second, a jury was not the only source of community input: "The community's voice is heard at least as clearly in the legislature when the death penalty is authorized and the particular circumstances in which death is appropriate are defined." That trial judges imposed sentences was a normal part of the judicial system. The Supreme Court continued, "In light of the facts that the Sixth Amendment does not require jury sentencing, that the demands of fairness and reliability in capital cases do not require it, and that neither the nature of, nor the purpose behind, the death penalty requires jury sentencing, we cannot conclude that placing responsibility on the trial judge to impose the sentence in a capital case is unconstitutional."

The court added that just because 30 out of 37 states let the jury make the sentencing decision did not mean states that let a judge decide were wrong. The court pointed out that there is no one right way for a state to establish its method of capital sentencing.

Writing for the dissenters, Justice Stevens indicated, "Because of its severity and irrevocability, the death penalty is qualitatively different from any other punishment, and hence must be accompanied by unique safeguards to ensure that it is a justified response to a given offense.... I am convinced that the danger of an excessive response can only be avoided if the decision to impose the death penalty is made by a jury rather than by a single governmental official [because a jury] is best able to 'express the conscience of the community on the ultimate question of life or death.'"

Justice Stevens also gave weight to the fact that 30 out of 37 states had the jury make the decision, attesting to the high "level of consensus" that communities strongly believe life-or-death decisions should remain with the people—as represented by the jury—rather than relegated to a single government official.

Alabama

In March 1988 Louise Harris asked a coworker, Lorenzo McCarter, with whom she was having an affair, to find someone to kill her husband. McCarter paid two accomplices $100, with a promise of more money after they killed the husband. McCarter testified against Harris in exchange for the prosecutor's promise that he would not seek the death penalty against McCarter. McCarter testified that Harris had asked him to kill her husband so they could share in his death benefits. An Alabama jury convicted Harris of capital murder. At the sentencing hearing, witnesses testified to her good background and strong character. She was rearing seven children, held three jobs simultaneously, and was active in her church.

Alabama law gives capital sentencing authority to the trial judge but requires the judge to "consider" an advisory jury verdict. The jury voted 7–5 to give Harris life imprisonment without parole. The trial judge then considered her sentence. He found one aggravating circumstance (the murder was committed for monetary gain), one statutory mitigating circumstance (Harris had no prior criminal record), and one nonstatutory mitigating circumstance (Harris was a hardworking, respected member of her church).

Noting that she had planned the crime, financed it, and stood to benefit from the murder, the judge felt that the aggravating circumstance outweighed the other mitigating circumstances and sentenced her to death. On appeal, the Alabama Supreme Court affirmed the conviction and sentence. It rejected Harris's arguments that the procedure was unconstitutional because Alabama state law did "not specify the weight the judge must give to the jury's recommendation and thus permits the arbitrary imposition of the death penalty."

On appeal, the U.S. Supreme Court upheld in *Harris v. Alabama* (513 U.S. 504 [1995]) the Alabama Supreme Court's decision. Alabama's capital-sentencing process is similar to Florida's. Both require jury participation during sentencing but give the trial judge the ultimate sentencing authority. Nevertheless, even though the Florida statute requires that a trial judge must give "great weight" to the jury recommendation, the Alabama statute requires only that the judge "consider" the jury's recommendation.

As in the *Spaziano* case, the high court ruled that the Eighth Amendment does not require the state "to define the weight the sentencing judge must give to an advisory jury verdict." The court stated, "Because the Constitution permits the trial judge, acting alone, to impose a capital sentence ... it is not offended when a State further requires the judge to consider a jury recommendation and trusts the judge to give it the proper weight."

JURY SENTENCING

In 2002 the Supreme Court decided a case concerning death sentencing in Arizona involving the Sixth Amendment right to an impartial jury (as opposed to the Eighth Amendment, which bars a cruel and unusual punishment).

Timothy Stuart Ring was convicted of murder in the armed robbery of an armored-car driver in 1994. According to Arizona law, Ring's offense was punishable by life imprisonment or death. He would only be eligible for the death penalty if the trial judge held a separate hearing and found that aggravating factors warranted the death penalty.

One of Ring's accomplices, who negotiated a plea bargain in return for a second-degree murder charge, testified against him at a separate sentencing hearing without a jury present. The same judge who had presided at Ring's trial concluded that Ring committed the murder and that the crime was committed "in an especially heinous, cruel or depraved manner." Weighing the two aggravating circumstances against the mitigating evidence of Ring's minimal criminal record, the judge sentenced Ring to death.

Ring appealed to the Arizona Supreme Court, claiming that the state's capital sentencing law violated his Sixth and 14th Amendment rights because it allowed a judge, rather than a jury, to make the factual findings that made him eligible for a death sentence. The court put aside Ring's argument against Arizona's judge-sentencing system in light of the U.S. Supreme Court's ruling in *Walton v. Arizona* (497 U.S. 639 [1990]). The court held in *Walton* that Arizona's sentencing procedure was constitutional because "the additional facts found by the judge qualified as sentencing considerations, not as 'element[s] of the offense of capital murder.'" Next, the Arizona Supreme Court threw out the trial judge's finding of the heinous nature of the crime but concluded that Ring's minimal criminal record was not enough to outweigh the aggravating evidence of "planned, ruthless robbery and killing." The court affirmed the death sentence.

Ring took his case to the U.S. Supreme Court. On June 24, 2002, by a 7–2 vote, the court ruled in *Ring v. Arizona* (536 U.S. 584) that only juries and not judges can determine the presence of aggravating circumstances that warrant the death sentence. This case differs from the *Harris* and *Spaziano* cases in which the court ruled simply that a judge could sentence a person to death after hearing a jury's recommendation. In the *Ring* opinion the court included a discussion of *Apprendi v. New Jersey* (530 U.S. 466 [2000]), in which it held that "the Sixth Amendment does not permit a defendant to be 'expose[d]...to a penalty exceeding the maximum he would receive if punished according to the facts reflected in the jury verdict alone.'" *Apprendi* involved a defendant in a noncapital case who received a prison term beyond the maximum sentence. This occurred because New Jersey law allowed sentencing judges to increase the penalty if they found that a crime was racially motivated. In *Apprendi*, the court held that any fact other than a prior conviction that increases the punishment for a crime beyond the maximum allowed by law must be found by a jury beyond a reasonable doubt. The court found *Walton* and *Apprendi* irreconcilable. The court

overruled *Walton* "to the extent that it allows a sentencing judge, sitting without a jury, to find an aggravating circumstance necessary for imposition of the death penalty." Justice Ruth Bader Ginsburg (1933–), who delivered the opinion of the court, wrote, "The right to trial by jury guaranteed by the Sixth Amendment would be senselessly diminished if it encompassed the factfinding necessary to increase a defendant's sentence by two years [referring to *Apprendi*], but not the factfinding necessary to put him to death. We hold that the Sixth Amendment applies to both."

However, Justice Antonin Scalia (1936–), joined by Justice Clarence Thomas (1948–), pointed out in a separate concurring opinion that under *Ring*, states that let judges impose the death sentence may continue to do so by requiring the finding of aggravating factors necessary to the imposition of the death penalty during the trial phase.

Justice Sandra Day O'Connor (1930–), in her dissenting opinion, joined by Chief Justice Rehnquist, claimed that just as the *Apprendi* decision has overburdened the appeals courts, the *Ring* decision will cause more federal appeals. O'Connor observed that *Ring v. Arizona* also invalidates the capital sentencing procedure of four other states. These included Idaho and Montana, where a judge had the sole sentencing authority, as well as Colorado and Nebraska, where a three-judge panel made the sentencing decisions. The court ruling also potentially affected Alabama, Delaware, Florida, and Indiana, where the jury rendered an advisory verdict, but the judge had the ultimate sentencing authority.

The *Ring* Decision Does Not Retroactively Apply to Those Already Sentenced for Murder

The Arizona death row inmate Warren Summerlin was convicted of brutally crushing the skull of the bill collector Brenna Bailey and then sexually assaulting her. Summerlin was convicted by a jury, and an Arizona trial judge sentenced him to death in 1982. After the *Ring* decision was handed down, the U.S. Court of Appeals for the Ninth Circuit ruled 8–3 in *Summerlin v. Stewart* (309 F.3d 1193 [9th Cir., 2003]) that in light of *Ring v. Arizona*, Summerlin's death sentence should be vacated. The appellate court held that the Supreme Court's ruling should apply retroactively, even to those inmates who have exhausted their appeals. The prosecution brought the case to the U.S. Supreme Court.

In *Schriro v. Summerlin* (No. 03-526 [2004]), the Supreme Court reversed the appellate court's decision in a 5–4 vote. The nation's highest court concluded that the *Ring* ruling changed only the procedures involved in a sentencing trial for capital punishment cases and did not alter those fundamental legal guidelines judges and juries follow when sentencing a person to death. As such, the *Ring* ruling does not call into question the accuracy of past convictions and should not be retroactive. Speaking for the majority, Justice Scalia wrote, "[We] give retroactive effect to only a small set of 'watershed rules of criminal procedure' implicating the fundamental fairness and accuracy of the criminal proceeding.... That a new procedural rule is 'fundamental' in some abstract sense is not enough; the rule must be one 'without which the likelihood of an accurate conviction is seriously diminished.'"

DOUBLE JEOPARDY

In 1991 David Sattazahn was convicted for the 1987 murder of a restaurant manager in Berks County, Pennsylvania. Sattazahn and an accomplice killed the manager in the process of robbing him of the day's receipts. The state sought the death sentence and included an aggravating circumstance: the commission of murder while perpetrating a felony. During the sentencing phase the jury could not reach a verdict as to life or death. The trial judge considered the jury as hung and imposed an automatic sentence of life imprisonment as mandated by state law.

On appeal to the Pennsylvania Superior Court, Sattazahn was granted a new trial. The court held that the trial judge had erred in jury instructions relating to his offenses and reversed his murder conviction. During the second trial the state again sought the death penalty, this time adding a second aggravating factor: the defendant's history of felony convictions of using or threatening violence to the victim. The jury convicted Sattazahn of first-degree murder and sentenced him to death.

Next, the Pennsylvania Supreme Court heard Sattazahn's case. The death row inmate claimed, among other things, that the U.S. constitution prohibits the imposition of the death penalty in his case because it guarantees protection from double jeopardy. The double jeopardy clause of the Fifth Amendment states that "no person shall ... be subject for the same offense to be twice put in jeopardy of life or limb." In other words, no person can be tried or punished twice for the same crime.

Relying on its ruling in *Commonwealth v. Martorano* (634 A.2d 1063,1071 [Pa. 1993]), the Pennsylvania Supreme Court affirmed both Sattazahn's conviction and death sentence. In *Martorano*, the court noted that the jury, as in Sattazahn's first trial, was deadlocked. The hung jury did not "acquit" the defendant of the death sentence. Therefore, there was no double jeopardy prohibition against the death penalty during the second trial.

In *Sattazahn v. Pennsylvania* (537 U.S. 101 [2003]), the U.S. Supreme Court, by a 5–4 vote, agreed with the ruling of the Pennsylvania Supreme Court. Justice Scalia, writing the majority opinion, concluded that double jeopardy did not exist in this case. According to the court, "The touchstone for double-jeopardy protection in capital-sentencing proceedings is whether there has been an 'acquittal.' Petitioner here cannot establish that the jury or

the court 'acquitted' him during his first capital-sentencing proceeding. As to the jury: The verdict form returned by the foreman stated that the jury deadlocked 9-to-3 on whether to impose the death penalty; it made no findings with respect to the alleged aggravating circumstance. That result—or more appropriately, that non-result—cannot fairly be called an acquittal."

Furthermore, the court added that the imposition of a life sentence by the judge did not "acquit" the defendant of the death penalty because the judge was just following the state law. "A default judgment does not trigger a double jeopardy bar to the death penalty upon retrial."

Justice Ginsburg, writing for the dissent, was joined by Justices Stevens, David H. Souter (1939–), and Stephen G. Breyer (1938–). The dissenters argued that jeopardy terminated after the judge imposed a final judgment of life imprisonment when the jury was deadlocked. Therefore, the defendant was "acquitted" of the death penalty the first time, which means that the state could not seek the death penalty the second time. Justice Ginsburg also pointed out that "the Court's holding confronts defendants with a perilous choice.... Under the court's decision, if a defendant sentenced to life after a jury deadlock chooses to appeal her underlying conviction, she faces the possibility of death if she is successful on appeal but convicted on retrial. If, on the other hand, the defendant loses her appeal, or chooses to forgo an appeal, the final judgment for life stands. In other words, a defendant in Sattazahn's position must relinquish either her right to file a potentially meritorious appeal, or her state-granted entitlement to avoid the death penalty."

SENTENCING PROCEDURES
Comparative Proportionality Review: Comparing Similar Crimes and Sentences

On July 5, 1978, in Mira Mesa, California, Robert Harris and his brother decided to steal a car they would need for a getaway in a planned bank robbery. Harris approached two teenage boys eating hamburgers in a car. He forced them at gunpoint to drive to a nearby wooded area. The teenagers offered to delay telling the police of the car robbery and even to give the authorities misleading descriptions of the two robbers. When one of the boys appeared to be fleeing, Harris shot both of them. Harris and his brother later committed the robbery, were soon caught, and confessed to the robbery and murders.

Harris was found guilty. In California, a convicted murderer could be sentenced to death or life imprisonment without parole only if "special circumstances" existed and the murder had been "willful, deliberate, premeditated, and committed during the commission of kidnapping and robbery." This had to be proven during a separate sentencing hearing.

The state showed that Harris was convicted of manslaughter in 1975; he was found in possession of a makeshift knife and garrote (an instrument used for strangulation) while in prison; he and other inmates sodomized another inmate; and he threatened that inmate's life. Harris testified that he had an unhappy childhood, had little education, and his father had sexually molested his sisters. The jury sentenced Harris to death, and the judge concurred.

Harris claimed the U.S. Constitution, as interpreted in previous capital punishment rulings, required the state of California to give his case comparative proportionality review to determine if his death sentence was not out of line with that of others convicted of similar crimes. In comparative proportionality review, a court considers the seriousness of the offense, the severity of the penalty, the sentences imposed for other crimes, and the sentencing in other jurisdictions for the same crime. Courts have occasionally struck down punishments that were inherently disproportionate and, therefore, cruel and unusual. Georgia, by law, and Florida, by practice, had incorporated such reviews in their procedures. Other states, such as Texas and California, had not.

When the case reached the U.S. Court of Appeals for the Ninth Circuit, the court agreed with Harris and ordered California to establish proportionality or lift the death sentence. In *Pulley v. Harris* (465 U.S. 37 [1984]), the U.S. Supreme Court, in a 7–2 decision, did not agree. The court noted that the California procedure contained enough safeguards to guarantee a defendant a fair trial and those convicted a fair sentence. The high court added, "That some [state statutes] providing proportionality review are constitutional does not mean that such review is indispensable. . . . To endorse the statute as a whole is not to say that anything different is unacceptable. . . . Examination of our 1976 cases makes clear that they do not establish proportionality review as a constitutional requirement."

Justice Brennan, joined by Justice Marshall, dissented. He noted that the Supreme Court had thrown out the existing death penalty procedures during the 1970s because they were deemed arbitrary (subject to individual judgment) and capricious. He believed they still were, but the introduction of proportionality might "eliminate some, if only a small part, of the irrationality that currently infects imposition of the death penalty by the various States."

Due Process and Advance Notice of Imposing the Death Penalty

Robert Bravence and Cheryl Bravence were beaten to death at their campsite near Santiam Creek, Idaho, in 1983. Two brothers, Bryan Lankford and Mark Lankford, were charged with two counts of first-degree murder. At the arraignment (a summoning before a court to hear and answer charges), the trial judge advised Bryan Lankford that, if convicted of either of the two charges (he was charged with both murders), the maximum punishment he might receive was either life imprisonment or death.

After the arraignment, Bryan Lankford's attorney made a deal with the prosecutor. Bryan Lankford entered a plea bargain in which he agreed to take two lie-detector tests in exchange for a lesser sentence. Even though the results were somewhat unclear, they convinced the prosecutor that Lankford's older brother, Mark, was primarily responsible for the crimes and was the actual killer of both victims. Bryan Lankford's attorney and the prosecutor agreed on an indeterminate sentence with a 10-year minimum in exchange for a guilty plea, subject to commitment from the trial judge that he would impose that sentence. The judge refused to make such a commitment, and the case went to trial.

The judge also refused to instruct the jury that a specific intent to kill was required to support a conviction of first-degree murder. The jury found Bryan Lankford guilty on both counts. The sentencing hearing was postponed until after Mark Lankford's trial. He was also charged with both murders.

Before the sentencing trial, at Bryan Lankford's request, the trial judge ordered the prosecutor to notify the court and Lankford whether it would seek the death penalty and, if so, to file a statement of the aggravating circumstance on which the death penalty would be based. The prosecutor notified the judge that the state would not recommend the death penalty. Several proceedings followed, including Lankford's request for a new attorney, a motion for a new trial, and a motion for continuance of the sentencing hearing. At none of the proceedings was there any mention that Lankford might receive the death penalty.

At the sentencing hearing, the prosecutor recommended a life sentence, with a minimum ranging between 10 and 20 years. The trial judge indicated that he considered Lankford's testimony unbelievable and that the seriousness of the crime warranted more severe punishment than recommended by the state. He sentenced Lankford to death.

Lankford appealed, asserting that the trial judge violated the U.S. Constitution by failing to give notice that he intended to impose the death penalty in spite of the state's earlier notice that it would not seek the death penalty. The judge maintained that the Idaho Code provided Lankford with sufficient notice. The judge added that the fact the prosecutor said he would not seek the death penalty had "no bearing on the adequacy of notice to petitioner that the death penalty might be imposed." The Idaho Supreme Court agreed with the judge's decision.

In *Lankford v. Idaho* (500 U.S. 110 [1991]), the U.S. Supreme Court reversed the state supreme court ruling and remanded the case (sent it back to the lower court for further proceedings) for a new trial. Writing for the majority, Justice Stevens stated that the due process clause of the 14th Amendment was violated. Stevens noted, "If defense counsel had been notified that the trial judge was contemplating a death sentence based on five specific aggravating circumstances, presumably she would have advanced arguments that addressed these circumstances; however, she did not make these arguments, because they were entirely inappropriate in a discussion about the length of petitioner's possible incarceration."

Stevens further indicated that the trial judge's silence, in effect, hid from Lankford and his attorney, as well as from the prosecutor, the principal issues to be decided.

In a dissenting opinion, Justice Scalia wrote that Lankford's due process rights were not violated because he knew that he had been convicted of first-degree murder, and the Idaho Code clearly states that "every person guilty of murder of the first degree shall be punished by death or by imprisonment for life." At the arraignment the trial judge told Lankford that he could receive either punishment. Scalia further noted that, in Idaho, the death penalty statute places full responsibility for determining the sentence on the judge.

CHAPTER 3

SUPREME COURT RULINGS II: CIRCUMSTANCES THAT DO AND DO NOT WARRANT THE DEATH PENALTY, RIGHT TO EFFECTIVE COUNSEL, APPEALS BASED ON NEW EVIDENCE, AND CONSTITUTIONALITY OF EXECUTION METHODS

CIRCUMSTANCES FOUND NOT TO WARRANT THE DEATH PENALTY

Rape of Adult Women and Kidnapping

On June 29, 1977, a 5–4 divided U.S. Supreme Court ruled in *Coker v. Georgia* (433 U.S. 584) that the death penalty may not be imposed for the crime of raping an adult woman that does not result in death. The court stated in *Coker*:

> Rape is without doubt deserving of serious punishment; but in terms of moral depravity and of the injury to the person and to the public, it does not compare with murder, which does involve the unjustified taking of human life. Although it may be accompanied by another crime, rape by definition does not include the death of or even the serious injury to another person. The murderer kills; the rapist, if no more than that, does not. Life is over for the victim of the murderer; for the rape victim, life may not be nearly so happy as it was, but it is not over and normally is not beyond repair. We have the abiding conviction that the death penalty, which "is unique in its severity and irrevocability," is an excessive penalty for the rapist who, as such, does not take human life.

Chief Justice Warren Burger (1907–1995), joined by Justice William H. Rehnquist (1924–2005), dissented. The justices stated:

> A rapist not only violates a victim's privacy and personal integrity, but inevitably causes serious psychological as well as physical harm in the process.... Rape is not a mere physical attack—it is destructive of the human personality. The remainder of the victim's life may be gravely affected, and this in turn may have a serious detrimental effect upon her husband and any children she may have.... Victims may recover from the physical damage of knife or bullet wounds, or a beating with fists or a club, but recovery from such a gross assault on the human personality is not healed by medicine or surgery. To speak blandly, as the plurality does, of rape victims who are "unharmed," or to classify the human outrage of rape, as does Mr. Justice Powell, in terms of "excessively brutal," versus "moderately brutal," takes too little account of the profound suffering the crime imposes upon the victims and their loved ones.

The court also held that kidnapping did not warrant the death penalty. Even though the victims usually suffered tremendously, they had not lost their lives. (If the kidnapped victim was killed, then the kidnapper could be tried for murder.)

Child Rape

The Supreme Court's rulings in *Coker v. Georgia* and *Eberheart v. Georgia* were interpreted to apply only to the rape of adult women. The constitutionality of applying the death penalty for child rape remained untested. In 2008 the issue was resolved when the court ruled in *Kennedy v. Louisiana* (554 U.S. ___) that a statute in Louisiana prescribing the death penalty for child rape violated the Eighth Amendment of the U.S. Constitution. The Eighth Amendment bars "cruel and unusual punishments."

In 2003 Patrick Kennedy was convicted of raping his eight-year-old stepdaughter in 1998. The girl was severely injured by the intercourse and required emergency surgery to stem excessive bleeding and repair internal injuries. At that time, Louisiana law allowed the death penalty for aggravated rape of a child under the age of 12 years. In 2007 the state supreme court upheld the sentence, noting that four other states—Georgia, Montana, Oklahoma, and South Carolina—had similar laws and that "children are a class that need special protection." However, Chief Justice Pascal Frank Calogero Jr. (1931–) of the Louisiana Supreme Court dissented with the ruling, arguing that the U.S. Supreme Court had "set out a bright-line and easily administered rule" that forbids capital punishment for crimes in which the victim survives.

In June 2008 the U.S. Supreme Court overturned the death sentence in a narrow 5–4 decision. Justice Anthony M. Kennedy (1936–) acknowledged the heinous nature of the crime, determining: "Petitioner's crime was one that cannot be recounted in these pages in a way sufficient to capture in full the hurt and horror inflicted on his victim or to convey the revulsion society, and the jury that represents it, sought to express by sentencing petitioner to death." Nevertheless, the majority of the justices held that there was no national consensus on the imposition of capital punishment for child rape. Only a handful of states had or were attempting to pass similar laws. In addition, Louisiana was the only state at the time with people on death row for child rape. (Another man, Richard Davis, had been sentenced to die for raping a five-year-old girl in 2006.)

The court's decision was extremely controversial and received harsh criticism from the Louisiana governor Bobby Jindal (1971–) and then–presidential candidates Senator John McCain (1936–) and Senator Barack Obama (1961–). In October 2008 Louisiana asked the court to reconsider its ruling after it came to light that the military penal code also allowed the death penalty for child rape—a fact not mentioned or apparently considered by the court in its original deliberations over the existence of a "national consensus" on the issue. The court refused to reopen the case. It did issue a modified opinion (October 2008, http://www.scotusblog.com/wp/wp-content/uploads/2008/10/07-343.pdf) that stated, "We find that the military penalty does not affect our reasoning or conclusions."

An Unconstitutionally Vague Statute

During a heated dispute with his wife of 28 years, Robert Godfrey threatened her with a knife. Mrs. Godfrey, saying she was leaving her husband, went to stay with relatives. That same day she went to court to file for aggravated assault. Several days later she initiated divorce proceedings and moved in with her mother. During subsequent telephone conversations, the couple argued over the wife's determination to leave Godfrey permanently.

About two weeks later Godfrey killed his wife and mother-in-law. Godfrey told police that his wife phoned him, telling him she expected all the money from the planned sale of their home. She also told Godfrey she was never reconciling with him. Godfrey confessed that he went to his mother-in-law's nearby trailer and shot his wife through a window, killing her instantly. He then entered the trailer, struck his fleeing 11-year-old daughter on the head with the gun, and shot his mother-in-law in the head, killing her. Godfrey believed his mother-in-law was responsible for his wife's reluctance to reconcile with him.

Godfrey was convicted of killing his wife and mother-in-law and of the aggravated assault on his daughter. The Georgia Code permits the imposition of the death penalty in the case of a murder that "was outrageously or wantonly vile, horrible, or inhuman in that it involved torture, depravity of mind, or an aggravated brutality to the victim." Aware of this law, the jury sentenced Godfrey to die. He appealed, claiming that the statute was unconstitutionally vague. After the Georgia Supreme Court upheld the lower court decision, the case was appealed to the U.S. Supreme Court.

The Supreme Court noted in *Godfrey v. Georgia* (446 U.S. 420 [1980]) that the victims were killed instantly (i.e., there was no torture), the victims had been "causing [Godfrey] extreme emotional trauma," and he acknowledged his responsibility. The high court concluded that, in this case, the Georgia law was unconstitutionally vague. Moreover, the Georgia Supreme Court did not attempt to narrow the definition of "outrageously or wantonly vile." In a concurring opinion, Justice Thurgood Marshall (1908–1993), joined by Justice William J. Brennan (1906–1997), found this to be an example of the inherently arbitrary (subject to individual judgment) and capricious (unpredictable) nature of capital punishment, because even the prosecutor in Godfrey's case observed many times that there was no torture or abuse involved.

CRIMINAL INTENT

On April 1, 1975, Sampson Armstrong and Jeanette Armstrong, on the pretext of requesting water for their overheated car, tried to rob Thomas Kersey at his home. Earl Enmund waited in the getaway car. Kersey called for his wife, who tried to shoot Jeanette Armstrong. The Armstrongs killed the Kerseys. Enmund was tried for aiding and abetting in the robbery-murder and sentenced to death.

In *Enmund v. Florida* (458 U.S. 782 [1982]), the Supreme Court ruled 5–4 that, in this case, the death penalty violated the Eighth and 14th Amendments to the U.S. Constitution. The majority noted that only nine of the 36 states with capital punishment permitted its use on a criminal who was not actually present at the scene of the crime. The exception was the case where someone paid a hit man to murder the victim.

Furthermore, over the years juries had tended not to sentence to death criminals who had not actually been at the scene of the crime. Certainly, Enmund was guilty of planning and participating in a robbery, but murder had not been part of the plan. Statistically, because someone is killed in 1 out of 200 robberies, Enmund could not have expected that the Kerseys would be murdered during the robbery attempt. The court concluded that, because Enmund did not kill or plan to kill, he should be tried only for his participation in the robbery. The court observed, "We have no doubt that robbery is a serious crime deserving serious punishment. It is not, however, a crime 'so grievous an affront to humanity that the only adequate response may be the penalty of death.' It does not compare with murder, which does involve the unjustified taking of human life.... The murderer kills; the [robber], if no more than that, does not. Life is over for the victim of the murderer; for the [robbery] victim, life ... is not over and normally is not beyond repair."

Writing for the minority, Justice Sandra Day O'Connor (1930–) concluded that intent is a complex issue. It should be left to the judge and jury trying the accused to decide intent, not a federal court far removed from the actual trial.

Enmund Revisited

However, just because a person had no intent to kill does not mean that he or she cannot be sentenced to death. In the early morning of September 22, 1978, Crawford Bullock and his friend Ricky Tucker had been drinking at a bar in Jackson, Mississippi, and were offered a ride home by Mark Dickson, an acquaintance.

During the drive an argument ensued over money that Dickson owed Tucker, and Dickson stopped the car. The argument escalated into a fistfight, and, outside the car, Bullock held Dickson while Tucker punched Dickson and hit him in the face with a whiskey bottle. When Dickson fell, Tucker smashed his head with a concrete block, killing him. Tucker and Bullock disposed of the body. The next day police spotted Bullock driving the victim's car. After his arrest Bullock confessed.

Under Mississippi law a person involved in a robbery that results in murder may be convicted of capital murder regardless of "the defendant's own lack of intent that any killing take place." The jury was never asked to consider whether Bullock in fact killed, attempted to kill, or intended to kill. He was convicted and sentenced to death as an accomplice to the crime. During the appeals process the Mississippi Supreme Court confirmed that Bullock was indeed a participant in the murder.

In January 1986 a divided U.S. Supreme Court modified the *Enmund* decision with a 5–4 ruling in *Cabana v. Bullock* (474 U.S. 376). The court indicated that even though *Enmund* had to be considered at some point during the judicial process, the initial jury trying the accused did not necessarily have to consider the *Enmund* ruling. The high court ruled that even though the jury had not been made aware of the issue of intent, the Mississippi Supreme Court had considered this question. Because *Enmund* did not require that intent be presented at the initial jury trial, only that it be considered at some time during the judicial process, the state of Mississippi had met that requirement.

The four dissenting justices claimed that it was difficult for any appeals court to determine intent from reading a typed transcript of a trial. Seeing the accused and others involved was important in helping determine who was telling the truth and who was not. This was why *Enmund* must be raised to the jury so it could consider the question of intent in light of what it had seen and heard directly.

"Reckless Indifference to the Value of Human Life"

Gary Tison was a convicted criminal who had been sentenced to life imprisonment for murdering a prison guard during an escape from the Arizona State Prison in Florence, Arizona. Tison's three sons, his wife, his brother, and other relatives planned a prison escape involving Tison and a fellow prisoner, Randy Greenawalt, also a convicted murderer.

On the day of the planned escape in July 1978, Tison's sons smuggled guns into the prison's visitation area. After locking up the guards and visitors, the five men fled in a car. They later transferred to another car and waited in an abandoned house for a plane to take them to Mexico. When the plane did not come, the men got back on the road. The car soon had flat tires. One son flagged down a passing car. The motorist who stopped to help was driving with his wife, their 2-year-old son, and a 15-year-old niece.

Gary Tison then told his sons to go get some water from the motorist's car, which was going to be left with the family they planned to abandon in the desert. While the sons were gone, Tison and Greenawalt shot and killed the family. Several days later two of Tison's sons and Greenawalt were captured. The third son was killed, and Tison escaped into the desert, where he later died of exposure.

The surviving Tisons and Greenawalt were found guilty and sentenced to death. The sons, citing *Enmund*, appealed, claiming that they had neither pulled the triggers nor intended the deaths of the family who had stopped to help them. In *Tison v. Arizona* (481 U.S. 137 [1987]), the Supreme Court ruled 5–4 to uphold the death sentence, indicating that the Tison sons had shown a "reckless indifference to the value of human life [which] may be every bit as shocking to the moral sense as an 'intent to kill.'"

The Tisons may not have pulled the triggers (and the court fully accepted the premise that they did not do the shootings or directly intend them to happen), but they released and then assisted two convicted murderers. They should have realized that freeing two killers and giving them guns could very well put innocent people in great danger. Moreover, they continued to help the escapees even after the family was killed.

"These facts," concluded Justice O'Connor for the majority, "not only indicate that the Tison brothers' participation in the crime was anything but minor; they also would clearly support a finding that they both subjectively appreciated that their acts were likely to result in the taking of innocent life." Unlike the situation in the *Enmund* case, they were not sitting in a car far from the murder scene. They were direct participants in the whole event. The death sentence would stand.

Writing for the minority, Justice Brennan observed that had a prison guard been murdered (Gary Tison had murdered a prison guard in a previous escape attempt), then the court's argument would have made sense. The murder of the family, however, made no sense and was not even necessary for the escape. The Tison sons were away from the murder scene getting water for the victims and could have done nothing to save them. Even though they were guilty of planning and carrying out an escape, the murder of the family who stopped to help them was an unexpected outcome of the escape.

Furthermore, the father had promised his sons that he would not kill during the escape, a promise he had kept despite several opportunities to kill during the actual prison escape. Therefore, it was not unreasonable for the sons to believe that their father would not kill in a situation that did not appear to warrant it. Justice Brennan concluded that "like Enmund, the Tisons neither killed nor attempted or intended to kill anyone. Like Enmund, the Tisons have been sentenced to death for the intentional acts of others which the Tisons did not expect, which were not essential to the felony, and over which they had no control."

In 1992 the Arizona Supreme Court overturned the death penalty sentences for the Tison sons. They were subsequently sentenced to life in prison. Greenawalt was executed in 1997.

RIGHT TO EFFECTIVE COUNSEL

In 1989 Kevin Eugene Wiggins received a death sentence for the 1988 drowning of an elderly Maryland woman in her home. The Maryland Court of Appeals affirmed his sentence in 1991. With the help of new counsel, Wiggins sought postconviction relief, challenging the quality of his initial lawyers. Wiggins claimed his lawyers failed to investigate and present mitigating evidence (evidence that may lessen responsibility for a crime) that he was physically and sexually abused as a child. The sentencing jury never heard that he was starved, that his mother punished him by burning his hand on the stove, and that after the state put him in foster care at age six, he suffered more physical and sexual abuse.

In 2001 a federal district court concluded that Wiggins's first lawyers should have conducted a more thorough investigation into his childhood abuse, which would have kept the jury from imposing a death sentence. However, the U.S. Court of Appeals for the Fourth Circuit reversed the district court decision, ruling that the original attorneys had made a "reasonable strategic decision" to concentrate their defense on raising doubts about Wiggins's guilt instead.

On June 26, 2003, the U.S. Supreme Court threw out the death sentence. In *Wiggins v. Smith* (539 U.S. 510), the court ruled 7–2 that Wiggins's lawyers violated his Sixth Amendment right to effective assistance of counsel. The court noted, "Counsel's investigation into Wiggins' background did not reflect reasonable professional judgment. . . . Given the nature and extent of the abuse, there is a reasonable probability that a competent attorney, aware of this history, would have introduced it at sentencing, and that a jury confronted with such mitigating evidence would have returned with a different sentence."

When Does the Right to Counsel End?

Joseph Giarratano was a Virginia death row prisoner. He received full counsel for his trial and for his initial appeal. Afterward, Virginia would no longer provide him with his own lawyer. He went to court, complaining that because he was poor the state of Virginia should provide him with counsel to help prepare postconviction appeals. Virginia permitted the condemned prisoner the right to use the prison libraries to prepare an appeal, but it did not provide the condemned with his own personal attorney.

Virginia had unit attorneys, who were assigned to help prisoners with prison-related legal matters. A unit attorney could give guidance to death row inmates but could not act as the personal attorney for any one particular inmate. This case became a class action in which the federal district court certified a class made up of "all current and future Virginia inmates awaiting execution who do not have and cannot afford counsel to pursue postconviction proceedings."

The federal district court and the federal court of appeals agreed with Giarratano, but the Supreme Court, in *Murray v. Giarratano* (492 U.S. 1 [1989]), disagreed. Writing for the majority, Chief Justice Rehnquist concluded that even though the Sixth and 14th Amendments to the Constitution ensure an impoverished defendant the right to counsel at the trial stage of a criminal proceeding, they do not provide for counsel for postconviction proceedings, as the court ruled in *Pennsylvania v. Finley* (481 U.S. 551 [1987]). Because *Finley* had not specifically considered prisoners on death row, but all prisoners in general, the majority did not believe the decision needed to be reconsidered just because death row prisoners had more at stake.

Chief Justice Rehnquist agreed that those facing the death penalty have a right to counsel for the trial and during the initial appeal. During these periods the defendant needs a heightened measure of protection because the death penalty is involved. Later appeals, however, involve more procedural matters that "serve a different and more limited purpose than either the trial or appeal."

In dissent, Justice John Paul Stevens (1920–), who was joined by Justices Brennan, Marshall, and Harry A. Blackmun (1908–1999), indicated that he thought condemned prisoners in Virginia faced three critical differences from those considered in *Finley*. First, the Virginia prisoners had been sentenced to death, which made their condition different from a sentence of life imprisonment. Second, Virginia's particular judicial decision forbids certain issues to be raised during the direct review or appeals process and forces them to be considered only during later postconviction appeals. This means that important issues may be considered without the benefit of counsel. Finally, "unlike the ordinary inmate, who presumably has ample time to use and reuse the prison library and to seek guidance from other prisoners experienced in preparing . . . petitions . . . a grim deadline imposes a finite limit on the condemned person's capacity for useful research."

He continued, quoting from the district court's decision on the matter, an "inmate preparing himself and his family for impending death is incapable of performing the mental functions necessary to adequately pursue his claims."

Federal Judges Can Delay Executions to Allow Habeas Corpus Reviews

In 1988 Congress passed the Anti-Drug Abuse Act, which guaranteed qualified legal representation for poor death row defendants wanting to file for habeas corpus (a prisoner's petition to be heard in federal court) so that the counsel could assist in the preparation of the appeal. In 1994 this law was brought to question before the Supreme Court by the death row inmate Frank McFarland.

In November 1989 a Texas jury found McFarland guilty of stabbing to death a woman he had met in a bar and sentenced him to death. The state appellate court upheld his conviction, and two lower federal courts refused his request for a stay (postponement) of execution. The federal courts ruled that they did not have jurisdiction to stop the execution until McFarland filed a habeas corpus. The inmate argued that without the stay, he would be executed before he could obtain a lawyer to prepare the petition.

The Supreme Court granted a stay of execution. In *McFarland v. Scott* (512 U.S. 849 [1994]), the court ruled 5–4 to uphold the 1988 federal law. Once a defendant requested counsel, the federal court could postpone execution so the lawyer would have time to prepare an appeal. Justice Blackmun stated that "by providing indigent [poor] capital defendants with a mandatory right to qualified legal counsel in these proceedings, Congress has recognized that Federal habeas corpus has a particularly important role to play in promoting fundamental fairness in the imposition of the death penalty."

Does the Right to Counsel Extend to Crimes That Have Not Been Charged?

In 1994 Raymond Levi Cobb confessed to burglarizing the home of Lindsey Owings the previous year. He claimed no knowledge, however, of the disappearances of Owings's wife and infant at the time of the burglary. The court subsequently assigned Cobb a lawyer to represent him in the burglary offense. With the permission of Cobb's lawyer, investigators twice questioned Cobb regarding the disappearance of the Owings family. Both times Cobb denied any knowledge of the missing pair.

In 1995, while free on bond for the burglary and living with his father, Cobb told his father that he killed Margaret Owings and buried her baby, while still alive, with her. The father reported his son's confession to the police. When brought in, Cobb confessed to the police and waived his Miranda rights, which include the right to counsel. Cobb was convicted of the murders and sentenced to death. On appeal, Cobb claimed that his confession, which was obtained in violation of his Sixth Amendment right to counsel, should have been suppressed. He argued that his right to counsel attached (went into full effect) when he was reported for the burglary case, and despite his open confession to the police, he never officially gave up this right to counsel.

The Texas Court of Criminal Appeals reversed Cobb's conviction, ordering a new trial. The court considered Cobb's confession to the murders inadmissible, holding that "once the right to counsel attaches to the offense charged [burglary], it also attaches to any other offense [in this case, murder] that is very closely related factually to the offense charged."

The state appealed to the U.S. Supreme Court. In *Texas v. Cobb* (532 U.S. 162 [2001]), the court, in a 5–4 decision, stated, "The Sixth Amendment right [to counsel] . . . is offense specific. It cannot be invoked once for all future prosecutions, for it does not attach until a prosecution is commenced, that is, at or after the initiation of adversary judicial criminal proceedings—whether by way of formal charge, preliminary hearing, indictment, information, or arraignment."

This means that Cobb's right to counsel did not extend to crimes with which he had not been charged. Because this right did not prohibit investigators from questioning him about the murders without first notifying his lawyer, Cobb's confession was admissible.

CASES INVOLVING ERROR BY THE PROSECUTION
Coerced Confessions

Oreste C. Fulminante called the Mesa, Arizona, police to report the disappearance of his 11-year-old stepdaughter, Jeneane Michelle Hunt. Fulminante was caring for the child while his wife, Jeneane's mother, was in the hospital. Several days later Jeneane's body was found in the desert east of Mesa with two shots to the head, fired at close range by a large-caliber weapon. There was a ligature (a cord used in tying or binding) around her neck. Because of the decomposed state of her body, it was not possible to determine whether she had been sexually assaulted.

Fulminante's statements about the child's disappearance and his relationship to her included inconsistencies that made him a suspect in her death. He was not, however, charged with the murder. Fulminante left Arizona for New Jersey, where he was eventually convicted on federal charges of unlawful possession of a firearm by a felon.

While incarcerated, he became friendly with Anthony Sarivola, a former police officer. Sarivola had been involved in loan-sharking for organized crime but then became a paid informant for the Federal Bureau of Investigation (FBI). In prison he masqueraded as an organized crime figure. When Fulminante was receiving some tough treatment from the other inmates, Sarivola offered him protection, but only on the condition that Fulminante tell him everything.

Fulminante was later indicted in Arizona for the first-degree murder of Jeneane. In a hearing before the trial, Fulminante moved to suppress the statement he had made to Sarivola in prison and then later to Sarivola's wife, Donna, following his release from prison. He maintained that the confession to Sarivola was coerced and that the second confession was the "fruit" of the first one.

The trial court denied the motion to remove the statements from the record, finding that, based on the specified facts, the confessions were voluntary. Fulminante was convicted of Jeneane's murder and subsequently sentenced to death.

In his appeal Fulminante argued, among other things, that his confession to Sarivola was coerced and that its use at the trial violated his rights of due process under the Fifth and 14th Amendments to the Constitution. The Arizona Supreme Court ruled that the confession was coerced but initially determined that the admission of the confession at the trial was a harmless error because of the overpowering evidence against Fulminante. In legal terms, harmless error refers to an error committed during the trial that has no bearing on the outcome of the trial, and as such, is not harmful enough to reverse the outcome of the trial on appeal.

After Fulminante motioned for reconsideration, however, the Arizona Supreme Court ruled that the U.S. Supreme Court had set a precedent that prevented the use of harmless error in the case of a coerced confession. The harmless-error standard, as stated in *Chapman v. California* (386 U.S. 18 [1967]), held that an error is harmless if it appears "beyond a reasonable doubt that the error complained of did not contribute to the verdict obtained." The Arizona Supreme Court reversed the conviction and ordered that Fulminante be retried without the use of his confession to Sarivola. Because of differences in the state and federal courts over the admission of a coerced confession with regard to harmless-error analysis, the U.S. Supreme Court agreed to hear the case.

In *Arizona v. Fulminante* (499 U.S. 279 [1991]), Justice Byron R. White (1917–2002), writing for the majority, stated that even though the question was a close one, the Arizona Supreme Court was right in concluding that Fulminante's confession had been coerced. He further noted, "The Arizona Supreme Court found a credible threat of physical violence unless Fulminante confessed. Our cases have made clear that a finding of coercion need not depend upon actual violence by a government agent; a credible threat is sufficient. As we have said, 'coercion can be mental as well as physical, and . . . the blood of the accused is not the only hallmark of an unconstitutional inquisition.'"

Justice White further argued that the state of Arizona had failed to meet its burden of establishing, beyond a reasonable doubt, that the admission of Fulminante's confession to Sarivola was harmless. He added, "A confession is like no other evidence. Indeed, 'the defendant's own confession is probably the most probative [providing evidence] and damaging evidence that can be admitted against him. . . . The admissions of a defendant come from the actor himself, the most knowledgeable and unimpeachable source of information about his past conduct. Certainly, confessions have profound impact on the jury, so much so that we may justifiably doubt its ability to put them out of mind even if told to do so.'"

Presumption of Malice

In February 1981 Dale Robert Yates and Henry Davis planned to rob a country store in Greenville County, South Carolina. When they entered the store, only the owner, Willie Wood, was present. Yates and Davis showed their weapons and ordered Wood to give them money from the cash register. Davis handed Yates $3,000 and ordered Wood to lie across the counter. Wood, who had a pistol beneath his jacket, refused.

Meanwhile, Yates was backing out of the store with his gun pointed at the owner. After being told to do so by Davis, Yates fired two shots. The first bullet wounded Wood; the second missed. Yates then jumped into the car and waited for Davis. When Davis did not appear, Yates drove off. Inside the store, although wounded, Wood pursued Davis. As the two struggled, Wood's mother, Helen, came in and ran to help her son. During the struggle Helen Wood was stabbed once in the chest and died at the scene. Wood then shot Davis five times, killing him.

After Yates was arrested and charged with murder, his primary defense was that Helen Wood's death was not the probable natural consequence of the robbery he had planned with Davis. He claimed that he had brought the weapon only to induce the owner to give him the cash and that neither he nor Davis intended to kill anyone during the robbery.

The prosecutor's case for murder hinged on the agreement between Yates and Davis to commit an armed robbery. He argued that they planned to kill any witness, thereby making homicide a probable or natural result of the robbery. The prosecutor concluded, "It makes no difference who actually struck the fatal blow, the hand of one is the hand of all."

The judge told the jury that under South Carolina law, murder is defined as "the unlawful killing of any human being with malice aforethought either express or implied." In his instructions to the jury, the judge said, "Malice is implied or presumed by the law from the willful, deliberate, and intentional doing of an unlawful act without any just cause or excuse. In its general signification, malice means the doing of a wrongful act, intentionally, without justification or excuse.... I tell you, also, that malice is implied or presumed from the use of a deadly weapon."

The judge continued to instruct the jury on the theory of accomplice liability. The jury returned guilty verdicts on the murder charge and on all other counts in the indictment. Yates was sentenced to death.

Yates petitioned the South Carolina Supreme Court, asserting that the jury charge that "malice is implied or presumed from the use of a deadly weapon" was an unconstitutional burden-shifting instruction. The case was twice reviewed by the South Carolina Supreme Court, which agreed that the jury instructions were unconstitutional, but that allowing the jury to presume malice was a harmless error, one that had no bearing on the outcome of the trial. The South Carolina court found that the jury did not have to rely on presumptions of malice because Davis's "lunging" at Helen Wood and stabbing her were acts of malice.

The U.S. Supreme Court, in *Yates v. Evatt* (500 U.S. 391 [1991]), reversed the decisions of the South Carolina Supreme Court and remanded the case (sent it back to the lower court for further proceedings). Justice David H. Souter (1939–), writing for the high court, ruled that the state supreme court failed to apply the proper harmless-error standard as stated in *Chapman*. "The issue under *Chapman* is whether the jury actually rested its verdict on evidence establishing the presumed fact beyond a reasonable doubt, independently of the presumption."

Justice Souter concluded by stating that there was clear evidence of Davis's attempt to kill Wood because he could have left the store with Yates but stayed to pursue Wood with a deadly weapon. The evidence that Davis intended to kill Helen Wood was not as clear. The record also showed that Yates heard a woman scream as he left the store but did not attempt to return and kill her.

The jury could have interpreted Yates's behavior to confirm his claim that he and Davis had not originally intended to kill anyone. Even the prosecutor, in summation, conceded that Helen Wood could have been killed inadvertently by Davis.

APPEALS BASED ON NEW EVIDENCE
Newly Discovered Evidence Does Not Stop Execution

On an evening in late September 1981, the body of Officer David Rucker of the Texas Department of Public Safety was found lying beside his patrol car. He had been shot in the head. At about the same time, Officer Enrique Carrisalez saw a vehicle speeding away from the area where Rucker's body had been found. Carrisalez and his partner chased the vehicle and pulled it over. Carrisalez walked to the car. The driver opened his door and exchanged a few words with the police officer before firing

at least one shot into Carrisalez's chest. The officer died nine days later.

Leonel Torres Herrera was arrested a few days after the shootings and charged with capital murder. In January 1982 he was tried and found guilty of murdering Carrisalez. In July 1982 he pleaded guilty to Rucker's murder.

At the trial Officer Carrisalez's partner identified Herrera as the person who fired the gun. He also testified that there was only one person in the car. In a statement by Carrisalez before he died, he also identified Herrera. The speeding car belonged to Herrera's girlfriend, and Herrera had the car keys in his pocket when he was arrested. Splatters of blood on the car and on Herrera's clothes were the same type as Rucker's. Strands of hair found in the car also belonged to Rucker. Finally, a handwritten letter, which strongly implied that he had killed Rucker, was found on Herrera when he was arrested.

In 1992, 10 years after the initial trial, Herrera appealed to the federal courts, alleging that he was innocent of the murders of Rucker and Carrisalez and that his execution would violate the Eighth and 14th Amendments. He presented affidavits (sworn statements) claiming that he had not killed the officers but that his now dead brother had. The brother's attorney, one of Herrera's cellmates, and a school friend all swore that the brother had killed the police officers. The dead brother's son also said that he had witnessed his father killing the police officers.

In *Herrera v. Collins* (506 U.S. 390 [1993]), the U.S. Supreme Court ruled 6–3 that executing Herrera would not violate the Eighth and 14th Amendments. The high court said that the trial—not the appeals process—judges a defendant's innocence or guilt. Appeals courts determine only the fairness of the proceedings.

Writing for the majority, Chief Justice Rehnquist stated:

A person when first charged with a crime is entitled to a presumption of innocence, and may insist that his guilt be established beyond a reasonable doubt.... Once a defendant has been afforded a fair trial and convicted of the offense for which he was charged, the presumption of innocence disappears.... Here, it is not disputed that the State met its burden of proving at trial that petitioner was guilty of the capital murder of Officer Carrisalez beyond a reasonable doubt. Thus, in the eyes of the law, petitioner does not come before the Court as one who is "innocent," but on the contrary, as one who has been convicted by due process of law of two brutal murders.

Based on affidavits here filed, petitioner claims that evidence never presented to the trial court proves him innocent....

Claims of actual innocence based on newly discovered evidence have never been held to state a ground for [court] relief absent an independent constitutional violation occurring in the underlying state criminal proceeding....

This rule is grounded in the principle that [appeals] courts sit to ensure that individuals are not imprisoned in violation of the Constitution—not to correct errors of fact.

Rehnquist continued that states all allow the introduction of new evidence. Texas was one of 17 states that require a new trial motion based on new evidence within 60 days. Herrera's appeal came 10 years later. The chief justice, however, emphasized that Herrera still had options, saying, "For under Texas law, petitioner may file a request for executive clemency.... Executive clemency has provided the 'fail-safe' in our criminal justice system.... It is an unalterable fact that our judicial system, like the human beings who administer it, is fallible. But history is replete with examples of wrongfully convicted persons who have been pardoned in the wake of after-discovered evidence establishing their innocence."

The majority opinion found the information presented in the affidavits inconsistent with the other evidence. The justices questioned why the affidavits were produced at the very last minute. The justices also wondered why Herrera had pleaded guilty to Rucker's murder if he had been innocent. They did note that some of the information in the affidavits might have been important to the jury, "but coming 10 years after petitioner's trial, this showing of innocence falls far short of that which would have to be made in order to trigger the sort of constitutional claim [to decide for a retrial]."

Speaking for the minority, Justice Blackmun wrote:

We really are being asked to decide whether the Constitution forbids the execution of a person who has been validly convicted and sentenced, but who, nonetheless, can prove his innocence with newly discovered evidence. Despite the State of Texas' astonishing protestation to the contrary...I do not see how the answer can be anything but "yes."

The Eighth Amendment prohibits "cruel and unusual punishments." This proscription is not static, but rather reflects evolving standards of decency. I think it is crystal clear that the execution of an innocent person is "at odds with contemporary standards of fairness and decency."...The protection of the Eighth Amendment does not end once a defendant has been validly convicted and sentenced.

Claim of Miscarriage of Justice

Lloyd Schlup, a Missouri prisoner, was convicted of participating in the murder of a fellow inmate in 1984 and sentenced to death. He had filed one petition for habeas corpus, arguing that he had inadequate counsel. He claimed the counsel did not call fellow inmates and other witnesses to testify that could prove his innocence. He filed a second petition, alleging that constitutional error at his trial deprived the jury of crucial evidence that would again have established his innocence.

Using a previous U.S. Supreme Court ruling (*Sawyer v. Whitley*, 505 U.S. 333 [1992]), the district court claimed that Schlup had not shown "by clear and convincing evidence that but for a constitutional error no reasonable jury would have found him guilty." Schlup's lawyers argued that the district court should have used another ruling (*Murray v. Carrier*, 477 U.S. 478 [1986]), in which a petitioner need only to show that "a constitutional violation has probably resulted in the conviction of one who is actually innocent." The appellate court affirmed the district court's ruling, noting that Schlup's guilt, which had been proven at the trial, barred any consideration of his constitutional claim.

The U.S. Supreme Court, on appeal, reviewed the case to determine whether the *Sawyer* standard provides enough protection from a miscarriage of justice that would result from the execution of an innocent person. In *Schlup v. Delo* (513 U.S. 298 [1995]), the court observed, "If a petitioner such as Schlup presents evidence of innocence so strong that a court cannot have confidence in the outcome of the trial...the petitioner should be allowed to...argue the merits of his underlying claims."

The justices concluded that the less stringent *Carrier* standard, as opposed to the rigid *Sawyer* standard, focuses the investigation on the actual innocence, allowing the court to review relevant evidence that might have been excluded or unavailable during the trial. The court noted "because both the Court of Appeals and the District Court evaluated the record under an improper standard, further proceedings are necessary." The case was remanded back to the district court. In 1999 Schlup was being retried when he pleaded guilty to noncapital murder as part of a plea deal and was given a life sentence with a chance for parole. As of September 2011, no information could be determined on Schlup's status; he was not found in a website search of the list of inmates incarcerated by the Missouri Department of Correction (https://web.mo.gov/doc/offSearchWeb/search Offender.do).

Schlup v. Delo Revisited in House v. Bell

In 2006 the Supreme Court heard a case involving the Tennessee prisoner Paul House, who had been convicted in 1985 of murdering Carolyn Muncey. The prosecution alleged that House, a paroled sex offender, murdered Muncey during an attempted rape. He was convicted based on circumstantial evidence and forensics tests that showed semen stains on Muncey's clothing were of House's blood type. More incriminating were small blood stains found on House's blue jeans that matched Muncey's blood type.

In 1996 House's lawyers filed a habeas corpus petition in the U.S. District Court and presented new evidence, including deoxyribonucleic acid tests showing that the semen on Muncey's clothing was from her husband, not House. Several witnesses testified that Hubert Muncey Jr.

had confessed to them while he was drunk that he did commit the murder. They also testified that he had a history of beating his wife. In addition, the original blood evidence came into question, due to allegations of the mishandling of blood that was collected during the autopsy. The defense attorneys argued that some of the autopsy blood spilled on House's pants before they were tested at the FBI laboratory in Washington, D.C. The state admitted that the autopsy blood was improperly sealed and transported and spilled, but argued that the spill occurred after the pants were tested. The district court ruled that the new evidence did not demonstrate actual innocence as required under *Schlup v. Delo* and failed to show that House was ineligible for the death penalty under *Sawyer v. Whitley*. The ruling was eventually upheld on appeal.

In *House v. Bell* (No. 04-8990 [2006]), the U.S. Supreme Court ruled 5–3 that House's habeas petition should proceed, because the new evidence constituted a "stringent showing" under *Schlup v. Delo*. (Note that only eight justices, rather than the usual nine justices, decided this case, because of its timing. The case was argued on January 11, 2006, and decided on June 12, 2006. Neither Justice O'Connor nor Justice Samuel A. Alito Jr. [1950–], her successor, participated in the case because Alito replaced O'Connor on January 31, 2006.) The court concluded:

> This is not a case of conclusive exoneration. Some aspects of the State's evidence—Lora Muncey's memory of a deep voice, House's bizarre evening walk, his lie to law enforcement, his appearance near the body, and the blood on his pants—still support an inference of guilt. Yet the central forensic proof connecting House to the crime—the blood and the semen—has been called into question, and House has put forward substantial evidence pointing to a different suspect. Accordingly, and although the issue is close, we conclude that this is the rare case where—had the jury heard all the conflicting testimony—it is more likely than not that no reasonable juror viewing the record as a whole would lack reasonable doubt.

Supporters of House's innocence, including members of the state legislature, petitioned the governor for a pardon. Eventually, in 2008 the U.S. Supreme Court determined that the jury that convicted House did not hear testimony at the time that could have cleared him of the murder. During the spring of 2009 prosecutors dropped their charges against House, who had contracted multiple sclerosis and was confined to a wheelchair. Shortly thereafter he was released from prison and moved in with his mother.

Suppressed Evidence Means a New Trial

Curtis Lee Kyles was convicted by a Louisiana jury of the first-degree murder of a woman in a grocery store parking lot in 1984. He was sentenced to death. It was revealed on review that the prosecutor had never disclosed certain evidence favorable to the defendant. Among the evidence were conflicting statements by an informant who, the defense believed, wanted to get rid of Kyles to get his girlfriend. The state supreme court, the federal district court, and the Fifth Circuit Court denied Kyles's appeals. The U.S. Supreme Court, in *Kyles v. Whitley* (514 U.S. 419 [1995]), reversed the lower courts' decisions. The high court ruled, "Favorable evidence is material, and constitutional error results from its suppression by the government, if there is a 'reasonable probability' that, had the evidence been disclosed to the defense, the result of the proceeding would have been different.... [The] net effect of the state-suppressed evidence favoring Kyles raises a reasonable probability that its disclosure would have produced a different result at trial."

The conviction was overturned. Four mistrials followed. On February 18, 1998, after his fifth and final trial ended with a hung jury, Kyles was released from prison. He had spent 14 years on death row.

CHALLENGING THE ANTITERRORISM AND EFFECTIVE DEATH PENALTY ACT OF 1996

The Antiterrorism and Effective Death Penalty Act (AEDPA) became law in April 1996, shortly after the first anniversary of the Oklahoma City bombing. The AEDPA aims in part to "provide for an effective death penalty." After passage of the law the lower courts differed in their interpretations of certain core provisions. For the first time, on April 18, 2000, the U.S. Supreme Court addressed these problems.

Federal Habeas Corpus Relief and the AEDPA

The AEDPA restricts the power of federal courts to grant habeas corpus relief to state inmates who have exhausted their state appeals. Through the writ of habeas corpus, an inmate could have a court review his or her conviction or sentencing. The AEDPA bars a federal court from granting an application for a writ of habeas corpus unless the state court's decision "was contrary to, or involved an unreasonable application of, clearly established federal law, as determined by the Supreme Court of the United States." The idea was to curtail the amount of habeas reviews filed by convicts and thus save the overbooked federal courts time and money.

In 1986 Terry Williams, while incarcerated in a Danville, Virginia, city jail, wrote to the police that he had killed two people and that he was sorry for his acts. He also confessed to stealing money from one of the victims. He was subsequently convicted of robbery and capital murder.

During the sentencing hearing the prosecutor presented many crimes Williams had committed besides the murders for which he was convicted. Two state witnesses also testified to the defendant's future dangerousness.

Williams's lawyer, however, called on his mother to testify to his being a nonviolent person. The defense also played a taped portion of a psychiatrist's statement, who said that Williams admitted to him that during a previous robbery he had removed bullets from a gun so as not to harm anyone. During his closing statement, however, the lawyer noted that the jury would probably find it hard to give his client mercy because he did not show mercy to his victims. The jury sentenced Williams to death, and the trial judge imposed the sentence.

In 1988 Williams filed a state habeas corpus petition. The Danville Circuit Court found Williams's conviction valid. The court found, however, that the defense lawyer's failure to present several mitigating factors at the sentencing phase violated Williams's right to effective assistance of counsel as prescribed by *Strickland v. Washington* (466 U.S. 668 [1984]). The mitigating circumstances included early childhood abuse and borderline mental retardation. The habeas corpus hearing further revealed that the state expert witnesses had testified that if Williams were kept in a "structured environment," he would not be a threat to society. The circuit court recommended a new sentencing hearing.

In 1997 the Virginia Supreme Court rejected the circuit court's recommendation for a new sentencing hearing, concluding that the omitted evidence would not have affected the sentence. In making its ruling, the state supreme court relied on what it considered to be an established U.S. Supreme Court precedent.

Next, Williams filed a federal habeas corpus petition. The federal trial judge ruled not only that the death sentence was "constitutionally infirm" but also that defense counsel was ineffective. However, the U.S. Court of Appeals for the Fourth Circuit reversed the federal trial judge's decision, holding that the AEDPA prohibits a federal court from granting habeas corpus relief unless the state court's decision "was contrary to, or involved an unreasonable application of, clearly established federal law, as determined by the Supreme Court of the United States."

On April 18, 2000, the U.S. Supreme Court, in *Williams v. Taylor* (529 U.S. 362 [2000]), reversed the Fourth Circuit Court's ruling by a 6–3 decision. The court concluded that the Virginia Supreme Court's decision rejecting Williams's claim of ineffective assistance was contrary to a Supreme Court–established precedent (*Strickland v. Washington*), as well as an unreasonable application of that precedent. This was the first time the Supreme Court had granted relief on such a claim.

In November 2000, during a court hearing, Williams accepted a plea agreement of a life sentence without parole after prosecutors agreed not to seek the death penalty.

Federal Evidentiary Hearings for Constitutional Claims

Under an AEDPA provision, if the petitioner has failed to develop the facts of his or her challenges of a constitutional claim in state court proceedings, the federal court shall not hold a hearing on the claim unless the facts involve an exception listed by the AEDPA.

In 1993, after robbing the home of Morris Keller Jr. and his wife, Mary Elizabeth, Michael Wayne Williams and his friend Jeffrey Alan Cruse raped the woman and then killed the couple. In exchange for the state's promise not to seek capital punishment, Cruse described details of the crimes. Williams received the death sentence for the capital murders. The prosecution told the jury about the plea agreement with Cruse. The state later revoked the plea agreement after discovering that Cruse had also raped the wife and failed to disclose it. After Cruse's court testimony against Williams, however, the state gave Cruse a life sentence, which Williams alleged amounted to a second, informal plea agreement.

Williams filed a habeas petition in state court, claiming he was not told of the second plea agreement between the state and his codefendant. The Virginia Supreme Court dismissed the petition (1994) and the U.S. Supreme Court refused to review the case (1995).

In 1996, on appeal, a federal district court agreed to an evidentiary hearing of Williams's claims of the undisclosed second plea agreement. The defendant had also claimed that a psychiatric report about Cruse, which was not revealed by the prosecution, could have shown that Cruse was not credible. Moreover, a certain juror might have had possible bias, which the prosecution failed to disclose. Before the hearing could be held, the state concluded that the AEDPA prohibited such a hearing. Consequently, the federal district court dismissed Williams's petition.

When the case was brought before the U.S. Court of Appeals for the Fourth Circuit, the court, interpreting the AEDPA, concluded that the defendant had failed to develop the facts of his claims. On April 18, 2000, in *Williams v. Taylor* (529 U.S. 420), a unanimous U.S. Supreme Court did not address Williams's claim of the undisclosed plea agreement between Cruse and the state. Instead, the high court held that the defendant was entitled to a federal district court evidentiary hearing regarding his other claims. According to the court, "Under the [AEDPA], a failure to develop the factual basis of a claim is not established unless there is lack of diligence, or some greater fault, attributable to the prisoner or the prisoner's counsel. . . . We conclude petitioner has met the burden of showing he was diligent in efforts to develop the facts supporting his juror bias and prosecutorial misconduct claims in collateral proceedings before the Virginia Supreme Court."

High Court Upholds Restriction on Federal Appeals

Even though the Supreme Court ruled in favor of new resentencing hearings for Terry Williams and Michael Williams, it stressed that the AEDPA places a new restriction on federal courts with respect to granting habeas relief to state inmates. The court noted in *Williams v. Taylor* (529 U.S. 362) that under the AEDPA:

> The writ may issue only if one of the following two conditions is satisfied—the state-court adjudication resulted in a decision that (1) "was contrary to . . . clearly established Federal law, as determined by the Supreme Court of the United States," or (2) "involved an unreasonable application of . . . clearly established Federal law, as determined by the Supreme Court of the United States." Under the "contrary to" clause, a federal habeas court may grant the writ if the state court arrives at a conclusion opposite to that reached by this court on a question of law or if the state court decides a case differently than this court has on a set of materially indistinguishable facts. Under the "unreasonable application" clause, a federal habeas court may grant the writ if the state court identifies the correct governing legal principle from this court's decisions but unreasonably applies that principle to the facts of the prisoner's case.

METHODS OF EXECUTION

The Role of the U.S. Food and Drug Administration

The injection of a deadly combination of drugs has become the method of execution in most states permitting capital punishment. Condemned prisoners from Texas and Oklahoma, two of the first states to introduce this method, brought suit claiming that even though the drugs used had been approved by the U.S. Food and Drug Administration (FDA) for medical purposes, they had never been approved for use in or tested for human executions.

The FDA commissioner refused to act, claiming serious questions whether the agency had jurisdiction in the area. The U.S. District Court for the District of Columbia disagreed with the condemned prisoners that the FDA had a responsibility to determine if the lethal mixture used during execution was safe and effective. The court noted that decisions by a federal agency not to take action were not reviewable in court.

A divided U.S. Court of Appeals for the District of Columbia reversed the lower court ruling. A generally irritated U.S. Supreme Court agreed to hear the case "to review the implausible result that the FDA is required to exercise its enforcement power to ensure that States only use drugs that are 'safe and effective' for human execution."

In *Heckler v. Chaney* (470 U.S. 821 [1985]), the unanimous court agreed that, in this case, the FDA did not have jurisdiction.

Is Execution by Hanging Constitutional?

Washington state law imposes capital punishment either by "hanging by the neck" or, if the condemned chooses, by lethal injection. Charles Rodham Campbell was convicted of three counts of murder in 1982 and sentenced to death. Campbell, in challenging the constitutionality of hanging under the Washington statute, claimed that execution by hanging violated his Eighth Amendment right because it was a cruel and unusual punishment. Furthermore, the direction that he be hanged unless he chose lethal injection was a cruel and unusual punishment. He claimed that such instruction further violated his First Amendment right by forcing him to participate in his own execution to avoid hanging.

In *Campbell v. Wood* (18 F.3d. 662 [9th Cir. 1994]), the U.S. Court of Appeals for the Ninth Circuit noted, "We do not consider hanging to be cruel and unusual simply because it causes death, or because there may be some pain associated with death. . . . As used in the Constitution, 'cruel' implies 'something inhuman and barbarous, something more than the mere extinguishment of life.' . . . Campbell is entitled to an execution free only of 'the unnecessary and wanton infliction of pain.'"

According to the court, just because the defendant was given a choice of method of execution did not mean that he was being subjected to a cruel and unusual punishment: "We believe that benefits to prisoners who may choose to exercise the option and who may feel relieved that they can elect lethal injection outweigh the emotional costs to those who find the mere existence of an option objectionable."

Campbell argued that the state was infringing on his First Amendment right of free exercise of his religion. He claimed that it was against his religion to participate in his own execution by being allowed to elect lethal injection over hanging.

The court contended that Campbell did not have to choose an execution method or participate in his own execution. "He may remain absolutely silent and refuse to participate in any election. The statute provides for imposition of the death penalty by hanging, and does not require him to choose the method of his execution." On appeal (*Campbell v. Wood*, No. 93-8931 [1994]), the U.S. Supreme Court decided not to hear the case. In 1994 Campbell was executed by hanging. He refused to cooperate during the execution and had to be pepper sprayed and strapped to a board to carry out the hanging.

Is Execution by Lethal Gas Constitutional?

On April 17, 1992, three California death row inmates—David Fierro, Alejandro Gilbert Ruiz, and Robert Alton Harris—filed a suit on behalf of themselves and all others under sentence of execution by lethal gas. In *Fierro v. Gomez* (790 F. Supp. 966 [N.D. Cal. 1992]), the inmates alleged that California's method of execution by lethal gas violated the Eighth and 14th Amendments. Harris was scheduled to be executed four days later, on April 21—an execution that was carried out.

The district court prohibited James Gomez, the director of the California Department of Corrections, and Arthur Calderon, the warden of San Quentin Prison, from executing any inmate until a hearing was held. On appeal from Gomez and Calderon, the U.S. Court of Appeals for the Ninth Circuit vacated (annulled) the district court's ruling. On his execution day Harris had filed a habeas corpus petition with the California Supreme Court, challenging the constitutionality of the gas chamber. The court declined to review the case, and Harris was put to death that day. In the aftermath of Harris's execution, the California legislature amended in 1993 its death penalty statute, providing that, if lethal gas "is held invalid, the punishment of death shall be imposed by the alternative means," lethal injection.

In October 1994 a federal district judge, Marilyn Hall Patel (1938–), ruled that execution by lethal gas "is inhumane and has no place in civilized society" (865 F. Supp. at 1415). She then ordered California's gas chamber closed and that lethal injection be used instead. This was the first time a federal judge had ruled that any method of execution violated the Eighth and 14th Amendments. Even though the state of California maintained that cyanide gas caused almost instant unconsciousness, the judge referred to doctors' reports and witnesses' accounts of gas chamber executions, which indicated that the dying inmates stayed conscious for 15 seconds to a minute or longer and suffered "intense physical pain."

Gomez and Calderon appealed Judge Patel's ruling on the unconstitutionality of the gas chamber before the U.S. Court of Appeals for the Ninth Circuit. The court also appealed the permanent injunction against the use of lethal gas as a method of execution. In February 1996, in *Fierro v. Gomez* (77 F.3d. 301 [9th Cir.]), the appellate court affirmed Judge Patel's ruling.

Gomez and Calderon appealed the case to the U.S. Supreme Court. In October 1996 a 7–2 Supreme Court, in *Gomez v. Fierro* (519 U.S. 918), vacated the appellate court's ruling and returned the case to the appellate court for additional proceedings, citing the death penalty statute amended in 1993 (lethal injection as an alternative to lethal gas). As of September 2011, Fierro remained on death row. Ruiz died of natural causes in early 2007.

Does Electrocution Constitute a Cruel and Unusual Punishment?

During the 1990s, even though Florida had three botched executions using the electric chair, the state supreme court ruled each time that electrocution does not constitute a cruel and unusual punishment. In 1990 and 1997 flames shot

out from the headpiece worn by the condemned inmate. On July 8, 1999, Allen Lee Davis developed a nosebleed during his execution in the electric chair.

Thomas Provenzano, who was scheduled to be electrocuted after Davis, challenged the use of the electric chair as Florida's sole method of execution. In *Provenzano v. Moore* (No. 95973 [1999]), the Florida Supreme Court ruled 4–3 that the electric chair was not a cruel and unusual punishment. The court further reported that Davis's nosebleed occurred before the execution and did not result from the electrocution.

Subsequently, the court, as it routinely does with all its rulings, posted the *Provenzano* decision on the Internet. Three photographs of Davis covered with blood were posted as part of the dissenting opinion of Justice Leander J. Shaw Jr. (1930–). The photographs brought public outcry worldwide. Justice Shaw claimed that Davis was "brutally tortured to death."

In October 1999, for the first time, the U.S. Supreme Court agreed to consider the constitutionality of electrocution. The death row inmate Anthony Braden Bryan asked the court to review his case, based on the unreliability of the electric chair. Before the high court could hear the case, however, the Florida legislature voted in a special session to replace electrocution with lethal injection as the primary method of execution, but allowed a condemned person to choose the electric chair as an alternative.

On January 24, 2000, the Supreme Court dismissed *Bryan v. Moore* (No. 99-6723) as moot (irrelevant), based on Florida's new legislation. Governor Jeb Bush (1953–) agreed to sign the bill in conjunction with a second bill that limits, in most cases, death row inmates to two appeals in state courts, with the second appeal to be filed within six months of the first. This provision cut in half the time limit for the second appeal.

In 2001 the Georgia Supreme Court became the first appellate court to rule a method of execution unconstitutional. On October 5 the court held that electrocution was a cruel and unusual punishment in violation of the state constitution. In 2000 the Georgia legislature had passed a law making lethal injection the sole method of execution. Before the state supreme court ruling in October 2001, that law applied only to those sentenced after May 1, 2000.

Throughout the first decade of the 21st century, all other death penalty states made lethal injection their primary (and sometimes only) method of execution. Nebraska was the last state to do so. In 2008 the Nebraska Supreme Court ruled that execution by electrocution was unconstitutional because "electrocution inflicts intense pain and agonizing suffering." The following year the Nebraska legislature passed legislation that established lethal injection as the state's only method of execution. As will be explained in Chapter 5, some states still allow alternative means of execution (i.e., electrocution, lethal gas, hanging, or firing squad) under certain circumstances.

Challenges to Lethal Injection

In April 2006 the U.S. Supreme Court considered a case in which the Florida inmate Clarence E. Hill challenged the state's form of lethal injection as unnecessarily painful and thus a violation of his Eighth Amendment rights. Hill was convicted in 1983 for the capital murder of Officer Stephen Taylor and sentenced to death. After exhausting his state appeals, he filed for a federal writ of habeas corpus, which was denied. As Hill's execution loomed in January 2006, his lawyers filed a new challenge, this time against the lethal injection procedure itself. A trial court dismissed the claim, because Hill had already exhausted his federal habeas corpus appeals. Federal law prohibits multiple appeals of this type. The ruling was upheld by the Florida Supreme Court.

In *Hill v. McDonough* (No. 05-8794 [2006]), the U.S. Supreme Court issued a unanimous 9–0 opinion that Hill's challenge of the form of execution did not constitute a second habeas corpus appeal, but was a new action of a different type. The decision came only minutes before Hill was to be executed. He was already strapped to a gurney and hooked up to intravenous lines. However, the reprieve proved to be temporary. Florida courts refused to hear Hill's challenge, arguing that it was presented too late. His execution date was reset, and the Supreme Court denied a second appeal. In September 2006 Hill was executed by lethal injection.

In September 2007 the U.S. Supreme Court agreed to hear another case pertaining to lethal injection. Two Kentucky death row inmates—Ralph Baze and Thomas Bowling—petitioned the court after lower courts rejected their challenges to the three-drug protocol used for lethal injection in Kentucky. Neither of the men, who had been convicted in separate double murders, had execution dates set at that time. Because the lethal injection protocol in question was widely used by other death penalty states, the court's agreement to hear the case triggered a national moratorium (suspension) on pending executions. In April 2008 the court issued its opinion in *Baze v. Rees* (553 U.S. ___). The court ruled 7–2 that Kentucky's three-drug protocol for lethal injection did not violate the Eighth Amendment's ban on cruel and unusual punishment.

The protocol included the administration of sodium thiopental (to render the prisoner unconscious) followed by pancuronium bromide (a paralyzing agent) and potassium chloride, which causes cardiac arrest resulting in death. Even though the court acknowledged that improper administration of the drugs (particularly the sodium thiopental) could result in a painful death, it rejected the petitioners' claim that there was a "significant risk" that the protocol would not be properly followed. The court also refused to consider the petitioners' claim that an alternative single-drug protocol for lethal injection offered far less risk of pain. It noted that pursuing such claims in numerous death row cases "would embroil the courts in ongoing scientific controversies beyond their expertise, and would substantially intrude on the role of state legislatures in implementing execution procedures." However, the court warned that states that refused to adopt suitable alternative protocols in the future might violate the Eighth Amendment. The court noted that an alternative protocol would be considered suitable if it was "feasible, readily implemented, and in fact significantly reduced a substantial risk of severe pain." As of September 2011, Baze and Bowling remained on death row in Kentucky.

DOES EXTENDED STAY ON DEATH ROW CONSTITUTE A CRUEL AND UNUSUAL PUNISHMENT?

In 2002 Charles Kenneth Foster, a Florida inmate, asked the U.S. Supreme Court to consider whether his long wait for execution constitutes a cruel and unusual punishment prohibited by the Eighth Amendment. Foster had been on death row since 1975 for a murder conviction. In 1981 and again in 1984 the defendant was granted a stay of execution to allow his federal habeas corpus petition.

Justice Stephen G. Breyer (1938–) dissented from the court's refusal to hear the case (*Foster v. Florida*, No. 01-10868 [2002]). Justice Breyer pointed out that the defendant's long wait on death row resulted partly from Florida's repeated errors in proceedings. The justice added, "Death row's inevitable anxieties and uncertainties have been sharpened by the issuance of two death warrants and three judicial reprieves. If executed, Foster, now 55, will have been punished both by death and also by more than a generation spent in death row's twilight. It is fairly asked whether such punishment is both unusual and cruel."

Concurring with the court opinion not to hear Foster's case, Justice Clarence Thomas (1948–) observed that the defendant could have ended the "anxieties and uncertainties" of death row had he submitted to execution, which the people of Florida believe he deserves. As of September 2011, Foster remained on death row in Florida.

In *Thompson v. McNeil* (No. 08-7369 [2009]) the Supreme Court refused to hear a similar case involving a Florida man who had been on death row for 32 years. William Thompson was sentenced to death for the kidnapping, torture, and murder of Sally Ivester in 1976. Justices Breyer and Stevens expressed their displeasure with the court's decision. Breyer noted that the state of Florida "was in significant part responsible" for Thompson's long stay on death row due to judicial errors during his sentencing trial. Stevens described "the especially severe conditions of confinement" in which Thompson had been held on death row and remarked on the psychological toll that an impending execution takes when a prisoner experiences a long wait for the execution to be administered. He concluded, "Executing defendants after such long delays is unacceptably cruel." However, Justice Thomas noted that Thompson had taken advantage of the many appeals processes allowed under the law and was now complaining about a delayed execution. Thomas recounted the gruesome details of Thompson's crime and the brutal manner in which Ivester was tortured to death. He notes, "Three juries recommended that petitioner receive the death penalty for this heinous murder, and petitioner has received judicial review of his sentence on at least 17 occasions." He concluded, "It is the crime—and not the punishment imposed by the jury or the delay in petitioner's execution—that was 'unacceptably cruel.'" As of September 2011, Thompson was still on death row in Florida.

CHAPTER 4

SUPREME COURT RULINGS III: MITIGATING CIRCUMSTANCES, YOUTH, INSANITY, MENTAL RETARDATION, THE ADMISSIBILITY OF VICTIM IMPACT STATEMENTS, AND THE INFLUENCE OF RACE IN CAPITAL CASES

MITIGATING CIRCUMSTANCES

Mitigating circumstances may lessen the responsibility for a crime, whereas aggravating circumstances may add to the responsibility for a crime. In 1978 an Ohio case highlighted the issue of mitigating circumstances before the U.S. Supreme Court after Sandra Lockett was convicted of capital murder for her role in a pawnshop robbery that resulted in the shooting death of the storeowner. Lockett helped plan the robbery, drove the getaway car, and hid her accomplices in her home, but she was not present in the store at the time the storeowner was shot. According to the Ohio death penalty statute, capital punishment had to be imposed on Lockett unless "(1) the victim induced or facilitated the offense; (2) it is unlikely that the offense would have been committed but for the fact that the offender was under duress, coercion, or strong provocation; or (3) the offense was primarily the product of the offender's psychosis or mental deficiency." Lockett was found guilty and sentenced to die.

Lockett appealed, claiming that the Ohio law did not give the sentencing judge the chance to consider the circumstances of the crime, the defendant's criminal record, and the defendant's character as mitigating factors, lessening her responsibility for the crime. In July 1978 the Supreme Court, in *Lockett v. Ohio* (438 U.S. 586), upheld Lockett's contention. Chief Justice Warren Burger (1907–1995) observed, "A statute that prevents the sentencer in capital cases from giving independent mitigating weight to aspects of the defendant's character and record and to the circumstances of the offense proffered in mitigation creates the risk that the death penalty will be imposed in spite of factors that may call for a less severe penalty, and when the choice is between life and death, such risk is unacceptable and incompatible with the commands of the Eighth and Fourteenth Amendments."

Mitigating Circumstances Must Always Be Considered

In *Hitchcock v. Dugger* (481 U.S. 393 [1987]), a unanimous Supreme Court further emphasized that all mitigating circumstances had to be considered before the convicted murderer could be sentenced. A Florida judge had instructed the jury not to consider evidence of mitigating factors that were not specifically indicated in the Florida death penalty law. Writing for the court, Justice Antonin Scalia (1936–) stressed that a convicted person had the right "to present any and all relevant mitigating evidence that is available."

CAN A MINOR BE SENTENCED TO DEATH?

On April 4, 1977, 16-year-old Monty Lee Eddings and several friends were pulled over by a police officer as they traveled in a car in Oklahoma. Eddings had several guns in the car, which he had taken from his father. When the police officer approached the car, Eddings shot and killed him. Eddings was tried as an adult even though he was 16 at the time of the murder. He was convicted of first-degree murder for killing a police officer and was sentenced to death.

At the sentencing hearing following the conviction, Eddings's lawyer presented substantial evidence of a turbulent family history, beatings by a harsh father, and serious emotional disturbance. The judge refused, as a matter of law, to consider the mitigating circumstances of Eddings's unhappy upbringing and emotional problems. He ruled that the only mitigating circumstance was the petitioner's youth, which was insufficient to outweigh the aggravating circumstances.

In *Eddings v. Oklahoma* (455 U.S. 104 [1982]), the Supreme Court, in a 5–4 opinion, ordered the case remanded (sent back to the lower courts for further proceedings). The justices based their ruling on *Lockett v. Ohio*, which required the trial court to consider and weigh all the mitigating evidence concerning the petitioner's family background and personal history.

By implication, because the majority did not reverse the case on the issue of age, the ruling let stand Oklahoma's decision to try Eddings as an adult. Meanwhile, Chief Justice Burger, who filed the dissenting opinion in which Justices Byron R. White (1917–2002), Harry A. Blackmun (1908–1999), and William H. Rehnquist (1924–2005) joined, observed, "The Constitution does not authorize us to determine whether sentences imposed by state courts are sentences we consider 'appropriate'; our only authority is to decide whether they are constitutional under the Eighth Amendment. The Court stops far short of suggesting that there is any constitutional proscription against imposition of the death penalty on a person who was under age 18 when the murder was committed."

Hence, even though the high court did not directly rule on the question of minors being sentenced to death, the sense of the court would appear to be that it would uphold such a sentencing. Eddings's sentence was subsequently changed to life in prison.

Not at 15 Years Old

With three adults, William Thompson brutally murdered a former brother-in-law in Oklahoma. Thompson was 15 at the time of the murder, but the state determined that Thompson, who had a long history of violent assault, had "virtually no reasonable prospects for rehabilitation . . . within the juvenile system and . . . should be held accountable for his acts as if he were an adult and should be certified to stand trial as an adult." Thompson was tried as an adult and found guilty. As in *Eddings*, Thompson's age was considered a mitigating circumstance, but the jury still sentenced him to death.

Thompson appealed, and even though the Court of Criminal Appeals of Oklahoma upheld the decision, the U.S. Supreme Court, in *Thompson v. Oklahoma* (487 U.S. 815 [1988]), did not. In a 5–3 majority vote, with Justice Sandra Day O'Connor (1930–) agreeing to vacate (annul) the sentence but not agreeing with the majority reasoning, the case was reversed. (Justice Anthony M. Kennedy [1936–] took no part in the decision.)

Writing for the majority, Justice John Paul Stevens (1920–) observed that "inexperience, less education, and less intelligence make the teenager less able to evaluate the consequences of his or her conduct while at the same time he or she is much more apt to be motivated by mere emotion or peer pressure than is an adult. The reasons why juveniles are not trusted with the privileges and responsibilities of an adult also explain why their irresponsible conduct is not as morally reprehensible as that of an adult."

Justice Stevens noted that 18 states required the age of at least 16 years before the death penalty could be considered. Counting the 14 states prohibiting capital punishment, a total of 32 states did not execute people under the age of 16 years.

Justice O'Connor agreed with the judgment of the court that the appellate court's ruling should be reversed.

O'Connor pointed out, however, that even though most 15-year-old criminals are generally less blameworthy than adults who commit the same crimes, some may fully understand the horrible deeds they have done. Individuals, after all, have different characteristics, including their capability to distinguish right from wrong.

Writing for the minority, Justice Scalia found no national consensus forbidding the execution of a person who was 16 years old at the commission of the murder. The justice could not understand the majority's calculations establishing a "contemporary standard" that forbade the execution of young minors. He reasoned that abolitionist states (states with no death penalty) should not be considered in the issue of executing minors because they did not have executions in the first place. Rather, the 18 states that prohibited the execution of offenders who were younger than 16 when they murdered should be compared with the 19 states that applied the death penalty to young offenders.

For a Number of Years Minors Could Be Sentenced to Death at Age 16 or 17

In 1988 a majority of the court, with Justice O'Connor straddling the fence, found the death penalty unacceptable for an offender who was less than 16 years old when he or she committed murder. A majority of the court, however, found the death sentence acceptable for a minor who was aged 16 or 17 years during the commission of murder. The Supreme Court, in two jointly considered cases, *Stanford v. Kentucky* and *Wilkins v. Missouri* (492 U.S. 361 [1989]), ruled that inmates who committed their crimes at ages 16 or 17 could be executed for murder.

In January 1981, 17-year-old Kevin Stanford and an accomplice raped Barbel Poore, an attendant at a Kentucky gas station they were robbing. They then took the woman to a secluded area near the station, where Stanford shot her in the face and in the back of the head. Stressing the seriousness of the offense and Stanford's long history of criminal behavior, the court certified him as an adult. He was tried, found guilty, and sentenced to death.

In July 1985, 16-year-old Heath Wilkins stabbed Nancy Allen to death while he was robbing the convenience store where she worked. Wilkins indicated he murdered Allen because "a dead person can't talk." Based on his long history of juvenile delinquency, a Missouri court ordered Wilkins to be tried as an adult. He was found guilty and sentenced to death.

Writing for the majority, Justice Scalia could find no national consensus that executing minors aged 16 and 17 years constituted a cruel and unusual punishment. Scalia observed that of the 37 states whose statutes allowed the death penalty, just 15 states refused to impose it on 16-year-old offenders and only 12 states refused to impose it on 17-year-old offenders. Thus, overall, 22 out of 37 states allowed the death penalty for 16-year-old offenders, and 25 out of 37 states allowed the death penalty for 17-year-old offenders.

Furthermore, Justice Scalia saw no connection between the defendant's argument that those under the age of 18 years were denied the right to drive, drink, or vote because they were not considered mature enough to do so responsibly and whether this standard of maturity should be applied to a minor's understanding that murder is terribly wrong. Scalia added, "Even if the requisite degrees of maturity were comparable, the age statutes in question would still not be relevant.... These laws set the appropriate ages for the operation of a system that makes its determinations in gross, and that does not conduct individualized maturity tests for each driver, drinker, or voter.... In the realm of capital punishment in particular, 'individualized consideration [is] a constitutional requirement,' ... and one of the individualized mitigating factors that sentencers must be permitted to consider is the defendant's age."

Writing for the minority, Justice William J. Brennan (1906–1997) found a national consensus among 30 states when he added the 15 states forbidding the execution of a person who was 16 years old during the commission of the crime to those with no capital punishment, and the states that, in practice if not in law, did not execute minors. Justice Brennan, taking serious exception to the majority's observation that they had to find a national consensus in the laws passed by the state legislatures, stated, "Our judgment about the constitutionality of a punishment under the Eighth Amendment is informed, though not determined ... by an examination of contemporary attitudes toward the punishment, as evidenced in the actions of legislatures and of juries. The views of organizations with expertise in relevant fields and the choices of governments elsewhere in the world also merit our attention as indicators whether a punishment is acceptable in a civilized society."

In 1996 Wilkins was retried in Missouri and sentenced to three life terms. Stanford remained on Kentucky's death row until 2003, when his sentence was commuted to life without parole by Governor Paul E. Patton (1937–).

The Supreme Court Reverses Its Decision Regarding Minors

For 16 years the nation's highest court held fast on its decision to allow for the execution of minors who committed capital crimes. The Supreme Court even rejected another appeal by Stanford in 2002. In *Roper v. Simmons* (543 U.S. 551 [2005]), however, the court reversed its earlier opinion when it ruled that executing Christopher Simmons was cruel and unusual based on the fact that Simmons was a minor when he committed murder.

In 1993, 17-year-old Simmons and two friends, John Tessmer and Charles Benjamin, planned the elaborate burglary and murder of Shirley Cook, who lived in Fenton, Missouri. The three teenagers wanted to experience the thrill of the crime, reasoning that they would not be held accountable because they were under the age of 18 years. On the night of the murder, Tessmer and Simmons broke into Cook's house. (Benjamin backed out.) When Cook identified who the boys were, they covered her eyes and mouth with duct tape and bound her hands. The teenagers drove Cook to a state park, wrapped more duct tape over her entire face, tied her hands and feet with electrical wire, and threw her off a railroad trestle into a river.

The next day Simmons began bragging about the murder at school and was picked up by the police along with the two other teenagers. Simmons confessed on videotape and was tried and sentenced to death. He made a number of unsuccessful appeals and pleas for habeas corpus (a petition to be heard in federal court). Just weeks before he was scheduled to die, the Missouri Supreme Court called off the execution and reopened the debate in light of the U.S. Supreme Court's *Atkins* decision. (In *Atkins v. Virginia* [536 U.S. 304 (2002)], the court ruled that executing mentally retarded criminals was a violation of the Eighth Amendment because the mentally retarded do not have as strong a sense of lasting consequences or of right and wrong as normal adults.) The state court overturned Simmons's death sentence 6–3, stating that a national consensus had developed against executing minors since *Stanford* and *Wilkins* were decided. Simmons was resentenced to life without parole.

The U.S. Supreme Court upheld the Missouri court's decision in a 5–4 vote, reversing *Stanford*. The majority reasoned that adolescents do not have the emotional maturity and understanding of lasting consequences that adults have. As such, they cannot be held to as high of a standard and should not be sentenced to death. The majority also agreed with the Missouri court in that a national and international consensus had changed over the past 15 years. The court noted, "To implement this framework we have established the propriety and affirmed the necessity of referring to 'the evolving standards of decency that mark the progress of a maturing society.'"

Justices O'Connor, Scalia, Rehnquist, and Clarence Thomas (1948–) dissented, claiming that the guidelines for executing minors should not be inflexible and that a great many U.S. citizens still favor the death penalty for teenagers who commit especially heinous crimes. Scalia stated that the majority was bowing to international pressures. In his dissent, he wrote, "Though the views of our own citizens are essentially irrelevant to the Court's decision today, the views of other countries and the so-called international community take center stage."

Youth: A Mitigating Circumstance Even for Those over the Age of 18 Years

On March 23, 1986, Dorsie Lee Johnson Jr. and an accomplice staked out a convenience store in Snyder, Texas, with the intention of robbing it. They learned that only one employee worked during the predawn hours. Agreeing to leave no witnesses to the crime, the 19-year-old Johnson shot and killed the clerk, Jack Huddleston. They then emptied the cash register and stole some cigarettes.

The following month Johnson was arrested and subsequently confessed to the robbery and murder. During jury selection the defense attorneys asked potential jurors whether they believed that people were capable of change and whether they, the potential jurors, had ever done things in their youth that they would not now do.

The only witness the defense called was Johnson's father, who told of his son's drug use, grief over the death of his mother two years before the crime, and the murder of his sister the following year. He spoke of his son's youth and the fact that, at age 19, he did not evaluate things the way a person of 30 or 35 would.

Johnson was tried and convicted of capital murder. Under Texas law the homicide qualified as a capital offense because Johnson intentionally or knowingly caused Huddleston's death. Moreover, the murder was carried out in the course of committing a robbery.

In the sentencing phase of the trial, the judge instructed the jury to answer two questions: (1) whether Johnson's actions were deliberate and intended to kill, and (2) whether there was a possibility that he would continue to commit violent crimes and be a threat to society. If the jury answered "yes" to both questions, Johnson would be sentenced to death. If the jury returned a "no" answer to either question, the defendant would be sentenced to life in prison. The jury was not to consider or discuss the possibility of parole.

Of equal importance was the instruction that the jury could consider all the evidence, both aggravating and mitigating, in either phase of the trial. The jury unanimously answered yes to both questions, and Johnson was sentenced to death.

Five days after the state appellate court denied Johnson's motions for a rehearing, the U.S. Supreme Court issued its opinion in *Penry v. Lynaugh* (492 U.S. 302 [1989]), in which it held that the jury should have been instructed that it could consider mental retardation as a mitigating factor during the penalty phase. Based on the *Penry* ruling, Johnson appealed once more, claiming that a separate instruction should have been given to the jurors that would have allowed them to consider his youth. Again, the appellate court rejected his petition.

Affirming the Texas appellate court decision, Justice Kennedy delivered the opinion of the Supreme Court in *Johnson v. Texas* (509 U.S. 350 [1993]). He was joined by Justices Rehnquist, White, Scalia, and Thomas. Kennedy noted that the Texas special-issues system (two

questions asked of the jury and instruction to consider all evidence) allowed for adequate consideration of Johnson's youth. Justice Kennedy stated:

> Even on a cold record, one cannot be unmoved by the testimony of petitioner's father urging that his son's actions were due in large part to his youth. It strains credulity to suppose that the jury would have viewed the evidence of petitioner's youth as outside its effective reach in answering the second special issue. The relevance of youth as a mitigating factor derives from the fact that the signature qualities of youth are transient; as individuals mature, the impetuousness and recklessness that may dominate in younger years can subside.... As long as the mitigating evidence is within "the effective reach of the sentencer," the requirements of the Eighth Amendment are satisfied.

Justice O'Connor, in a dissenting opinion joined by Justices Blackmun, Stevens, and David H. Souter (1939–), stated that the jurors were not allowed to give full effect to his strongest mitigating circumstance: his youth. Hearing of his less than exemplary youth, a jury might easily conclude, as Johnson's did, that he would continue to be a threat to society.

In 1997 Johnson was executed by lethal injection in the state of Texas.

ROLE OF PSYCHIATRISTS
Validity of a Psychiatrist's Testimony

In 1978 Thomas Barefoot was convicted of murdering a police officer in Bell County, Texas. During the sentencing phase of his trial the prosecution put two psychiatrists on the stand. Neither psychiatrist had actually interviewed Barefoot, nor did either ask to do so. Both psychiatrists agreed that an individual with Barefoot's background and who had acted as Barefoot had in murdering the policeman represented a future threat to society. Partially based on their testimony, the jury sentenced Barefoot to death.

Barefoot's conviction and sentence were appealed many times, and in 1983 his case was argued before the U.S. Supreme Court. Among the issues debated was the validity of the psychiatrists' testimony. Barefoot's lawyers questioned whether it was necessary for the psychiatrists to have interviewed Barefoot or if it was enough for them to answer hypothetical questions that pertained to a hypothetical individual who acted like Barefoot.

Barefoot's attorneys claimed that psychiatrists could not reliably predict that a particular offender would commit other crimes in the future and be a threat to society. They further argued that psychiatrists should also not be allowed to testify about an offender's future dangerousness in response to hypothetical situations presented by the prosecutor and without having first examined the offender.

In *Barefoot v. Estelle* (463 U.S. 880 [1983]), the Supreme Court ruled 6–3 that local juries were in the best position to decide guilt and impose a sentence. The court referred to *Jurek v. Texas* (428 U.S. 262 [1976]), an earlier case that, among other things, upheld the testimony of laypeople concerning a defendant's possible future actions. Therefore, the court looked on psychiatrists as just another group of people presenting testimony to the jury for consideration. The court claimed that like all evidence presented to the jury, a psychiatric observation "should be admitted and its weight left to the factfinder, who would have the benefit of cross-examination and contrary evidence by the opposing party. Psychiatric testimony predicting dangerousness may be countered not only as erroneous in a particular case but also as generally so unreliable that it should be ignored. If the jury may make up its mind about future dangerousness unaided by psychiatric testimony, jurors should not be barred from hearing the views of the State's psychiatrists along with opposing views of the defendant's doctors."

The high court dismissed the amicus curiae brief (a friend-of-the-court brief prepared to enlighten the court) presented by the American Psychiatric Association (APA), indicating that psychiatric testimony was "almost entirely unreliable" in determining future actions. The court countered that such testimony had been traditionally accepted. The high court also observed that arguments, such as the APA brief, were founded "on the premise that a jury will not be able to separate the wheat from the chaff," a sentiment with which the court did not agree.

The high court also dismissed Barefoot's contention that the psychiatrists should have personally interviewed him. Such methods of observation and conclusion were quite normal in courtroom procedures, and the psychiatric observations had been based on established facts. Barefoot's appeal was denied.

Justice Blackmun strongly dissented from the majority decision. He declared, "In the present state of psychiatric knowledge, this is too much for me. One may accept this in a routine lawsuit for money damages, but when a person's life is at stake—no matter how heinous his offense—a requirement of greater reliability should prevail. In a capital case, the specious testimony of a psychiatrist, colored in the eyes of an impressionable jury by the inevitable untouchability of a medical specialist's words, equates with death itself."

The state of Texas executed Barefoot by lethal injection in 1984.

A Prisoner Maintains Rights during Psychiatric Examination

During the commission of a robbery in 1973, Ernest Smith's accomplice fatally shot a grocery clerk (Smith had tried to shoot the clerk, but his weapon had jammed). The state of Texas sought the death penalty against Smith based on the Texas law governing premeditated murder.

Thereafter, the judge ordered a psychiatric examination of Smith by James P. Grigson to determine if Smith was competent to stand trial. Without permission from Smith's lawyer, Grigson interviewed Smith in jail for about 90 minutes and found him competent. Grigson then discussed his conclusions and diagnosis with the state attorney. Smith was eventually found guilty. During the sentencing phase of the trial, over the protests of the defendant's lawyers, Grigson testified that Smith was a "very severe sociopath," who would continue his previous behavior, which would get worse. The jury sentenced Smith to death.

Smith appealed his sentence, claiming he was not informed of his rights. Both the federal district court and the appeals court agreed. So did a unanimous Supreme Court. In *Estelle v. Smith* (451 U.S. 454 [1981]), the court ruled that the trial court had the right to determine if Smith was capable of standing trial. It had no right, however, to use the information gathered without first advising him of his Fifth Amendment right against self-incrimination. According to the court, the psychiatrist was "an agent of the state" about whom the defendant had not been warned, but who was reporting about the defendant. Noting *Miranda v. Arizona* (384 U.S. 436 [1966]), the court continued, "The Fifth Amendment privilege is available outside of criminal court proceedings and serves to protect persons in all settings in which their freedom of action is curtailed in any significant way from being compelled to incriminate themselves."

The court reiterated that the prosecution may not use any statements made by a suspect under arrest "unless it demonstrates the use of procedural safeguards effective to secure the privilege against self-incrimination."

In 1981 Smith was convicted of a lesser charge and sentenced to life in prison.

Needing a Psychiatrist to Prove Insanity

In 1979 Glen Burton Ake and Steven Hatch shot and killed the Reverend Richard Douglass and Marilyn Douglass and wounded their children, Brooks and Leslie, in Canadian County, Oklahoma. Before the trial, because of Ake's bizarre behavior, the trial judge ordered him examined by a psychiatrist to determine if he should be put under observation. The psychiatrist diagnosed Ake as a probable paranoid schizophrenic and reported that his client claimed "to be the 'sword of vengeance' of the Lord." The physician recommended a long-term psychiatric examination to determine Ake's competency to stand trial.

Ake's psychiatric evaluation confirmed his paranoid schizophrenia. Consequently, the court pronounced him incompetent to stand trial and ordered him committed to the state mental hospital.

Six weeks later the hospital psychiatrist informed the court that Ake had become competent to stand trial. Under daily treatment with an antipsychotic drug, he could stand trial. The state of Oklahoma resumed proceedings against the accused murderer.

Before the trial Ake's lawyer told the court of his client's insanity defense. He also informed the court that for him to defend Ake adequately, he needed to have Ake examined by a psychiatrist to determine his mental condition at the time he committed murder. During his stay at the mental hospital, Ake was evaluated as to his "present sanity" to stand trial but not his mental state during the murder. Because Ake could not afford a psychiatrist, his counsel asked the court to provide a psychiatrist or the money to hire one. The trial judge refused his request, claiming the state is not obligated to provide a psychiatrist, even to poor defendants in capital cases.

Ake was tried for two counts of first-degree murder and for two counts of shooting with intent to kill. During the trial Ake's only defense was insanity; however, none of the psychiatrists at the state mental hospital could testify to his mental state at the time of the crime.

The judge instructed the jurors that Ake could be found not guilty by reason of insanity if he could not distinguish right from wrong when he committed murder. The jurors were told they could presume Ake sane at the time of the crime unless he presented sufficient evidence to raise a reasonable doubt about his sanity during the crime. The jury found him guilty on all counts. The jury sentenced Ake to death based on the earlier testimony of the psychiatrist, who concluded that Ake was a threat to society. On appeal, the Oklahoma Court of Appeals agreed with the trial court that the state did not have the responsibility to provide an impoverished defendant with a psychiatrist to help with his defense.

The U.S. Supreme Court disagreed. In *Ake v. Oklahoma* (470 U.S. 68 [1985]), the court ruled 8–1 to reverse the lower court's ruling, finding that "there was no expert testimony for either side on Ake's sanity at the time of the offense." The high court further observed, "This Court has long recognized that when a State brings its judicial power to bear on an indigent [poor] defendant in a criminal proceeding, it must take steps to assure that the defendant has a fair opportunity to present his defense. This elementary principle, grounded in significant part on the Fourteenth Amendment's due process guarantee of fundamental fairness, derives from the belief that justice cannot be equal where, simply as a result of his poverty, a defendant is denied the opportunity to participate meaningfully in a judicial proceeding in which his liberty is at stake."

In 1986 Ake was retried, found guilty, and sentenced to life in prison.

INSANITY AND EXECUTION
Can an Insane Person Be Executed?

In 1974 Alvin Ford was convicted of murder and sentenced to death in Florida. There was no question that he was completely sane at the time of his crime, at his trial, and at his sentencing. Eight years later Ford began to show signs of delusion—from thinking that people were conspiring to force him to commit suicide to believing that family members were being held hostage in prison.

Ford's lawyers had a psychiatrist examine their client. After 14 months of evaluation and investigation, the doctor concluded that Ford suffered from a severe mental disorder that would preclude him from assisting in the defense of his life. A second psychiatrist concluded that Ford did not understand why he was on death row.

Florida law required the governor to appoint a panel of three psychiatrists to determine whether Ford was mentally capable of understanding the death penalty and the reasons he was being sentenced to death. The three state-appointed doctors met with Ford once for about 30 minutes and then filed separate reports. Ford's lawyers were present but were ordered by the judge not to participate in the examination in "any adversarial manner."

The three psychiatrists submitted different diagnoses, but all agreed that Ford was sane enough to be executed. Ford's lawyers attempted to submit to the governor the reports of the first two psychiatrists along with other materials. However, the governor refused to inform the lawyers whether he would consider these reports. He eventually signed Ford's death warrant.

Ford's appeals were denied in state and federal courts, but a 7–2 Supreme Court, in *Ford v. Wainwright* (477 U.S. 399 [1986]), reversed the earlier judgments. In light of the fact that there had been no precedent formed for such a case in U.S. history, the justices turned to English law. Writing for the majority, Justice Thurgood Marshall (1908–1993) observed that even though the reasons appear unclear, English common law forbade the execution of the insane. The English jurist William Blackstone (1723–1780) had labeled such a practice "savage and inhuman." Likewise, the other noted English judicial resource, Sir Edward Coke (1552–1634), observed that even though the execution of a criminal was to serve as an example, the execution of a madman was considered "of extream inhumanity and cruelty, and can be no example to others." Consequently, because the Eighth Amendment forbidding a cruel and unusual punishment was prepared by men who accepted English common law, there could be no question that the Eighth Amendment prohibited the execution of the insane.

The issue then became the method the state used to determine Ford's insanity. The high court noted that Florida did not allow the submission of materials that might be relevant to the decision whether or not to execute the condemned man. In addition, Ford's lawyers were not given the chance to question the state-appointed psychiatrists about the basis for finding their client competent.

Questions the defense could have asked included the possibility of personal bias on the doctors' part toward the death penalty, any history of error in their judgment, and their degree of certainty in reaching their conclusions. Finally, the justices pointed out that the greatest defect in Florida's practice is its entrusting the ultimate decision about the execution entirely to the executive branch. The high court observed, "Under this procedure, the person who appoints the experts and ultimately decides whether the State will be able to carry out the sentence that it has long sought is the Governor, whose subordinates have been responsible for initiating every stage of the prosecution of the condemned from arrest through sentencing. The commander of the State's corps of prosecutors cannot be said to have the neutrality that is necessary for reliability in the factfinding proceeding."

The high court further observed that even though a prisoner has been sentenced to death, he is still protected by the Constitution. Therefore, ascertaining his sanity as a basis for a legal execution is as important as other proceedings in a capital case.

In dissent, Justice Rehnquist, joined by Chief Justice Burger, thought the Florida procedure was consistent with English common law, which had left the decision to the executive branch. Rehnquist warned, "A claim of insanity may be made at any time before sentence and, once rejected, may be raised again; a prisoner found sane two days before execution might claim to have lost his sanity the next day, thus necessitating another judicial determination of his sanity and presumably another stay of his execution."

Ford remained on Florida's death row until 1991, when he died of natural causes.

Can an Insane Person Stabilized by Drugs Be Executed?

In 1979 Charles Singleton stabbed Mary Lou York twice in the neck after robbing her grocery store in Hamburg, Arkansas. He was tried, convicted, and sentenced to death. He was sane during the murder and throughout the trial.

However, Singleton developed schizophrenia while in prison. At one point during his incarceration, Singleton claimed his prison cell was possessed by demons. When given antipsychotic medication, however, Singleton regained his sanity. Fearing a psychotic outburst from Singleton, the prison forced medication on him when he refused to take it. Singleton filed several habeas corpus petitions in state and federal courts, claiming that in light of *Ford*, he was not competent enough to be executed. He also argued that the forcible administration of antipsychotic medication was a violation of the Eighth Amendment, which forbids a cruel and unusual punishment.

The case was taken up by the U.S. Court of Appeals for the Eighth Circuit. In *Singleton v. Norris* (319 F.3d 1018 [8th Cir., 2003]), the appellate court upheld the death penalty for Singleton in a 5–4 decision. The majority felt that as long as Singleton was on medication and in full control of his faculties, his execution was not a violation of the Eighth Amendment. Singleton appealed to the U.S. Supreme Court, but the high court turned the case down, effectively endorsing the decision of the appellate court. Singleton was executed by the state of Arkansas on January 6, 2004.

CAN A MENTALLY RETARDED PERSON BE EXECUTED?
Penry I

In 1979 Pamela Carpenter was brutally raped, beaten, and stabbed with a pair of scissors in Livingston, Texas. Before she died, she was able to describe her attacker, and as a result, Johnny Paul Penry was arrested for, and later confessed to, the crime. At the time of the crime, Penry was out on parole for another rape. He was found guilty for the murder of Carpenter and sentenced to death.

Among the issues considered in his appeal was whether the state of Texas could execute a mentally retarded person. At Penry's competency hearing a psychiatrist testified that the defendant had an intelligence quotient (IQ) of 54. Penry had been tested in the past as having an IQ between 50 and 63, indicating mild to moderate retardation. (It is generally accepted that an IQ below 70 is evidence of mental retardation. Normal IQ is considered 90 and above.) According to the psychiatrist, during the commission of the crime the 22-year-old Penry had the mental age of a child six-and-a-half years old and the social maturity of someone who was nine to 10 years old. Penry's attorneys argued, "Because of their mental disabilities, mentally retarded people do not possess the level of moral culpability to justify imposing the death sentence.... There is an emerging national consensus against executing the mentally retarded."

Writing for the majority regarding the execution of mentally retarded people, Justice O'Connor, in *Penry v. Lynaugh* (492 U.S. 302 [1989]), found no emerging national consensus against such executions. Furthermore, even though profoundly retarded people had not been executed for murder historically, Penry did not fall into this group.

Justice O'Connor noted that Penry was found competent to stand trial. He was able to consult rationally with his lawyer and understood the proceedings against him. She thought that the defense was guilty of lumping all mentally retarded people together, ascribing, among other things, a lack of moral capacity to be culpable for actions that call for the death punishment. O'Connor wrote:

> Mentally retarded persons are individuals whose abilities
> and experiences can vary greatly. [If the mentally

retarded were not treated as individuals, but as an undifferentiated group,] a mildly mentally retarded person could be denied the opportunity to enter into contracts or to marry by virtue of the fact that he had a "mental age" of a young child. . . . In light of the diverse capacities and life experiences of mentally retarded persons, it cannot be said on the record before us today that all mentally retarded people, by definition, can never act with the level of culpability associated with the death penalty.

Furthermore, the majority could find no national movement toward any type of consensus on this issue. Even though *Penry* produced several public opinion polls that indicated strong public opposition to executing the retarded, almost none of this public opinion was reflected in death penalty legislation. Only the federal Anti-Drug Abuse Act of 1988 and the states of Georgia and Maryland at the time banned the execution of retarded people found guilty of a capital crime.

Justice Brennan disagreed. Even though he agreed that lumping mentally retarded people together might result in stereotyping and discrimination, he believed there are characteristics that fall under the clinical definition of mental retardation. Citing the amicus curiae brief prepared by the American Association on Mental Retardation, he noted, "'Every individual who has mental retardation'—irrespective of his or her precise capacities or experiences—has 'a substantial disability in cognitive ability and adaptive behavior.' . . . Though individuals, particularly those who are mildly retarded, may be quite capable of overcoming these limitations to the extent of being able to 'maintain themselves independently or semi-independently in the community,' nevertheless, the mentally retarded by definition 'have a reduced ability to cope with and function in the everyday world.'"

Justice Brennan did not believe that executing a person not fully responsible for his or her actions would serve the "penal goals of deterrence or retribution." What is the point of executing someone who did not fully recognize the terrible evil that he or she had done? Furthermore, he argued, executing a mentally retarded person would not deter nonretarded people, those who would be aware of the possibility of an execution.

Even though the Supreme Court held that executing people with mental retardation was not a violation of the Eighth Amendment, it ruled that Penry's Eighth Amendment right was violated because the jury was not instructed that it could consider mental retardation as a mitigating factor during sentencing. The case was sent back to the lower court. In 1990 Texas retried Penry, and he was again found guilty of capital murder. During the sentencing phase the prosecution used a specific portion of a psychiatric report to point out the doctor's opinion that, if released from custody, Penry would be a threat to society. Penry appealed his case all the way to the

Supreme Court. Ten years later, in November 2000, with Penry less than three hours from being put to death, the Supreme Court granted a stay of execution to hear Penry's claims.

Penry II

Penry once again appealed to the Supreme Court after his case was retried. In his appeal to the Supreme Court, Penry argued that the use of a portion of an old psychiatric report at his 1990 retrial violated his Fifth Amendment right against self-incrimination. In 1977 Penry was arrested in connection with another rape. During this rape case the state of Texas provided Penry with a psychiatrist at the request of his lawyer. The psychiatrist was to determine the defendant's competency to stand trial. In 2000 Penry argued that the psychiatrist was an "agent of the State" and that the prosecution's use of his report in the 1990 retrial for murder violated Penry's right against self-incrimination. Penry also claimed jury instructions were inadequate.

On June 4, 2001, the Supreme Court ruled 6–3 in *Penry v. Johnson* (532 U.S. 782) that the admission of the psychiatrist's report did not violate Penry's Fifth Amendment right. The court held that this case was different from *Estelle v. Smith*, in which the justices found that the psychiatrist's testimony about the defendant's future dangerousness based on the defendant's statements without his lawyer present violated his Fifth Amendment right. The justices emphasized that *Estelle* was restricted to that particular case.

The justices, however, sent the case back to the trial court for resentencing because, as in the original *Penry* case, the state did not give the sentencing jury adequate instructions about how to weigh mental retardation as a mitigating factor.

The Court Revisits Mental Retardation

Daryl Renard Atkins was convicted and sentenced to death for a 1996 abduction, armed robbery, and capital murder. On appeal to the Virginia Supreme Court, Atkins argued that he could not be executed because he was mentally retarded. Relying on *Penry v. Lynaugh*, the court affirmed the conviction. The court ordered a sentencing retrial because the trial court had used the wrong verdict form. As with the first penalty trial, a psychologist testified that Atkins was "mildly mentally retarded," having an IQ of 59. The jury sentenced Atkins to death for a second time. Atkins again appealed to the Virginia Supreme Court, which upheld the trial court ruling.

The U.S. Supreme Court unanimously agreed to hear Atkins's case. Thirteen years after ruling that executing the mentally retarded does not violate the Constitution, the Supreme Court, in a 6–3 decision, reversed its 1989 *Penry* decision. On June 20, 2002, in *Atkins v. Virginia*

(536 U.S. 304), most of the court held that "executions of mentally retarded criminals are 'cruel and unusual punishments' prohibited by the Eighth Amendment."

Justice Stevens delivered the opinion of the court. Justices O'Connor, Kennedy, Souter, Ruth Bader Ginsburg (1933–), and Stephen G. Breyer (1938–) joined the opinion. According to the court, since *Penry*, many states had concluded that death is not a suitable punishment for mentally retarded offenders, reflecting society's sentiments that these individuals are less culpable than average offenders. The court observed, "Mentally retarded persons . . . have diminished capacities to understand and process information, to communicate, to abstract from mistakes and learn from experience, to engage in logical reasoning, to control impulses, and to understand the reactions of others. . . . Their deficiencies do not warrant an exemption from criminal sanctions, but they do diminish their personal culpability."

The justices also noted that even though the theory is that capital punishment would serve as deterrence to those contemplating murder, this theory does not apply to the mentally retarded because their diminished mental capacities prevent them from appreciating the possibility of execution as punishment. Moreover, the lesser culpability of mentally retarded criminals does not warrant the severe punishment of death.

Justice Scalia disagreed with the ruling that a person who is slightly mentally retarded does not possess the culpability to be sentenced to death. He claimed that the ruling finds "no support in the text or history of the Eighth Amendment." The justice also noted that current social attitudes do not support the majority decision. He pointed out that the state laws that the majority claimed reflect society's attitudes against executing the mentally retarded are still in their infancy and have not undergone the test of time.

On the relationship between a criminal's culpability and the deserved punishment, Justice Scalia stated:

Surely culpability, and deservedness of the most severe retribution, depends not merely (if at all) upon the mental capacity of the criminal (above the level where he is able to distinguish right from wrong) but also upon the depravity of the crime—which is precisely why this sort of question has traditionally been thought answerable not by a categorical rule of the sort the Court today imposes upon all trials, but rather by the sentencer's weighing of the circumstances (both degree of retardation and depravity of crime) in the particular case. The fact that juries continue to sentence mentally retarded offenders to death for extreme crimes shows that society's moral outrage sometimes demands execution of retarded offenders. By what principle of law, science, or logic can the Court pronounce that this is wrong? There is none. Once the Court admits (as it does) that mental retardation does not render the offender morally blameless . . . there is no basis for saying that the death penalty is never appropriate retribution, no matter how heinous the crime.

Penry's Sentence Revisited

On July 3, 2002, about two weeks after the Supreme Court ruled that it is unconstitutional to execute a mentally retarded person, a Texas jury concluded that Penry was not mentally retarded. He was resentenced to death. Three years later the Texas Court of Criminal Appeals ruled that the jury had not fully considered Penry's claim of mental retardation and ordered a new sentencing hearing. The Texas attorney general appealed the decision. In 2008 Penry's sentence was converted to three life terms in prison without the chance of parole. As part of a plea deal agreement, Penry had to apologize to the victim's family and concede that he was not mentally retarded.

COMPETENCY STANDARD

In Las Vegas, Nevada, on August 2, 1984, Richard Allen Moran fatally shot a bartender and a patron four times each. Several days later he went to the home of his former wife and fatally shot her, then turned the gun on himself. However, his suicide attempt failed, and Moran confessed to his crimes. Later, the defendant pleaded not guilty to three counts of first-degree murder. Two psychiatrists examined Moran and concluded that he was competent to stand trial. Approximately 10 weeks after the evaluations, the defendant decided to dismiss his attorneys and change his plea to guilty. After review of the psychiatric reports, the trial court accepted the waiver for counsel and the guilty plea. The defendant was later sentenced to death.

Seven months later Moran appealed his case, claiming that he had been "mentally incompetent to represent himself." The appellate court reversed the conviction, ruling that "competency to waive constitutional rights requires a higher level of mental functioning than that required to stand trial." A defendant is considered competent to stand trial if he can understand the proceedings and help in his defense. Yet, for a defendant to be considered competent to waive counsel or to plead guilty, he has to be capable of "'reasoned choice' among the alternatives available to him." The appellate court found Moran mentally incapable of the reasoned choice needed to be in a position to waive his constitutional rights.

The Supreme Court ruled 7–2 in *Godinez v. Moran* (509 U.S. 389 [1993]) to reverse the judgment of the court of appeals, holding that the standard for measuring a criminal defendant's competency to plead guilty or to waive his right to counsel is not higher than the standard for standing trial. The high court then sent the case back to the lower courts for further proceedings. Moran was executed in March 1996.

VICTIM IMPACT STATEMENTS

First, They Are Not Constitutional

John Booth and Willie Reid stole money from elderly neighbors to buy heroin in 1983. Booth, knowing his neighbors could identify him, tied up the elderly couple and then repeatedly stabbed them in the chest with a kitchen knife. The couple's son found their bodies two days later. Booth and Reid were found guilty.

The state of Maryland permitted a victim impact statement to be read to the jury during the sentencing phase of the trial. The victim impact statement prepared in this case explained the tremendous pain caused by the murder of the parents and grandparents to the family. A 5–4 Supreme Court, in *Booth v. Maryland* (482 U.S. 496 [1987]), while recognizing the agony caused to the victims' family, ruled that victim impact statements, as required by Maryland's statute, were unconstitutional and could not be used during the sentencing phase of a capital murder trial.

Writing for the majority, Justice Lewis F. Powell Jr. (1907–1998) indicated that a jury must determine whether the defendant should be executed, based on the circumstances of the crime and the character of the offender. These factors had nothing to do with the victim. The high court noted that it is the crime and the criminal that are at issue. Had Booth and Reid viciously murdered a homeless man, the crime would have been just as horrible. Furthermore, some families could express the pain and disruption they suffered as a result of the murder better than other families, and a sentencing should not depend on how well a family could express its grief.

Reid's sentence was later converted to two life terms. As of September 2011, Booth, who has since changed his last name to Booth-el, remained on Maryland's death row.

... And Then They Are

Pervis Tyrone Payne of Tennessee spent the morning and early afternoon of June 27, 1987, injecting cocaine and drinking beer. Later, he drove around the town with a friend, each of them taking turns looking at a pornographic magazine. In mid-afternoon, Payne went to his girlfriend's apartment, who was away visiting her mother in Arkansas. Charisse Christopher lived across the hall from the apartment. Payne entered Christopher's apartment and made sexual advances toward Christopher, who resisted. Payne became violent.

When the police arrived, they found Christopher on the floor with 42 direct knife wounds and 42 defensive wounds on her arms and hands. Her two-year-old daughter had suffered stab wounds to the chest, abdomen, back, and head. The murder weapon, a butcher knife, was found at her feet. Christopher's three-year-old son, despite several stab wounds that went completely through his body, was still alive. Payne was arrested, and a Tennessee jury convicted him of the first-degree murders of Christopher and her daughter and of the first-degree assault, with intent to murder, of Christopher's son, Nicholas.

During the sentencing phase of the trial, Payne called his parents, his girlfriend, and a clinical psychologist to testify about the mitigating aspects of his background and character. The prosecutor, however, called Nicholas's grandmother, who testified how much the child missed his mother and baby sister. In arguing for the death penalty, the prosecutor commented on the continuing effects the crime was having on Nicholas and his family. The jury sentenced Payne to death on each of the murder counts. The state supreme court agreed, rejecting Payne's claim that the admission of the grandmother's testimony and the state's closing argument violated his Eighth Amendment rights under *Booth v. Maryland*.

On hearing the appeal, the U.S. Supreme Court ruled 6–3 in *Payne v. Tennessee* (501 U.S. 808 [1991]) to uphold the death penalty and overturned *Booth v. Maryland*. In *Payne*, the court ruled that the Eighth Amendment does not prohibit a jury from considering, at the sentencing phase of a capital trial, victim impact evidence relating to a victim's personal characteristics and the emotional impact of the murder on the victim's family. The Eighth Amendment also does not bar a prosecutor from arguing such evidence at the sentencing phase.

The court reasoned that the assessment of harm caused by a defendant as a result of a crime has long been an important concern of criminal law in determining both the elements of the offense and the appropriate punishment. Victim impact evidence is simply another form or method of informing the sentencing jury or judge about the specific harm caused by the crime in question.

The *Booth* case unfairly weighted the scales in a capital trial. No limits were placed on the mitigating evidence the defendant introduced relating to his own circumstances. The state, however, was potentially barred from offering a glimpse of the life of the victim or from showing the loss to the victim's family or to society. *Booth* was decided by narrow margins, the court continued, and had been questioned by members of the Supreme Court as well as by the lower courts.

Dissenting, Justice Stevens stated that a victim impact statement "sheds no light on the defendant's guilt or moral culpability, and thus serves no purpose other than to encourage jurors to decide in favor of death rather than life on the basis of their emotions rather than their reason."

As of September 2011, Payne remained on Tennessee's death row.

THE ISSUE OF RACE IN CAPITAL CASES

In 1978 Willie Lloyd Turner, an African-American, robbed a jewelry store in Franklin, Virginia. Angered because the owner had set off a silent alarm, Turner first shot the owner in the head, wounding him, and then shot him twice in the chest, killing him for "snitching." Turner's lawyer submitted to the judge the following question for the jurors: "The defendant, Willie Lloyd Turner, is a member of the Negro race. The victim, W. Jack Smith, Jr., was a white Caucasian. Will these facts prejudice you against Willie Lloyd Turner or affect your ability to render a fair and impartial verdict based solely on the evidence?"

The judge refused to allow this question to be asked. A jury of eight whites and four African-Americans convicted Turner and then, in a separate sentencing hearing, recommended the death sentence, which the judge imposed.

Turner appealed his conviction, claiming that the judge's refusal to ask prospective jurors about their racial attitudes deprived him of his right to a fair trial. Even though his argument failed to persuade state and federal appeals courts, the U.S. Supreme Court heard his case. The high court ruled 7–2 in *Turner v. Murray* (476 U.S. 28 [1986]) to overturn Turner's death sentence, but not his conviction.

Writing for the majority, Justice White noted that, in considering a death sentence, every juror makes a subjective decision that is uniquely his or her own regarding what punishment should be meted out to the offender. White further stated:

> Because of the range of discretion entrusted to a jury in a capital sentencing hearing, there is a unique opportunity for racial prejudice to operate but remain undetected. On the facts of this case, a juror who believes that blacks are violence prone or morally inferior might well be influenced by that belief in deciding whether petitioner's crime involved the aggravating factors specified under Virginia law. Such a juror might also be less favorably inclined toward petitioner's evidence of mental disturbance as a mitigating circumstance. More subtle, less consciously held racial attitudes could also influence a juror's decision in this case. Fear of blacks, which could easily be stirred up by the violent facts of petitioner's crime, might incline a juror to favor the death penalty.

The high court recognized that the death sentence differs from all other punishments and, therefore, requires a more comprehensive examination of how it is imposed. The lower court judge, by not asking prospective jurors about their racial attitudes, had not exercised this thorough examination. Consequently, the Supreme Court reversed Turner's death sentence. Justice Powell, in his dissent, observed that the court ruling seemed to be "based on what amounts to a constitutional presumption that jurors in capital cases are racially biased. Such presumption unjustifiably suggests that criminal justice in our courts of law is meted out on racial grounds."

In 1987 a Virginia court resentenced Turner to death. After completing the appeals process he was executed in 1995.

Limits to Consideration of Racial Attitudes

On May 13, 1978, Warren McCleskey and three armed men robbed a furniture store in Fulton County, Georgia. A police officer, responding to a silent alarm, entered the store, was shot twice, and died. McCleskey was African-American; the officer was white. McCleskey admitted taking part in the robbery but denied shooting the police officer. The state proved that at least one shot came from the weapon McCleskey was carrying and produced two witnesses who had heard McCleskey admit to the shooting. A jury found him guilty, and McCleskey, offering no mitigating circumstances during the sentencing phase, received the death penalty.

McCleskey eventually appealed his case all the way to the U.S. Supreme Court. Part of his appeal was based on two major statistical studies of more than 2,000 Georgia murder cases that occurred during the 1970s. Prepared by David C. Baldus, Charles A. Pulanski Jr., and George Woodworth, the statistical analyses were referred to as the Baldus study. (The two studies were "Comparative Review of Death Sentences: An Empirical Study of the Georgia Experience" [*Journal of Criminal Law and Criminology*, vol. 74, no. 3, Autumn 1983] and "Monitoring and Evaluating Contemporary Death Sentencing Systems: Lessons from Georgia" [*University of California Davis Law Review*, vol. 18, no. 1375, 1985].)

The Baldus study found that defendants charged with killing white people received the death penalty in 11% of cases, but defendants charged with killing African-Americans received the death penalty in only 1% of the cases. The study also found a reverse racial difference, based on the defendant's race—4% of the African-American defendants received the death penalty, as opposed to 7% of the white defendants.

Furthermore, the Baldus study reported on the cases based on the combination of the defendant's race and that of the victim. The death penalty was imposed in 22% of the cases involving African-American defendants and white victims, in 8% of the cases involving white defendants and white victims, in 3% of the cases involving white defendants and African-American victims, and in 1% of the cases involving African-American defendants and African-American victims.

The Baldus study also found that prosecutors sought the death penalty in 70% of the cases involving African-American defendants and white victims, in 32% of the cases involving white defendants and white victims, in 19% of the cases involving white defendants and African-American victims, and in 15% of the cases involving African-American defendants and African-American victims.

Finally, after taking account of variables that could have explained the differences on nonracial grounds, the study concluded that defendants charged with killing white victims were 4.3 times as likely to receive the death penalty as defendants charged with killing African-Americans. In addition, African-American defendants were 1.1 times as likely to get a death sentence as other defendants were. Therefore, McCleskey, who was African-American and killed a white victim, had the greatest likelihood of being sentenced to death.

In court testimony, Baldus testified that, in really brutal cases where there is no question the death penalty should be imposed, racial discrimination on the part of the jurors tends to disappear. The racial factors usually come into play in midrange cases, such as McCleskey's, where the jurors were faced with choices.

Even though the federal district court did not accept the Baldus study, both the court of appeals and the U.S. Supreme Court accepted the study as valid. However, a 5–4 Supreme Court, in *McCleskey v. Kemp* (481 U.S. 279 [1987]), rejected McCleskey's appeal. McCleskey had to show that the state of Georgia had acted in a discriminatory manner in his case, and the Baldus study was not enough to support the defendant's claim that any of the jurors had acted with discrimination.

Justice Powell noted that statistics, at most, may show that a certain factor might likely enter some decision-making processes. The court recognized that a jury's decision could be influenced by racial prejudice, but the majority believed previous rulings had built in enough safeguards to guarantee equal protection for every defendant. The court declared, "At most, the Baldus study indicates a discrepancy that appears to correlate with race. Apparent disparities in sentencing are an inevitable part of our criminal justice system.... We hold that the Baldus study does not demonstrate a constitutionally significant risk of racial bias affecting the Georgia capital sentencing process."

The court expressed concern that if it ruled that Baldus's findings did represent a risk, the findings might well be applied to lesser cases. It further noted that it is the job of the legislative branch to consider these findings and incorporate them into the laws to guarantee equal protection in courts of law.

Justice Brennan, who, along with Justice Marshall, believed capital punishment constitutes a cruel and unusual punishment and, therefore, is unconstitutional, thought the Baldus study powerfully demonstrated that it is impossible to eliminate arbitrariness in the imposition of the death penalty. Therefore, he argued, the death penalty must be abolished altogether because the court cannot rely on legal safeguards to guarantee an African-American defendant a fair sentencing. Even though the Baldus study did not show that racism necessarily led to McCleskey's death sentence, it had surely shown that McCleskey faced a considerably greater likelihood of being sentenced to death because he was an African-American man convicted of killing a white man.

Also writing in dissent, Justice Blackmun thought the court majority had concentrated too much on the potential racial attitudes of the jury. As important, he thought, were the racial attitudes of the prosecutor's office, which the Baldus study found to be much more likely to seek the death penalty for an African-American person who had killed a white person than for other categories.

The district attorney for Fulton County had testified that no county policy existed on how to prosecute capital cases. Decisions to seek the death penalty were left to the judgment of the assistant district attorneys who handled the cases. Blackmun thought that such a system was certainly open to abuse. Without guidelines, the prosecutors could let their racial prejudices influence their decisions.

Blackmun also noted that the court majority had totally dismissed Georgia's history of racial prejudice as past history. Even though it should not be the overriding factor, this bias should be considered in any case presented to the high court, he thought. Justice Blackmun found most disturbing the court's concern that, if the Baldus findings were upheld, they might be applied to other cases, leading to constitutional challenges. Blackmun thought that a closer scrutiny of the effects of racial discrimination would benefit the criminal justice system and, ultimately, society.

In 1991 McCleskey was executed in the electric chair by the state of Georgia.

Prosecutor's Racially Based Use of Peremptory Challenges in Jury Selection

James Ford, an African-American, was charged with the kidnapping, rape, and murder of a white woman on February 29, 1984. The state of Georgia informed Ford that it planned to seek the death penalty. Before the trial, Ford filed a "Motion to Restrict Racial Use of Peremptory Challenges," claiming that the prosecutor had consistently excluded African-Americans from juries where the victims were white.

At a hearing on the defendant's motion, Ford's lawyer noted that it had been his experience that the district attorney and his assistants had used their peremptory challenges (the right to reject a juror without giving a reason) to excuse potential African-American jurors. Ford's lawyer asked the trial judge to prevent this from happening by ordering the district attorney to justify on the record his reasons for excusing potential African-American jurors.

The prosecutor denied any discrimination on his part. He referred to the U.S. Supreme Court decision in *Swain v. Alabama* (380 U.S. 202 [1965]), which said, in part, "It would be an unreasonable burden to require an attorney for either side to justify his use of peremptory challenges." The judge denied the defense attorney's motion because he had previously seen the district attorney passing over prospective white jurors in favor of potential African-American jurors.

During jury selection the prosecutor used nine of his 10 peremptory challenges to dismiss prospective African-American jurors, leaving only one African-American member seated on the jury. In closed sessions, the judge allowed Ford's attorney's observation, for the record, that nine of the 10 African-American prospective members had been dismissed on peremptory challenges by the prosecutor. The judge, however, told the prosecutor that he did not have to offer any reasons for his peremptory actions.

Ford was convicted on all counts and sentenced to death. His attorney, believing that the jury did not represent a fair cross-section of the community, called for a new trial and claimed that Ford's "right to an impartial jury as guaranteed by Sixth Amendment to the United States Constitution was violated by the prosecutor's exercise of his peremptory challenges on a racial basis." On appeal, the Georgia Supreme Court affirmed the conviction.

Ford appealed to the U.S. Supreme Court. In *Ford v. Georgia* (498 U.S. 411 [1991]), the high court reversed the decision of the Georgia Supreme Court. The court vacated Ford's conviction and ruled that its decision in *Batson v. Kentucky* (476 U.S. 79 [1986]) could be applied retroactively to Ford's case, which had been tried in 1984. In 1986 the high court had superseded *Swain* when it ruled in *Batson* that a defendant could make a case claiming the denial of equal protection of the laws solely on evidence that the prosecutor had used peremptory challenges to exclude members of the defendant's race from the jury.

Delivering the opinion for a unanimous court, Justice Souter held that the Georgia Supreme Court had erred when it ruled that Ford had failed to present a proper equal protection claim. Even though Ford's pretrial motion did not mention the equal protection clause (of the 14th Amendment), and his new trial motion had cited the Sixth Amendment rather than the 14th Amendment, the motion referring to a pattern of excluding African-American members "'over a long period of time' constitutes the assertion of an equal protection claim." As of September 2011, Ford was in the Georgia State Prison serving a sentence of life without the possibility of parole.

Using Race/Ethnicity to Obtain a Death Sentence

On June 5, 2000, the Supreme Court, in a summary disposition, ordered the Texas Court of Criminal Appeals to hold a new sentencing hearing for Victor Saldano, an Argentine national on death row. In a summary disposition, the court decides a case in a simple proceeding without a jury. Generally, a summary disposition is rare in criminal cases. In this instance, the crime was committed by a foreign national and thus fell outside of a trial jury's mandate. In *Saldano v. Texas* (No. 99-8119), the court cited the confession of error by the Texas attorney general John Cornyn (1952–) regarding the use of race as a factor in sentencing the defendant.

Texas death penalty statutes require that the jury consider a defendant's future dangerousness to determine whether or not to impose the death penalty. At the sentencing hearing Walter Quijano, the court-appointed psychologist, testified that Saldano was "a continuing threat to society" because he is Hispanic. Quijano told the jury that because Hispanics are "over-represented" in prisons they are more likely to be dangerous. Following this decision, other death row inmates whose cases reflected similar circumstances were granted new sentencing hearings. Saldano's own case continued in the courts; in March 2004 the U.S. Court of Appeals for the Fifth Circuit refused to reinstate Saldano's death sentence. As of September 2011, Saldano remained on Texas's death row.

CHAPTER 5

DEATH PENALTY LAWS: STATE, FEDERAL, AND U.S. MILITARY

STATE DEATH PENALTY LAWS

Before the late 1960s U.S. death penalty laws varied considerably from state to state and from region to region. Few national standards existed on how a murder trial should be conducted or which types of crimes deserved the death penalty. In South Carolina, for instance, a person could be executed for rape or robbery. In Georgia and in a number of other states, juries were given complete discretion in delivering a sentence along with the conviction. Though verdicts were swift, the punishments such juries meted out could be arbitrary and discriminatory.

During the late 1960s and early 1970s the U.S. Supreme Court undertook a series of cases that questioned the constitutionality of state capital punishment laws. In *Furman v. Georgia* (408 U.S. 238 [1972]), the court ruled that the death penalty, as it was then being administered, constituted a cruel and unusual punishment in violation of the Eighth and 14th Amendments to the U.S. Constitution. According to the court, the state laws that were then in effect led to arbitrary sentencing of the death penalty. As a result, many states changed their laws to conform to standards set by the *Furman* decision. Since *Furman*, review of individual state statutes has continued as appeals of capital sentences reach state courts or the U.S. Supreme Court. In particular, the use of capital punishment against the insane (*Ford v. Wainwright*, 477 U.S. 399 [1986]), the mentally retarded (*Atkins v. Virginia*, 536 U.S. 304 [2002]), and juveniles (*Roper v. Simmons*, 543 U.S. 551 [2005]) has been found to be unconstitutional by the U.S. Supreme Court.

Court decisions have also affected state trial and sentencing procedures. Under revised laws, most states now use a bifurcated (two-part) trial system, where the first trial is used to determine a defendant's guilt, and the second trial determines the sentence of a guilty defendant. In most trials jurors are usually only given the option of either sentencing a convicted felon to life in prison or to death. During a sentencing hearing, juries must consider all the aggravating circumstances presented by the prosecution and the mitigating circumstances presented by the defense. Mitigating circumstances may lessen the responsibility for a crime, whereas aggravating circumstances may add to the responsibility for a crime.

Capital Offenses under State Laws

State laws, statutes, and criminal codes specifically lay out which crimes are to be handled as capital cases. Table 5.1 lists capital offenses by state in 2009 per the U.S. Department of Justice's Bureau of Justice Statistics. Note that Illinois eliminated the death penalty in 2011. In addition, New York's capital punishment law has been found, in part, to be unconstitutional, which will be described in Chapter 8.

Different types of capital murder are specified by legal definition. Even though varying somewhat from one jurisdiction to another, the types of homicide most commonly specified are murder carried out during the commission of a felony (serious offense such as rape, robbery, or arson); murder of a peace officer, corrections employee, or firefighter engaged in the performance of official duties; murder by an inmate serving a life sentence; and murder for hire (contract murder). Different statutory terminology may be used in different states to designate essentially similar crimes. Terms such as *capital murder, first-degree murder, capital felony,* or *murder Class 1 felony* may indicate the same offense in different states.

NONHOMICIDE CRIMES. As described in Chapter 3, the imposition of the death penalty for some nonhomicide crimes has been ruled unconstitutional by the courts. The notable examples are rape and kidnapping in which the victim survives. However, other offenses (such as treason and air piracy or hijacking) that carry the death penalty under law have not yet had their constitutionality tested.

Under Texas law a person who is party to, but does not actually commit, a murder can receive the death

TABLE 5.1

Capital offenses, by state, 2009

State	Offense
Alabama	Intentional murder with 18 aggravating factors (Ala. Stat. Ann.13A-5-40(a)(1)-(18)).
Arizona	First-degree murder accompanied by at least 1 of 14 aggravating factors (A.R.S. § 13-703(F)).
Arkansas	Capital murder (Ark. Code Ann. 5-10-101) with a finding of at least 1 of 10 aggravating circumstances; treason.
California	First-degree murder with special circumstances; sabotage; train wrecking causing death; treason; perjury causing execution of an innocent person; fatal assault by a prisoner serving a life sentence.
Colorado	First-degree murder with at least 1 of 17 aggravating factors; first-degree kidnapping resulting in death; treason.
Connecticut	Capital felony with 8 forms of aggravated homicide (C.G.S. § 53a-54b).
Delaware	First-degree murder with at least 1 statutory aggravating circumstance (11 Del. C. § 4209).
Florida	First-degree murder; felony murder; capital drug trafficking; capital sexual battery.
Georgia	Murder; kidnapping with bodily injury or ransom when the victim dies; aircraft hijacking; treason.
Idaho	First-degree murder with aggravating factors; first-degree kidnapping; perjury resulting in death.
Illinois	First-degree murder with 1 of 21 aggravating circumstances (720 Ill. Comp. Stat. 5/9-1).
Indiana	Murder with 16 aggravating circumstances (IC 35-50-2-9).
Kansas	Capital murder with 8 aggravating circumstances (KSA 21-3439, KSA 21-4625, KSA 21-4636).
Kentucky	Murder with aggravating factors; kidnapping with aggravating factors (KRS 532.025).
Louisiana	First-degree murder; treason (La. R.S. 14:30 and 14:113).
Maryland	First-degree murder, either premeditated or during the commission of a felony, provided that certain death eligibility requirements are satisfied.
Mississippi	Capital murder (Miss. Code Ann. § 97-3-19(2)); aircraft piracy (Miss. Code Ann. § 97-25-55(1)).
Missouri	First-degree murder (565.020 RSMO 2000).
Montana	Capital murder with 1 of 9 aggravating circumstances (Mont. Code Ann. § 46-18-303); aggravated sexual intercourse without consent (Mont. Code Ann. § 45-5-503).
Nebraska	First-degree murder with a finding of at least 1 statutorily-defined aggravating circumstance.
Nevada	First-degree murder with at least 1 of 15 aggravating circumstances (NRS 200.030, 200.033, 200.035).
New Hampshire	Murder committed in the course of rape, kidnapping, or drug crimes; killing of a law enforcement officer; murder for hire; murder by an inmate while serving a sentence of life without parole (RSA 630:1, RSA 630:5).
New York*	First-degree murder with 1 of 13 aggravating factors (NY Penal Law § 125.27).
North Carolina	First-degree murder (NCGS § 14-17).
Ohio	Aggravated murder with at least 1 of 10 aggravating circumstances (O.R.C. secs. 2903.01, 2929.02, and 2929.04).
Oklahoma	First-degree murder in conjunction with a finding of at least 1 of 8 statutorily-defined aggravating circumstances; sex crimes against a child under 14 years of age.
Oregon	Aggravated murder (ORS 163.095-150).
Pennsylvania	First-degree murder with 18 aggravating circumstances.
South Carolina	Murder with 1 of 12 aggravating circumstances (§ 16-3-20(C)(a)).
South Dakota	First-degree murder with 1 of 10 aggravating circumstances.
Tennessee	First-degree murder with 1 of 15 aggravating circumstances (Tenn. Code Ann. § 39-13-204).
Texas	Criminal homicide with 1 of 9 aggravating circumstances (Tex. Penal Code § 19.03).
Utah	Aggravated murder (76-5-202, Utah Code Annotated).
Virginia	First-degree murder with 1 of 15 aggravating circumstances (VA Code § 18.2-31).
Washington	Aggravated first-degree murder.
Wyoming	First-degree murder; murder during the commission of sexual assault, sexual abuse of a minor, arson, robbery, escape, resisting arrest, kidnapping, or abuse of a minor under 16 (W.S.A. § 6-2-101 (a)).

*The New York Court of Appeals has held that a portion of New York's death penalty sentencing statute (CPL 400.27) was unconstitutional (People v. Taylor, 9 N.Y.3d 129 (2007)). As a result, no defendants can be sentenced to death until the legislature corrects the errors in this statute.

SOURCE: Tracy L. Snell, "Table 1. Capital Offenses, by State, 2009," in *Capital Punishment, 2009—Statistical Tables*, U.S. Department of Justice, Office of Justice Programs, Bureau of Justice Statistics, December 2010, http://bjs.ojp.usdoj.gov/content/pub/pdf/cp09st.pdf (accessed July 5, 2011)

penalty. Section 7.02 of the Texas Penal Code took effect in 1974 and allows prosecutors to charge an accomplice with capital murder if the accomplice should have anticipated that the murder was going to occur. This is known informally as "the law of parties" and is explained by Jordan Smith in "Wrong Place, Wrong Time" (*Austin Chronicle*, February 11, 2005). The law of parties received national attention when it was used in 1997 to impose a death sentence against Kenneth Foster for his role as the getaway driver in a murder. Foster and three other men were arrested in 1996. They had been robbing people at gunpoint when they saw an attractive woman in a suburban neighborhood. One of the men, Mauriceo Brown, left the car to talk to the woman and wound up shooting and killing her boyfriend, Michael LaHood Jr. Allegedly, Brown was at least 80 feet (24 m) away from the car when the shooting occurred. He fled back to the car containing the other three men and they sped from the scene. Brown was sentenced to death; he was executed in 2006. The other two men involved were not charged with capital murder.

Foster garnered the support of abolitionists (people against the death penalty), who argued that a death sentence was too harsh a penalty for his crime. After exhausting all appeals Foster faced execution on August 31, 2007. Just hours before the scheduled execution, the Texas governor Rick Perry (1950–) granted clemency—a very rare occurrence in the state. Foster's sentence was changed to life imprisonment with a possibility for parole.

Recent State Law Revisions

The Death Penalty Information Center (DPIC) is a private nonprofit organization that is opposed to the death penalty. The DPIC tracks capital punishment legislation across the country and lists proposed and passed bills, by year and state, at "Recent Legislative Activity" (http://www.deathpenaltyinfo.org/recent-legislative-activity). The following legislative list is based in large part on the DPIC's information:

- In 2009 Maryland legislators voted to limit capital cases to only those in which deoxyribonucleic acid evidence, videotaped confessions, or videotape linking the defendant to the murder are available.

- In 2010 Louisiana passed a law allowing death row inmates to waive their direct appeals. Bills that would expedite the appeals process were considered, but not passed, in 2010 and 2011 in California, Connecticut, Florida, Nevada, and Utah.

- In 2010 seven states—Illinois, Kansas, Kentucky, Nebraska, Pennsylvania, South Dakota, and Washington—considered bills that would have abolished the death penalty. None of the bills passed.

- In 2010 and 2011 Alaska, Hawaii, Massachusetts, New Jersey, New Mexico, and West Virginia considered, but did not pass, bills to reinstate the use of capital punishment.

- In 2010 and 2011 Florida, Indiana, Maryland, New Hampshire, Oklahoma, Tennessee, Texas, and Virginia considered bills to expand their capital statutes to cover more types of murders. The bills passed in Florida (victims who have petitioned for protective injunctions), New Hampshire (victims killed during home invasions), Tennessee (pregnant victims), Texas (victims under the age of 11 years), and Virginia (victims who are auxiliary police officers or fire marshals).

- Between January and September 2011 abolition bills had been introduced in 15 states: California, Connecticut, Florida, Illinois, Indiana, Kansas, Kentucky, Maryland, Missouri, Montana, Nebraska, Ohio, Pennsylvania, Texas, and Washington. Only the Illinois bill passed.

ACTS OF TERRORISM. In the aftermath of the September 11, 2001, attacks on the World Trade Center and the Pentagon, several states expanded their death penalty statutes to apply to acts of terrorism. Because acts of terrorism generally include "regular" criminal offenses already defined by state law, terrorism statutes include additional criteria to define terrorist acts. For example, Florida Criminal Code 775.30 (2011, http://www.leg.state.fl.us/Statutes/index.cfm?mode=View%20Statutes&SubMenu=1&App_mode=Display_Statute&Search_String=775.30&URL=0700-0799/0775/Sections/0775.30.html) defines terrorism as an activity that violates the state's criminal code and "is intended to: (a) [i]ntimidate, injure, or coerce a civilian population; (b) [i]nfluence the policy of a government by intimidation or coercion; or (c) [a]ffect the conduct of government through destruction of property, assassination, murder, kidnapping, or aircraft piracy."

As of September 2011, however, all defendants accused of murder during terrorist acts in relation to the September 11, 2001, attacks and the nation's subsequent so-called war on terror had been prosecuted by federal or military authorities.

Hybrid Systems

In most death penalty states the sentencing decision is made by juries. As of 2011 Alabama, Delaware, and Florida allowed trial judges to override jury-imposed sentences in capital cases. Thus, the jury recommends a sentence, and the trial judge can accept the recommendation or override it. This system is variously called a hybrid, judicial override, or jury override system. As described in Chapter 2, the constitutionality of judicial override in Florida and Alabama was upheld by the U.S. Supreme Court in *Spaziano v. Florida* (1984) and *Harris v. Alabama* (1995), respectively.

The Equal Justice Institute (EJI) is a private nonprofit legal organization based in Alabama that is opposed to capital punishment. In *The Death Penalty in Alabama: Judge Override* (July 2011, http://eji.org/eji/files/Override_Report.pdf), the EJI notes that Florida law has long required a judge to give "great weight" to a jury's recommendation and strictly limits judicial override of a life sentence with a death sentence. Delaware law is based on Florida law in this respect. As a result, judicial overrides in these two states have been rare. According to the EJI, Alabama law, by contrast, only requires that the trial judge "consider" the jury's recommendation. This distinction has meant that since 1976, 98 jury recommendations for life sentences in Alabama have been overridden by judges imposing death sentences. Only nine jury recommendations for death sentences have been overridden by judges to life sentences.

The Appeals Process in State Capital Cases

The appeals process in capital cases varies slightly from state to state but generally includes the steps shown in Figure 5.1.

The appeals process begins with the automatic direct appeal. In *Gregg v. Georgia* (428 U.S. 153 [1976]), the U.S. Supreme Court ruled that any death sentence must be appealed from the trial court directly to the highest court in the state with criminal jurisdiction. The highest court of the state may be either the state supreme court or the highest court of criminal appeals. The state high court evaluates the trial court records for constitutional or legal errors. If the high court upholds the conviction and sentence, the defendant can appeal directly to the U.S. Supreme Court using a writ of certiorari. A writ of certiorari is a petition to the Supreme Court to review only the issues brought up in the direct appeal in the state's high court. If the Supreme Court denies certiorari, the trial court's ruling stands.

FIGURE 5.1

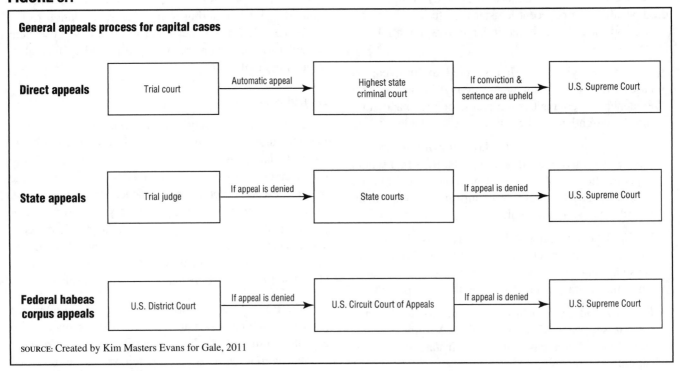

General appeals process for capital cases

Direct appeals	Trial court	→Automatic appeal→	Highest state criminal court	→If conviction & sentence are upheld→	U.S. Supreme Court

State appeals	Trial judge	→If appeal is denied→	State courts	→If appeal is denied→	U.S. Supreme Court

Federal habeas corpus appeals	U.S. District Court	→If appeal is denied→	U.S. Circuit Court of Appeals	→If appeal is denied→	U.S. Supreme Court

SOURCE: Created by Kim Masters Evans for Gale, 2011

If the direct appeals fail, the inmate may then pursue a state appeals process. This second round of appeals differs from the direct appeal in that the condemned may raise issues that were not and could not have been raised during the direct appeal. These issues include the incompetence of the defense lawyer, jury bias, or the suppression of evidence by police or the prosecution. This appeal is also the time that the inmate's attorney can present any newly discovered exculpatory evidence (evidence that is favorable to the inmate) that was not available during the original trial. Some states call this process the collateral appeal, because it does not directly challenge the original conviction or sentence, but raises collateral issues. Other states call it a state habeas corpus procedure. Habeas corpus is a Latin phrase that literally means "have the body." The rest of the phrase "brought before me" is implied. A writ (or order) of habeas corpus is a command from one court to another court (or to a lesser authority, such as a prison warden) to produce an inmate and explain why that inmate is being detained. Whatever the name, the scope of the state appeals process is limited to collateral issues and typically begins with the trial judge. If turned down by the trial judge, the convict may petition the first level of state appellate courts and finally the state's highest court. If the state review is denied, the condemned can again appeal directly to the U.S. Supreme Court.

A death row inmate who has exhausted all state appeals can then file a petition for a federal habeas corpus review on grounds of violation of his or her constitutional rights. The right may involve a violation of the Sixth Amendment to the U.S. Constitution (the right to have the assistance of counsel for defense), the Eighth Amendment (the ban against a cruel and unusual punishment), or the 14th Amendment (the right to due process). The inmate files the appeal with the district court with jurisdiction over the city or county in which he or she was convicted. If the district court denies the appeal, the inmate can proceed to the U.S. Circuit Court of Appeals in the region. As of 2011, there were 94 federal judicial districts and 12 U.S. Circuit Courts of Appeal in the United States. (See Figure 5.2; note that the 12th circuit is the District of Columbia.) Finally, if the circuit court denies the appeal, the condemned can for a third time ask the U.S. Supreme Court for a certiorari review.

Execution of "Volunteers"

Death row inmates can choose to waive their appeals to speed their execution date. These so-called volunteers often pursue appeals on first being condemned and then abandon their efforts at a later point, typically after spending many years on death row. As a result, the mental competency of execution volunteers is hotly debated.

In 2004 John Blume of the Cornell Law School published a study on the volunteer phenomena. In *Killing the Willing: "Volunteer," Suicide, and Competency* (September 15, 2004, http://scholarship.law.cornell.edu/cgi/view content.cgi?article=1015&context=lsrp_papers), Blume notes that 106 of the 885 executions that took place in the United States between 1977 and 2003 involved volunteers. He presents data indicating that at least 93 of the volunteers (or 88% of the total) suffered from "documented mental illness or severe substance-abuse disorders."

FIGURE 5.2

Geographic boundaries of United States Courts of Appeals and United States District Courts

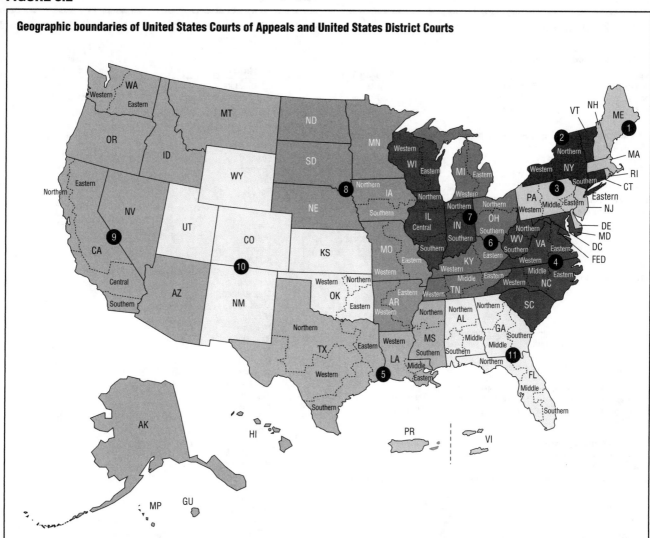

SOURCE: "Geographic Boundaries of United States Courts of Appeals and United States District Courts," in *District Courts*, Administrative Office of the U.S. Courts, undated, http://www.uscourts.gov/uscourts/images/CircuitMap.pdf (accessed July 27, 2011)

The DPIC lists in "Information on Defendants Who Were Executed since 1976 and Designated as 'Volunteers'" (May 9, 2011, http://www.deathpenaltyinfo.org/information-defendants-who-were-executed-1976-and-designated-volunteers) 133 inmates executed between 1976 and May 2011 that reportedly waived their appeals rights. Texas had the highest number (27), followed by Nevada (11), Florida (9), and South Carolina (9). The most recent volunteer was Jeffrey Motts of South Carolina, who was executed in May 2011. The article "South Carolina Executes Man Who Strangled Prison Inmate" (Reuters, May 6, 2011) reports that Motts murdered his cellmate Charles Martin in 2005. At the time of the murder, Motts was serving two life sentences for murdering two elderly relatives, Clyde Camby and Etta Osteen. Following his capital conviction, Motts asked the South Carolina Supreme Court to allow him to waive his appeals. In April 2011 the court found him mentally competent and allowed his execution to proceed.

In 2005 Michael Ross of Connecticut became one of the most famous execution volunteers in the country, because he was the first person executed in that state (and in all of New England) since 1960. Ross was on death row for the 1983–84 murders of Wendy Baribeault, April Brunias, Leslie Shelley, and Robin Stavinsky, but was suspected of murdering at least four other women and girls. For nearly two decades he actively pursued appeals before abandoning his efforts. Death penalty opponents, mental health professionals, and members of his family sought court orders delaying his execution, but were only temporarily successful. According to the article "Serial Killer Sent Taunting Note before Execution" (Associated Press, June 14, 2005), Ross publicly said he was speeding his execution to avoid further traumatizing his victims' families; however, in a letter to his girlfriend he allegedly said the reason was that he could no longer bear living on death row.

TABLE 5.2

Clemency process by state

States in which the governor has sole authority (14)

Alabama	New Jersey[d]	South Carolina
California[a]	New Mexico[e]	Virginia
Colorado	New York[d]	Washington
Kansas	North Carolina	Wyoming
Kentucky	Oregon	

States in which the governor must have the recommendation of clemency from a board or advisory group (8)

Arizona	Louisiana	Pennsylvania
Delaware	Montana	Texas
Florida[b]	Oklahoma	

States in which the governor may receive a non-binding recommendation of clemency from a board or advisory group (11)

Arkansas	Maryland	Ohio
Idaho	Mississippi	South Dakota
Illinois[c]	Missouri	Tennessee
Indiana	New Hampshire	

States in which a board or advisory group determines clemency (3)

Connecticut
Georgia
Utah

[a]California's governor may not grant a pardon or commutation to a person twice convicted of a felony except on recommendation of the state Supreme Court, with at least four judges concurring.
[b]Florida's governor must have recommendation of the board, on which s/he sits.
[c]Illinois no longer has the death penalty, as of 2011.
[d]New York and New Jersey no longer have the death penalty, as of 2007.
[e]New Mexico no longer has the death penalty for future cases as of 2009, but 2 inmates remain on death row. For federal death row inmates, the president alone has pardon power.

SOURCE: "Clemency Process by State," in *Clemency*, Death Penalty Information Center, 2011, http://www.deathpenaltyinfo.org/clemency (accessed July 23, 2011)

Clemency

If a convict exhausts all appeals and is still on death row, the only way the sentence can be altered is through the power of clemency. The power of clemency may rest solely with a state's governor, with a clemency board, or with the governor and a board of advisers. (See Table 5.2.) All states provide for clemency, which may take the form of a reprieve, a commutation, or a pardon. A reprieve, which typically involves a stay of execution, is just a temporary measure to allow further investigation of a case. A commutation involves the reduction of a criminal sentence after a criminal conviction. In the context of capital punishment, a commutation typically means replacing the death sentence with a lesser sentence, such as life without parole. As shown in Table 5.3, the Department of Justice reports that 365 state and federal death penalty sentences were commuted between 1973 and 2009. Illinois had the most commutations (156), followed by Texas (56) and Florida (18).

Neither a reprieve nor a commutation removes a person's responsibility for the crime. A pardon, however, frees from punishment a person who has been convicted of a crime and removes his or her criminal record as if the conviction never happened. Pardons are generally only given if investigators can prove beyond any doubt that a

TABLE 5.3

Number of death sentences commuted, by jurisdiction, 1973–2009

Jurisdiction	Sentence commuted
U.S. total	365
Federal	1
Alabama	2
Arizona	7
Arkansas	2
California	15
Colorado	1
Connecticut	0
Delaware	0
Florida	18
Georgia	9
Idaho	3
Illinois	156
Indiana	6
Kansas	0
Kentucky	2
Louisiana	7
Maryland	4
Massachusetts	2
Mississippi	0
Missouri	2
Montana	2
Nebraska	2
Nevada	4
New Hampshire	0
New Jersey	8
New Mexico	5
New York	0
North Carolina	8
Ohio	15
Oklahoma	3
Oregon	0
Pennsylvania	6
Rhode Island	0
South Carolina	3
South Dakota	0
Tennessee	4
Texas	56
Utah	1
Virginia	11
Washington	0
Wyoming	0

Note: In 1972, the U.S. Supreme Court invalidated capital punishment statutes in several states (*Furman v. Georgia*, 408 U.S. 238 [1972]), effecting a moratorium on executions. Executions resumed in 1977 when the Supreme Court found that revisions to several state statutes had effectively addressed the issues previously held unconstitutional (*Gregg v. Georgia*, 428 U.S. 153 [1976] and its companion cases). Some inmates executed since 1977 or currently under sentence of death were sentenced prior to 1977. For those persons sentenced to death more than once, the numbers are based on the most recent death sentence.

SOURCE: Adapted from Tracy L. Snell, "Table 20. Number Sentenced to Death and Number of Removals, by Jurisdiction and Reason for Removal, 1973–2009," in *Capital Punishment, 2009—Statistical Tables*, U.S. Department of Justice, Office of Justice Programs, Bureau of Justice Statistics, December 2010, http://bjs.ojp.usdoj.gov/content/pub/pdf/cp09st .pdf (accessed July 5, 2011)

death row inmate did not commit the crime of which he or she was convicted.

According to the DPIC, in "Clemency" (2011, http:// www.deathpenaltyinfo.org/clemency), 268 clemencies were granted by states and the federal government "for humanitarian reasons" between 1976 and 2011. (See Table 5.4.)

The DPIC notes that humanitarian reasons include "doubts about the defendant's guilt or conclusions of the

TABLE 5.4

Clemencies granted, by state, 1976–2011

Clemencies granted by state since 1976	Number of clemencies
Illinois	187
Ohio	15
New Jersey	8
Virginia	8
Florida	6
Georgia	7
New Mexico	5
North Carolina	5
Oklahoma	4
Indiana	3
Tennessee	3
Missouri	3
Maryland	2
Kentucky	2
Louisiana	2
Texas	2
Alabama	1
Arkansas	1
Idaho	1
Montana	1
Nevada	1
Federal	1
Total	**268**

SOURCE: "Clemencies Granted by State since 1976," in *Clemency*, Death Penalty Information Center, 2011, http://www.deathpenaltyinfo.org/clemency (accessed July 23, 2011)

governor regarding the death penalty process." The vast majority (187) of the humanitarian-based clemencies occurred in Illinois. In 2003 the Illinois governor George Ryan (1934–) commuted the death sentences or pardoned all of the state's death row prisoners. However, capital punishment remained legal in Illinois and death sentences continued to be given out until 2011, when capital punishment was abolished.

The DPIC reports that there were five humanitarian-reason clemencies in 2010: three in Ohio and one each in Oklahoma and Tennessee. Another 18 humanitarian-reason clemencies had been granted between January and September 2011: 15 in Illinois (all remaining inmates on death row) and one each in Missouri, Ohio, and Tennessee.

It should be noted that death penalty sentences have also been commuted on technical or legal grounds, particularly following U.S. Supreme Court decisions ruling that certain practices are unconstitutional, namely the execution of the mentally retarded (2002) and minors (2005). The DPIC explains that commutations to lower sentences have also been granted by states for "judicial expediency," for example, to avoid capital case retrials following the overturning of death sentences by appeals courts. The DPIC describes these commutations as being for the "state's convenience."

State Death Penalty Methods

Tracy L. Snell of the Department of Justice reports in *Capital Punishment, 2009—Statistical Tables* (December

2010, http://bjs.ojp.usdoj.gov/content/pub/pdf/cp09st.pdf) that 36 states used lethal injection as the primary method of execution in 2009. (See Table 5.5.) Some states also authorized one or more alternative methods: electrocution, lethal gas, hanging, or death by firing squad. According to Snell, the choice of method is generally left up to the condemned, depending on when the sentence was imposed. Note that Illinois ended its capital punishment system in 2011.

As explained in Chapter 3, a national moratorium (suspension) of executions was triggered in 2007, when the U.S. Supreme Court agreed to hear a case challenging the constitutionality of the three-drug protocol that was used for lethal injection in Kentucky. In 2008 the court ruled in *Baze v. Rees* (553 U.S. ___) that the protocol is constitutional. At that time the protocol used by Kentucky, and by many other states, was sodium thiopental (a sedative), followed by pancuronium bromide (a paralyzing agent) and potassium chloride (to stop the heart). In May 2008 executions resumed, and according to Snell, 37 inmates were executed throughout the remainder of the year. Another 52 executions were carried out in 2009 and 46 in 2010. As shown in Figure 5.3, executions during 2010 took place in 12 states: Texas (17), Ohio (8), Alabama (5), Mississippi (3), Oklahoma (3), Virginia (3), Georgia (2), Arizona (1), Florida (1), Louisiana (1), Utah (1), and Washington (1).

In 2008 Nebraska's sole reliance on the electric chair as a means of execution was ruled unconstitutional by the state's supreme court. In 2009 a new state law established lethal injection as Nebraska's sole means of execution and directed corrections officials to develop a suitable protocol for carrying it out. According to the DPIC, in "2009 Proposed or Passed Legislation" (2011, http://www.deathpenaltyinfo.org/2009-proposed-or-passed-legislation), Idaho passed legislation in 2009 to conform its lethal injection protocol to that used in Kentucky. The state also eliminated a firing squad as an alternative method of execution.

In 2009 two events happened that would force death penalty states to reconsider their lethal injection drug protocols. First, the domestic producer of sodium thiopental, Hospira Inc., stopped producing the drug. Kevin Sack reports in "Executions in Doubt in Fallout over Drug" (*New York Times*, March 16, 2011) that the company ceased production because it was unable to obtain one of the ingredients that are used to produce the drug. Also in 2009 Ohio executioners tried and failed in 18 attempts over a period of two hours to find a suitable vein in which to deliver lethal drugs to the convicted murderer Romell Broom (1956–). Governor Ted Strickland (1941–) halted the execution and imposed a temporary moratorium on further executions in Ohio until alternative injection protocols could be developed. In "Capital Punishment in Ohio" (March 21, 2011, http://drc.ohio.gov/Public/capital.htm),

TABLE 5.5

Method of execution, by state, 2009

State	Lethal injection	Electrocution	Lethal gas	Hanging	Firing squad
Total	36	9	4	3	2
Alabama	X	X			
Arizona[a]	X		X		
Arkansas[b]	X	X			
California	X		X		
Colorado	X				
Connecticut	X				
Delaware[c]	X			X	
Florida	X	X			
Georgia	X				
Idaho	X				
Illinois[d]	X	X			
Indiana	X				
Kansas	X				
Kentucky[e]	X	X			
Louisiana	X				
Maryland	X				
Mississippi	X				
Missouri	X		X		
Montana	X				
Nebraska	X				
Nevada	X				
New Hampshire[f]	X			X	
New York	X				
North Carolina	X				
Ohio	X				
Oklahoma[g]	X	X			X
Oregon	X				
Pennsylvania	X				
South Carolina	X	X			
South Dakota	X				
Tennessee[h]	X	X			
Texas	X				
Utah[i]	X				X
Virginia	X	X			
Washington	X			X	
Wyoming[j]	X		X		

Note: The method of execution of federal prisoners is lethal injection, pursuant to 28 CFR, Part 26. For offenses prosecuted under the Violent Crime Control and Law Enforcement Act of 1994, the execution method is that of the state in which the conviction took place (18 U.S.C. 3596).

[a]Authorizes lethal injection for persons sentenced after November 15,1992; inmates sentenced before that date may select lethal injection or gas.
[b]Authorizes lethal injection for those whose offense occurred on or after July 4,1983; inmates whose offense occurred before that data may select lethal injection or electrocution.
[c]Authorizes lethal injection for those whose capital offense occurred on or after June 13,1986; those who committed the offense before that date may select lethal injection or hanging.
[d]Authorizes electrocution only if lethal injection is held illegal or unconstitutional.
[e]Authorizes lethal injection for persons sentenced on or after March 31,1998; inmates sentenced before that data may select lethal injection or electrocution.
[f]Authorizes hanging only if lethal injection cannot be given.
[g]Authorizes electrocution if lethal injection is held to be unconstitutional, and firing squad if both lethal injection and electrocution are held to be unconstitutional.
[h]Authorizes lethal injection for those whose capital offense occurred after December 31,1998; those who committed the offense before that date may select electrocution by written waiver.
[i]Authorizes firing squad if lethal injection is held unconstitutional. Inmates who selected execution by firing squad prior to May 3, 2004, may still be entitled to execution by that method.
[j]Authorizes lethal gas if lethal injection is held to be unconstitutional.

SOURCE: Tracy L. Snell, "Table 2. Method of Execution, by State, 2009," in *Capital Punishment, 2009—Statistical Tables*, U.S. Department of Justice, Office of Justice Programs, Bureau of Justice Statistics, December 2010, http://bjs.ojp.usdoj.gov/content/pub/pdf/cp09st.pdf (accessed July 5, 2011)

the Ohio Department of Rehabilitation and Correction notes that in November 2009 Ohio "became the first state in the country to adopt a one-drug protocol for lethal injections." Sodium thiopental alone was used that month to execute Kenneth Biros, a man on death row for the 1991 murder of Tami L. Engstrom.

In January 2011 Hospira announced in the press release "Hospira Statement Regarding Pentothal (Sodium Thiopental) Market Exit" (http://phx.corporate-ir.net/phoenix.zhtml?c=175550&p=irol-newsArticle&ID=1518610&highlight=) that it would not resume domestic production of sodium thiopental. The company noted that it had intended to

produce the drug at a plant in Italy; however, Italian authorities disapproved of the drug's use in capital punishment in the United States. Fearing liability issues, the company decided to exit the market completely. By this time state correctional officials were running low on supplies of sodium thiopental. According to Sack, the typical shelf life of the drug is approximately two years.

In March 2011 the Drug Enforcement Administration (DEA) seized a shipment of sodium thiopental that Georgia correctional officials had imported from a distributor in England. Sack notes that the seizure was "presumably" spurred by a complaint that was filed with the U.S.

FIGURE 5.3

Executions, by state, 2010

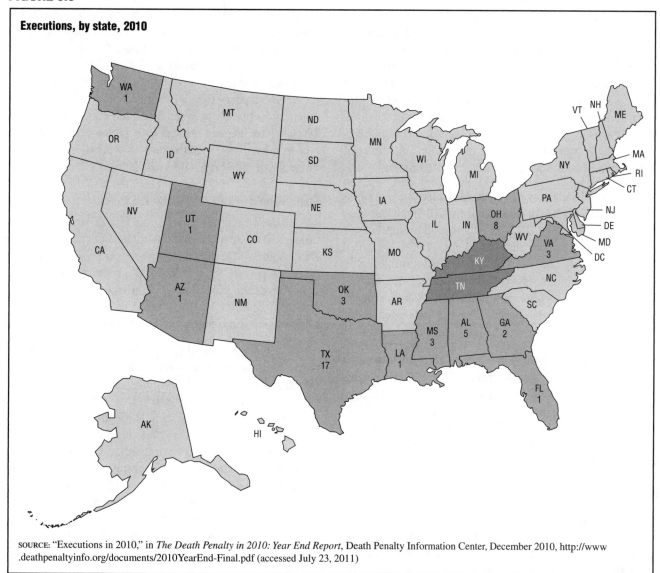

SOURCE: "Executions in 2010," in *The Death Penalty in 2010: Year End Report*, Death Penalty Information Center, December 2010, http://www .deathpenaltyinfo.org/documents/2010YearEnd-Final.pdf (accessed July 23, 2011)

attorney general Eric Holder (1951–) the previous month by John T. Bentivoglio, a lawyer representing an inmate on Georgia's death row. Bentivoglio alleged that Georgia did not have a federal license to import controlled substances. In "Seeking Execution Drug, States Cut Legal Corners" (*New York Times*, April 13, 2011), John Schwartz reports that by 2011 lawsuits had been filed "in many states" over concerns about how correctional officials were obtaining the drug. According to Schwartz, death penalty states had established a "legally questionable swap club," in which states with ample supplies of the drug shared it with states that were running low. Meanwhile, some states allegedly continued to import the drug from foreign distributors.

Katie Zezima indicates in "2 More States Turn over a Drug Used in Executions" (*New York Times*, April 1, 2011) that in April 2011 Tennessee and Kentucky relinquished their supplies of sodium thiopental to the DEA. Zezima notes that both states, along with California and Arizona,

were believed to have obtained the drug from foreign suppliers. She also reports that the British government had instituted a ban on exporting drugs to the United States that will be used in executions.

As supplies of sodium thiopental dwindled in late 2010 and early 2011 some states turned to an alternative sedative: pentobarbital. According to the Ohio Department of Rehabilitation and Correction, the state announced in January 2011 a new one-drug protocol for executions using pentobarbital. That drug was subsequently used in March 2011 to execute Johnnie Baston for the 1994 murder of Chong-Hoon Mah. Baston is believed to be the first death row inmate executed using a single dose of pentobarbital. Sack notes that Oklahoma and Texas decided in late 2010 and early 2011, respectively, to substitute pentobarbital for sodium thiopental in their three-drug execution cocktail.

In July 2011 the Danish pharmaceutical company Lundbeck announced distribution restrictions in the United

States for its sodium pentobarbital drug Nembutal. In "Danish Company Blocks Sale of Drug for U.S. Executions" (*New York Times*, July 1, 2011), David Jolly reports that the company issued a statement saying that it "adamantly opposes the distressing misuse of our product in capital punishment." Lundbeck said it will implement ordering and delivery restrictions that are intended to prevent prisons in death penalty states from obtaining the drug. According to Jolly, the decision was significant, because as of July 2011 Nembutal was the only injectable form of sodium pentobarbital available in the United States.

The DPIC indicates in "Execution List 2011" (http://www.deathpenaltyinfo.org/execution-list-2011) that between January and September 2011, 32 inmates had been executed. Seven inmates executed through March 2011 were killed using a three-drug cocktail that included sodium thiopental. An additional four inmates (in Ohio) were executed using only sodium thiopental or only pentobarbital. The remaining 21 inmates were killed using a three-drug cocktail that included pentobarbital.

In "Death Penalty in Flux" (2011, http://www.death penaltyinfo.org/death-penalty-flux), the DPIC also notes that as of September 2011, Arkansas, California, Florida, Indiana, Kentucky, Maryland, Nebraska, Nevada, Ohio, and Tennessee were delaying executions due to drug shortages, court challenges to new drug protocols, or related lethal injection issues.

Witnesses to State Executions

Death penalty states have statutes or policies (or both) that specify which witnesses may be present during an execution. Witnesses usually include prison officials, physicians, the condemned inmate's relatives, the victim's relatives, spiritual advisers, selected state citizens, and reporters. In celebrated cases, however, such as that of Julius Rosenberg (1918–1953) and Ethel Rosenberg (1915–1953), who were convicted spies, the notorious California killer Caryl Chessman (1921–1960), and the convicted Oklahoma City bomber Timothy McVeigh (1968–2001), the witnesses made up a larger group.

FEDERAL DEATH PENALTY LAWS

In modern times, capital punishment has generally fallen under the states' purview. Each year, the federal government pursues the death penalty in far fewer cases than most states with death penalty statutes. The reason for this is simple: Most crimes are state crimes. Generally speaking, the federal government is only involved in prosecuting a relatively small number of crimes—those that cross state boundaries, those that are committed on federal property, or those that affect federal officials or the working of the federal government. Table 5.6 lists federal capital offenses by law as of 2009.

The federal government, however, has been executing criminals almost since its formation. In 1790 Thomas Bird became the first inmate to be executed under the federal death penalty. He was hanged in Maine for murder. In "Federal Executions 1927–2003" (2011, http://www.deathpenaltyinfo.org/federal-executions-1927-2003), the DPIC reports that 34 people were executed by the federal government between 1927 and 1963. On March 15, 1963, Victor Feguer was hanged in Iowa for kidnapping and murder. This was the last execution by the federal government until nearly 40 years later.

Expansion of the Federal Death Penalty

In 1988 Congress enacted the first of several laws that broadened the scope of the federal death penalty. The Anti-Drug Abuse Act included a drug-kingpin provision, allowing the death penalty for murder resulting from large-scale illegal drug dealing. The act did not specify the method of federal execution. In 1993 President George H. W. Bush (1924–) authorized the use of lethal injection under this law.

In 1994 the Violent Crime Control and Law Enforcement Act (also known as the Federal Death Penalty Act) added more than 50 crimes punishable by death. Among the federal crimes were murder of certain government officials, kidnapping resulting in death, murder for hire, fatal drive-by shootings, sexual abuse crimes resulting in death, carjacking resulting in death, and other crimes not resulting in death, such as running a large-scale illicit drug enterprise. The method of execution would be the same as that used in the state where the sentencing occurred. If the state did not allow the death penalty, the judge would choose a state with the death penalty.

Antiterrorism legislation came about in the wake of the Oklahoma City bombing in 1995 and the September 11, 2001, terrorist attacks. In 1996 Congress passed and President Bill Clinton (1946–) signed the Antiterrorism and Effective Death Penalty Act (AEDPA). Another capital crime was added in June 2002, as part of the Terrorist Bombings Convention Implementation Act. The law makes punishable by death the bombing of places of public use, government facilities, public transportation systems, and infrastructure facilities with the intent to cause death or serious physical injury or with intent to cause destruction resulting in major economic loss. The USA Patriot Act of 2001 and the USA Patriot Act Improvement and Reauthorization Act of 2005 expanded the list of terrorist acts deemed federal crimes that could be subject to the death penalty.

New Laws Lead to an Increase in Federal Capital Cases

In 1992 the Administrative Office of the U.S. Courts established the Federal Death Penalty Resource Counsel Project (FDPRCP) to serve as a clearinghouse for information helpful to defense attorneys who are appointed in federal death penalty cases. According to Richard Burr, David

TABLE 5.6

Federal crimes punishable by death, 2009

Statute	Description
8 U.S.C. 1342	Murder related to the smuggling of aliens.
18 U.S.C. 32–34	Destruction of aircraft, motor vehicles, or related facilities resulting in death.
18 U.S.C. 36	Murder committed during a drug-related drive-by shooting.
18 U.S.C. 37	Murder committed at an airport serving international civil aviation.
18 U.S.C. 115(b)(3) [by cross-reference to 18 U.S.C. 1111]	Retaliatory murder of a member of the immediate family of law enforcement officials.
18 U.S.C. 241, 242, 245, 247	Civil rights offenses resulting in death.
18 U.S.C. 351 [by cross-reference to 18 U.S.C. 1111]	Murder of a member of Congress, an important executive official, or a Supreme Court Justice.
18 U.S.C. 794	Espionage.
18 U.S.C. 844(d), (f), (i)	Death resulting from offenses involving transportation of explosives, destruction of government property, or destruction of property related to foreign or interstate commerce.
18 U.S.C. 924(i)	Murder committed by the use of a firearm during a crime of violence or a drug-trafficking crime.
18 U.S.C. 930	Murder committed in a federal government facility.
18 U.S.C. 1091	Genocide.
18 U.S.C. 1111	First-degree murder.
18 U.S.C. 1114	Murder of a federal judge or law enforcement official.
18 U.S.C. 1116	Murder of a foreign official.
18 U.S.C. 1118	Murder by a federal prisoner.
18 U.S.C. 1119	Murder of a U.S. national in a foreign country.
18 U.S.C. 1120	Murder by an escaped federal prisoner already sentenced to life imprisonment.
18 U.S.C. 1121	Murder of a state or local law enforcement official or other person aiding in a federal investigation; murder of a state correctional officer.
18 U.S.C. 1201	Murder during a kidnapping.
18 U.S.C. 1203	Murder during a hostage taking.
18 U.S.C. 1503	Murder of a court officer or juror.
18 U.S.C. 1512	Murder with the intent of preventing testimony by a witness, victim, or informant.
18 U.S.C. 1513	Retaliatory murder of a witness, victim, or informant.
18 U.S.C. 1716	Mailing of injurious articles with intent to kill or resulting in death.
18 U.S.C. 1751 [by cross-reference to 18 U.S.C. 1111]	Assassination or kidnapping resulting in the death of the president or vice president.
18 U.S.C. 1958	Murder for hire.
18 U.S.C. 1959	Murder involved in a racketeering offense.
18 U.S.C. 1992	Willful wrecking of a train resulting in death.
18 U.S.C. 2113	Bank-robbery-related murder or kidnapping.
18 U.S.C. 2119	Murder related to a carjacking.
18 U.S.C. 2245	Murder related to rape or child molestation.
18 U.S.C. 2251	Murder related to sexual exploitation of children.
18 U.S.C. 2280	Murder committed during an offense against maritime navigation.
18 U.S.C. 2281	Murder committed during an offense against a maritime fixed platform.
18 U.S.C. 2332	Terrorist murder of a U.S. national in another country.
18 U.S.C. 2332a	Murder by the use of a weapon of mass destruction.
18 U.S.C. 2340	Murder involving torture.
18 U.S.C. 2381	Treason.
21 U.S.C. 848(e)	Murder related to a continuing criminal enterprise or related murder of a federal, state, or local law enforcement officer.
49 U.S.C. 1472–1473	Death resulting from aircraft hijacking.

SOURCE: Tracy L. Snell, "Table 3. Federal Capital Offenses, by Statute, 2009," in *Capital Punishment, 2009—Statistical Tables*, U.S. Department of Justice, Office of Justice Programs, Bureau of Justice Statistics, December 2010, http://bjs.ojp.usdoj.gov/content/pub/pdf/cp09st.pdf (accessed July 5, 2011)

Bruck, and Kevin McNally of the FDPRCP, in "An Overview of the Federal Death Penalty Process" (August 2009, http://www.capdefnet.org/), between 1988, when the Anti-Drug Abuse Act was signed into law, and August 2009, the U.S. attorney general authorized the government to seek the death penalty against 461 defendants. Of these, 261 were tried, of which three were executed: McVeigh and Juan Raul Garza (c. 1957–) in 2001 and Louis Jones Jr. (1950–) in 2003. Most of the rest of the defendants received life sentences from juries or judges or through plea bargain agreements.

Federal Government Resumes Executions

Timothy McVeigh was sentenced to death for conspiracy and murder in 1997 for the bombing of the Alfred P. Murrah Federal Building in Oklahoma City, Oklahoma, on April 19, 1995, which killed 168 people. On June 11, 2001, the execution was carried out.

Eight days later, on June 19, 2001, the Texas drug boss Juan Raul Garza became the second federal prisoner to be executed since 1963. He was the first person to be executed under the Anti-Drug Abuse Act of 1988 for murders resulting from a drug enterprise. Garza received the death sentence in 1993 for the 1990 murders of three associates.

Louis Jones Jr., a retired soldier, was executed by the U.S. government on March 18, 2003. In 1995 Jones was convicted of killing a female soldier. He admitted to kidnapping Tracie Joy McBride from an air force base in Texas. The federal government prosecuted Jones because his crime originally occurred at a U.S. military facility. As of September 2011, Jones was the last person to have been executed by the federal government.

The Federal Death Penalty Resource Council (FDPRC) is an independent organization that was established by the U.S. Courts to provide consulting and informational services regarding the federal death penalty. According to the FDPRC, in "Federal Death Penalty" (http://www.capdefnet.org/FDPRC/pubmenu.aspx?menu_id=94&id=2094), as of September 2011, the U.S. attorney general had authorized the death penalty for 472 defendants since 1988. More than half of the defendants (272) had been tried and 140 received life sentences. Another 13 were acquitted, and one was granted clemency. In federal cases, the president alone has clemency power. In 2001 President Clinton commuted the death sentence of David Ronald Chandler to life in prison with no parole. As of September 2011, Chandler was still incarcerated in a federal prison; at that time, his was the most recent federal commutation to take place. As noted earlier, since 1963 only three inmates have been executed by the federal government. All three executions occurred during President George W. Bush's (1946–) first administration (January 2001–January 2005). No executions were carried out during Bush's second administration (January 2005–January 2009). Likewise, as of September 2011, no executions had been conducted under the administration of Barack Obama (1961–), who took office in January 2009.

The federal government's death row and execution chamber are located in Terre Haute, Indiana. According to the DPIC (http://www.deathpenaltyinfo.org/federal-death-row-prisoners), 58 inmates were on federal death row as of August 2011. The inmates who had been on federal death row the longest were Richard Tipton, Cory Johnson, and James H. Roane Jr., who were sentenced to death in 1993 for their murderous roles in a crack cocaine ring. All were scheduled to be executed in May 2006, but those executions were put on hold when lawyers for the inmates filed lawsuits challenging the federal lethal injection protocol.

In "Federal Prisons Run out of Key Execution Drug" (Associated Press, March 10, 2011), Andrew Welsh-Huggins notes that in March 2011 Attorney General Holder notified death penalty states in a letter that the Department of Justice did not have supplies of sodium thiopental. Holder reportedly informed the states that the shortage "is a serious concern" and that the federal government was researching alternative protocols. As of September 2011, the still unresolved 2006 challenge to the federal government's lethal injection protocol and the anticipated changes to that protocol (which will likely trigger additional court challenges) made it extremely unlikely that any federal executions would take place in the near future. The DPIC notes in "Federal Death Penalty" (2011, http://www.deathpenaltyinfo.org/federal-death-penalty) that the federal government must provide notice of an upcoming execution at least 120 days before it is to take place. As of September 2011, the Federal Bureau of Prisons (http://www.bop.gov/news/press_releases.jsp) had no pending execution dates.

Federal Capital Punishment in Non–death Penalty States

According to Department of Justice policy, federal criminal law can be enacted in any state and U.S. territory. In 2000 federal prosecutors in Puerto Rico (a U.S. territory) sought the death penalty against two men for kidnapping and murder. Puerto Rico had its last execution in 1927 and had banned the death penalty in 1929. In August 2003 a federal jury voted to acquit the defendants.

Massachusetts outlawed capital punishment in 1975, but in 2000 the federal government sought the death penalty in the case of Kristen Gilbert in Massachusetts. Gilbert was charged with killing four patients at the Veterans Affairs Medical Center in Northampton, a federal hospital. The jury found Gilbert guilty of first-degree murder but was deadlocked on the death sentence. As a result, Judge Michael A. Ponsor (1946–) sentenced the defendant to life imprisonment without the possibility of parole.

In September 2003 Massachusetts was once again the scene of a federal death penalty case. The Federal Death Penalty Act of 1994 allowed federal prosecutors to seek the death penalty in the case of Gary Lee Sampson, who killed two men in separate carjacking incidents in 2001. Before the trial phase began, Sampson pleaded guilty to the crimes. The case proceeded to the penalty phase, in which a federal jury sentenced him to death. As of September 2011, Sampson remained on federal death row.

Michigan has not executed an inmate under state law since it joined the Union in 1837. In 1938 Anthony Cherboris was executed in the state under federal law for killing a bystander during a bank robbery. This was the last federal death sentence in Michigan until March 2002, when Marvin Gabrion received the death penalty for killing Rachel Timmerman in 1997 on federal property in Manistee National Forest. In August 2011, a federal appeals court overturned Gabrion's death sentence due to a procedural error that was committed during his original trial. As of September 2011, he had not been resentenced.

According to the DPIC, in "Federal Death Penalty," as of September 2011, six of the 58 inmates on federal death row had been sentenced for crimes that occurred in states that did not have the death penalty: two in Iowa and one each in Massachusetts, Michigan, North Dakota, and Vermont. The sentence in North Dakota was particularly notable because it involved a crime that began in neighboring Minnesota, also a non–death penalty state. In 2003 Dru Sjodin, a student at the University of North Dakota, was kidnapped, raped, and murdered. Her body was found in Minnesota. Alfonso Rodriguez Jr. was convicted of the crime and sentenced to death. The judge ordered the execution to take place in South Dakota, which allows the death penalty by means of lethal injection.

In 2011 the Rhode Island governor Lincoln D. Chafee (1953–) made national headlines when he refused to turn over to federal authorities a defendant who was charged with killing a man at a Rhode Island bank. Federal authorities have jurisdiction over crimes at federally insured banks. In "R.I. Aims to Block Death-Penalty Trial" (*Boston Globe*, July 28, 2011), Milton J. Valencia reports that Jason W. Pleau murdered David M. Main in September 2010 and agreed to plead guilty to the murder in state court in exchange for a life sentence without parole. Rhode Island does not have the death penalty. In June 2011 Chafee refused to relinquish custody of Pleau to federal authorities; Pleau would likely face capital charges for the murder. In the editorial "Lincoln D. Chafee: My Pleau Stand Affirms Core R.I. Values" (*Providence Journal*, August 24, 2011), Chafee acknowledges that Pleau is "a career criminal with an extensive record of deplorable acts," but argues that "this does not justify the abandonment of Rhode Island's long-standing abolition of capital punishment." As of September 2011, the issue had not been resolved in state courts and was expected to ultimately reach the U.S. Supreme Court.

Limiting Federal Appeals

The AEDPA applied new restrictions and filing deadlines regarding appeals by death row inmates. It restricts death row inmates' use of habeas corpus petitions. The law requires death row inmates to file their habeas corpus petitions in the appropriate district courts within six months of the final state appeal. Before the enactment of this law, no filing deadline existed. Under the 1996 law, a defendant who fails to challenge his or her conviction or sentence within the time specified cannot file another petition unless approved by a three-judge appellate court. The AEDPA further dictates that federal judges must defer to the rulings of the state courts, unless the rulings violate the U.S. Constitution or U.S. laws or contradict "the Supreme Court's recognition of a new federal right that is made retroactively applicable."

Some opponents feared that the limitations on federal habeas corpus petitions required by the AEDPA would contribute to the execution of innocent people. In addition, they believed that the unclear language of the AEDPA allowed for varying interpretations in federal appeals courts. In 2000 the U.S. Supreme Court addressed, in *Williams v. Taylor* (529 U.S. 362) and *Williams v. Taylor* (529 U.S. 420), the lower courts' interpretation of the AEDPA, ultimately ruling that the AEDPA was valid as long as the state appellate courts did not uphold rulings contrary to the precedents laid down by the U.S. Supreme Court.

Federal Death Penalty Methods

The federal government currently authorizes the method of execution under two different laws. Crimes prosecuted under Code 28, Part 26, of the Federal Regulations call for execution by lethal injection, whereas offenses covered by the Violent Crime Control and Law Enforcement Act of 1994 (also known as the Federal Death Penalty Act of 1994) are referred to the state where the conviction occurred.

U.S. MILITARY DEATH PENALTY LAWS

The U.S. military has its own death penalty law: the Uniform Code of Military Justice (UCMJ) found under U.S. Code, Title 10, Chapter 47. Lethal injection is the method of execution. For crimes that occurred on or after November 17, 1997, the UCMJ provides the alternative sentence of life without the possibility of parole. As commander in chief, the president of the United States can write regulations and procedures to implement the UCMJ provisions. The military needs the president's approval to implement a death sentence.

The first U.S. soldier to be executed since the Civil War (1861–1865) was Private Edward Slovik of the U.S. Army. In 1944 he was charged with desertion while assigned to the European theater during World War II (1939–1945). Even though Slovik was just one of hundreds of U.S. soldiers who were convicted of desertion and sentenced to death, he was the only one executed. It is believed that, among other reasons, the military wanted to use his case as a deterrent to future desertions. Slovik died by firing squad on January 31, 1945, in France. Since then no other soldier has been executed for desertion. The last military execution occurred on April 13, 1961, when Private John A. Bennett of the U.S. Army was hanged for the 1955 rape and murder of an 11-year-old girl.

In "The U.S. Military Death Penalty" (http://www.deathpenaltyinfo.org/us-military-death-penalty), the DPIC reports that there were six men on military death row in 2011: four African-Americans and two whites. All were convicted of premeditated murder or felony murder (murder that occurs during the commission of another serious crime, such as arson). The military's death row is located at the U.S. Disciplinary Barracks at Fort Leavenworth, Kansas. It is important to note that capital defendants can be tried and convicted in both state court and military court; this is not considered double jeopardy under the U.S. Constitution. As explained in Chapter 2, the constitutional prohibition against double jeopardy means that a person cannot be tried or punished twice for the same crime.

The military death penalty received little notice until 2008, when President Bush signed a death warrant for Ronald Gray (1966–), a former army private who was charged with murdering several women during the late 1980s. As explained by the article "Bush Approves Execution of American Soldier Ronald Gray" (*Times* [London,

England], July 29, 2008), Gray was first convicted in North Carolina, because his crimes occurred in Fayetteville, near Fort Bragg, the army base at which Gray was stationed. He received eight life sentences in exchange for a guilty plea for raping and murdering Kimberly Anne Ruggles and Laura Lee Vickery Clay and raping and attempting to murder another woman. In 1988 Gray was found guilty in a court-martial (military trial) for the same crimes and was sentenced to death. Only days before his scheduled execution date in December 2008, he received a stay of execution from a federal judge to allow more time for appeals in the case. As of September 2011, a new execution date had not been set for Gray.

In 2009 dozens of people were killed at Fort Hood, an army base near Killeen, Texas, during a shooting rampage. The alleged killer was Nidal Malik Hasan (1970–), a U.S. Army major who is believed to have conducted the killings as revenge for U.S. actions during the so-called war on terror that was initiated after the September 11, 2001, terror attacks on the United States. As of September 2011, Hasan was scheduled to be court-martialed in early 2012 and was expected to receive the death penalty.

In "Military Often Botches Death Penalty Cases" (*Sacramento Bee*, August 28, 2011), Marisa Taylor details alleged problems with the military's capital punishment system that have resulted in capital sentences being overturned on appeals due to trial mistakes by inexperienced military lawyers and judges. Taylor reports that 10 of the 16 men sentenced to death by the military since 1984 have since been resentenced to life in prison. She notes, "Critics say the military botched the cases because its judicial system lags behind civilian courts and isn't equipped to handle the complex legal and moral questions that capital cases raise." She points to the appeal that was granted to Gray and the overturning of the death sentence in 1996 of Jessie Quintanilla, who was convicted of murdering his superior officer, Daniel Kidd, and attempting to kill two other marines. Quintanilla ultimately received a sentence of life in prison. The military judicial system is not really one system, but three separate systems that are operated by the three branches of the service: the U.S. Army, the U.S. Navy, and the U.S. Marine Corps. As a result, Taylor suggests that this system makes it difficult for "sweeping" reforms to be implemented.

CHAPTER 6

STATISTICS: DEATH SENTENCES, CAPITAL CASE COSTS, AND EXECUTIONS

STATISTICAL SOURCES

On a nationwide basis there are three primary sources of statistical information regarding death sentences, inmates on death row, and executions. The first is the Bureau of Justice Statistics (BJS), a division of the Office of Justice Programs under the U.S. Department of Justice (DOJ). Since 1993 the BJS has published an annual report titled *Capital Punishment* (http://bjs.ojp.usdoj.gov/index .cfm?ty=pbtp&tid=1) that summarizes data collected by the U.S. Census Bureau from state correctional offices as part of the National Prisoner Statistics program. The reports for 1993 through 2005 are available in both paper and electronic format and include detailed information and data analysis. The reports for 2006 through 2009 (the most recent available as of September 2011) are electronic versions only and include a limited number of statistical tables with no detailed analysis. *Capital Punishment, 2009—Statistical Tables* (December 2010, http:// bjs.ojp.usdoj.gov/content/pub/pdf/cp09st.pdf) by Tracy L. Snell of the BJS provides statistics on death row inmates and executions conducted through 2009. In some cases in this chapter, the BJS statistics are updated with data for 2010 that were collected from two other notable sources: the Death Penalty Information Center (DPIC) and the Criminal Justice Project of the National Association for the Advancement of Colored People's Legal Defense and Educational Fund Inc. (LDF).

The DPIC is a private nonprofit organization that provides a comprehensive array of news, statistics, and other information about capital punishment and the inmates on death row. Since 1996 the DPIC has published in December an annual report known as its year-end report (http:// www.deathpenaltyinfo.org/reports). As of September 2011, the most recent report available was *The Death Penalty in 2010: Year End Report* (December 2010, http://www.death penaltyinfo.org/documents/2010YearEnd-Final.pdf). The LDF (2011, http://naacpldf.org/about-ldf) calls itself

"America's premier legal organization fighting for racial justice." Since 2000 the organization's Criminal Justice Project has published a series of reports titled *Death Row U.S.A.* (http://naacpldf.org/death-row-usa) that list the names of all inmates known to be on death row or to have been executed. The race and gender of death row defendants is included. Information is also provided on the race and gender of executed defendants and their victims on a state-by-state basis. As of September 2011, the most recent report available was *Death Row U.S.A.: Winter 2011* (August 24, 2011, http://naacpldf.org/files/publications/DRUSA_Winter _2011.pdf) by Deborah Fins. The DPIC and the LDF are opposed to capital punishment.

DEATH ROW

Table 6.1 lists the cities and states in which death row facilities are located around the country. Most states house men and women inmates under sentence of death in different cities.

It should be noted that the number of inmates on death row is constantly changing. New death sentences increase the number, but existing death sentences may be overturned during the appeals process. Commutations (replacement of the death sentence with a lesser sentence), pardons, executions, and deaths due to causes other than execution also reduce the number of prisoners on death row in any given year.

Death Row Demographics: Year-End 2009

As noted earlier, the BJS publication *Capital Punishment, 2009: Statistical Tables* provides statistics on death row inmates as of year-end 2009. Table 6.2 shows the breakdown of death row entries and exits during 2009 for the state and federal prison systems. At the end of 2008, 3,210 prisoners were under sentence of death. The vast majority of prisoners (3,159) were on state death rows. Only 51 of the inmates were on federal death row. The

TABLE 6.1

Death row locations, by state

Alabama	Atmore (Women: Wetumpka)
Arizona	Florence (Women: Perryville)
Arkansas	Grady (Women: Pine Bluff)
California	San Quentin (Women: Chowchilla)
Colorado	Canon City
Connecticut	Somers
Delaware	Smyrna (Women: Claymont)
Federal system	Terre Haute, IN
Florida	Stark (Women: Lowell)
Georgia	Jackson (Women: Atlanta)
Idaho	Boise (Women: Pocatello)
Illinois	Pontiac (Women: Dwight)
Indiana	Michigan City (Women: Indianapolis)
Kansas	El Dorado (Women: Topeka)
Kentucky	Eddyville (Women: Pee Wee Valley)
Louisiana	Angola (Women: St. Gabriel)
Maryland	Cresaptown
Mississippi	Parchman (Women: Pearl)
Missouri	Mineral Point (Women: Fulton)
Montana	Deer Lodge (Women: Warm Springs)
Nebraska	Tecumseh (Women: York)
Nevada	Ely (Women: Carson City)
New Hampshire	Concord
New Jersey	Trenton
New Mexico	Santa Fe
North Carolina	Raleigh
Ohio	Youngstown and Mansfield (Women: Marysville)
Oklahoma	McAlester (Women: McLoud)
Oregon	Salem
Pennsylvania	SCI Greene (Waynesburg) or SCI Graterford (Women: Muncy)
South Carolina	Ridgville (Women: Columbia)
South Dakota	Sioux Falls
Tennessee	Nashville
Texas	Livingston (Women: Gatesville)
U.S. Military	Fort Leavenworth—Kansas
Utah	Draper
Virginia	Waverly
Washington	Walla Walla
Wyoming	Rawlins (Women: Lusk)

SOURCE: Adapted from *State by State Database*, Death Penalty Information Center, 2011, http://www.deathpenaltyinfo.org/state_by_state (accessed July 27, 2011)

overall racial makeup of the death row prisoners at that time was 1,795 white inmates (56% of total) and 1,343 African-American inmates (42% of total). Even though the number of death row prisoners of other races is not provided, it made up 2% of the total at year-end 2008.

As shown in Table 6.2, 112 new prisoners were received by corrections officials under sentence of death during 2009. Another 97 prisoners were removed from death row for causes other than execution. Fifty-two prisoners on death row were executed in 2009. As a result, there were 3,173 prisoners under sentence of death at year-end 2009. Nearly all (3,118) were on state death rows, while 55 were on federal death row. Overall, 1,780 (56%) of the condemned prisoners were white, and 1,317 (42%) were African-Amerian—the same ratio that was reported at the end of 2008. The other 2% of death row prisoners at year-end 2009 were of other races.

NEW ENTRIES DURING 2009. Table 6.3 provides additional details for the 112 inmates that entered death row during 2009. Nearly all (108) were sentenced under state laws. The remaining four prisoners were sentenced under federal laws. Of the 108 inmates sentenced to state death rows in 2009, the largest number (49 inmates, or 44% of the total) were sentenced in the South. The three southern states with the largest number of death row entries were Florida (15 inmates), Alabama (nine inmates), and Texas (eight inmates). Each of the other regions sent far fewer numbers to death row in 2009. The western states added 44 inmates, or 39% of the total. The vast majority of these prisoners were sentenced in California, which added 29 inmates to death row in 2009. The midwestern states had seven new inmates under sentence of death, and the northeastern states sent eight new prisoners to death row in 2009, all in Pennsylvania.

TABLE 6.2

Prisoners under sentence of death, by race, 2008 and 2009

Region and jurisdiction	Prisoners under sentence of death, 12/31/08			Received under sentence of death, 2009			Removed from death row (excluding executions), 2009[a]			Executed, 2009			Prisoners under sentence of death, 12/31/09		
	Total[b]	White[c]	Black[c]	Total[b]	White[c]	Black[c]	Total[b]	White[c]	Black[c]	Total[b]	White[c]	Black[c]	Total[b]	White[c]	Black[c]
U.S. total	3,210	1,795	1,343	112	65	42	97	49	47	52	31	21	3,173	1,780	1,317
Federal[d]	51	23	27	4	3	1	0	0	0	0	0	0	55	26	28
State	3,159	1,772	1,316	108	62	41	97	49	47	52	31	21	3,118	1,754	1,289

Note: Some figures shown for yearend 2008 are revised from those reported in *Capital Punishment, 2008—Statistical Tables*, NCJ 228662. The revised figures include 13 inmates who were either reported late to the National Prisoner Statistics program or were not in custody of state correctional authorities on December 31, 2008 (4 in Ohio, 3 in Texas, 2 in Indiana, and 1 each in Nebraska, Florida, Tennessee, and Nevada). The revised figures also exclude 10 inmates who were relieved of a death sentence before December 31, 2008 (3 in Idaho, and 1 each in Delaware, Oklahoma, Texas, Arizona, California, Nevada, and Oregon).
[a]Includes 23 deaths from natural causes (8 in California; 5 each in Alabama and Florida; and 1 each in Pennsylvania, Georgia, Kentucky, Texas, and Oregon) and 4 deaths from suicide (1 each in Pennsylvania, Georgia, California, and Nevada).
[b]Includes American Indians, Alaska Natives, Asians, Native Hawaiians, and other Pacific Islanders.
[c]The reporting of race and Hispanic origin differs from that presented in other tables in this document. In this table, counts of white and black inmates include persons of Hispanic/Latino origin.
[d]Excludes persons held under armed forces jurisdiction with a military death sentence for murder.

SOURCE: Adapted from Tracy L. Snell, "Table 4. Prisoners under Sentence of Death, by Region, Jurisdiction, and Race, 2008 and 2009," in *Capital Punishment, 2009—Statistical Tables*, U.S. Department of Justice, Office of Justice Programs, Bureau of Justice Statistics, December 2010, http://bjs.ojp.usdoj.gov/content/pub/pdf/cp09st.pdf (accessed July 5, 2011)

TABLE 6.3

Prisoners received under sentence of death, by jurisdiction, region, and race, 2009

Region and jurisdiction	Received under sentence of death, 2009		
	Total[a]	White[b]	Black[b]
U.S. total	112	65	42
Federal[c]	4	3	1
State	108	62	41
Northeast	8	3	5
Connecticut	0	0	0
New Hampshire	0	0	0
New York	0	0	0
Pennsylvania	8	3	5
Midwest	7	5	2
Illinois	1	1	0
Indiana	1	1	0
Kansas	1	1	0
Missouri	2	2	0
Nebraska	1	0	1
Ohio	1	0	1
South Dakota	0	0	0
South	49	29	19
Alabama	9	6	2
Arkansas	0	0	0
Delaware	0	0	0
Florida	15	10	5
Georgia	2	1	1
Kentucky	0	0	0
Louisiana	3	2	1
Maryland	0	0	0
Mississippi	2	1	1
North Carolina	2	1	1
Oklahoma	2	1	1
South Carolina	2	1	1
Tennessee	3	1	2
Texas	8	5	3
Virginia	1	0	1
West	44	25	15
Arizona	14	9	4
California	29	15	11
Colorado	0	0	0
Idaho	0	0	0
Montana	0	0	0
Nevada	1	1	0
New Mexico	0	0	0
Oregon	0	0	0
Utah	0	0	0
Washington	0	0	0
Wyoming	0	0	0

Note: Some figures shown for yearend 2008 are revised from those reported in *Capital Punishment, 2008—Statistical Tables*, NCJ 228662. The revised figures include 13 inmates who were either reported late to the National Prisoner Statistics program or were not in custody of state correctional authorities on December 31, 2008 (4 in Ohio, 3 in Texas, 2 in Indiana, and 1 each in Nebraska, Florida, Tennessee, and Nevada). The revised figures also exclude 10 inmates who were relieved of a death sentence before December 31, 2008 (3 in Idaho, and 1 each in Delaware, Oklahoma, Texas, Arizona, California, Nevada, and Oregon).

[a]Includes American Indians, Alaska Natives, Asians, Native Hawaiians, and other Pacific Islanders.

[b]The reporting of race and Hispanic origin differs from that presented in other tables in this document. In this table, counts of white and black inmates include persons of Hispanic/Latino origin.

[c]Excludes persons held under armed forces jurisdiction with a military death sentence for murder.

SOURCE: Adapted from Tracy L. Snell, "Table 4. Prisoners under Sentence of Death, by Region, Jurisdiction, and Race, 2008 and 2009," in *Capital Punishment, 2009—Statistical Tables*, U.S. Department of Justice, Office of Justice Programs, Bureau of Justice Statistics, December 2010, http://bjs.ojp.usdoj.gov/content/pub/pdf/cp09st.pdf (accessed July 5, 2011)

NEW REMOVALS IN 2009. As shown in Table 6.4, in 2009 a total of 149 inmates were removed from death row. Fifty-two inmates were executed. The largest numbers were in Texas (24), Alabama (6), and Ohio (5). Twenty-seven death row inmates died of causes other than execution in 2009. Overall, 70 prisoners were removed from death row and remained alive. Forty-two inmates had their death sentences overturned and 22 had their convictions overturned. Another four inmates were removed because of changes in capital statutes. Two inmates had their sentences commuted.

Of the 70 inmates who were removed from death row in 2009, the largest number (42 inmates, or 60% of the total) were in the South, followed by 11 inmates (16% of the total) in the Northeast (Pennsylvania only), nine inmates (13% of the total) in the Midwest, and eight inmates (11% of the total) in the West.

GENDER, RACE, EDUCATIONAL BACKGROUND, AND MARITAL STATUS. Table 6.5 provides a summary of certain demographic information for the 3,173 state and federal prisoners under sentence of death at year-end 2009. Nearly all (98.1%) were male, whereas only 1.9% were female. Concerning the racial and ethnic background of the death row prisoners, 56.1% were white, 41.5% were African-American, and 2.4% were other races. A large majority (86.5%) of the inmates were non-Hispanic, while 13.5% were Hispanic. However, the Hispanic origin of 396 inmates on death row was unknown.

The BJS also reports the regional makeup of the death row population. (See Table 7.2 in Chapter 7.) The southern states had the largest number (1,656 prisoners, or 52% of the total), followed by the western states (965 prisoners, or 30% of the total), the midwestern states (268 prisoners, or 8% of the total), and the northeastern states (229 prisoners, or 7% of the total). Overall, the five states with the largest numbers of death row inmates at year-end 2009 were California (684 inmates), Florida (389 inmates), Texas (331 inmates), Pennsylvania (218 inmates), and Alabama (200 inmates).

The educational background of death row inmates at year-end 2009 is shown in Table 6.6. Only 9% of the prisoners had attended college. The largest percentage (41.5%) had graduated from high school or received a general equivalency diploma. More than one-third (36%) had completed school through the ninth to the 11th grades. Another 13.5% had completed school through the eighth grade or lower. The median grade completed was the 12th grade, meaning that half of the inmates had completed that grade or more, and half had completed that grade or less. It should be noted that the educational status of 532 death row inmates was unknown.

Table 6.7 provides information about the marital status of death row prisoners at year-end 2009. More than half (54.7%) had never been married. Less than one-fourth (21.9%) of the inmates on death row were married at the

TABLE 6.4

Prisoners removed from under sentence of death, by jurisdiction and method of removal, 2009

Region and jurisdiction	Inmates removed from under sentence of death, 2009						
	Total	Execution	Other death	Appeals or higher courts overturned:			Sentence commuted
				Capital statute	Conviction	Sentence	
U.S. total	149	52	27	4	22	42	2
Northeast	**13**	**0**	**2**	**0**	**2**	**9**	**0**
Pennsylvania	13	0	2	0	2	9	0
Midwest	**16**	**7**	**0**	**0**	**1**	**7**	**1**
Indiana	2	1	0	0	0	1	0
Missouri	1	1	0	0	0	0	0
Ohio	12	5	0	0	1	5	1
South Dakota	1	0	0	0	0	1	0
South	**101**	**45**	**14**	**2**	**18**	**21**	**1**
Alabama	14	6	5	0	1	2	0
Arkansas	1	0	0	1	0	0	0
Delaware	2	0	0	1	1	0	0
Florida	17	2	5	0	5	5	0
Georgia	6	3	2	0	1	0	0
Kentucky	1	0	1	0	0	0	0
Louisiana	4	0	0	0	3	1	0
Mississippi	2	0	0	0	0	2	0
North Carolina	4	0	0	0	0	4	0
Oklahoma	7	3	0	0	3	1	0
South Carolina	5	2	0	0	1	2	0
Tennessee	2	2	0	0	0	0	0
Texas	33	24	1	0	3	4	1
Virginia	3	3	0	0	0	0	0
West	**19**	**0**	**11**	**2**	**1**	**5**	**0**
Arizona	1	0	0	0	0	1	0
California	13	0	9	0	1	3	0
Nevada	2	0	1	0	0	1	0
Oregon	3	0	1	2	0	0	0

SOURCE: Tracy L. Snell, "Table 11. Inmates Removed from under Sentence of Death, by Jurisdiction and Method of Removal, 2009," in *Capital Punishment, 2009—Statistical Tables*, U.S. Department of Justice, Office of Justice Programs, Bureau of Justice Statistics, December 2010, http://bjs.ojp.usdoj.gov/content/pub/pdf/cp09st.pdf (accessed July 5, 2011)

time. A slightly smaller percentage (20.5%) were divorced or separated. Only 2.8% of the inmates were widowed. The BJS could not determine the marital status of 376 death row inmates.

LENGTH OF TIME ON DEATH ROW. Because the capital punishment appeals process is so lengthy, many condemned inmates at year-end 2009 had been on death row for many years. Table 6.8 lists the mean (average) and median number of months that prisoners had been on death row. Overall, the average amount of time was 152 months (12 years and eight months). The median amount of time was 146 months (12 years and two months). In general, white and African-American inmates had the longest average time on death row—155 months (12 years and 11 months)—compared with inmates of Hispanic origin. Overall, the male occupants of death row at year-end 2009 had been there for an average of 153 months (12 years and nine months), compared with an average of 118 months (nine years and 10 months) for female inmates.

Table 6.9 compares jurisdictions in terms of the average number of years that inmates had spent under sentence of death as of year-end 2009. Note that averages were not

calculated for states with fewer than 10 death row inmates. The highest averages were for Idaho (16.7 years), Utah (16.4 years), and Nevada (16.1 years). However, these states had relatively small numbers of death row inmates overall. For the five jurisdictions with the most death row inmates at year-end 2009, the averages were Florida (14.4 years), California (14.2 years), Pennsylvania (13.8 years), Texas (10.8 years), and Alabama (10.7 years). The five jurisdictions (excluding Illinois, which abolished the death penalty in 2011) that had the lowest averages were Virginia (5.4 years), the federal system (6 years), and Delaware, Nebraska, and Oklahoma (8.9 years each).

Table 6.10 provides a breakdown of inmates sentenced to death by year of sentencing and by jurisdiction between 1974 and 2009. Of the 3,173 total inmates on death row as of year-end 2009, 113 inmates had been sentenced to death between 1974 and 1982. The vast majority of these inmates were in California (36 inmates), Florida (33 inmates), and Texas (11 inmates). Overall, 669 inmates (or 21% of the total) entered death row between 1974 and 1990. Another 1,446 inmates (or 46% of the total) were sentenced to death between 1991 and 2000. The remaining 1,058 inmates (or 33% of the total) entered death row between 2001 and 2009.

TABLE 6.5

Sex, race, and Hispanic origin of prisoners under sentence of death, 2009

| Characteristic | Prisoners under sentence of death, 2009 | | |
	Yearend	Admissions	Removals
Total inmates	3,173	112	149
Sex			
Male	98.1%	98.2%	100%
Female	1.9	1.8	0.0
Race[a]			
White	56.1%	58.0%	53.7%
Black	41.5	37.5	45.6
All other races[b]	2.4	4.5	0.7
Hispanic origin			
Hispanic	13.5%	19.4%	12.4%
Non-Hispanic	86.5	80.6	87.6
Number unknown	396	19	12

Note: Calculations are based on those cases for which data were reported. Detail may not add to total due to rounding.
[a]Includes persons of Hispanic/Latino origin.
[b]At yearend 2009, inmates in "all other races" consisted of 26 American Indians, 36 Asians, and 14 self-identified Hispanics. During 2009, 1 Asian and 4 self-identified Hispanic inmates were admitted, and 1 American Indian was removed.

SOURCE: Adapted from Tracy L. Snell, "Table 5. Demographic Characteristics of Prisoners under Sentence of Death, 2009," in *Capital Punishment, 2009—Statistical Tables*, U.S. Department of Justice, Office of Justice Programs, Bureau of Justice Statistics, December 2010, http://bjs.ojp.usdoj.gov/content/pub/pdf/cp09st.pdf (accessed July 5, 2011)

TABLE 6.6

Educational level of prisoners under sentence of death, 2009

| Characteristic | Prisoners under sentence of death, 2009 | | |
	Yearend	Admissions	Removals
Education			
8th grade or less	13.5%	8.1%	10.5%
9th–11th grade	36.0	38.4	49.2
High school graduate/GED	41.5	47.7	29.0
Any college	9.0	5.8	11.3
Median	12th	12th	11th
Number unknown*	532	26	25

Notes: Calculations are based on those cases for which data were reported. Detail may not add to total due to rounding. GED = General equivalency diploma.
*Due to a large number of cases with missing data on the education variable, users are advised to use caution when interpreting the distribution on this variable.

SOURCE: Adapted from Tracy L. Snell, "Table 5. Demographic Characteristics of Prisoners under Sentence of Death, 2009," in *Capital Punishment, 2009—Statistical Tables*, U.S. Department of Justice, Office of Justice Programs, Bureau of Justice Statistics, December 2010, http://bjs.ojp.usdoj.gov/content/pub/pdf/cp09st.pdf (accessed July 5, 2011)

In comparing the two-year sentencing periods between 1974 and 2009, the largest addition of death row inmates occurred in 1997–98, when 337 inmates were added. However, on a state-by-state basis California added the most inmates (74) in 1995–96, Florida added the most (39) in 1991–92, and Texas added the most (51) in 2003–04. As of year-end 2009, these three states held 1,404 death row inmates, or 44% of the total.

TABLE 6.7

Marital status of prisoners under sentence of death, 2009

| Characteristic | Prisoners under sentence of death, 2009 | | |
	Yearend	Admissions	Removals
Marital status			
Married	21.9%	17.0%	25.0%
Divorced/separated	20.5	33.0	21.3
Widowed	2.8	1.1	4.4
Never married	54.7	48.9	49.3
Number unknown	376	18	13

Note: Calculations are based on those cases for which data were reported. Detail may not add to total due to rounding.

SOURCE: Adapted from Tracy L. Snell, "Table 5. Demographic Characteristics of Prisoners under Sentence of Death, 2009," in *Capital Punishment, 2009—Statistical Tables*, U.S. Department of Justice, Office of Justice Programs, Bureau of Justice Statistics, December 2010, http://bjs.ojp.usdoj.gov/content/pub/pdf/cp09st.pdf (accessed July 5, 2011)

TABLE 6.8

Elapsed time since sentencing for inmates under sentence of death on December 31, 2009, by gender, race, and Hispanic origin

| Inmates under sentence of death | Elapsed time since sentencing | |
	Mean	Median
Total	152 mo	146 mo
Male	153	147
Female	118	115
White*	155	150
Black*	155	151
Hispanic	133	129

Note: For those persons sentenced to death more than once, the data are based on the most recent death sentence.
*Excludes persons of Hispanic/Latino origin.

SOURCE: Tracy L. Snell, "Table 9. Elapsed Time since Sentencing for Inmates under Sentence of Death, by Sex, Race, and Hispanic Origin, December 31, 2009," in *Capital Punishment, 2009—Statistical Tables*, U.S. Department of Justice, Office of Justice Programs, Bureau of Justice Statistics, December 2010, http://bjs.ojp.usdoj.gov/content/pub/pdf/cp09st.pdf (accessed July 5, 2011)

The BJS also compiles statistics on the length of time that condemned prisoners spend on death row before being executed. (See Table 6.11.) An inmate executed in 1984 had spent an average of 74 months (six years and two months) on death row. By 1999 that time had nearly doubled to 143 months (11 years and 11 months). An inmate executed in 2009 had spent an average of 169 months (14 years and one month) on death row.

AGE OF DEATH ROW INMATES. Table 6.12 shows the age breakdown of condemned inmates at year-end 2009. The age category containing the largest percentage (17.9%) of inmates was 45 to 49 years old. The next two largest categories were inmates aged 40 to 44 years (17%) and inmates aged 35 to 39 years (16.8%). Very few condemned inmates were in their early 20s (1.2%), late 20s (5.5%), or 65 years or older (2.6%). The mean age on death row was 44 years old.

TABLE 6.9

Average number of years under sentence of death, as of December 31, 2009

Jurisdiction	Average number of years under sentence of death as of 12/31/09
California	14.2
Florida	14.4
Texas	10.8
Arizona	12.3
Georgia	13.3
Nevada	16.1
Alabama	10.7
Tennessee	14.9
Mississippi	11.9
Pennsylvania	13.8
Arkansas	11.8
Idaho	16.7
Kentucky	15.0
Missouri	10.4
Ohio	14.4
Maryland	*
South Carolina	9.0
Oklahoma	8.9
Indiana	10.0
Montana	*
Louisiana	11.2
Utah	16.4
Nebraska	8.9
North Carolina	11.8
Connecticut	9.3
Oregon	10.1
Delaware	8.9
Washington	*
Federal system	6.0
South Dakota	*
Colorado	*
New Mexico	*
Virginia	5.4
Kansas	*
Illinois	3.5
Wyoming	*
New Hampshire	*
Total	**12.7**

Note: For those persons sentenced to death more than once, the numbers are based on the most recent death sentence.

*Averages not calculated for fewer than 10 inmates.

SOURCE: Adapted from Tracy L. Snell, "Table 18. Prisoners under Sentence of Death, by Jurisdiction and Year of Sentencing, December 31, 2009," in *Capital Punishment, 2009—Statistical Tables*, U.S. Department of Justice, Office of Justice Programs, Bureau of Justice Statistics, December 2010, http://bjs.ojp.usdoj.gov/content/pub/pdf/cp09st.pdf (accessed July 5, 2011)

CRIMINAL HISTORY. BJS statistics indicate that most prisoners on death row at year-end 2009 were already convicted felons when they were arrested for their capital crimes. (See Table 6.13.) Nearly two-thirds (65.7%) of the prisoners under sentence of death had prior felony convictions. Nearly 9% of the death row inmates had prior homicide convictions. However, 60.6% of the inmates had no particular legal status at the time of their capital offense. Another 15.2% were on parole, 10.5% were on probation, and 7.7% had charges pending when they were arrested. Small percentages of inmates had committed their capital offenses while they were incarcerated (4.1%) or had escaped from incarceration (1.5%). It should be noted that the legal history and status of 347 death row inmates at year-end 2009 could not be determined.

HISTORICAL DEATH ROW DISPOSITIONS. A number of prisoners are removed from death row each year for reasons other than execution: resentencing, retrial, commutation, or death while awaiting execution (natural death, murder, or suicide). As shown in Table 6.14, 8,115 inmates were under sentence of death between 1973 and 2009. Of these, 1,188 (15%) were executed, while 2,939 (36%) were removed from death row due to appeals or higher court decisions. Another 416 (5%) death row inmates died by means other than execution and 365 (4%) had their death sentences commuted. It should be noted that the BJS did not provide or did not know the reason for removal of 34 death row inmates. Thus, the breakdown as of year-end 2009 for all 8,115 inmates sentenced to death since 1973 was as follows (see Figure 6.1):

- Executed—1,118 (15%)

- Died due to causes other than execution—416 (5%)

- Removed from death row due to appeals or higher court decisions—2,939 (36%)

- Sentence commuted—365 (5%)

- Remained on death row—3,173 (39%)

In addition, 34 (0.4%) condemned inmates had been removed from death row for other or unknown reasons.

Table 6.15 provides a breakdown by state of the status of the 8,115 condemned inmates. The states with the largest numbers sentenced to death between 1973 and 2009 were:

- Texas—1,040 inmates (13% of the total)

- Florida—977 inmates (12% of the total)

- California—927 inmates (11% of the total)

- North Carolina—528 inmates (7% of the total)

- Alabama—412 inmates (5% of the total)

Together, these five states accounted for nearly half (48%, or 3,884) of the inmates sentenced to death.

As shown in Table 6.15, the states with the largest numbers of inmates executed between 1973 and 2009 were:

- Texas—447 inmates (38% of the total)

- Virginia—105 inmates (9% of the total)

- Oklahoma—91 inmates (8% of the total)

- Florida—68 inmates (6% of the total)

- Missouri—67 inmates (6% of the total)

Together, these five states accounted for nearly two-thirds (65%, or 778) of the inmates executed.

Of the 416 death row inmate deaths due to reasons other than execution, the most deaths occurred in California (73), followed by Florida (53), Texas (38), Alabama (31), and Pennsylvania (24).

TABLE 6.10

Prisoners sentenced to death, by year of sentencing and jurisdiction, 1974–2009

Jurisdiction	1974–1982	1983–1984	1985–1986	1987–1988	1989–1990	1991–1992	1993–1994	1995–1996	1997–1998	1999–2000	2001–2002	2003–2004	2005–2006	2007	2008	2009	Under sentence of death, 12/31/09
California	36	31	29	43	57	56	53	74	64	73	39	32	39	9	20	29	684
Florida	33	17	15	28	24	39	37	27	26	32	17	19	25	18	17	15	389
Texas	11	6	2	12	10	23	14	22	32	43	46	51	25	14	12	8	331
Arizona	5	5	4	11	10	12	13	7	8	1	1	13	13	8	6	14	131
Georgia	5	0	5	5	5	10	8	8	20	12	3	5	5	5	3	2	101
Nevada	5	7	5	7	6	4	5	16	7	7	0	3	3	2	2	1	80
Alabama	4	1	5	7	11	7	18	20	27	17	13	13	27	12	9	9	200
Tennessee	4	6	10	5	6	6	3	7	11	6	10	7	3	1	1	3	89
Mississippi	3	0	0	0	4	4	8	7	7	6	9	3	5	2	0	2	60
Pennsylvania	3	7	16	17	16	17	26	19	18	19	16	10	13	8	5	8	218
Arkansas	1	0	0	0	1	3	7	5	7	5	3	1	2	2	3	0	40
Idaho	1	0	2	1	2	2	1	2	0	0	1	2	0	0	0	0	14
Kentucky	1	3	4	2	0	3	4	1	5	5	2	0	4	0	0	0	35
Missouri	1	1	2	1	0	4	1	8	7	3	4	5	5	1	6	2	51
Ohio	0	11	14	11	11	14	13	21	21	9	13	10	8	5	3	1	165
Maryland	0	3	0	0	0	0	0	1	1	0	0	0	0	0	0	0	5
South Carolina	0	3	0	0	3	0	2	4	6	5	6	9	7	4	4	2	55
Oklahoma	0	1	1	3	1	1	2	7	11	12	7	11	8	3	9	2	79
Indiana	0	1	0	1	0	0	1	0	2	2	2	1	2	0	1	1	14
Montana	0	1	0	0	0	1	0	0	0	0	0	0	0	0	0	0	2
Louisiana	0	0	3	4	1	3	4	13	18	13	7	5	6	0	3	3	83
Utah	0	0	2	1	1	1	1	2	0	1	0	0	0	1	1	0	10
Nebraska	0	0	1	0	0	0	0	2	0	2	1	1	2	1	0	1	11
North Carolina	0	0	0	0	2	8	28	34	25	25	11	9	10	3	1	2	159
Connecticut	0	0	1	0	1	2	0	1	0	0	0	1	2	2	1	0	10
Oregon	0	0	0	0	0	3	2	4	5	5	3	4	3	2	0	0	31
Delaware	0	0	0	0	0	2	2	2	1	0	5	3	3	0	1	0	17
Washington	0	0	0	0	0	1	2	1	2	0	2	0	0	0	0	0	8
Federal system	0	0	0	0	0	0	2	2	4	4	6	12	12	6	3	4	55
South Dakota	0	0	0	0	0	0	1	0	1	0	0	0	0	0	0	0	2
Colorado	0	0	0	0	0	0	0	1	0	0	0	0	0	0	1	0	2
New Mexico	0	0	0	0	0	0	0	1	0	0	1	0	0	0	0	0	2
Virginia	0	0	0	0	0	0	0	0	1	1	1	4	3	1	1	1	13
Kansas	0	0	0	0	0	0	0	0	0	0	2	2	2	0	2	1	9
Illinois	0	0	0	0	0	0	0	1	0	0	0	5	4	3	3	0	16
Wyoming	0	0	0	0	0	0	0	0	0	0	0	1	0	1	0	0	13
New Hampshire	0	0	0	0	0	0	0	0	0	0	0	0	0	0	1	0	1
Total	**113**	**104**	**121**	**159**	**172**	**226**	**258**	**317**	**337**	**308**	**231**	**243**	**241**	**112**	**119**	**112**	**3,173**

Note: For those persons sentenced to death more than once, the numbers are based on the most recent death sentence.

SOURCE: Adapted from Tracy L. Snell, "Table 18. Prisoners under Sentence of Death, by Jurisdiction and Year of Sentencing, December 31, 2009," in *Capital Punishment, 2009—Statistical Tables*, U.S. Department of Justice, Office of Justice Programs, Bureau of Justice Statistics, December 2010, http://bjs.ojp.usdoj.gov/content/pub/pdf/cp09st.pdf (accessed July 5, 2011)

TABLE 6.11

Time under sentence of death by year of execution, 1977–2009

Year	Number of inmates executed	Average elapsed time from sentence to execution for all inmates
1977	1	*mo.
1979	2	*
1981	1	*
1982	2	*
1983	5	*
1984	21	74
1985	18	71
1986	18	87
1987	25	86
1988	11	80
1989	16	95
1990	23	95
1991	14	116
1992	31	114
1993	38	113
1994	31	122
1995	56	134
1996	45	125
1997	74	133
1998	68	130
1999	98	143
2000	85	137
2001	66	142
2002	71	127
2003	65	131
2004	59	132
2005	60	147
2006	53	145
2007	42	153
2008	37	139
2009	52	169

Note: In 1972, the U.S. Supreme Court invalidated capital punishment statutes in several states (*Furman v. Georgia*, 408 U.S. 238 [1972]), effecting a moratorium on executions. Executions resumed in 1977 when the Supreme Court found that revisions to several state statutes had effectively addressed the issues previously held unconstitutional (*Gregg v. Georgia*, 428 U.S. 153 [1976] and its companion cases). Average time was calculated from the most recent sentencing date.
*Averages not calculated for fewer than 10 cases.

SOURCE: Tracy L. Snell, "Table 12. Average Time between Sentencing and Execution, by Year, 1977–2009," in *Capital Punishment, 2009—Statistical Tables*, U.S. Department of Justice, Office of Justice Programs, Bureau of Justice Statistics, December 2010, http://bjs.ojp.usdoj.gov/content/pub/pdf/cp09st.pdf (accessed July 5, 2011)

TABLE 6.12

Age of prisoners under sentence of death, 2009

Characteristic	Prisoners under sentence of death, 2009		
	Yearend	Admissions	Removals
Age			
20–24	1.2%	11.6%	0.0%
25–29	5.5	14.3	4.7
30–34	12.3	18.8	7.4
35–39	16.8	19.6	16.1
40–44	17.0	5.4	12.1
45–49	17.9	16.1	19.5
50–54	13.3	5.4	19.5
55–59	7.8	4.5	5.4
60–64	5.6	3.6	10.7
65 or older	2.6	0.9	4.7
Mean age	44	38	47
Median age	44	36	47

Note: Calculations are based on those cases for which data were reported. Detail may not add to total due to rounding.

SOURCE: Adapted from Tracy L. Snell, "Table 5. Demographic Characteristics of Prisoners under Sentence of Death, 2009," in *Capital Punishment, 2009—Statistical Tables*, U.S. Department of Justice, Office of Justice Programs, Bureau of Justice Statistics, December 2010, http://bjs.ojp.usdoj.gov/content/pub/pdf/cp09st.pdf (accessed July 5, 2011)

TABLE 6.13

Criminal history profile of prisoners under sentence of death, by race and Hispanic origin, 2009

	Percent of prisoners under sentence of death[a]			
	All[b]	White[c]	Black[c]	Hispanic
U.S. total	100%	100%	100%	100%
Prior felony convictions				
Yes	65.7%	62.1%	71.4%	61.8%
No	34.3	37.9	28.6	34.3
Number unknown	257			
Prior homicide convictions				
Yes	8.6%	8.8%	9.0%	6.7%
No	91.4	91.2	91.0	93.3
Number unknown	56			
Legal status at time of capital offense				
Charges pending	7.7%	8.6%	7.6%	5.0%
Probation	10.5	9.1	11.7	11.4
Parole	15.2	12.9	16.5	19.2
On escape	1.5	2.0	0.9	1.5
Incarcerated	4.1	4.5	3.9	3.5
Other status	0.5	0.4	0.5	0.6
None	60.6	62.5	58.9	58.9
Number unknown	347			

[a]Percentages are based on those offenders for whom data were reported. Detail may not add to total because of rounding.
[b]Includes American Indians, Alaska Natives, Asians, Native Hawaiians, and other Pacific Islanders.
[c]Excludes persons of Hispanic/Latino origin.

SOURCE: Tracy L. Snell, "Table 10. Criminal History Profile of Prisoners under Sentence of Death, by Race and Hispanic Origin, 2009," in *Capital Punishment, 2009—Statistical Tables*, U.S. Department of Justice, Office of Justice Programs, Bureau of Justice Statistics, December 2010, http://bjs.ojp.usdoj.gov/content/pub/pdf/cp09st.pdf (accessed July 5, 2011)

Table 6.15 notes that 2,939 death row inmates had their sentence or conviction overturned between 1973 and 2009. The largest numbers occurred in the following states:

- Florida—447 inmates (15% of the total)
- North Carolina—297 inmates (10% of the total)
- Ohio—168 inmates (6% of the total)
- Texas—167 inmates (6% of the total)
- Oklahoma—165 inmates (6% of the total)

Together, these five states accounted for 40% (1,244) of the total.

Also shown in Table 6.15 is a breakdown by jurisdiction of the 365 death sentences that were commuted between 1973 and 2009. The most commutations were granted in Illinois (156), followed by Texas (56), Florida (18), California (15), and Ohio (15). Illinois, by far, accounted for the most commutations, as was explained in Chapter 5.

TABLE 6.14

Prisoners sentenced to death and outcome of the sentence, by year of sentencing, 1973–2009

| | | | | Number of prisoners removed from under sentence of death | | | | | |
| | | | | Appeal or higher courts overturned | | | | | |
Year of sentence	Number sentenced to death	Execution	Other death	Death penalty statute	Conviction	Sentence	Sentence commuted	Other or unknown reasons	Number under sentence of death, 2/31/2009
1973	42	2	0	14	9	8	9	0	0
1974	149	11	4	65	15	30	22	1	1
1975	298	6	4	171	24	67	21	2	3
1976	233	14	6	136	17	43	15	0	2
1977	137	19	5	40	26	33	7	0	7
1978	185	36	7	21	36	65	8	0	12
1979	151	28	14	2	28	59	6	1	13
1980	173	45	15	4	30	52	12	0	15
1981	223	56	14	0	42	80	12	1	18
1982	267	67	23	0	40	82	12	1	42
1983	251	67	23	1	28	68	15	2	47
1984	286	69	19	2	46	72	13	8	57
1985	261	48	14	1	43	87	13	4	51
1986	300	73	23	1	50	64	14	5	70
1987	287	55	27	7	45	74	7	7	65
1988	289	57	18	1	35	70	14	0	94
1989	256	43	18	0	33	59	13	1	89
1990	251	46	17	1	36	50	17	1	83
1991	268	42	13	2	37	60	11	0	103
1992	287	42	19	0	28	54	21	0	123
1993	287	61	21	3	20	41	15	0	126
1994	313	64	11	9	33	50	14	0	132
1995	313	57	20	6	19	42	13	0	156
1996	315	39	16	4	20	60	15	0	161
1997	268	27	9	3	18	40	9	0	162
1998	294	35	10	4	22	39	9	0	175
1999	277	26	12	8	19	33	10	0	169
2000	224	20	10	4	11	31	9	0	139
2001	159	11	8	3	5	25	2	0	105
2002	166	10	4	3	2	16	5	0	126
2003	152	9	5	1	4	11	0	0	122
2004	140	2	0	1	5	10	1	0	121
2005	139	1	4	0	4	4	0	0	126
2006	123	0	1	0	5	1	1	0	115
2007	120	0	2	2	4	0	0	0	112
2008	119	0	0	0	0	0	0	0	119
2009	112	0	0	0	0	0	0	0	112
Total, 1973–2009	8,115	1,188	416	520	839	1,580	365	34	3,173

Note: In 1972, the U.S. Supreme Court invalidated capital punishment statutes in several states (*Furman v. Georgia*, 408 U.S. 238 [1972]), effecting a moratorium on executions. Executions resumed in 1977 when the Supreme Court found that revisions to several state statutes had effectively addressed the issues previously held unconstitutional (*Gregg v. Georgia*, 428 U.S. 153 [1976] and its companion cases). Some inmates executed since 1977 or currently under sentence of death were sentenced prior to 1977. For those persons sentenced to death more than once, the numbers are based on the most recent death sentence.

SOURCE: Tracy L. Snell, "Table 19. Prisoners Sentenced to Death and Outcome of the Sentence, by Year of Sentencing, 1973–2009," in *Capital Punishment, 2009—Statistical Tables*, U.S. Department of Justice, Office of Justice Programs, Bureau of Justice Statistics, December 2010, http://bjs.ojp.usdoj.gov/content/pub/pdf/cp09st.pdf (accessed July 5, 2011)

Death Row Demographics: January 2011

According to Fins, in *Death Row U.S.A.: Winter 2011*, there were 3,251 inmates on death row as of January 1, 2011. (See Table 6.16.) The vast majority of the inmates (3,191, or 98.2% of the total) were male, whereas only 60 inmates (1.9% of the total) were female. Fins notes that 1,420 of the inmates (43.7% of the total) were white and 1,358 (41.8% of the total) were African-American. Another 394 inmates (12.1% of the total) were Hispanic. Much smaller numbers were Asian-American or Native American.

DEATH ROW POPULATION OVER TIME. As shown in Figure 6.2, in 1953 the nation's death row population was only 131 inmates. By 1971 the number had grown to 642, before plummeting to 134 in 1973. This drop was due to the landmark 1972 decision by the U.S. Supreme Court, which ruled in *Furman v. Georgia* (408 U.S. 238) that the death penalty was unconstitutional. The ruling forced states to develop more uniform systems for applying capital punishment. During the late 1970s the death row population began to grow once more. It underwent a long and steady increase that persisted for more than two decades. In 2000 the number of prisoners under sentence of death reached its highest level ever: 3,601 inmates. The number then dipped slightly and ranged between 3,100 and 3,400 from 2001 through 2009. Fins's estimate of 3,251 death row inmates as of January 1, 2011, also fits within this range.

FIGURE 6.1

Prisoners sentenced to death and number of removals, 1973–2009

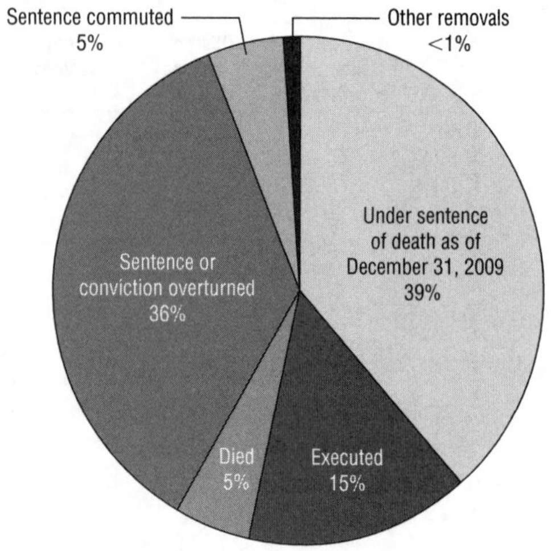

SOURCE: Adapted from Tracy L. Snell, "Table 20. Number Sentenced to Death and Number of Removals, by Jurisdiction and Reason for Removal, 1973–2009," in *Capital Punishment, 2009—Statistical Tables*, U.S. Department of Justice, Office of Justice Programs, Bureau of Justice Statistics, December 2010, http://bjs.ojp.usdoj.gov/content/pub/pdf/cp09st.pdf (accessed July 5, 2011)

WOMEN ON DEATH ROW. According to the BJS, 60 women were on death row at year-end 2009. (See Table 6.17.) Forty-two (70%) of the women were white and 15 (25%) were African-American. California (16) had the largest contingent of women under sentence of death, followed by Texas (10) and five each in Alabama, North Carolina, and Pennsylvania.

HISPANICS ON DEATH ROW. As shown in Table 6.18, 376 Hispanics were on death row at year-end 2009. The largest number under state jurisdiction were in California (157), followed by Florida (32), Pennsylvania (20), Nevada (8), and four each in Nebraska and North Carolina. Six Hispanic inmates were reported on the federal death row.

DEATH SENTENCES DECLINE AS HOMICIDES DECLINE

During the late 1990s the number of defendants sentenced to death each year began to decline. (See Figure 6.3.) In 1973 only 42 death sentences were handed out in the United States. During the 1980s and early 1990s between 250 and 300 defendants per year were regularly sentenced to die. The number of death sentences peaked in 1996 at 315 and then began a dramatic decline, dropping to 112 in 2009, the lowest number in more than three decades. In *Death Penalty in 2010*, the DPIC estimates that 114 defendants were sentenced to death in 2010. The decline in death sentences beginning in the late 1990s may be linked to the

corresponding decrease in the nation's homicide rate. As shown in Figure 1.5 in Chapter 1, the homicide rate dropped dramatically from 9.8 homicides per 100,000 population in 1991 to 5 homicides per 100,000 population in 2009.

FINANCIAL COSTS OF THE DEATH PENALTY

As noted in Chapter 1, capital cases are more expensive to litigate than noncapital homicides. This is due in part to the lengthy appeals process that is built in to the death penalty process. An additional expense is the cost of specialized housing and extra security provided on death rows. Since the last half of the first decade of the 21st century, several studies have been performed to analyze the financial costs that are associated with capital punishment systems. Some of these studies have been conducted and/or funded by private organizations that may or may not be opposed to the death penalty or take no public stance on it either way. Other studies have been published by government agencies or commissions at the state or federal level. More casual studies on the costs of capital punishment are conducted by journalists for publication by newspapers or other news outlets.

California

In June 2011 the Loyola Law School in Los Angeles published a study by Arthur L. Alarcón, a federal judge in the United States Courts for the Ninth Circuit (which includes California), and Paula Mitchell, a professor at the school. In *Executing the Will of the Voters?: A Roadmap to Mend or End the California Legislature's Multibillion-Dollar Death Penalty Debacle* (http://llr.lls.edu/docs/44-SIalarcon.pdf), the researchers estimate that between 1978 and 2011 California had spent more than $4 billion on its "dysfunctional" capital punishment system. Because only 13 executions took place during that time, the cost per execution was around $308 million. Alarcón and Mitchell complain that "billions of taxpayer dollars have been spent to create a bloated system, in which condemned inmates languish on death row for decades before dying of natural causes and in which executions rarely take place." The researchers put much of the blame for the delays on the state legislature, which they suggest has failed to fund programs to provide "adequate" legal counsel for death row inmates during the appeals process.

California spends an estimated $144 million annually on housing, medical care, and legal costs for death row inmates. At the time the report was written, the state had more than 700 death row inmates. Alarcón and Mitchell estimate that it will take more than 20 years to resolve those cases unless reforms are implemented to eliminate the delays and backlog. They conclude that reforming the state's capital punishment system will require "tens of millions of dollars annually on a statewide basis" until the backlog is reduced. Limiting application of the death penalty to "the worst of the worst" offenders would

TABLE 6.15

Number sentenced to death and number of removals, by jurisdiction and reason for removal, 1973–2009

Jurisdiction	Total sentenced to death, 1973–2009	Number of removals, 1973–2009					Under sentence of death, 12/31/09
		Executed	Died	Sentence or conviction overturned	Sentence commuted	Other removals	
U.S. total	8,115	1,188	416	2,939	365	34	3,173
Federal	65	3	0	6	1	0	55
Alabama	412	44	31	135	2	0	200
Arizona	286	23	14	110	7	1	131
Arkansas	110	27	3	38	2	0	40
California	927	13	73	142	15	0	684
Colorado	21	1	2	15	1	0	2
Connecticut	13	1	0	2	0	0	10
Delaware	56	14	0	25	0	0	17
Florida	977	68	53	447	18	2	389
Georgia	320	46	16	147	9	1	101
Idaho	42	1	3	21	3	0	14
Illinois	307	12	15	96	156	12	16
Indiana	100	20	4	54	6	2	14
Kansas	12	0	0	3	0	0	9
Kentucky	81	3	6	35	2	0	35
Louisiana	238	27	6	114	7	1	83
Maryland	53	5	3	36	4	0	5
Massachusetts	4	0	0	2	2	0	0
Mississippi	190	10	5	112	0	3	60
Missouri	182	67	10	52	2	0	51
Montana	15	3	2	6	2	0	2
Nebraska	32	3	4	12	2	0	11
Nevada	147	12	15	36	4	0	80
New Hampshire	1	0	0	0	0	0	1
New Jersey	52	0	3	33	8	8	0
New Mexico	28	1	1	19	5	0	2
New York	10	0	0	10	0	0	0
North Carolina	528	43	21	297	8	0	159
Ohio	401	33	20	168	15	0	165
Oklahoma	350	91	12	165	3	0	79
Oregon	58	2	2	23	0	0	31
Pennsylvania	399	3	24	148	6	0	218
Rhode Island	2	0	0	2	0	0	0
South Carolina	203	42	5	98	3	0	55
South Dakota	5	1	1	1	0	0	2
Tennessee	221	6	15	105	4	2	89
Texas	1,040	447	38	167	56	1	331
Utah	27	6	1	9	1	0	10
Virginia	150	105	6	14	11	1	13
Washington	38	4	1	25	0	0	8
Wyoming	12	1	1	9	0	0	1

Note: In 1972, the U.S. Supreme Court invalidated capital punishment statutes in several states (*Furman v. Georgia*, 408 U.S. 238 [1972]), effecting a moratorium on executions. Executions resumed in 1977 when the Supreme Court found that revisions to several state statutes had effectively addressed the issues previously held unconstitutional (*Gregg v. Georgia*, 428 U.S. 153 [1976] and its companion cases). Some inmates executed since 1977 or currently under sentence of death were sentenced prior to 1977. For those persons sentenced to death more than once, the numbers are based on the most recent death sentence.

SOURCE: Adapted from Tracy L. Snell, "Table 20. Number Sentenced to Death and Number of Removals, by Jurisdiction and Reason for Removal, 1973–2009," in *Capital Punishment, 2009—Statistical Tables*, U.S. Department of Justice, Office of Justice Programs, Bureau of Justice Statistics, December 2010, http://bjs.ojp.usdoj.gov/content/pub/pdf/cp09st.pdf (accessed July 5, 2011).

provide "immediate" savings of millions of dollars to the state. So would abolishing the death penalty in favor of life sentences with no chance of parole. Alarcón and Mitchell estimate that this option would save "billions of dollars over the next 20 years."

The California Commission on the Fair Administration of Justice (CCFAJ; 2011, http://www.ccfaj.org/) was created in 2004 by the state legislature to examine California's criminal justice system and make recommendations to remedy any problems. The CCFAJ examined numerous issues that were associated with the state's capital punishment system, many of which had cost implications. In June

2008 its findings and recommendations were published *California Commission on the Fair Administration of Justice: Report and Recommendations on the Administration of the Death Penalty in California* (http://www.ccfaj.org/documents/reports/dp/official/FINAL%20REPORT%20DEATH%20PENALTY.pdf).

The CCFAJ noted that one particularly expensive component of the state's capital punishment system is the lengthy amount of time that prisoners spend on death row. The average time between death sentence and execution in California is 20 to 25 years. This is about twice the national average for other death penalty states. The

CCFAJ complained, "Just to keep cases moving at this snail's pace, we spend large amounts of taxpayers' money each year: by conservative estimates, well over one hundred million dollars annually." Part of the problem, noted the CCFAJ, is a lack of funding for qualified attorneys to handle death sentence appeals and habeas corpus proceedings, which has resulted in a huge backlog of cases.

The CCFAJ made numerous recommendations to the California legislature for reform of the capital punishment system. However, Alarcón and Mitchell complain that the legislature failed to act on these recommendations. In "Death Penalty Costs California $184 Million a Year, Study Says" (*Los Angeles Times*, June 20, 2011), Carol J. Williams reports that "none of the remedies"

described by the CCFAJ "has been adopted by lawmakers or put to the public for a vote."

Alarcón and Mitchell's report is generally regarded to be fair and unbiased, even by death penalty advocates. Williams notes that even though Mitchell has publicly voiced her opposition to capital punishment, Alarcón is not opposed to the death penalty and prosecuted capital cases earlier in his career. Debra J. Saunders, a conservative columnist who favors capital punishment, admits in "Death Penalty Foes' Self-Fulfilling Prophecies" (*San Francisco Chronicle*, July 17, 2011) that Alarcón and Mitchell did "a solid job quantifying how much taxpayers must pay for the death penalty." However, she suggests that they "gloss over the role of frivolous appeals and bonehead rulings by federal judges." The latter complaint relates to the Ninth Circuit of Appeals, which has reversed approximately 70% of the capital cases that have come before it and is widely criticized by death penalty advocates as having an anti-capital punishment bias. Saunders concludes that "for decades, capital punishment opponents have tried to thwart California's 1978 death-penalty law with frivolous appeals that clog courts, delay punishment and burn through taxpayers' dollars. They now have been so successful that they can argue that California's death penalty doesn't work and costs too much."

Maryland

In March 2008 the Urban Institute published *The Cost of the Death Penalty in Maryland* (http://www.urban.org/UploadedPDF/411625_md_death_penalty.pdf) by John Roman et al. The Urban Institute is a nonprofit organization based in Washington, D.C. According to the institute (2011, http://www.urban.org/about/), it "gathers

TABLE 6.16

Total number of death row inmates as reported by the NAACP, January 1, 2011

[Total: 3,251]

Race of defendant		
White	1,420	43.68%
Black	1,358	41.77%
Latino/Latina	394	12.12%
Native American	36	1.11%
Asian	42	1.29%
Unknown at this issue	1	0.03%
Gender		
Male	3,191	98.15%
Female	60	1.85%

SOURCE: Adapted from "Death Row Statistics," in *Death Row USA Winter 2011*, NAACP Legal Defense and Educational Fund, Inc., 2011, http://naacpldf.org/files/publications/DRUSA_Winter_2011.pdf (accessed September 19, 2011)

FIGURE 6.2

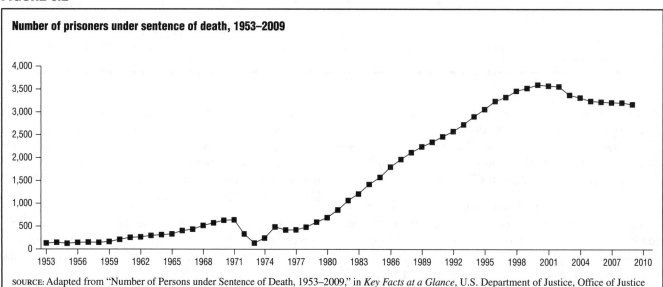

Number of prisoners under sentence of death, 1953–2009

SOURCE: Adapted from "Number of Persons under Sentence of Death, 1953–2009," in *Key Facts at a Glance*, U.S. Department of Justice, Office of Justice Programs, Bureau of Justice Statistics, November 5, 2010, http://bjs.ojp.usdoj.gov/content/glance/sheets/dr.csv (accessed July 5, 2011)

TABLE 6.17

Women under sentence of death, by race and jurisdiction, yearend 2009

Region and jurisdiction	Under sentence of death, 12/31/09		
	Total[a]	White[b]	Black[b]
U.S. total	**60**	**42**	**15**
Federal	2	2	0
State	58	40	15
Northeast	**5**	**2**	**3**
Pennsylvania	5	2	3
Midwest	**2**	**1**	**1**
Indiana	1	0	1
Ohio	1	1	0
South	**32**	**22**	**9**
Alabama	5	3	2
Florida	1	1	0
Georgia	1	1	0
Kentucky	1	1	0
Louisiana	2	1	1
Mississippi	3	3	0
North Carolina	5	2	2
Oklahoma	1	1	0
Tennessee	2	2	0
Texas	10	6	4
Virginia	1	1	0
West	**19**	**15**	**2**
Arizona	2	2	0
California	16	12	2
Idaho	1	1	0

Note: No women were removed from under sentence of death during 2009.
[a]Includes American Indians, Alaska Natives, Asians, Native Hawaiians, and other Pacific Islanders.
[b]The reporting of race and Hispanic origin differs from that presented in other tables in this document. In this table, counts of white and black inmates include persons of Hispanic/Latino origin.

SOURCE: Adapted from Tracy L. Snell, "Table 6. Women under Sentence of Death, by Region, Jurisdiction, and Race, 2008 and 2009," in *Capital Punishment, 2009—Statistical Tables*, U.S. Department of Justice, Office of Justice Programs, Bureau of Justice Statistics, December 2010, http://bjs.ojp.usdoj.gov/content/pub/pdf/cp09st.pdf (accessed July 5, 2011)

TABLE 6.18

Hispanics under sentence of death, by jurisdiction, year-end 2009

Region and jurisdiction	Under sentence of death, 12/31/09
U.S. total	**376**
Federal	6
State	370
Northeast	**21**
Connecticut	1
Pennsylvania	20
Midwest	**10**
Illinois	2
Indiana	1
Nebraska	4
Ohio	3
South	**147**
Alabama	2
Delaware	2
Florida	32
Georgia	2
Kentucky	1
Louisiana	2
North Carolina	4
Oklahoma	2
South Carolina	1
Tennessee	1
Texas	98
West	**192**
Arizona	20
California	157
Idaho	1
Nevada	8
New Mexico	1
Oregon	2
Utah	3

SOURCE: Adapted from Tracy L. Snell, "Table 7. Hispanics under Sentence of Death, by Region and Jurisdiction, 2008 and 2009," in *Capital Punishment, 2009—Statistical Tables*, U.S. Department of Justice, Office of Justice Programs, Bureau of Justice Statistics, December 2010, http://bjs.ojp.usdoj.gov/content/pub/pdf/cp09st.pdf (accessed July 5, 2011)

FIGURE 6.3

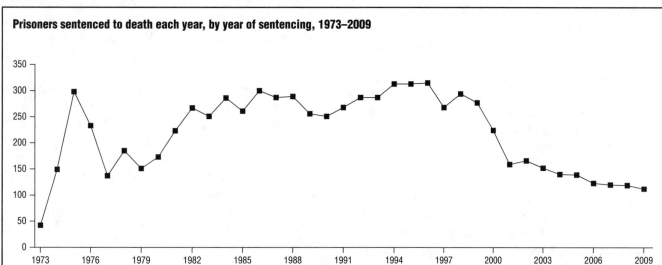

Prisoners sentenced to death each year, by year of sentencing, 1973–2009

SOURCE: Adapted from Tracy L. Snell, "Table 19. Prisoners Sentenced to Death and Outcome of the Sentence, by Year of Sentencing, 1973–2009," in *Capital Punishment, 2009—Statistical Tables*, U.S. Department of Justice, Office of Justice Programs, Bureau of Justice Statistics, December 2010, http://bjs.ojp.usdoj.gov/content/pub/pdf/cp09st.pdf (accessed July 5, 2011)

data, conducts research, evaluates programs, offers technical assistance overseas, and educates Americans on social and economic issues—to foster sound public policy and effective government." Roman et al.'s research was funded by the Abell Foundation (2011, http://www.abell.org/aboutthefoundation/index.html) of Baltimore, Maryland, a private organization that is devoted to helping "the disadvantaged in the Baltimore community and the region."

Roman et al. note that since 1978 Maryland had 56 cases resulting in a death sentence. Five of these inmates were executed. As of 2008 the state had five inmates on death row. The researchers examine the costs of adjudication (the process of judging) and incarceration for 1,136 cases that occurred between 1978 and 1999 in which the defendant was eligible for the death penalty. Note this does not mean that the prosecution sought a death sentence, only that the defendant was eligible for capital punishment under state law. Roman et al. conclude that an average case in which a death sentence was not sought cost more than $1.1 million. An average case in which a death sentence was sought, but not imposed, cost $1.8 million. An average case in which a death sentence was sought and imposed cost just over $3 million. The breakdown for the latter was about $1.7 million for adjudication costs and about $1.3 million for incarceration costs.

New Hampshire

In 2009 the New Hampshire legislature created a commission to study the state's capital punishment system. (As noted in Table 6.15, New Hampshire only sentenced one person to death between 1973 and 2009. In 2008 Michael Addison was sentenced to death for killing the police officer Michael Briggs.) In December 2010 the Commission to Study the Death Penalty in New Hampshire issued *Final Report on HB 520, Chapter 284, Laws of 2009* (http://gencourt.state.nh.us/statstudcomm/reports/2009.pdf), which discussed many issues related to the death penalty including costs. The commission found that the cost of prosecuting and incarcerating inmates in capital cases was "significantly" higher than in noncapital murder cases. However, the commission concluded that "the death penalty is pursued sparingly in this state and those costs are necessary to provide both a high quality of prosecution and a vigorous defense."

New Jersey

In 2006 the governor of New Jersey appointed the New Jersey Death Penalty Study Commission (NJDPSC) to assess the state's capital punishment system and issue recommendations regarding its continued usage. At that time, New Jersey only had eight prisoners on death row and had not executed anyone in more than two decades. In January 2007 the NJDPSC published *New Jersey Death Penalty Study Commission Report* (http://www.njleg.state.nj.us/

committees/dpsc_final.pdf), which recommended replacing the state's death sentence with a sentence of life imprisonment without the chance of parole. The decision was based on a number of factors, including costs. The commission noted, "The costs of the death penalty are greater than the costs of life in prison without parole, but it is not possible to measure these costs with any degree of precision." However, estimates provided from state agencies indicated that eliminating the death penalty in favor of lifetime incarceration would save nearly $1.5 million per year in public defender costs for the 19 capital cases active at that time and would save approximately $1 million per death row inmate in incarceration costs. The potential cost savings in court-related expenses could not be estimated, and it was concluded that no cost savings would be achieved by prosecutor offices in the state.

In December 2007 New Jersey abolished the death penalty in the state and replaced it with lifetime incarceration without parole.

Washington

In December 2006 the Washington State Bar Association (WSBA) published *Final Report of the Death Penalty Subcommittee of the Committee on Public Defense* (http://www.nacdl.org/public.nsf/defenseupdates/deathpenalty004?OpenDocument). At that time there had been 79 death penalty cases in Washington in the previous 25 years. However, only four executions had taken place, the most recent in 2001. The WSBA reviewed previous statistical reports on costs associated with the state's death penalty and surveyed prosecutors and defense attorneys who had been involved in capital cases regarding trial costs and attorney compensation. Data were also collected on state and federal costs during the appeals process.

The WSBA notes that quantifying and comparing costs between criminal cases is very difficult. It estimates that trying a death penalty case in Washington costs an average of $467,000 more than a comparable noncapital case. This figure includes the extra expenses incurred by the prosecutor and the defense. Fees and costs at the appellate level were estimated to be at least $100,000 more for a capital case than for a comparable noncapital case. The WSBA concludes that "it costs significantly more to try a capital case to final verdict than to try the same case as an aggravated murder case where the penalty sought is life without possibility of parole." However, the WSBA does not foresee that eliminating the death penalty in Washington would reduce the budgets of prosecutor offices. Instead, the cost savings would likely be devoted to other cases.

Federal Death Penalty Costs

Since the passage of the Anti-Drug Abuse Act in 1988 and the Violent Crime Control and Law Enforcement Act of 1994 (also known as the Federal Death Penalty Act), the number of federal prosecutions, including crimes punishable by death, has risen. As described in Chapter 5, between 1988 and August 2009 the U.S. attorney general authorized the government to seek the death penalty against 461 defendants. Two hundred sixty-one of the defendants were tried, and of these three were executed. Most of the rest of the defendants received life sentences from juries or judges or through plea bargain agreements. In the federal system defendants are deemed death-eligible if their crime is considered a death penalty crime under federal law. The U.S. attorney general chooses which death-eligible defendants will face a death sentence at trial. These cases are called death-authorized cases.

In September 2010 the Office of Defender Services (ODS) of the Administrative Office of the U.S. Courts published its second-phase report titled *Report to the Committee on Defender Services, Judicial Conference of the United States: Update on the Cost and Quality of Defense Representation in Federal Death Penalty Cases* (http://www.deathpenaltyinfo.org/documents/FederalDP Cost2010.pdf) by Jon B. Gould and Lisa Greenman. The report was an update of a 1998 study on the federal death penalty system that specifically examined funding for defense services provided to defendants in capital cases. For the updated report the ODS analyzed cost data for federal death penalty cases from 1998 to 2004 in which the government provided public defenders (at taxpayer expense) for the defendants. The results included medians for total costs of defense representation, meaning that half the values were less than the median value and the other half of the values were greater than the median value. The median cost for a death-authorized case was $353,185. The median cost for a death-eligible but nondeath-authorized case was $44,809.

Gould and Greenman also issue recommendations on the federal death penalty system. In regards to cost, they note that "the median cost of a case in which the Attorney General authorized seeking the death penalty was nearly eight times greater than the cost of a case that was eligible for capital prosecution but in which the death penalty was *not* authorized." The median cost of a death-authorized case that proceeded to trial was more than twice the cost of a death-authorized case that was resolved through a plea bargain agreement. Furthermore, Gould and Greenman report that the cost of defending federal capital cases "increased substantially" during the first decade of the 21st century for a number of reasons, including legal and forensic factors.

EXECUTIONS

Until 1930 the U.S. government did not keep any record of the number of people executed under the death penalty. As shown in Table 6.19, from 1930 through 2009 a

TABLE 6.19

Number of persons executed, by jurisdiction, 1930–2009 and 1977–2009

	Number executed	
Jurisdiction	Since 1930	Since 1977
U.S. total	**5,047**	**1,188**
Texas	744	447
Georgia	412	46
New York	329	0
North Carolina	306	43
California	305	13
Florida	238	68
Ohio	205	33
South Carolina	204	42
Virginia	197	105
Alabama	179	44
Mississippi	164	10
Louisiana	160	27
Pennsylvania	155	3
Oklahoma	151	91
Arkansas	145	27
Missouri	129	67
Kentucky	106	3
Illinois	102	12
Tennessee	99	6
New Jersey	74	0
Maryland	73	5
Arizona	61	23
Indiana	61	20
Washington	51	4
Colorado	48	1
Nevada	41	12
District of Columbia	40	0
West Virginia	40	0
Federal system	36	3
Massachusetts	27	0
Delaware	26	14
Connecticut	22	1
Oregon	21	2
Utah	19	6
Iowa	18	0
Kansas	15	0
Montana	9	3
New Mexico	9	1
Wyoming	8	1
Nebraska	7	3
Idaho	4	1
Vermont	4	0
South Dakota	2	1
New Hampshire	1	0

Note: Statistics on executions under civil authority have been collected by the federal government annually since 1930. These data exclude 160 executions carried out by military authorities between 1930 and 1961.

SOURCE: Tracy L. Snell, "Table 17. Number of Persons Executed, by Jurisdiction, 1930–2009," in *Capital Punishment, 2009—Statistical Tables*, U.S. Department of Justice, Office of Justice Programs, Bureau of Justice Statistics, December 2010, http://bjs.ojp.usdoj.gov/content/pub/pdf/cp09st.pdf (accessed July 5, 2011)

total of 5,047 executions were conducted under civil authority in the United States. Military authorities carried out an additional 160 executions between 1930 and 1961, the date of the last military execution.

Between 1930 and 1939 a total of 1,667 inmates were executed, the highest number of people put to death in any decade. The number of executions generally declined between the 1930s and the 1960s. In 1930, 155 executions took place, reaching a high of 199 in 1935. (See Figure 1.3

in Chapter 1.) By 1950 executions were down to 82, further dropping to 49 each in 1958 and 1959, and then rising slightly to 56 in 1960. In 1967 a 10-year moratorium (temporary suspension) of the death penalty began as states waited for the U.S. Supreme Court to determine a constitutionally acceptable procedure for carrying out the death penalty.

The moratorium ended in 1976, but no executions occurred that year. The first execution following the moratorium occurred in Utah in January 1977. In 1999, 98 inmates were put to death, the most in a one-year period after the death penalty was reinstated. (See Figure 1.3 in Chapter 1.) As shown in Table 6.19, between 1977 and the end of 2009, 1,188 people were put to death. Figure 6.4 shows the number of executions conducted by year between 1977 and 2010. Figure 6.5 shows the cumulative number of executions during this same period.

Locations of Executions

Table 6.19 shows the number of prisoners executed by state between 1930 and 2009 and between 1977 and 2009. Texas, by far, had the most executions during both periods—744 executions between 1930 and 2009 and 447 executions between 1977 and 2009.

Overall, 35 jurisdictions carried out executions between 1977 and 2009. (See Table 6.19.) The federal government executed three inmates. As mentioned previously, the largest number of executions in a single state occurred in

FIGURE 6.4

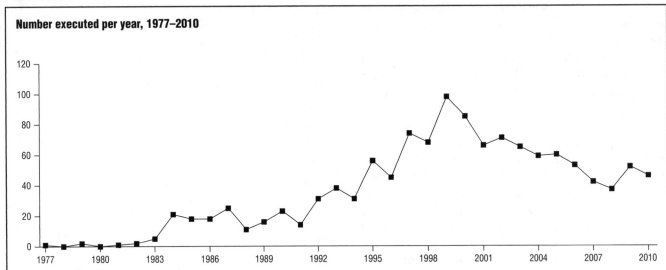

Number executed per year, 1977–2010

SOURCE: Adapted from "Number of Persons Executed in the United States, 1930–2010," in *Key Facts at a Glance*, U.S. Department of Justice, Office of Justice Programs, Bureau of Justice Statistics, January 20, 2011, http://bjs.ojp.usdoj.gov/content/glance/sheets/exe.csv (accessed July 5, 2011)

FIGURE 6.5

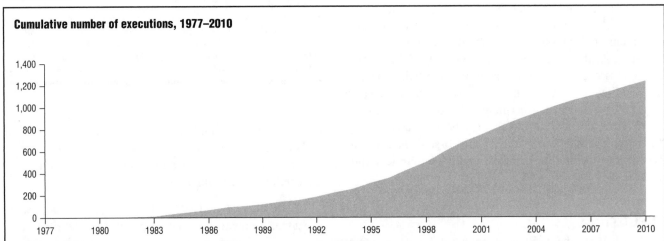

Cumulative number of executions, 1977–2010

SOURCE: Adapted from "Number of Persons Executed in the United States, 1930–2010," in *Key Facts at a Glance*, U.S. Department of Justice, Office of Justice Programs, Bureau of Justice Statistics, January 20, 2011, http://bjs.ojp.usdoj.gov/content/glance/sheets/exe.csv (accessed July 5, 2011)

FIGURE 6.6

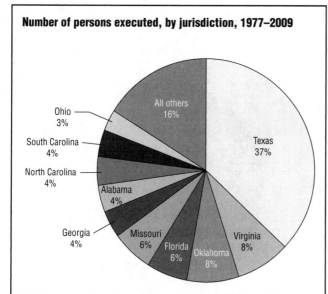

Number of persons executed, by jurisdiction, 1977–2009

Texas 37%
All others 16%
Ohio 3%
South Carolina 4%
North Carolina 4%
Alabama 4%
Georgia 4%
Missouri 6%
Florida 6%
Oklahoma 8%
Virginia 8%

SOURCE: Adapted from Tracy L. Snell, "Table 17. Number of Persons Executed, by Jurisdiction, 1930–2009," in *Capital Punishment, 2009—Statistical Tables*, U.S. Department of Justice, Office of Justice Programs, Bureau of Justice Statistics, December 2010, http://bjs.ojp .usdoj.gov/content/pub/pdf/cp09st.pdf (accessed July 5, 2011)

TABLE 6.20

Number of persons executed, by jurisdiction, 2010

Jurisdiction	Number of executions
Texas	17
Ohio	8
Alabama	5
Mississippi	3
Oklahoma	3
Virginia	3
Georgia	2
Florida	1
Louisiana	1
Arizona	1
Utah	1
Washington	1
Total	**46**

Note: Of the 46 executions carried out during this period, 44 were by lethal injection. One execution in Virginia was carried out by electrocution, and 1 in Utah was carried out by firing squad. One woman was executed in Virginia.

SOURCE: Tracy L. Snell, "Table 21. Advance Count of Executions: January 1, 2010–December 31, 2010," in *Capital Punishment, 2009—Statistical Tables*, U.S. Department of Justice, Office of Justice Programs, Bureau of Justice Statistics, December 2010, http://bjs.ojp.usdoj.gov/content/pub/pdf/cp09st .pdf (accessed July 5, 2011)

Texas (447), followed by Virginia (105), Oklahoma (91), Florida (68), Missouri (67), Georgia (46), Alabama (44), and North Carolina (43). Together, these eight states carried out just over three-quarters (77%, or 911) of all executions between 1977 and 2009. (See Figure 6.6.) The breakdown by state for executions conducted during 2010 is shown in Table 6.20. In total, 46 executions took place. Texas conducted 17 executions, by far, the most of any state.

Gender

The BJS does not provide state or yearly breakdowns of the number of women executed in the United States. However, Victor L. Streib of Ohio Northern University has been compiling information on female offenders and the death penalty in the United States since 1984. In *Death Penalty for Female Offenders: January 1, 1973, through June 30, 2009* (June 30, 2009, http://www.death penaltyinfo.org/files/FemDeathJune2009.pdf), Streib notes that between 1632 and the time of his report 568 documented executions of women had been reported. Of this number, 50 women were put to death between 1900 and 2005, the last execution of a female up until mid-2009. According to Fins, in *Death Row U.S.A.: Winter 2011*, 12 women have been executed since the 1976 reinstatement of the death penalty.

Streib notes that the first female to be put to death since the reinstatement of capital punishment was Velma Barfield, who was executed in 1984 in North Carolina for poisoning her boyfriend. The next, Karla Faye Tucker of Texas, was convicted of beating two people to death with a pickax. In 1998 Tucker became the first woman to be executed in Texas since the Civil War (1861–1865). (In 1863 Chipita Rodriguez, the last woman before Tucker to be executed in Texas, was put to death by hanging. She had been convicted of the ax murder of a horse trader.) In Florida Judias Buenoano was convicted of poisoning her husband with arsenic. She was also convicted of drowning her paraplegic son and of trying to kill her boyfriend. In 1998 Buenoano became the first woman to be executed in Florida since 1848, when a freed slave named Celia was hanged for killing her former owner.

In 2000 Betty Lou Beets was executed in Texas for killing her fifth husband. Christina Marie Riggs, convicted of killing her two children, was executed in Arkansas that same year. The last woman put to death in Arkansas before Riggs—Lavinia Burnett—was hanged in 1845 for being an accessory to murder.

In 2001 Oklahoma executed three female inmates: Wanda Jean Allen, Marilyn Kay Plantz, and Lois Nadean Smith. Allen was the first woman to be executed in Oklahoma since 1903. She was also the first African-American woman to be put to death in the United States since 1954. She was convicted of murdering her gay lover in 1988. Plantz was executed for the 1988 murder of her husband. She had hired two men to kill him. One of the men, William Bryson, was executed in June 2000 for the murder, and the other, Clinton McKimble, received a life sentence in exchange for his testimony against Plantz and Bryson. Smith was convicted of killing her son's girlfriend in 1982.

Lynda Lyon Block and her husband, George Sibley Jr., murdered a police officer in 1993. In 2002 Alabama executed Block, making her the first woman to be executed in the state in 45 years. Sibley was executed in 2005.

Aileen Wuornos, convicted of killing six men in Florida, was put to death by lethal injection in 2002. In 2005 Frances Elaine Newton of Texas was executed for murdering her husband and their two small children. As of September 2011, the last woman executed in the United States was Teresa Lewis of Virginia. She was executed by lethal injection in 2010 for paying for the murder of her husband and stepson.

RACE AND ETHNICITY

Figure 6.7 shows the racial and ethnic makeup of prisoners executed between 1977 and 2009. The majority (56%) of those executed were white, while slightly more than a third (35%) were African-American. Eight percent of the total executed were Hispanic. Other races, including Native American, accounted for 1%.

METHOD OF EXECUTION

As shown in Table 6.21, among the 1,188 prisoners executed between 1977 and 2009, 1,016 (86%) received lethal injection, followed by electrocution (156, or 13%). Eleven executions were carried out by lethal gas, three by hanging, and two by firing squad. Texas, the state with the largest number of prisoners executed, used lethal injection in all 447 cases. Virginia executed 76 inmates by lethal injection and 29 inmates by electrocution. Oklahoma put to death 91 prisoners, all by lethal injection. Table 6.22 provides a breakdown of executed inmates by method and racial and ethnic heritage between 1977 and 2009. Out of the 672 white inmates executed, the vast majority (576, or 86% of the total whites executed) were killed using lethal injection. Eighty-three of the white inmates, or 12% of the total whites exe-

FIGURE 6.7

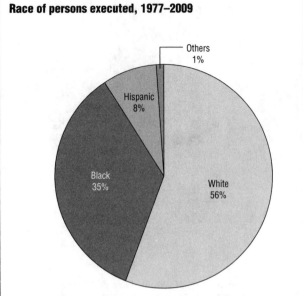

Race of persons executed, 1977–2009

SOURCE: Adapted from Tracy L. Snell, "Table 13. Number of Inmates Executed, by Race and Hispanic Origin, 1977–2009," in *Capital Punishment, 2009—Statistical Tables*, U.S. Department of Justice, Office of Justice Programs, Bureau of Justice Statistics, December 2010, http://bjs.ojp.usdoj.gov/content/pub/pdf/cp09st.pdf (accessed July 5, 2011)

cuted, were put to death by electrocution. Among African-American inmates executed, 338 (82% of the total African-Americans executed) were killed using lethal injection. Seventy of the African-American inmates (or 17% of the total African-Americans executed) went to the electric chair. Similar breakdowns are provided for other racial and ethnic backgrounds.

TABLE 6.21

Executions, by jurisdiction and method, 1977–2009

Jurisdiction	Number executed	Method of execution				
		Lethal injection	Electrocution	Lethal gas	Hanging	Firing squad
U.S. total	1,188	1,016	156	11	3	2
Federal	3	3	0	0	0	0
Alabama	44	20	24	0	0	0
Arizona	23	21	0	2	0	0
Arkansas	27	26	1	0	0	0
California	13	11	0	2	0	0
Colorado	1	1	0	0	0	0
Connecticut	1	1	0	0	0	0
Delaware	14	13	0	0	1	0
Florida	68	24	44	0	0	0
Georgia	46	23	23	0	0	0
Idaho	1	1	0	0	0	0
Illinois	12	12	0	0	0	0
Indiana	20	17	3	0	0	0
Kentucky	3	2	1	0	0	0
Louisiana	27	7	20	0	0	0
Maryland	5	5	0	0	0	0
Mississippi	10	6	0	4	0	0
Missouri	67	67	0	0	0	0
Montana	3	3	0	0	0	0
Nebraska	3	0	3	0	0	0
Nevada	12	11	0	1	0	0
New Mexico	1	1	0	0	0	0
North Carolina	43	41	0	2	0	0
Ohio	33	33	0	0	0	0
Oklahoma	91	91	0	0	0	0
Oregon	2	2	0	0	0	0
Pennsylvania	3	3	0	0	0	0
South Carolina	42	35	7	0	0	0
South Dakota	1	1	0	0	0	0
Tennessee	6	5	1	0	0	0
Texas	447	447	0	0	0	0
Utah	6	4	0	0	0	2
Virginia	105	76	29	0	0	0
Washington	4	2	0	0	2	0
Wyoming	1	1	0	0	0	0

Note: In 1972, the U.S. Supreme Court invalidated capital punishment statutes in several states (*Furman v. Georgia*, 408 U.S. 238 [1972]), effecting a moratorium on executions. Executions resumed in 1977 when the Supreme Court found that revisions to several state statutes had effectively addressed the issues previously held unconstitutional (*Gregg v. Georgia*, 428 U.S. 153 [1976] and its companion cases).

SOURCE: Tracy L. Snell, "Table 16. Number of Executions, by Jurisdiction and Method, 1977–2009," in *Capital Punishment, 2009—Statistical Tables*, U.S. Department of Justice, Office of Justice Programs, Bureau of Justice Statistics, December 2010, http://bjs.ojp.usdoj.gov/content/pub/pdf/cp09st.pdf (accessed July 5, 2011)

TABLE 6.22

Number of persons executed, by race, Hispanic origin, and method, 1977–2009

Method of execution	Number of persons executed				
	White*	Black*	Hispanic	American Indian*	Asian*
Total	672	411	91	8	6
Lethal injection	576	338	89	7	6
Electrocution	83	70	2	1	0
Lethal gas	8	3	0	0	0
Hanging	3	0	0	0	0
Firing squad	2	0	0	0	0

Note: In 1972, the U.S. Supreme Court invalidated capital punishment statutes in several states (*Furman v. Georgia*, 408 U.S. 238 [1972]), effecting a moratorium on executions. Executions resumed in 1977 when the Supreme Court found that revisions to several state statutes had effectively addressed the issues previously held unconstitutional (*Gregg v. Georgia*, 428 U.S. 153 [1976] and its companion cases).
*Excludes persons of Hispanic/Latino origin.

SOURCE: Tracy L. Snell, "Table 15. Number of Persons Executed, by Race, Hispanic Origin, and Method, 1977–2009," in *Capital Punishment, 2009—Statistical Tables*, U.S. Department of Justice, Office of Justice Programs, Bureau of Justice Statistics, December 2010, http://bjs.ojp.usdoj.gov/content/pub/pdf/cp09st.pdf (accessed July 5, 2011)

CHAPTER 7
ISSUES OF FAIRNESS

In February 1967 the President's Commission on Law Enforcement and Administration of Justice published the report *The Challenge of Crime in a Free Society* (http://www.ncjrs.gov/pdffiles1/nij/42.pdf), which examined in detail many aspects of the nation's criminal justice system. In regards to capital punishment, the commission concluded, "Finally there is evidence that the imposition of the death sentence and the exercise of dispensing power by the courts and the executive follow discriminatory patterns. The death sentence is disproportionately imposed and carried out on the poor, the Negro, and the members of unpopular groups." This statement was quoted by Justice William O. Douglas (1898–1980) of the U.S. Supreme Court in his concurring opinion in *Furman v. Georgia* (408 U.S. 238 [1972]), in which the court ruled that capital punishment was unconstitutional. As described in Chapter 1, this landmark decision resulted in major reforms in state laws in an effort to create a more uniform death penalty system that eliminates arbitrary and discriminatory factors in capital sentencing.

In the 21st century there are still many concerns about the fairness with which the death penalty is applied in the United States. Capital punishment opponents raise fairness challenges that avoid emotionally charged arguments about the moral rightness or wrongness of capital punishment to focus on more legally definable issues, such as discrimination and the denial of legal rights. An enduring idea of U.S. jurisprudence (the philosophy of law) is that "justice is blind." In other words, the merits of a criminal case should be decided without regard to the race, ethnicity, or economic status of the accused. Death penalty opponents argue that death sentences are applied unfairly and provide evidence of geographical and racial bias and poor legal representation. These factors, they suggest, prove that the U.S. capital punishment system is flawed and should be eliminated. Death penalty advocates counter that the judicial process contains adequate safeguards to ensure that defendants receive fair trials. They believe that

if any discrepancies do exist in capital convictions and sentences, they should be remedied by applying the death penalty more often, not less often.

GEOGRAPHICAL DISPARITIES

Capital punishment is supposed to be applied in a uniform manner across the jurisdictions in which it is allowed. Statistics, however, indicate that there are huge geographical differences in the numbers of death sentences that are imposed and carried out.

Differences between Death Penalty States

As shown in Table 7.1, between 1973 and 2009, 8,115 inmates were sentenced to death across the nation. Nearly half were sentenced in only five states: Texas (1,040, or 13% of the total), Florida (977, or 12%), California (927, or 11%), North Carolina (528, or 7%), and Alabama (412, or 5%). Likewise, Figure 6.6 in Chapter 6 shows that two-thirds (65%) of the 1,188 executions conducted between 1977 and 2009 were concentrated in only a handful of states: Texas (37%), Virginia (8%), Oklahoma (8%), Florida (6%), and Missouri (6%). On a regional basis, the South had more inmates on state death row than any other region as of December 31, 2009. (See Table 7.2.) Of the 3,118 prisoners under sentence of death at that time, more than half (1,656, or 53% of the total) were in southern states. The West had 965 (31%) death row inmates, followed by the Midwest (268, or 9%) and the Northeast (229 or 7%).

Death penalty opponents often point to these differences between states (and between regions) as proof that capital punishment is applied inconsistently and unfairly. In particular, the large death sentencing and execution rates in southern states are often seen as indicators of lingering racial bias against African-Americans, as will be explained later in this chapter. Critics counter that legitimate factors can account for varying death penalty rates between states and between regions. These include variations in murder rates and the

TABLE 7.1

Total number sentenced to death, by jurisdiction, 1973–2009

Total sentenced to death, 1973–2009	
U.S. total	**8,115**
Texas	1,040
Florida	977
California	927
North Carolina	528
Alabama	412
Ohio	401
Pennsylvania	399
Oklahoma	350
Georgia	320
Illinois	307
Arizona	286
Louisiana	238
Tennessee	221
South Carolina	203
Mississippi	190
Missouri	182
Virginia	150
Nevada	147
Arkansas	110
Indiana	100
Kentucky	81
Federal	65
Oregon	58
Delaware	56
Maryland	53
New Jersey	52
Idaho	42
Washington	38
Nebraska	32
New Mexico	28
Utah	27
Colorado	21
Montana	15
Connecticut	13
Kansas	12
Wyoming	12
New York	10
South Dakota	5
Massachusetts	4
Rhode Island	2
New Hampshire	1

SOURCE: Adapted from "Table 20. Number Sentenced to Death and Number of Removals, by Jurisdiction and Reason for Removal, 1973–2009," in *Capital Punishment, 2009—Statistical Tables*, U.S. Department of Justice, Office of Justice Programs, Bureau of Justice Statistics, December 2010, http://bjs.ojp.usdoj.gov/content/pub/pdf/cp09st.pdf (accessed July 5, 2011)

TABLE 7.2

Prisoners on death row, by jurisdiction, region, and race, December 31, 2009

Region and jurisdiction	Prisoners under sentence of death, 12/31/09		
	Total[a]	White[b]	Black[b]
U.S. total	**3,173**	**1,780**	**1,317**
Federal[c]	55	26	28
State	3,118	1,754	1,289
Northeast	**229**	**84**	**136**
Connecticut	10	4	6
New Hampshire	1	0	1
New York	0	0	0
Pennsylvania	218	80	129
Midwest	**268**	**144**	**121**
Illinois	16	11	5
Indiana	14	11	3
Kansas	9	5	4
Missouri	51	29	22
Nebraska	11	8	2
Ohio	165	78	85
South Dakota	2	2	0
South	**1,656**	**909**	**724**
Alabama	200	103	96
Arkansas	40	16	24
Delaware	17	9	8
Florida	389	254	135
Georgia	101	52	48
Kentucky	35	29	6
Louisiana	83	29	53
Maryland	5	1	4
Mississippi	60	28	31
North Carolina	159	65	85
Oklahoma	79	43	32
South Carolina	55	25	30
Tennessee	89	49	38
Texas	331	200	127
Virginia	13	6	7
West	**965**	**617**	**308**
Arizona	131	109	17
California	684	402	250
Colorado	2	0	2
Idaho	14	14	0
Montana	2	2	0
Nevada	80	47	32
New Mexico	2	2	0
Oregon	31	27	3
Utah	10	8	1
Washington	8	5	3
Wyoming	1	1	0

Note: Some figures shown for yearend 2008 are revised from those reported in *Capital Punishment, 2008—Statistical Tables*, NCJ 228662. The revised figures include 13 inmates who were either reported late to the National Prisoner Statistics program or were not in custody of state correctional authorities on December 31, 2008 (4 in Ohio, 3 in Texas, 2 in Indiana, and 1 each in Nebraska, Florida, Tennessee, and Nevada). The revised figures also exclude 10 inmates who were relieved of a death sentence before December 31, 2008 (3 in Idaho, and 1 each in Delaware, Oklahoma, Texas, Arizona, California, Nevada, and Oregon).
[a]Includes American Indians, Alaska Natives, Asians, Native Hawaiians, and other Pacific Islanders.
[b]The reporting of race and Hispanic origin differs from that presented in other tables in this document. In this table, counts of white and black inmates include persons of Hispanic/Latino origin.
[c]Excludes persons held under armed forces jurisdiction with a military death sentence for murder.

SOURCE: Adapted from Tracy L. Snell, "Table 4. Prisoners under Sentence of Death, by Region, Jurisdiction, and Race, 2008 and 2009," in *Capital Punishment, 2009—Statistical Tables*, U.S. Department of Justice, Office of Justice Programs, Bureau of Justice Statistics, December 2010, http://bjs.ojp.usdoj.gov/content/pub/pdf/cp09st.pdf (accessed July 5, 2011)

number of aggravating factors that make defendants eligible for a death sentence. Certainly, public opinion also plays a role, with some states and regions showing greater willingness than others to use capital punishment.

Differences within Death Penalty States

State capital cases are prosecuted at the local level, that is, by county or city prosecutors, and are decided by juries made up of local residents. During a criminal trial these decision makers typically reflect the attitudes about crime and punishment that are prominent in their local areas. Thus, death penalty sentencing rates can (and do) vary significantly between local jurisdictions within a state. In "The Geography of the Death Penalty" (October 17, 2010, http://www.unc.edu/~fbaum/Innocence/NC/Baumgartner-geography-of-capital-punishment-oct-17-2010.pdf), Frank

R. Baumgartner of the University of North Carolina presents geographical data regarding the 1,229 executions that were conducted in the United States between 1977 and October 2010. He states that only 454 counties out of the 3,146 total counties in death penalty states "have carried out any executions." Furthermore, only 14 counties accounted for nearly one-third (30%) of the national execution total. Harris County in southeastern Texas is the undisputed death penalty capital of the nation; Houston is the county seat. According to Baumgartner, Harris County was responsible for 115 (9%) of the total executions between 1977 and October 2010, followed by Dallas County, Texas (44 executions), Oklahoma County, Oklahoma (36 executions), Tarrant County, Texas (34 executions), and Bexar County, Texas (31 executions). The Texas Department of Corrections provides in "County of Conviction for Offenders on Death Row" (http://www.tdcj.state.tx.us/stat/countyconviction.htm) a breakdown by county of conviction for the 313 inmates on the state's death row as of July 2011. Of these, 106 inmates (34%) were convicted in Harris County.

In "See Where Murderers Most Often Get the Death Penalty" (*Sacramento Bee*, March 21, 2011), Phillip Reese provides a map showing large disparities between California counties regarding death sentences that were handed out per 100 homicide arrests between 2000 and 2009. (It should be noted that not all homicide arrests end in homicide convictions, and not all homicides are capital cases.) Reese includes excerpts from an interview that was conducted in 2009 with Rod Pacheco, the former district attorney of Riverside County, a county with one of the highest death sentence rates in the state. Between 2000 and 2009 Riverside County had 752 homicide arrests and handed out 28 death sentences. By contrast, San Francisco County had 288 homicide arrests and no death sentences. Pacheco noted, "The people here have a very different view of public safety than the people in San Francisco."

Death penalty opponents point to county disparities in death sentences as evidence that capital punishment is applied unevenly and unfairly. Critics disagree, noting that county death sentencing rates vary based on differing murder rates, financial resources (death penalty cases are more expensive to prosecute than noncapital homicides), and local attitudes about crime and punishment.

Differences between Federal Judicial Districts

Table 5.6 in Chapter 5 lists dozens of capital offenses that are prosecuted at the federal level. A federal death penalty trial is typically conducted in the federal judicial district in which the crime occurred. As of September 2011, the country was divided into 94 federal judicial districts. Like the nation's counties, these federal judicial districts show large geographic disparities in death sentencing. In "The Racial Geography of the Federal Death Penalty" (*Washington Law Review*, vol. 85, no. 3, 2010),

G. Ben Cohen and Robert J. Smith present data indicating that only six of the districts accounted for a third of all 460 death-authorized cases since 1988. Likewise, only seven of the districts accounted for about 40% of the 57 inmates on federal death row as of August 2010. Cohen and Smith suggest that the discrepancy cannot be explained by differences in murder rates between jurisdictions, noting that "while there is no shortage of death-eligible murders in the United States each year, the number of murders in a particular location bears little relationship to the number of defendants from that jurisdiction who are sentenced to death federally." Instead, they believe the discrepancy is directly related to the racial demographics of the federal judicial districts, as will be explained in the next section.

RACIAL BIAS IN THE DEATH PENALTY?

One of the most contentious and long-standing issues within the death penalty debate is race. Since the 1980s numerous statistical studies have been conducted to examine the role of racial bias in the administration of the death penalty. In general, these studies have found almost no evidence of racial bias based solely on the race of the defendant (the accused). Even capital punishment opponents agree that, overall, the reforms enacted since the *Furman v. Georgia* decision have eliminated this type of bias. The Constitution Project, a nonprofit organization based in Washington, D.C., and a vocal critic of the nation's capital punishment system, notes in "Death Penalty" (2010, (http://www.constitutionproject.org/cjp/death penalty.php) that "procedural safeguards are deeply flawed and assurances of fundamental fairness are lacking." In a November 2007 radio interview with PBS's *NewsHour* (http://www.pbs.org/newshour/insider/social_issues/july-dec07/deathpenalty_1107.html), Virginia Sloan of the Constitution Project stated that studies have not shown the race of the defendant to be a "major factor" in death penalty decisions. Instead, death penalty opponents argue that many studies demonstrate that the race of the victim is a major factor in capital cases, specifically, that defendants who kill white victims are more likely to get the death penalty than defendants who kill African-American victims.

Since the 1980s many statistical studies at the national and state levels have been published that show this bias. One of the most famous is the Baldus study.

The Baldus Study

In 1986 lawyers appealing the case of Warren McCleskey (1947?–1991), a convicted murderer, brought before the U.S. Supreme Court the Baldus study, an analysis of 2,000 cases in Georgia during the 1970s by David C. Baldus, Charles A. Pulanski Jr., and George Woodworth. (The study actually consisted of two studies: "Comparative Review of Death Sentences: An Empirical Study of the Georgia Experience" [*Journal of Criminal Law and Criminology*, vol. 74, no. 3, Autumn 1983] and "Monitoring and

Evaluating Contemporary Death Sentencing Systems: Lessons from Georgia" [*University of California Davis Law Review*, vol. 18, no. 1375, 1985].)

This study found that African-American defendants who were convicted of killing whites were more likely to receive death sentences than white murderers or African-Americans who had killed African-Americans. In *McCleskey v. Kemp* (481 U.S. 279 [1987]), the justices rejected McCleskey's appeal by noting that:

> To evaluate McCleskey's challenge, we must examine exactly what the Baldus study may show. Even Professor Baldus does not contend that his statistics prove that race enters into any capital sentencing decisions, or that race was a factor in McCleskey's particular case. Statistics, at most, may show only a likelihood that a particular factor entered into some decisions. There is, of course, some risk of racial prejudice influencing a jury's decision in a criminal case. There are similar risks that other kinds of prejudice will influence other criminal trials.... The question "is at what point that risk becomes constitutionally unacceptable." ...McCleskey asks us to accept the likelihood allegedly shown by the Baldus study as the constitutional measure of an unacceptable risk of racial prejudice influencing capital sentencing decisions. This we decline to do.

ANOTHER BALDUS STUDY. David C. Baldus et al. find in "Racial Discrimination and the Death Penalty in the Post-*Furman* Era: An Empirical and Legal Analysis with Recent Findings from Philadelphia" (*Cornell Law Review*, vol. 83, 1998) evidence of race-of-victim disparities in 26 out of 29 death penalty states. The researchers note that the race of the victim was related to whether capital punishment was imposed. A defendant was more likely to receive the death penalty if the victim was white than if the victim was African-American.

The U.S. General Accounting Office Study

These studies were consistent with a February 1990 U.S. government study of capital punishment. The U.S. General Accounting Office (GAO; now the U.S. Government Accountability Office), in *Death Penalty Sentencing: Research Indicates Pattern of Racial Disparities* (http://archive.gao.gov/t2pbat11/140845.pdf), reviewed 28 studies on race and the death penalty. The GAO reported that "in 82% of the studies, the race of the victim was found to influence the likelihood of being charged with capital murder or receiving the death penalty." The GAO found that when the victim was white, the defendant, whether white or African-American, was more likely to get the death sentence.

The GAO added that in the small number of horrendous murders, death sentences were more likely to be imposed, regardless of race. Nevertheless, when the offender killed a person while robbing the person or when the murderer had a previous record, the race of the victim played a role. The

GAO also explained that for crimes of passion, the convicted person (regardless of race) rarely received the death penalty.

U.S. Department of Justice Study of Racial and Ethnic Bias, 2000

In July 2000 President Bill Clinton (1946–) ordered the U.S. Department of Justice to review the administration of the federal death penalty system. This order came in the aftermath of a request for clemency by Juan Raul Garza (c. 1957–2001), who was granted a stay by President Clinton, but who was ultimately executed in June 2001. Garza's lawyer contended that it was unfair to execute his client because the federal death penalty discriminated against members of minorities.

In September 2000 the Justice Department released *The Federal Death Penalty System: A Statistical Survey (1988–2000)* (http://www.usdoj.gov/dag/pubdoc/dpsurvey .html), which provided information on the federal death penalty since the passage of the first federal capital punishment law in 1988 (the Anti-Drug Abuse Act). From 1988 to 1994 prosecutors in the 94 federal districts were required to submit to the U.S. attorney general for review and approval only those cases that the attorney general deemed worthy for the death penalty. During this period the prosecutors sought the death penalty in 52 cases and received authorization from the attorney general in 47 cases.

In 1995 the Justice Department adopted a new protocol that required U.S. attorneys to submit for review all cases in which a defendant was charged with a crime subject to the death penalty, regardless of whether they intended to seek authorization to pursue the death penalty. These cases were first reviewed by the attorney general's Review Committee on Capital Cases, a committee of senior Justice Department lawyers.

Between January 27, 1995, and July 20, 2000, at every phase of the federal process, minority defendants were overrepresented. Of the 682 defendants whose cases were submitted for review by federal prosecutors, 47.5% were African-American, 28.6% were Hispanic, and 19.6% were white. The prosecutors recommended seeking the death penalty for 183 out of the 682 cases submitted for review. Of these 183 cases, two-thirds were members of minorities (44.3% were African-American and 21.3% were Hispanic). The attorney general reviewed 588 of the cases and authorized the U.S. attorneys to seek the death penalty in 159 cases. Of the 159 defendants, 44.7% were African-American and 20.1% were Hispanic. Only 27.7% were white.

Racial Disparity in Plea Bargaining?

It should be noted that the attorney general's decision to seek the death penalty may be changed up until the jury has returned a sentencing verdict. This change may be sought by the defense lawyer, the U.S. attorney, the Review Committee, or the attorney general. A plea agreement is one avenue that may result in the withdrawal of the death penalty. This means that the defendant enters into an agreement with the U.S. attorney resulting in a guilty plea, saving him or her from the death penalty. From 1995 to 2000, after the attorney general sought the death penalty for 159 defendants, 51 defendants entered into plea agreements. Almost twice as many white defendants (48%, or 21 out of 44) as African-American defendants (25%, or 18 out of 71) received a plea agreement. About 28% (9 out of 32) of Hispanic defendants entered into a plea agreement.

GOVERNMENT DEFENDS DATA. The National Institute of Justice (NIJ) observes in *Research into the Investigation and Prosecution of Homicide: Examining the Federal Death Penalty System* (July 20, 2001, http://www .ncjrs.gov/pdffiles1/nij/sl000490.pdf) that, "generally speaking, once submitted for review [to obtain a death penalty authorization], minorities proceeded to the next stages in the death penalty process at lower rates than whites." The NIJ reports that the attorney general authorized the death penalty for 38% (44 out of 115) of white defendants being considered, compared with 25% (71 out of 287) of African-American defendants and 20% (32 out of 160) of Hispanic defendants.

Justice Department Supplemental Study of Racial and Ethnic Bias, 2001

In June 2001 the Justice Department released a supplement to the September 2000 report—*The Federal Death Penalty System: Supplementary Data, Analysis, and Revised Protocols for Capital Case Review* (http://www.usdoj.gov/ dag/pubdoc/deathpenaltystudy.htm). That same month the U.S. attorney general John D. Ashcroft (1942–) told the Committee on the Judiciary of the U.S. House of Representatives that the report confirmed that the subsequent study of the administration of the federal death penalty showed no indication of racial or ethnic bias.

The follow-up study had been ordered by his predecessor, U.S. attorney general Janet Reno (1938–). Besides the 682 cases submitted by federal prosecutors for review in the first study of the federal death penalty, another 291 cases were analyzed, for a total of 973 cases. These included cases that should have been submitted for review for the first report but were not, those in which the defendant eventually entered into a plea agreement for a lesser sentence, and cases in which the death penalty could have been sought but was not. Among the 973 defendants, 408 (42%) were African-American, 350 (36%) were Hispanic, and 166 (17%) were white.

According to the supplement, of the 973 defendants who were eligible for capital charges between 1995 and 2000, federal prosecutors requested authorization to pursue the death penalty against 81% of whites, 79% of African-Americans, and 56% of Hispanics. The attorney general ultimately authorized seeking the death penalty for 27% of the white defendants, 17% of the African-American defendants, and 9% of the Hispanic defendants.

Critics of the supplementary report pointed out that the second federal review failed to address many issues. In "Federal Death Row: Is It Really Color-Blind? Analysis of June 6 Department of Justice Report on the Federal Death Penalty" (June 14, 2001, http://www.aclu.org/capital/ general/10574pub20010614.html), the American Civil Liberties Union (ACLU) noted that, unlike the September 2000 Justice Department report, the June 2001 report did not include information on whether the supplemental 291 cases were from all or just some districts and, therefore, whether or not they represented all the death penalty–eligible cases between 1995 and 2000. The ACLU also indicated that even though the report found that federal prosecutors were less likely to submit cases with African-American and Hispanic defendants to the attorney general for death penalty authorizations and that the attorney general authorized capital punishment for a higher proportion of whites than African-Americans and Hispanics, there was no information about the decision-making process behind prosecuting on the federal level and offering of plea agreements.

A Kentucky Study

In 1992 the Kentucky legislature commissioned a report on racial bias in the state's capital punishment system. The result was *Race and the Death Penalty in Kentucky Murder Trials, 1976–1991: A Study of Racial Bias as a Factor in Capital Sentencing* (September 1993) by Thomas J. Keil and Gennaro F. Vito. Vito summarizes the findings of the study in "The Racial Justice Act in Kentucky" (*Northern Kentucky Law Review*, vol. 37, no. 2, 2010). Vito notes that the study identified four murder case factors that tended to elicit death penalty sentences: more than one victim, murders committed to "silence" someone, more than one aggravating circumstance, and murders in which white victims were killed by African-American defendants. He states that the study concluded "that juries considered the killing of a white by a black more deserving of the death penalty than other offender/victim racial combinations."

KENTUCKY RACIAL JUSTICE ACT OF 1998. In March 1998 Kentucky passed legislation that allows defendants to use statistical studies on racial bias in the state's capital punishment cases to argue that such bias affected their sentence. Vito notes that racial bias claims must be made by the defense prior to the start of the trial and that the prosecution can rebut any bias evidence that is presented by the defense.

A North Carolina Study

In April 2001 Isaac Unah and John Charles Boger of the University of North Carolina released the most comprehensive study of North Carolina's death penalty system in the state's history: *Race and the Death Penalty in North Carolina—An Empirical Analysis: 1993–1997* (http://www.deathpenaltyinfo.org/race-and-death-penalty-north-carolina). The researchers studied 3,990 homicide cases that occurred in North Carolina between January 1, 1993, and December 31, 1997, including defendants who received death sentences, as well as those sentenced to life imprisonment.

On first analysis of all homicide cases, Unah and Boger found that, overall, the death-sentencing rate for white victims (3.7%) was almost twice as high as the rate where the victims were nonwhite (1.9%). In addition, the death-sentencing rate for nonwhite defendants/white victims (6.4%) was over two times higher than the rate for white defendants/white victims (2.6%).

When Unah and Boger confined their investigation to death-eligible cases (those imposing the death penalty, such as a case involving the murder of a police officer), race determined whether the defendant received the death sentence. The death-sentencing rate in all death-eligible cases was much higher in white-victim cases (8%) than in nonwhite-victim cases (4.7%). As with all cases, nonwhite defendants in white-victim homicides received the death sentence at a higher rate (11.6%) than white defendants who murdered whites (6.1%).

After the initial analysis, Unah and Boger performed a more comprehensive investigation involving 502 defendants, collecting 113 factors about each crime. These factors included the circumstances of the homicide, the evidence, the charges brought against the defendant, the character and background of the defendant and the victim, the presence or absence of aggravating or mitigating circumstances as specified under the law, as well as the presence or absence of aggravating or mitigating circumstances not specified under the law. The researchers also looked into other factors that might have influenced the imposition of the death penalty, such as the coming reelection of the district attorney prosecuting the crime. Unah and Boger found that race—specifically the race of the victim—played a role in the imposition of capital punishment in North Carolina between 1993 and 1997. On average, the odds of receiving the death penalty were increased by a factor of 3.5 times when the victim was white.

NORTH CAROLINA RACIAL JUSTICE ACT OF 2009. In August 2009 North Carolina passed legislation allowing death row inmates the right to use county prosecutorial statistics to prove that bias was a factor in their death penalty conviction, thus gaining the right to have a sentence converted to life imprisonment. Simply put, if race was found to be a contributing factor in a death penalty case, then the conviction would not stand. Promoters of the bill saw it as a way to overcome racial disparities in death sentences. Opponents insisted it was a way to effectively end the death penalty in North Carolina and maintained that

the argument from statistics was flawed: just because disproportionately more men than women were under a death sentence, they noted, did not prove a prosecutorial bias against men. In addition, some observers expected all 163 death row inmates in North Carolina at the time to pursue an appeal based on the new statute, a caseload that would overtax the state's legal system and decimate the criminal justice budget.

Anne Blythe reports in "Racial Justice Act for Death Row Inmates Survives Court Challenge" (*News and Observer* [Raleigh, North Carolina], February 10, 2011) that county prosecutors challenged the law in court in February 2011, arguing that it is too broad and does not specify the types of racial bias that should be considered. The suit was rejected. Blythe notes that 154 of the state's inmates had cases pending that alleged racial bias under the act. In June 2011 the North Carolina House of Representatives voted to repeal the act; however, the North Carolina Senate failed to vote on the measure before adjourning. According to the article "Repeal of NC Racial Bias Review Delayed by Senate" (Associated Press, June 17, 2011), a repeal of the act is expected to be reconsidered by the North Carolina legislature in May 2012.

A Maryland Study

In January 2003 Raymond Paternoster et al. released *An Empirical Analysis of Maryland's Death Sentencing System with Respect to the Influence of Race and Legal Jurisdiction* (http://www.newsdesk.umd.edu/pdf/finalrep.pdf), a state-commissioned study of the use of the death penalty in Maryland. The researchers reviewed 1,311 death-eligible cases out of 6,000 murder cases that were prosecuted between 1978 and 1999. Of the 1,311 death-eligible cases, state attorneys filed a formal notice to seek the death penalty in 353 (27%) cases. Of the 353 cases, state attorneys dropped the death penalty notice in 140 (40%) cases. The death penalty notice was retained in 213 (60%) cases, out of which 180 (84%) cases proceeded to the penalty phase.

Paternoster et al. examined the four decision stages in the death penalty sentencing system: the prosecutor's decision to seek the death penalty, the prosecutor's decision to drop or stick with the death penalty notice, the case's proceeding to a penalty trial, and the court's decision to impose the death sentence. The researchers "found no evidence that the race of the defendant matter[ed] in the processing of capital cases in the state." However, the race of the victim had an impact on whether the prosecutor sought the death penalty. Prosecutors were more likely to seek the death penalty for killers of white victims and were more likely to stick with their death penalty notification when the victims were white.

The study also revealed that jurisdictions affected whether state attorneys sought the death penalty. For example, a defendant in Baltimore County was 13 times more likely to face the death penalty and nearly 23 times more likely to receive a sentence of death than a defendant in a similar case in Baltimore City.

A California Study

Glenn L. Pierce and Michael L. Radelet reviewed in "The Impact of Legally Inappropriate Factors on Death Sentencing for California Homicides, 1990–99" (*Santa Clara Law Review*, vol. 46, no. 1, 2005) data from all homicides that were committed in California between 1990 and 1999 and compared those that did and did not result in a death sentence. To examine any potential racial biases in conviction and sentencing, they excluded cases in which killers had multiple victims of different races.

Pierce and Radelet found that convicted murderers with non-Hispanic white victims were 4.7 times more likely to receive a death sentence than those who killed Latinos and 3.7 times more likely to receive a death sentence than those who killed African-Americans.

A 2004 National Study

In "Explaining Death Row's Population and Racial Composition" (*Journal of Empirical Legal Studies*, vol. 1, no. 1, March 2004), John Blume, Theodore Eisenberg, and Martin T. Wells compared 23 years of death row statistics to state murder rates. They found that between 1977 and 1999 the number of death row inmates in most states, including those with a reputation for sending a high number of defendants to death row, was nearly proportional to the number of murders in that state.

Overall, the number of inmates on death row in each state was between 0.4% (Colorado) and 6% (Nevada) of murders in that state, and the mean (average) "death sentencing rate" among all states was 2.2%. Despite having the highest number of executions per year, Texas came in below this average with a death row to murder ratio of 2%. Even though Texas juries sentenced 776 people to death row, a total of 37,879 murders had been committed during the study period. Florida, which had a total death row population of 735 inmates, had experienced 21,837 murders and a death sentencing rate of 3.4%. By contrast, Nevada had 124 death row inmates, but only 2,072 murders, giving the state a death sentencing rate three times that of Texas. California, Maryland, New Mexico, Virginia, and Washington all had death sentencing rates below 1.5%.

To explain the discrepancy between states, Blume, Eisenberg, and Wells looked at the states' statutes, politics, and other factors that might influence sentencing rates. They found that death sentencing rates were nearly twice as high in states where a judge handed out the sentence as opposed to a jury (4.1% versus 2.1%). State statutes also made a big difference. States with more open-ended statutes that allowed a jury to base their verdicts on subjective standards, such as the heinousness of the murder, had

sentencing rates of 2.7%. Sentencing rates dropped to 1.9% in states where specific murders, such as the murder of a pregnant woman or police officer, warranted the death sentence.

Blume, Eisenberg, and Wells then compared the race of the death row inmates to the number of murders committed by race across the country. Nationwide, African-Americans committed 51.5% of murders between 1977 and 1999, but they made up only 41.3% of death row. The researchers analyzed data from seven states—Georgia, Indiana, Maryland, Nevada, Pennsylvania, South Carolina, and Virginia—to determine why these percentages did not match.

Generally, what Blume, Eisenberg, and Wells found was that juries give the death sentence to a far smaller percentage of African-American murderers when the victim was also African-American, rather than white. In South Carolina, for instance, only 0.3% of African-Americans who killed African-Americans received the death penalty, whereas 6.8% of African-Americans who murdered whites were sentenced to death. Because 94% of African-American homicide victims were killed by African-Americans, the percentage of African-Americans on death row tended to be lower than the percentage of African-American murderers. Even though the researchers speculated that racism may figure into these percentages, they also believed that African-American juries in communities with a great deal of "black-on-black" crime were less likely to hand out the death sentence.

An Ohio Study

The Ohio Associated Press (AP) published an extensive study on the Ohio death penalty system in May 2005. The news organization reviewed 2,543 reported cases in which prisoners were brought up on capital charges between 1981 and 2002. This number was narrowed to 1,936 after analysts weeded out charges that were dismissed or erroneously reported. Roughly 270 of the indictments led to a death sentence. The AP analyzed the indictments to find any discrepancies in sentencing involving race, sex, or jurisdiction. The results were presented by Andrew Welsh-Huggins, in "Death Penalty Unequal" (Associated Press, May 7, 2005); Kate Roberts, in "Capital Cases Hard for Smaller Counties" (Associated Press, May 8, 2005); and John Seewer, in "Two Killers; One Spared" (Associated Press, May 9, 2005).

With respect to race, those indicted (formally accused) of capital murder in Ohio were much more likely to receive the death sentence if the victim was white. Some 17.9% of indictments led to a death sentence if the victim was white, as opposed to 8.5% if the victim was African-American. However, unlike the Baldus study, these percentages were not dependent on the race of the defendant. In cases where the offender and victim were both white, 18.3% of offenders received the death sentence. Roughly the same number of African-American offenders (17.9%) were sentenced to death if the victim was white. If the victim was African-American, 8.4% of African-American offenders were sentenced to death, compared with 8.7% of white offenders.

Jurisdiction had a bigger impact than race on who received the death sentence in Ohio. The AP looked at indictments by county and compared the numbers with those aspects of each county that might influence death penalty verdicts. The news organization found that the politics of a county played a significant role in determining the percentage of defendants who received the death penalty. Hamilton County (Cincinnati metropolitan area) and Cuyahoga County (Cleveland metropolitan area) are both large counties that paid their defense attorneys reasonably well. However, only 8% of all capital cases ended with a death sentence in Democratic Cuyahoga County, as opposed to 43% in the largely Republican Hamilton County.

The Ohio report also found that compensation for lawyers who represent poor defendants varied drastically from county to county. The limits ranged from $3,000 maximum per death penalty case in rural Coshocton County (east-central Ohio) up to $75,000 in the more affluent Montgomery County (Dayton metropolitan area). Generally, death penalty cases place an enormous strain on the resources of a small county court as opposed to a large county court. Rural judges reported having to dedicate all their resources for several months when capital cases came through their courts.

Death Penalty Advocates Speak about the Race Issue

The Criminal Justice Legal Foundation (CJLF) is a California-based group that supports capital punishment. Kent S. Scheidegger of the CJLF points out in *Mend It, Don't End It: A Report to the Connecticut General Assembly on Capital Punishment* (April 2011, http://www.cjlf.org/ deathpenalty/ConnDPReport2011.pdf) that the statistical models used in the 1980s-era Baldus study were found to be flawed by the federal district court that heard the *McCleskey v. Kemp* case before it was ultimately appealed to the Supreme Court. The latter assumed that the study was valid, but rejected the claim that it proved bias against McCleskey.

Scheidegger argues that many of the studies that appear to show a race-of-victim bias fail to take into account key factors that affect death penalty sentencing decisions: the strength of the evidence in the case, the heinousness of the crime, the criminal status of the victim (e.g., the murder of a fellow drug dealer versus the murder of an innocent victim), and the jurisdiction. Jurisdictional factors, in particular, are cited by death penalty advocates as the main cause of perceived race-of-victim bias.

According to Scheidegger, polls show that capital punishment receives higher support from whites than from African-Americans. Thus, the death penalty is applied less often in predominantly African-American jurisdictions, even though these areas have large numbers of African-American murder victims. Scheidegger states, "We should not be surprised if an urban community jaded by chronic violence defines the worst murders more restrictively than a community where violence is comparatively rare."

Charles Lane notes in *Stay of Execution: Saving the Death Penalty* (2010) that "above all, prosecutors do not seek the death penalty unless they think they can actually persuade a jury to impose it. In jurisdictions with large African-American populations, where most black-on-black crime occurs, persuading a jury to sentence a defendant to death is relatively difficult."

REMEDYING A RACIAL BIAS? In February 2006 the U.S. Senate Committee on the Judiciary Subcommittee on the Constitution, Civil Rights, and Human Rights conducted the hearing "An Examination of the Death Penalty in the United States." One of the scholars who testified was John McAdams of Marquette University (http://judiciary .senate.gov/hearings/hearing.cfm?id=e655f9e2809e54768 62f735da10e0680). McAdams noted that death penalty opponents often play "the race card" in debates over capital punishment. He acknowledged that studies do show "a huge bias" against African-American victims of homicide. He testified, "This is clearly unjust, but it leaves open the question of whether the injustice should be remedied by executing nobody at all, or rather executing more offenders who have murdered black people."

Scheidegger presents a similar argument, noting "if the death penalty is imposed less often when the victim is black, that means that there are perpetrators in black-victim cases who should have been sentenced to death but were not."

Racial Makeup of Death Row

Figure 7.1 shows a racial breakdown of death row prisoners between 1968 and 2009 according to the Justice Department's Bureau of Justice Statistics (BJS). The BJS notes that since 1976 more than 50% of death row inmates have been white. Table 7.2 provides racial and geographical information for the 3,173 prisoners under sentence of death as of December 31, 2009. There were 1,780 whites (56% of total) and 1,317 African-Americans (42% of total) on death row. The African-American-to-white ratios of death row prisoners by region were as follows:

- Northeast—229 total, including 84 white inmates (37% of the regional total) and 136 African-American inmates (59% of the total)

- Midwest—268 total, including 144 white inmates (54% of the regional total) and 121 African-American inmates (45% of the total)

FIGURE 7.1

Prisoners on death row, by race, 1968–2009

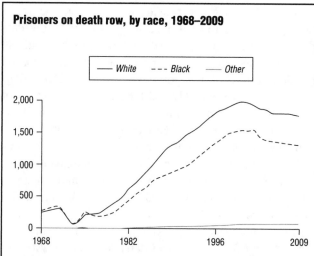

SOURCE: "Prisoners on Death Row, by Race, 1968–2009," in *Key Facts at a Glance*, U.S. Department of Justice, Office of Justice Programs, Bureau of Justice Statistics, July 27, 2011, http://bjs.ojp.usdoj.gov/content/glance/drrace.cfm# (accessed July 27, 2011)

- South—1,656 total, including 909 white inmates (55% of the regional total) and 724 African-American inmates (44% of the total)

- West—965 total, including 617 white inmates (64% of the regional total) and 308 African-American inmates (32% of the total)

According to Deborah Fins, in *Death Row U.S.A.: Winter 2011* (August 24, 2011, http://naacpldf.org/files/publications/DRUSA_Winter_2011.pdf), there were 3,251 inmates on death row as of January 1, 2011. Fins reports that 1,420 of the inmates (43.7% of the total) were white and 1,358 (41.8% of the total) were African-American. Another 394 inmates (12.1% of the total) were classified as Hispanic. Much smaller numbers were believed to be Asian-American or Native American.

Race of Executed Prisoners

Table 7.3 shows BJS statistics regarding the racial makeup of prisoners executed between 1977 and 2009.

TABLE 7.3

Executions, by year, race, and Hispanic origin, 1977–2009

Year of execution	Number executed				
	All executions	White[a]	Black[a]	Hispanic	All other races[a, b]
Total	**1,188**	**672**	**411**	**91**	**14**
1977	1	1	0	0	0
1979	2	2	0	0	0
1981	1	1	0	0	0
1982	2	1	1	0	0
1983	5	4	1	0	0
1984	21	13	8	0	0
1985	18	9	7	2	0
1986	18	9	7	2	0
1987	25	11	11	3	0
1988	11	6	5	0	0
1989	16	6	8	2	0
1990	23	16	7	0	0
1991	14	6	7	1	0
1992	31	17	11	2	1
1993	38	19	14	4	1
1994	31	19	11	1	0
1995	56	31	22	2	1
1996	45	29	14	2	0
1997	74	41	26	5	2
1998	68	40	18	8	2
1999	98	53	33	9	3
2000	85	43	35	6	1
2001	66	45	17	3	1
2002	71	47	18	6	0
2003	65	41	20	3	1
2004	59	36	19	3	1
2005	60	38	19	3	0
2006	53	25	20	8	0
2007	42	22	14	6	0
2008	37	17	17	3	0
2009	52	24	21	7	0

Note: In 1972, the U.S. Supreme Court invalidated capital punishment statutes in several states (*Furman v. Georgia*, 408 U.S. 238 [1972]), effecting a moratorium on executions. Executions resumed in 1977 when the Supreme Court found that revisions to several state statutes had effectively addressed the issues previously held unconstitutional (*Gregg v. Georgia*, 428 U.S. 153 [1976] and its companion cases).
[a]Excludes persons of Hispanic/Latino origin.
[b]Includes American Indians, Alaska Natives, Asians, Native Hawaiians, and other Pacific Islanders.

SOURCE: Tracy L. Snell, "Table 13. Number of Inmates Executed, by Race and Hispanic Origin, 1977–2009," in *Capital Punishment, 2009—Statistical Tables*, U.S. Department of Justice, Office of Justice Programs, Bureau of Justice Statistics, December 2010, http://bjs.ojp.usdoj.gov/content/pub/pdf/cp09st.pdf (accessed July 5, 2011)

Of the 1,188 inmates executed during this period, 672 (57% of the total) were white and 411 (35% of the total) were African-American. Ninety-one of the inmates, or 8% of the total, were Hispanic.

The BJS also publishes data on the number of death row prisoners that are executed or removed from a sentence of death for various reasons. As Table 7.4 shows, 7,773 inmates were under sentence of death between 1977 and 2009. Of these, 1,188 (15.3%) were executed and 3,412 (43.9%) received other dispositions (i.e., they were removed from death row for reasons other than execution, including vacated sentences, pardons, and death by other means). As of year-end 2009 a slightly larger percentage of whites (17.8%) than African-Americans (12.9%) or Hispanics (13.1%) on death row had been executed. African-American inmates on death row were slightly more likely to receive a disposition other than execution between 1977 and 2009; 46% of African-American death row inmates were removed without execution, compared with 44.3% of white inmates and 32.7% of Hispanic inmates.

Race of Victims of Executed Prisoners

The BJS does not provide statistics on the racial makeup of the victims of executed prisoners. These data are difficult to collect and verify and may not be available for all victims. However, some private organizations do provide estimates. Fins reports in *Death Row U.S.A.: Winter 2011* that between 1977 and January 1, 2011, 77.3% of the victims of executed inmates were white and 14.9% were African-American. However, an additional 21 defendants were executed for murdering multiple victims of different races. An examination of the defendant-victim racial combination reveals that between 1977 and January 1, 2011, 52.5% of cases involved a white defendant and a white victim, 20.3% of cases involved an African-American defendant and a white victim, 11.4% of cases involved an African-American defendant and an African-American victim, and 1.2% of cases involved a white defendant and an African-American victim. (See Table 7.5.)

Figure 7.2 contains data on victim race reported by the Death Penalty Information Center (DPIC) in "Facts about

TABLE 7.4

Executions and other dispositions of inmates sentenced to death, by race and Hispanic origin, 1977–2009

Race/Hispanic origin	Total under sentence of death 1977–2009[b]	Prisoners executed		Prisoners who received other dispositions[a]	
		Number	Percent of total	Number	Percent of total
Total	7,773	1,188	15.3%	3,412	43.9%
White[c]	3,774	672	17.8	1,672	44.3
Black[c]	3,184	411	12.9	1,466	46.0
Hispanic	694	91	13.1	227	32.7
All other races[c, d]	121	14	11.6	47	38.8

Note: In 1972, the U.S. Supreme Court invalidated capital punishment statutes in several states (*Furman v. Georgia*, 408 U.S. 238 [1972]), effecting a moratorium on executions. Executions resumed in 1977 when the Supreme Court found that revisions to several state statutes had effectively addressed the issues previously held unconstitutional (*Gregg v. Georgia*, 428 U.S. 153 [1976] and its companion cases).
[a]Includes persons removed from a sentence of death because of statutes struck down on appeal, sentences or convictions vacated, commutations, or death by other than execution.
[b]Includes 6 persons sentenced to death prior to 1977 who were still under sentence of death on December 31, 2009; 374 persons sentenced to death prior to 1977 whose death sentence was removed between 1977 and December 31, 2009; and 7,393 persons sentenced to death between 1977 and 2009.
[c]Excludes persons of Hispanic/Latino origin.
[d]Includes American Indians, Alaska Natives, Asians, Native Hawaiians, and other Pacific Islanders.

SOURCE: Tracy L. Snell, "Table 14. Executions and Other Dispositions of Inmates Sentenced to Death, by Race and Hispanic Origin, 1977–2009," in *Capital Punishment, 2009—Statistical Tables*, U.S. Department of Justice, Office of Justice Programs, Bureau of Justice Statistics, December 2010, http://bjs.ojp.usdoj.gov/content/pub/pdf/cp09st.pdf (accessed July 5, 2011)

TABLE 7.5

Breakdown of defendant and victim racial combinations in execution cases, 1977–January 1, 2011

	White victim		Black victim		Latino/a victim		Asian victim		Native American victim	
White defendant	648	52.51%	15	1.22%	16	1.30%	5	0.41%	0	0%
Black defendant	251	20.34%	140	11.35%	17	1.38%	11	0.89%	0	0%
Latino/a defendant	40	3.24%	3	0.24%	42	3.40%	2	0.16%	0	0%
Asian defendant	2	0.16%	0	0%	0	0%	5	0.41%	0	0%
Native Amer. def.	14	1.13%	0	0%	0	0%	0	0%	2	0.16%
Total	955	77.39%	158	12.80%	75	6.08%	23	1.86%	2	0.16%

Note: In addition, there were 21 defendants executed for the murders of multiple victims of different races. Of those, 11 defendants were white, 7 black and 3 Latino. (1.70%)

SOURCE: "Defendant-Victim Racial Combinations," in *Death Row USA Winter 2011*, NAACP Legal Defense and Educational Fund, Inc., 2011, http://naacpldf.org/files/publications/DRUSA_Winter_2011.pdf (accessed September 19, 2011)

FIGURE 7.2

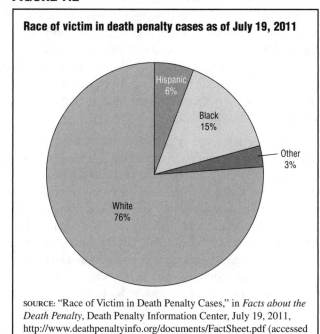

Race of victim in death penalty cases as of July 19, 2011

SOURCE: "Race of Victim in Death Penalty Cases," in *Facts about the Death Penalty*, Death Penalty Information Center, July 19, 2011, http://www.deathpenaltyinfo.org/documents/FactSheet.pdf (accessed July 21, 2011)

African-Americans. Cases of "black-on-white" and "white-on-black" homicide are relatively uncommon.

A similar pattern is apparent in 2009 data reported by the Federal Bureau of Investigation (FBI) in *Crime in the United States* (September 2010, http://www2.fbi.gov/ucr/cius2009/index.html). The FBI notes that racial information was known for 6,631 murder cases in 2009 involving a single offender and a single victim. Of the 3,518 white victims, the vast majority (2,963, or 84%) were killed by white offenders. Likewise, of the 2,867 African-American victims, 2,604 (91%) were killed by African-American offenders.

Racial Bias and Jury Selection

Another contentious racial issue in the death penalty debate involves jury selection. A venire is a pool of prospective jurors, who are typically selected at random using voter registration records or similar databases of local residents. In state capital cases the venire is usually drawn from the county in which the crime occurred and in which the trial will be held. In federal capital cases the venire is drawn from the judicial district in which the crime occurred and in which the trial will be held. As noted earlier, the United States is divided up into 94 federal judicial districts. Thus, each district may include many counties that are spread over a large geographical area. For example, Fed-Stats indicates in "Federal Judicial Districts" (April 20, 2007, http://www.fedstats.gov/mapstats/fjd/) that California contains 58 counties that are divided into four federal judicial districts.

ARE PEREMPTORY STRIKES MISUSED? Prior to the start of a criminal trial, the judge, the prosecutor, and the lawyer for the defendant can interview the potential jurors and strike (dismiss) individuals from serving on the jury. There are two types of dismissals: dismissals for cause and peremptory strikes. Dismissals for cause can be made by the judge or the attorneys (with the judge's approval) for specific allowable reasons, for example, a potential juror is related to the victim. Attorneys (not judges) make peremptory strikes, which are dismissals for which no reason has to be given to the court. Peremptory strikes are allowed in both federal and state capital trials.

In "Three Strikes and You're Out? Critics Seek Juror-Dismissal Cap" (*Wall Street Journal*, March 5, 2009), Nathan Koppel explains that lawyers for the prosecution and defense are allowed an unlimited number of challenges for cause, but are limited under state statute as to the number of peremptory strikes they can make per venire. According to Koppel, that number in 2009 ranged from six in Ohio, to 20 in California and New York, to 25 in Connecticut.

Peremptory strikes are forbidden by law to be based on the race or sex of the potential juror. The race provision stems from a U.S. Supreme Court decision in *Batson v. Kentucky* (476 U.S. 79 [1986]), in which the court

the Death Penalty" (July 19, 2011, http://www.deathpenalty info.org/documents/FactSheet.pdf). According to the DPIC, as of July 19, 2011, 76% of victims in death penalty cases were white, 15% were African-American, 6% were Hispanic, and 3% were of other races.

Race and Homicide Statistics

According to James Alan Fox and Marianne W. Zawitz of the BJS, in *Homicide Trends in the United States* (July 1, 2007, http://bjs.ojp.usdoj.gov/content/pub/pdf/htius.pdf), African-Americans are disproportionately represented among homicide offenders and victims. The researchers examined the U.S. homicide rate per 100,000 population between 1976 and 2005 for African-American and white murderers. Fox and Zawitz note that more than half of the offenders (52.2%) were African-American, whereas 45.8% were white. Furthermore, they report that in 2005 the offending rate for African-Americans (26.5 per 100,000 population) was more than seven times higher than the rate for whites (3.5). Their statistics also show that African-Americans made up a disproportionate percentage of homicide victims. Of all homicide victims between 1976 and 2005, 46.9% were African-American. White victims accounted for 50.9% of the total. In 2005 the homicide victimization rate for African-Americans (20.6 per 100,000 population) was six times higher than the rate for whites (3.3).

Fox and Zawitz indicate that the vast majority of homicides committed between 1976 and 2005 were intraracial: 86% of white victims were murdered by whites and 94% of African-American victims were murdered by

ruled that discriminatory jury selection is unconstitutional. However, critics claim that prosecutors often use peremptory strikes to eliminate African-Americans from capital case juries because African-Americans are known to have lower public support for the death penalty than whites.

The Equal Justice Institute (EJI), a nonprofit legal organization in Alabama, alleges in *Illegal Racial Discrimination in Jury Selection: A Continuing Legacy* (August 2010, http://eji.org/eji/files/EJI%20Race%20and%20Jury%20Report.pdf) that African-Americans are purposely struck by prosecutors from many juries, particularly in the South and especially in capital cases. The organization explains it examined jury selection practices in Alabama, Arkansas, Florida, Georgia, Louisiana, Mississippi, South Carolina, and Tennessee and found "shocking evidence of racial discrimination" in all these states. For example, in rural Houston County, Alabama, the EJI claims that prosecutors used peremptory strikes to dismiss 80% of African-American potential jurors from venires between 2005 and 2009. *Batson v. Kentucky* allows defense lawyers to object to prosecutors' peremptory strikes. The prosecutors must then provide to the court "race-neutral" explanations for the strikes to stand. The EJI presents dozens of reasons that were used by prosecutors as excuses to strike African-Americans from juries, including low intelligence, lack of education, wearing eyeglasses, chewing gum, marital status, age, being unemployed, having a child out of wedlock, looking like a drug dealer, having dyed red hair, and living in a high-crime neighborhood.

Since 2009 EJI lawyers have obtained new trials for two Alabama death row inmates—Jason Sharp and Earl McGahee—by arguing on appeal that African-American jurors were improperly struck from the original trial juries. Sharp, who is white, was convicted for the 1999 rape and murder of Tracy Lynn Morris, a white woman. McGahee, an African-American, is under sentence of death for the 1985 murders of Connie Brown and Cassandra Lee, also African-Americans. In the press release "Alabama Death Row Prisoner Wins New Trial from Appeals Court Due to Illegal Racial Discrimination in Jury Selection" (February 25, 2011, http://eji.org/eji/print/node/509), the EJI notes that seven African-Americans were struck from Sharp's venire for lacking "sophistication." An appeals court rejected this reason as "historically suspect." Likewise, African-Americans were struck from McGahee's venire for "low intelligence." Prosecutors claimed this was evidenced by the fact that the potential jurors were unemployed or held blue-collar jobs. An appeals court, however, found that whites who were unemployed were not struck from the venire. As of September 2011, Sharp and McGahee had not been retried.

RACIAL DISPARITIES IN FEDERAL JURIES. Claims of racial bias in jury selection are not limited to state capital cases. Similar claims are also made about federal death penalty cases. As noted earlier, Cohen and Smith have documented significant geographic disparities in federal capital sentences since 1988 indicating that only a few federal judicial districts account for significant numbers of federal inmates on death row. Cohen and Smith also allege that African-Americans are disproportionately sentenced to death in these districts due to the way that federal juries are selected.

Federal venires are drawn from the district at large, rather than from a single county. Thus, African-American defendants who might not be sentenced to death by a mostly African-American jury from their local city or county can end up with a mostly white jury that is drawn from the entire district. Cohen and Smith indicate that the highest death sentencing rates are in districts largely made up of an African-American–majority city or county that is surrounded by white-majority counties, such as New Orleans, Louisiana, in the Eastern District of Louisiana; St. Louis, Missouri, in the Eastern District of Missouri; Richmond, Virginia, in the Eastern District of Virginia; and Prince George's County in the District of Maryland. Twelve of the 57 inmates on the federal death row as of 2010 were prosecuted in these four districts and all were African-American. Cohen and Smith complain that "federal prosecutors are able to dilute minority-concentrated populations (obtaining far whiter jury pools) simply by prosecuting the same case in federal rather than state court." They also claim that data indicate death sentences have been infrequently given in districts that contain large minority populations or those in which the population demographics are similar throughout the district.

LEGAL REPRESENTATION: QUESTIONS ABOUT QUALITY

The Sixth Amendment to the U.S. Constitution guarantees the "assistance of counsel for . . . defense" in federal criminal prosecution. In *Gideon v. Wainwright* (372 U.S. 335 [1963]), the U.S. Supreme Court extended the right to counsel to state criminal prosecution of indigent (poor) people who are charged with felonies. In *Argersinger v. Hamlin* (407 U.S. 25 [1972]), the high court held that poor people who are charged with any crime that carries a sentence of imprisonment have the right to counsel.

The court later ruled in *Strickland v. Washington* (466 U.S. 688 [1984]) that the lawyers provided for poor defendants must abide by certain professional standards in criminal cases. Some of these standards include demonstrating loyalty to the client, avoiding conflicts of interest, keeping the defendant informed of important developments in the trial, and conducting reasonable factual and legal investigations that may aid the client's case.

Indigent Capital Defense in State Trials

States generally vary in fulfilling *Gideon*. Some states have undertaken the establishment and funding of an indigent defense system, whereas others have passed the responsibility on to individual counties. Across the United States different jurisdictions use one or a combination of three systems to provide counsel to poor defendants. The first system used by some jurisdictions has public defenders who are usually government employees. Under the second system, the court-assigned counsel system, a judge appoints private lawyers to represent the poor. A third system involves contract lawyers who bid for the job of providing indigent defense.

Court-assigned lawyers belong to a list of private lawyers who accept clients on a case-by-case basis. In jurisdictions that employ these lawyers, judges appoint lawyers from a list of private bar members and determine their pay. In most cases the pay is low.

A PHILADELPHIA CHALLENGE. In "Court-Appointed Death Penalty Lawyers Want More $$$" (*Philadelphia Inquirer*, April 6, 2011), Joseph A. Slobodzian reports that in April 2011 a group of court-appointed capital defense lawyers in Philadelphia, Pennsylvania, filed a petition in court against Philadelphia County protesting its pay structure. The petitioners alleged that the county "pays its court-appointed attorneys less to prepare a capital case than any remotely comparable jurisdiction in the country." According to Slobodzian, the county's pay schedule includes flat fees of $1,333 for pretrial preparation and $2,000 for the trial. By comparison, a private attorney in the Philadelphia area can charge as much as $50,000 to defend a murder case. Slobodzian notes in "Pennsylvania Supreme Court urged to Consider How Philadelphia Pays Death-Penalty Lawyers" (*Philadelphia Inquirer*, June 9, 2011) that in June 2011 the petitioners asked the Pennsylvania Supreme Court to hear the case after their petition was twice rejected by a lower court. As of September 2011, the case had not been resolved.

A STUDY OF HARRIS COUNTY, TEXAS. As noted earlier, Harris County, Texas, prosecuted 115 (9%) of the 1,229 total executions that were carried out in the United States between 1977 and October 2010. In "Legal Disparities in the Capital of Capital Punishment" (*Journal of Criminal Law and Criminology*, vol. 99, no. 3, Spring 2009), Scott Phillips of the University of Denver examines the method of legal representation of 504 defendants who were indicted for capital murder in Harris County between 1992 and 1999. Phillips notes that at that time Harris County was the largest metropolitan area in the country using a court-appointed system, rather than a public defender office. Of the 504 cases examined, the vast majority (369, or 73%) featured court-appointed lawyers. Hired lawyers represented only 31 (6%) of the defendants. The remaining 104 defendants used a mixture of court-appointed and hired lawyers throughout their legal proceedings. Phillips finds that the defendants with hired lawyers were approximately 20 times more likely to be acquitted than the

other defendants. He notes that "the relationship between legal counsel and acquittals is troubling. It does not seem plausible to conclude that defendants who hired counsel were actually twenty times more likely to be innocent." Rather, Phillips believes this discrepancy is due in large part to problems that are inherent to the county's court-appointed lawyer system:

- Flat-fee payments rather than hourly payments discourage appointed lawyers from spending large amounts of time on a particular case.

- A judge has to approve the hiring of any specialists, such as investigators or expert witnesses, and can limit the funding for them. Phillips notes that judges can be reluctant to spend funds on such specialists for fear of being perceived as sympathetic to defendants and "soft on crime."

- Judges appoint attorneys to handle cases. The lawyers vying for these positions can experience a conflict of interest between representing their clients aggressively in court (which risks antagonizing the judge) and maintaining a positive relationship with the judge to obtain additional appointments in the future.

- The judges also face a conflict of interest in that they are supposed to ensure that indigent defendants receive adequate representation, but are under funding pressures from the county government and political pressures to be tough on crime so they can be reelected.

- Political and personal factors can affect judges' appointment decisions, meaning that lawyers can be appointed to cases for reasons other than their legal skills or trial experience.

Phillips recommends that Harris County replace its court-appointment system with a capital defender office.

Molly Ryan reports in "Harris County Public Defender's Office Continues to Expand" (*Community Impact Newspaper* [Pflugerville, Texas], July 28, 2011) that in 2010 Harris County created a public defender office, which began accepting cases in February 2011. However, as of September 2011 the office handled only misdemeanor cases.

Ineffective Counsel?

Death penalty opponents claim that some lawyers who have defended capital cases were inexperienced, ill-trained, or incompetent. They point to cases in which the defense lawyers fell asleep during trial, drank to excess the night before, or even showed up in the courtroom intoxicated. They also cite the well-publicized cases of inmates who have been exonerated as a result of college students finding evidence that defense lawyers had failed to uncover.

In "In Pursuit of the Public Good: Lawyers Who Care" (April 9, 2001, http://www.supremecourt.gov/publicinfo/speeches/viewspeeches.aspx?Filename=sp_04-09-01a.html),

Justice Ruth Bader Ginsburg (1933–) of the U.S. Supreme Court expresses her concerns about proper representation in capital cases. She states, "I have yet to see a death case, among the dozens coming to the Supreme Court on eve of execution petitions, in which the defendant was well represented at trial.... Public funding for the legal representation of poor people in the United States is hardly generous. In capital cases, state systems for affording representation to indigent defendants vary from adequate to meager."

The American Bar Association (ABA) provides in "*Gideon*'s Broken Promise: America's Continuing Quest for Equal Justice" (December 2004, http://www.americanbar .org/) some insight into why poor defendants may receive inadequate counsel. The ABA analyzes the indigent defense system in 22 states and finds that lawyers who took on poor defendants received low pay and that judges tended to let legal protocols slide to clear overcrowded dockets. In noncapital cases involving lesser offenses, prosecutors and judges sometimes forced defendants to plead guilty before receiving counsel to move them through the system. In addition, the ABA notes that indigent defense systems lack the basic accountability and oversight needed to ensure decent legal representation or to correct these problems.

To remedy some of the problems inherent in death penalty trials, Congress passed and President George W. Bush (1946–) signed the Innocence Protection Act of 2004. This act launched a program in which state governments receive grants from the federal government to improve the quality of legal representation for poor defendants in state capital cases. To receive such a grant, a state's capital defense system has to meet a number of requirements, which include establishing minimum standards for defense attorneys and monitoring the performance of these attorneys.

MITIGATING EVIDENCE CASES. In June and July 2011 the U.S. Court of Appeals for the 11th Circuit reversed the death penalty sentences of three inmates—Richard Cooper and Terrell Johnson of Florida and Eric Ferrell of Georgia—based on claims of inadequate counsel. Cooper was under sentence of death for the 1982 murders of Steven Fridella, Gary Peterson, and Bobby Martindale during a home invasion. Johnson was sent to death row for killing James Dodson and Charles Himes during a robbery at a pawn shop in 1979. Ferrell was convicted of killing his grandmother, Willie Myrt Lowe, and 15-year-old cousin, Tony Kilgore, in 1987. In all three cases the court faulted the inmates' defense attorneys for failing to present mitigating evidence during the sentencing phases of their original trials; specifically, evidence of severe childhood abuse. As of September 2011, none of the inmates had been resentenced.

Counsel for Postconviction Review

Even though death row inmates have the right to seek review of their conviction and sentence, they do not have the right to counsel for postconviction proceedings per the Supreme Court ruling in *Murray v. Giarratano* (492 U.S. 1 [1989]).

According to the DPIC, in "Death Penalty Representation" (2011, http://www.deathpenaltyinfo.org/death-penalty-representation), 14 states (Arizona, California, Colorado, Florida [parts of the state], Idaho, Illinois, Indiana, Kentucky, Louisiana, Mississippi, Ohio, Oklahoma, Tennessee, and Texas) have capital postconviction offices that assist or represent indigent inmates after their direct appeals.

Indigent death row inmates in other states must find lawyers who are willing to handle appeals for free. In 1995 Congress discontinued federal funding of private organizations (called resource centers) that represented death row inmates in postconviction proceedings. As a result, private organizations and law firms, both proponents and opponents of the death penalty, that are concerned with the increasing problems in capital cases now volunteer their services. Some hold training seminars on the complex process of appellate review, whereas others provide research and investigation.

CHAPTER 8

EXONERATIONS AND MORATORIUMS

Since the 1990s dozens of death row inmates have been exonerated, meaning that the original capital charges against them have been dropped. In some cases new evidence came to light that cast doubt on their guilt. In other cases legal challenges changed the parameters that are used to determine who can be sentenced to capital punishment. Exonerations are heralded by death penalty opponents as proof that the U.S. capital punishment system is flawed and should be abandoned. Advocates of the death penalty argue that the importance of exonerations is exaggerated and their occurrence proves that the capital justice system protects the rights of defendants. Nevertheless, exonerations and other concerns about the capital punishment system have spurred several states to temporarily cease conducting executions. These temporary moratoriums allow officials time to reexamine their capital punishment systems and determine if there are systematic problems in their administration.

EXONERATIONS

The Death Penalty Information Center (DPIC) is opposed to capital punishment. In "Innocence: List of Those Freed from Death Row" (2011, http://www.death penaltyinfo.org/innocence-list-those-freed-death-row), the DPIC lists the names of 138 people that it says have been exonerated since 1973. The so-called Innocence List is often touted by death penalty opponents as proof that the U.S. capital punishment system is flawed. Defendants are added to the DPIC list in one of two ways: when their conviction is overturned and they are acquitted on retrial or all charges are dropped; or when they receive a governor's pardon because of new evidence of innocence.

It is important to note that the Innocence List is not limited solely to inmates who were on death row at the time of their exoneration. The list also includes inmates originally sentenced to death who have since been resentenced to noncapital sentences, for example, life in prison.

Figure 8.1 shows the number of exonerations per year between 1973 and October 2010. The largest numbers occurred in 2003 (12 exonerations), 2000 and 2009 (nine exonerations for each year), and 1987, 1996, and 1999 (eight exonerations for each year).

As of October 2010, Florida had the most exonerations (23), followed by Illinois (20), Texas (12), and Oklahoma (10). (See Figure 8.2.) Arizona and Louisiana each had eight exonerations. The DPIC reports in "Innocence: List of Those Freed from Death Row" that 85 of the exonerated had their charges dismissed, 46 were acquitted, and seven were pardoned. Seventeen defendants were exonerated based on deoxyribonucleic acid (DNA) evidence. The amount of time that elapsed between conviction and exoneration ranged from one year to 33 years. Overall, the average amount of time that passed between conviction and exoneration was 9.8 years.

Of the inmates reported exonerated, 71 were African-American and 53 were white. (See Table 8.1.) Twelve were Hispanic and two were classified as "other" races.

David Keaton: The First Exoneree

David Keaton (1952–), a Florida teenager who was convicted of murder in 1971, was the first person exonerated from death row in the modern era. His legal history is detailed by the Florida Commission on Capital Cases in *Case Histories: A Review of 24 Individuals Released from Death Row* (September 10, 2002, http://www.floridacapitalcases.state.fl.us/Publications/innocentsproject.pdf). Keaton was convicted of felony murder for the shooting of Thomas Revels during an armed robbery at a grocery store in Tallahassee in 1970. Keaton and four other men, known as the "Quincy Five," were indicted for the crime. Keaton was not accused of being the triggerman and initially he confessed to being involved in the robbery, but he later recanted. In 1971 Keaton was convicted and sentenced to death, based on his own confession and the testimony of

FIGURE 8.1

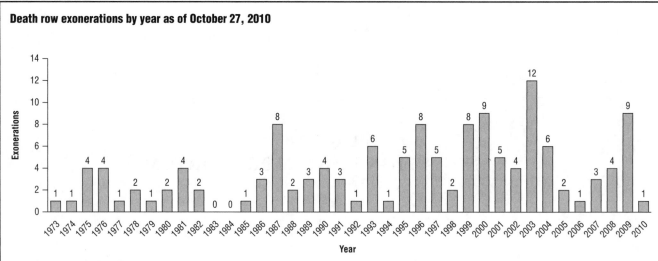

Death row exonerations by year as of October 27, 2010

SOURCE: "Exonerations by Year," in *Innocence and the Death Penalty*, Death Penalty Information Center, February 22, 2011, http://www.deathpenaltyinfo .org/innocence-and-death-penalty#inn-yr-rc (accessed July 24, 2011)

FIGURE 8.2

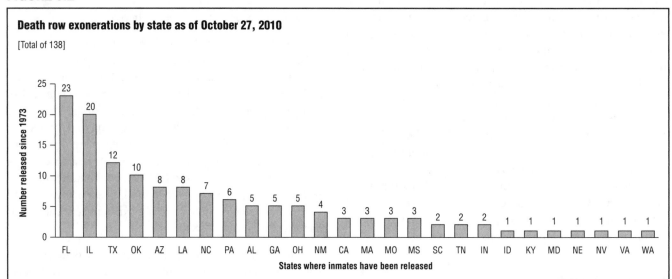

Death row exonerations by state as of October 27, 2010

[Total of 138]

SOURCE: "Death Row Exonerations by State, Total: 138," in *Facts about the Death Penalty*, Death Penalty Information Center, July 19, 2011, http://www .deathpenaltyinfo.org/documents/FactSheet.pdf (accessed July 21, 2011)

TABLE 8.1

Death row exonerations by race as of October 27, 2010

Race	Exonerations
Black	71
White	53
Latino	12
Other	2

SOURCE: "Exonerations by Race," in *Innocence and the Death Penalty*, Death Penalty Information Center, February 22, 2011, http://www.deathpenaltyinfo .org/innocence-and-death-penalty#inn-yr-rc (accessed July 24, 2011)

(408 U.S. 238 [1972]) that the death penalty, as then practiced, was unconstitutional.

Meanwhile, three other men were arrested for the murder of Revels based on fingerprint evidence and the testimony of an informant. In 1973 the Florida Supreme Court ordered a new trial for Keaton; however, the prosecutor decided not to retry the case. In "The Stigma Is Always There" (*St. Petersburg [FL] Times* July 4, 1999), Sydney P. Freedberg notes that the prosecutor claimed the original witnesses were too ill to testify at the retrial. However, Freedberg points out a number of problems with the original case against Keaton, including "threats and lies" that were used by sheriff's deputies to gain his confession (which did not even match the known facts)

eyewitnesses who placed him at the scene. The following year his sentence was converted to life in prison following the U.S. Supreme Court's finding in *Furman v. Georgia*

and a disreputable polygraph tester. Plus, Keaton—an African-American—was convicted by an all-white jury. At the time of his exoneration for murder, Keaton was serving a 20-year prison sentence for a separate robbery. He was released from prison in 1979 at the age of 27 years.

Kirk Bloodsworth: The First Exoneree Freed by DNA Evidence

Kirk Bloodsworth (1960–) was the first person exonerated from death row based on DNA evidence that proved his innocence. He was convicted in 1984 of raping and murdering nine-year-old Dawn Hamilton in Maryland. Details about the Bloodsworth case can be found on the website of the Center on Wrongful Conviction (CWC) at the Northwestern University School of Law (http://www.law.northwestern.edu/wrongfulconvictions/exonerations/mdBloodsworthSummary.html). According to the CWC, five eyewitnesses identified Bloodsworth as being with the victim on the day of the murder or at the scene where the crime later occurred. In addition, the prosecution claimed that shoe prints on Hamilton's body corresponded with shoes owned by Bloodsworth. He was convicted and given a death sentence in March 1985. The following year his conviction was overturned by the Maryland Court of Appeals because the prosecution had withheld potentially exculpatory evidence (evidence that is favorable to the defendant) from the defense. Bloodsworth was retried, found guilty, and sentenced to two life terms in prison. In 1988 that sentence was upheld on appeal. From his prison cell, Bloodsworth obtained court approval for DNA testing of crime scene evidence, and the DNA samples were found not to match Bloodsworth. The samples were retested by the Federal Bureau of Investigation, which also concluded that Bloodsworth's DNA did not match with crime scene evidence. Bloodsworth was released from prison in 1993, and the following year he was formally pardoned by the Maryland governor William D. Schaefer (1921–2011). In 2003 more DNA testing identified a man named Kimberly Shay Ruffner (1958–) as the perpetrator in Hamilton's murder. The following year Ruffner pleaded guilty to the murder and was sentenced to life in prison.

Since his release from prison Bloodsworth has become a vocal activist who speaks and writes about problems with the criminal justice system. In September 2008 Bloodsworth testified before the Maryland Commission on Capital Punishment (http://www.goccp.maryland.gov/capital-punishment/documents/transcript-sep-5.doc) saying, "I'm living proof that Maryland's capital punishment system is broken. And I'm living proof that Maryland gets it wrong." In early 2009 Maryland legislators voted to limit capital cases to only those in which DNA evidence, videotaped confessions, or videotape linking the defendant to the murder are available. The state of Maryland paid $300,000 to Bloodsworth to compensate him for lost income during his years in prison.

2010 Exoneration

As of September 2011, the most recent exoneration reported by the DPIC occurred in October 2010, when the Texas inmate Anthony Graves was freed from prison. In 1994 Graves was convicted for the 1992 slayings of Bobbie Davis, her daughter Nicole Davis, and Bobbie Davis's four grandchildren aged four to nine. The elder Davis died from multiple stab wounds and being beaten with a blunt object; her daughter was stabbed and shot multiple times; and her grandchildren were all stabbed to death. After the murders the bodies were doused in gasoline and the house set on fire. Robert Earl Carter, the biological father of the four-year-old child, was arrested several days after the murders. There was substantial evidence against him, including serious burns on his arms and face. He admitted to killing Nicole Davis and setting the house on fire, but testified in court that an accomplice, Anthony Graves, committed the rest of the murders. Both were found guilty and sentenced to death. Graves steadfastly denied any involvement in the crime.

In "Texas Sets Man Free from Death Row" (*Houston Chronicle*, October 27, 2010), Brian Rogers and Cindy George note that Graves's conviction was based largely on Carter's original accusations and "jailhouse statements purportedly overheard by law enforcement officers." In 2000, two weeks before his execution, Carter signed a sworn statement saying that he had lied when he implicated Graves in the murders. The Texas Department of Criminal Justice (June 24, 2008, http://www.tdcj.state.tx.us/stat/carterrobertlast.htm) notes that shortly before his execution, Carter claimed in his last statement that "it was me and me alone. Anthony Graves had nothing to do with it. I lied on him in court." In 2006 the U.S. Court of Appeals for the Fifth Circuit overturned Graves's conviction and granted him a new trial. According to Rogers and George, the court was swayed, in part, by new evidence that had been gathered by Graves's lawyers and journalism students at the University of St. Thomas with help from the Innocence Project, a nonprofit legal organization based at the Benjamin N. Cardozo School of Law at Yeshiva University.

In *Graves v. Dretke* (No. 05-70011 [2006]), the court noted that Carter made "several inconsistent statements" prior to the trial about whether or not he acted alone in the murders. However, the prosecutor did not disclose to Graves's attorney two of Carter's statements: one in which he said he was the only murderer and a second statement in which he implicated his wife, Cookie, as an accomplice. The court found, "If the defense had known about the statement placing Cookie at the scene and given Carter's continuing condition that he would only testify if he were not asked about Cookie's involvement, the defense could have explained every statement implicating Graves as a means of protecting Cookie."

Rogers and George report that by 2006 the original prosecutor in the case, Charles Sebesta, had left the prosecutor's office. The new prosecutor, Bill Parham, began preparing for Graves's retrial, but soon found that the evidence against Graves was insufficient for another conviction. In October 2010 Parham filed a motion to dismiss the charges against Graves, noting, "there is nothing that connects Anthony Graves to this crime." Graves was released from prison and in February 2011 he filed a lawsuit seeking monetary compensation for the 18 years he spent incarcerated. Robert Stanton notes in "Texan Who Was Wrongly Jailed Getting $80K a Year from State" (*Houston Chronicle*, June 21, 2011) that in June 2011 the Texas governor Rick Perry (1950–) signed a law authorizing $1.4 million be paid in compensation to Graves. Stanton indicates that Graves also sued the state's attorney general for a "declaration of innocence" in the case.

Sebesta publicly denied any prosecutorial misconduct in Graves's conviction. Rogers and George report that in 2009 Sebesta took out ads in local newspapers to dispute media claims that the prosecution had acted improperly in the case. As of September 2011, Sebesta maintained a website (http://www.charlessebesta.net/) in which he recounted in detail the evidence against Graves presented at the original trial and noted that Graves failed two polygraph examinations after he was arrested. Sebesta claimed that criticism of his prosecution of the case was driven by personal and political factors.

A New Exoneree?

In July 2011 a federal appeals judge overturned the conviction and death sentence of Justin Wolfe of Virginia. Wolfe was convicted in Prince William County in 2002 for the murder-for-hire of Daniel Petrole, a key participant in a drug ring operating in the region. Wolfe had allegedly purchased large amounts of marijuana from Petrole and hired a friend and fellow drug dealer named Owen Barber to kill him.

In "Death Sentence, Conviction of Innocence Project Clinic Client Overturned" (July 13, 2011, http://www.law.virginia.edu/html/news/2011_sum/innocence_wolfe.htm?ntype=feed), the Virginia Law School reports that law students participating in the school's Innocence Project Clinic played a key role in clearing Wolfe. The students pored over records, interviewed witnesses, and collaborated with attorneys who were representing Wolfe pro bono (without compensation) and the Virginia Capital Representation Resource Center, a nonprofit law firm that represents capital offenders.

Wolfe's legal team uncovered evidence that prosecutors had failed to disclose certain evidence to the defense during the original trial; chiefly, that Barber kept changing his story, sometimes denying that Wolfe had hired him to kill Petrole. The Virginia Law School notes in "Innocence Project Clinic Seeks to Overturn Death Sentence" (January 5, 2011, http://www.law.virginia.edu/html/news/2011_spr/in_clinic.htm) that Barber received a 38-year prison sentence in exchange for his testimony against Wolfe at the trial. During the appeals process Wolfe's lawyers obtained an evidentiary hearing in November 2010 at which they presented evidence in support of his claim of innocence. Barber officially recanted his previous testimony about Wolfe's role in the murder. The appeals court ruled that the prosecutor in the original trial had deprived the jury of "critical information" that could have prevented Wolfe's conviction. As of September 2011, Wolfe had not been retried on the murder charge. The article "Justin Wolfe Could Soon Be Released from Prison" (Associated Press, September 2, 2011) reports that Virginia appealed the decision overturning Wolfe's conviction. However, in late August 2011 another judge dismissed all remaining drug and gun charges against Wolfe, meaning that he could soon be released from prison. The article notes that the Prince William County prosecutor intended to retry Wolfe on the murder charge.

The Innocence List Disputed

Proponents of the death penalty are critical of the DPIC's Innocence List, claiming that it exaggerates the number of innocent people who are on death row. In 2000 the DPIC reported the 100th addition to the list, an event that was widely publicized in the media. In response, Ramesh Ponnuru attacked the list in "Bad List: A Suspect Roll of Death Row 'Innocents'" (*National Review*, September 16, 2002). Ponnuru claimed that most of the exonerations resulted from legal technicalities, rather than from actual innocence. He recounted the violent criminal records of some of the exonerees and the formidable evidence introduced at trial against them. He described legal motions and maneuvers that ultimately resulted in the reversal of their sentences. He complained that "the list leads people to think that innocence has been proven when the most that can be said is that the legal system cannot establish guilt beyond a reasonable doubt."

Ponnuru argued that approximately 32 of the 102 exonerees on the list at that time could truly be regarded as innocent. He noted that more than 7,000 people had been on death row since 1973; thus, the percentage of actual innocence cases was extremely low.

In *Critique of DPIC List ("Innocence: Freed from Death Row")* (2002, http://www.prodeathpenalty.com/DPIC.htm), Ward A. Campbell, the supervising deputy attorney general in California, investigated the 102 cases of exonerated death row inmates on the DPIC list at that time. He concluded that at least 68 of the 102 inmates on the list should not have been included. Campbell found that "many defendants on the List were not 'actually innocent.'" Some defendants had pleaded guilty to lesser charges and had their sentences commuted. Campbell noted that "an acquittal because the prosecution has not proven guilt beyond a reasonable doubt does not mean that the defendant did not actually commit the crime."

In June 2002 the Florida Commission on Capital Cases released *Case Histories: A Review of 24 Individuals Released from Death Row*, which listed the results of its investigation into 24 cases on the DPIC list. The commission concluded, "Of these 24 inmates, none were found 'innocent,' even when acquitted, because no such verdict exists. A defendant is found guilty or not guilty, never innocent. The guilt of only four defendants, however, was subsequently doubted by the prosecuting office or the Governor and Cabinet members.... An analysis of the remaining 20 inmates can be divided into three categories that account for their releases: (1) seven cases were remanded due to evidence issues, (2) an additional seven were remanded in light of witness issues, and (3) the remaining six were remanded as a result of issues involving court officials."

QUESTIONS ABOUT LEGAL ERRORS IN DEATH PENALTY CASES
Liebman Study

James S. Liebman, Jeffrey Fagan, and Valerie West conducted the first study of its kind—a statistical study of modern U.S. capital appeals—for the U.S. Senate Committee on the Judiciary. The study, called *A Broken System: Error Rates in Capital Cases, 1973–1995* (June 12, 2000, http://www2.law.columbia.edu/instructionalservices/liebman/liebman_final.pdf), examined all death penalty sentences (5,760) that had been imposed in the United States over a 23-year period.

On direct appeal, the state high courts reviewed 4,578 death sentences. Liebman, Fagan, and West found that 68% of the death sentences reviewed by courts across the country were found to have serious errors. For every 100 death sentences, 41 were returned to the courts during state appeal because of serious errors. Of the 59 death sentences that reached the second state appeal, another six went back to court because of errors. At the third level of appeal—with the federal courts—21 more cases were remanded (sent back) to the lower courts because of errors found. In all, of the original 100 death penalty sentences, 68 had serious errors that required retrial. Of the 68 defendants who were retried, 82% (56) did not receive the death penalty at their retrial. Another five inmates were found not guilty of the capital crime for which they received the death sentence.

THE LIEBMAN STUDY IS ANALYZED. Critics challenged the results of the Liebman study. Appearing before the Senate Committee on the Judiciary hearing on "Reducing the Risk of Executing the Innocent: The Report of the Illinois Governor's Commission on Capital Punishment" (June 12, 2002, http://www.gpo.gov/fdsys/pkg/CHRG-

107shrg86544/html/CHRG-107shrg86544.htm), Senator Strom Thurmond (1902–2003; R-SC) warned:

> A Columbia University report known as the Liebman study is often cited as proof that capital punishment in this country is deeply flawed. This study ... alleged that from 1973 to 1995, 70% of death penalty convictions were reversed on appeal. The implication is that 70% of the time, innocent people were sentenced to death. This study should be viewed carefully because during the time period addressed by this study, the Supreme Court issued a series of retroactive rules that nullified a number of verdicts. These reversals were not based on the actual innocence of defendants, but rather were based on procedural rules.

Latzer Study

In "Capital Appeals Revisited" (*Judicature*, vol. 84, no. 2, September–October 2000), Barry Latzer and James N. G. Cauthen noted that their reexamination of the Liebman study found that about one-fourth (27%)—and not two-thirds (68%)—of capital convictions were reversed between 1973 and 1995. Latzer and Cauthen stated that the Liebman study did not differentiate between reversals of convictions and reversals of death sentences.

Latzer and Cauthen conducted their own investigation, based on the theory that many of the appeals resulted in reversed sentences (reversals addressing the defendant's sentence but not his or her guilt or innocence) but not reversed convictions (reversals addressing the defendant's guilt or innocence). The study covered the period 1990 to 1999, using reversal data in the same 26 states studied by Liebman and his colleagues. Latzer and Cauthen wanted more recent data of the death penalty system that would provide more complete reversal rate differences.

Latzer and Cauthen found that of the 837 death penalty reversals in state-level direct appeal or postconviction review, 61% were sentence reversals and 39% were conviction reversals. Using the Liebman study's conclusion that five out of 10 capital judgments were reversed at either the direct-appeal phase or the postconviction review phase, Latzer and Cauthen applied this finding to their study and concluded that, of the five reversals, three were sentence reversals and two were conviction reversals.

Latzer and Cauthen also investigated reversals at the federal level—the third stage of death penalty judgment review—using data from the U.S. Court of Appeals for the Ninth Circuit, the largest of the circuit courts. Of the 29 capital cases reversed by the court during the 10-year period, 21 (72.4%) were sentence reversals and eight (27.7%) were conviction reversals. This was consistent with their findings regarding direct-appeal and postconviction sentence reversals at the state level. Using the Liebman study's finding that 68 out of 100 capital judgments were reversed, Latzer and Cauthen concluded, "If 68 of 100 capital decisions are reversed after direct, post-conviction, and federal habeas corpus review, and 39 percent of these are conviction reversals, then convictions in 26.52 (39 percent of 68) of 100 capital decisions are reversed."

FORENSIC SCIENCE

Forensic science is the application of scientific knowledge to legal problems. In the modern era the criminal justice system relies heavily on forensic science to reveal the guilt (or innocence) of suspects. Examples include fingerprint analysis, firearms testing, DNA testing, autopsies, arson and explosives investigations, and analysis of bloodstains, handwriting, bite marks, and so on. DNA testing, in particular, plays a major role in capital case investigations. DNA, which stores the genetic code of the human body, is found in saliva, skin tissue, bones, blood, semen, vaginal secretions, and the root of hair.

The science of DNA testing is improving rapidly. When DNA testing was first used in criminal trials starting in the mid-1980s, DNA samples had to be not only fresh but also contain thousands of cells. As DNA technology has become more sophisticated, scientists are able to test a single cell for DNA patterns that can link suspects to hair or body fluids found on a victim.

Postconviction DNA Testing

Before DNA testing became available as proof of identity, the U.S. Supreme Court held the view that U.S. appellate courts could not reverse a murder conviction based on newly discovered post-trial evidence. In *Herrera v. Collins* (506 U.S. 390 [1993]), the Supreme Court ruled that newly discovered evidence does not constitute grounds for a federal habeas relief if there is no evidence of a constitutional violation occurring during state criminal proceedings. (In this case, Leonel Torres Herrera [1947–1993] alleged 10 years after his initial trial that he was innocent of a double murder, presenting evidence that his brother, who had since died, had committed the crime.) However, the National Commission on the Future of DNA Evidence stated in *Postconviction DNA Testing: Recommendations for Handling* (September 1999, https://www.ncjrs.gov/txtfiles1/nij/177626.txt) that with the availability of DNA testing, "the possibility of demonstrating actual innocence has moved from the realm of theory to the actual."

The federal Innocence Protection Act became law in October 2004. The law established the conditions under which a federal prisoner who pleads not guilty can receive postconviction DNA testing. If a trial defendant is convicted, the act calls for the preservation of the defendant's biological evidence. A five-year, $25 million grant program was also established to help eligible states pay for postconviction testing. The act expired in 2009;

as of September 2011, legislation to reauthorize the act had not been passed.

A CIVIL RIGHTS ISSUE? In March 2011 the U.S. Supreme Court issued a stay of execution in a case in which a Texas death row inmate—Henry Skinner—alleged that the state violated his civil rights when it refused to conduct postconviction DNA testing of certain physical evidence that had been collected at the crime scene. Skinner was convicted and sentenced to death in 1995 for the 1993 murders of his girlfriend, Twila Busby, and her two adult sons, Randy Busby and Elwin Caler. The four shared the same residence. Twila Busby was bludgeoned and stabbed to death, and her two sons were stabbed to death. At the original trial the prosecution presented fingerprint and DNA results for some, but not all, of the physical evidence that had been collected at the crime scene. In particular, the untested items included a bloodied ax handle, knives, the victims' fingernail clippings, and vaginal swabs taken from Busby. Skinner was found by police soon after the murders in a closet at the residence; his clothes were smeared with the victims' blood. Other physical evidence also linked him to the crime. He admitted that he was in the house at the time of the murders, but claimed that he did not commit the murders because he was passed out after ingesting a large amount of alcohol and codeine.

Throughout his appeals process Skinner sought unsuccessfully to force the state to test the evidence that was not previously tested. In 2001 the Texas legislature passed a rule allowing for postconviction DNA testing under limited circumstances. Skinner was unable to qualify under this rule. When he exhausted the last of his appeals, he was scheduled to be executed on March 24, 2010. After Skinner finished his "last meal" and minutes before his execution was to take place, the U.S. Supreme Court issued a temporary stay of execution so it could consider whether or not to hear his civil rights claim, which had been denied by an appeals court. Nearly a year later, on March 6, 2011, the court overturned the appeals court's decision and remanded the case (returned it to the lower court). In May 2011 the appeals court remanded the decision back to the district court that had originally heard (and denied) Skinner's civil rights claim. As of September 2011, the case had not been reheard in district court.

In June 2011 Governor Perry signed into law a bill that modified the state's Code of Criminal Procedure to greatly expand defendant access to postconviction testing of biological evidence that is collected at crime scenes.

Backlog of DNA Testing

Given the high price of analyzing DNA samples, DNA evidence from crime scenes often goes untested. Such testing, however, could exonerate death row inmates who have been falsely accused. In December 2000 Congress authorized the U.S. Department of Justice to provide funding to state crime laboratories to analyze the backlog of DNA samples that had been collected but never tested.

In *Report to the Attorney General on Delays in Forensic DNA Analysis* (March 2003, http://www.ncjrs.gov/pdffiles1/nij/199425.pdf), the National Institute of Justice (NIJ) revealed that a task force assembled by the NIJ found a continuing backlog in the testing of DNA samples collected at crime scenes. Even though an estimated 350,000 rape and homicide DNA samples needed testing at that time, just 10% of the samples were in forensic crime laboratories. Most of the evidence samples were in the custody of law enforcement agencies because most laboratories lacked the proper storage facilities for preventing damage to the evidence.

Even if the laboratories had the proper storage facilities, the analysis of DNA samples could not take place because of the shortage of trained forensic scientists. Newly hired scientists need on-the-job training that requires an experienced scientist to spend time working one-on-one with new hires. The task force found that even when these problems were confronted, public crime laboratories could not retain their staff because of their lower compensation, compared with that paid by private companies.

According to the NIJ, in "Backlog Reduction Funding Awards, 2004–2010" (2011, http://www.nij.gov/topics/forensics/lab-operations/capacity/backlog-reduction-funding.htm), $64.8 million in funding to states was provided by the Forensic DNA Backlog Reduction Program in fiscal year 2010. Between fiscal years 2004 and 2010 a total of $394.9 million was given out. The largest recipients were California ($51.6 million), Texas ($35.7 million), and Florida ($33.6 million).

Questions about the Validity of Forensic Science

The Science, State, Justice, Commerce, and Related Agencies Appropriations Act of 2006 authorized the National Academy of Sciences to create an independent Forensic Science Committee (FSC) to assess the conditions and needs of the nation's forensic science community, specifically state and local crime laboratories, medical examiners, and coroners. In August 2009 the FSC issued the 352-page report *Strengthening Forensic Science in the United States: A Path Forward* (https://www.ncjrs.gov/pdffiles1/nij/grants/228091.pdf).

The FSC acknowledges the valuable role that forensic science has played in the U.S. justice system in recent decades in terms of convicting the guilty and exonerating the innocent. However, serious problems are described regarding the scientific basis of some procedures and general practices that characterize the forensic community. The committee notes, "There is no uniformity in the certification of forensic practitioners, or in the accreditation of crime laboratories. Indeed, most jurisdictions do not require forensic practitioners to be certified, and most forensic

science disciplines have no mandatory certification programs. Moreover, accreditation of crime laboratories is not required in most jurisdictions." The FSC also finds that "in some cases, substantive information and testimony based on faulty forensic science analyses may have contributed to wrongful convictions of innocent people." Regarding scientific validity, the FSC states, "The simple reality is that the interpretation of forensic evidence is not always based on scientific studies to determine its validity. This is a serious problem. Although research has been done in some disciplines, there is a notable dearth of peer-reviewed, published studies establishing the scientific bases and validity of many forensic methods."

The FSC also recognizes as problems the significant backlogs at crime laboratories around the country and the lack of educational and training requirements among medical examiners and coroners' offices. It notes that state and local forensic laboratories are "underresourced and understaffed." The committee calls for upgrades to systems and organizational structures, better training, and widespread adaptation of uniform training, certification, and accreditation procedures. Even though the FSC supports national oversight of the forensic community, it recommends against assigning that responsibility to a unit of the Department of Justice or to any entity that is principally devoted to law enforcement. The committee states that forensic science should be "equally available to law enforcement officers, prosecutors, *and* defendants in the criminal justice system."

Some of the problems identified by the FSC have already received public attention. For example, in "Tarnish on the 'Gold Standard': Recent Problems in Forensic DNA Testing" (*The Champion*, January–February 2006), William C. Thompson describes problems that have been uncovered at numerous crime laboratories around the country. Thomson cites incidences of poor quality control procedures, mishandling of samples, testing errors, and dishonest analysts. He notes that in some cases postconviction DNA testing has brought laboratory problems to light when the postconviction test results do not match the pretrial results.

Innocent Men Executed?

As noted earlier, more than 100 men who were once on death row have been exonerated. Since the turn of the 21st century two executions have taken place in which serious concerns arose either before or after the executions about the innocence of the condemned men.

CAMERON WILLINGHAM. The validity of forensic science techniques, specifically arson investigations, has taken center stage in the debate over the possible innocence of a man who was executed in Texas in 2004. Cameron Todd Willingham (1968–2004) was executed for setting a house fire that killed his three young children in 1991. His conviction rested largely on expert testimony from the state fire marshal that the fire had been deliberately set. Steve Mills and Maurice Possley describe in "Man Executed on Disproved Forensics" (*Chicago Tribune*, December 9, 2004) the findings of several arson investigators who were hired by the *Chicago Tribune* to review the trial evidence. All of the investigators disputed the original finding that the fire was definitely arson.

In 2008 the Innocence Project filed a formal complaint regarding the Willingham case with the Texas Forensic Science Commission (TFSC; http://www.fsc.state.tx.us/), which had been created in 2005 by the Texas legislature. In August 2009 a private company hired by the TFSC issued a scathing report criticizing the lack of scientific methods that were employed by the original fire investigators. A copy of the report, *Analysis of the Fire Investigation Methods and Procedures Used in the Criminal Arson Cases against Ernest Ray Willis and Cameron Todd Willingham* (August 17, 2009, http://www.deathpenaltyinfo.org/documents/BeylerArsonRpt082509.pdf), has been made public by the DPIC. The report details numerous shortcomings in the original investigation and describes subsequent development of fire science standards by the National Fire Protection Association (NFPA). The report concludes, "The investigators had poor understandings of fire science and failed to acknowledge or apply the contemporaneous understanding of the limitations of fire indicators. Their methodologies did not comport with the scientific method or the process of elimination. A finding of arson could not be sustained based upon the standard of care expressed by NFPA 921, or the standard of care expressed by fire investigation texts and papers in the period 1980–1992."

The controversial case continued to develop in late 2009, when Governor Perry replaced the chairman Sam Bassett and three other members of the TFSC just days before a scheduled hearing on the Willingham case at which the commission planned to review the report. Perry's critics suggested that the commission appointments were politically motivated and were a preemptive move that was designed to stall inquiry into the Willingham execution. Perry defended his decision not to stay the execution in 2004, stating that Willingham's death sentence had been upheld at every level of the Texas court system and that reports challenging forensic testimony amounted to little more than opinions. According to James C. McKinley Jr., in "Controversy Builds in Texas over an Execution" (*New York Times*, October 19, 2009), Perry said, "Willingham was a monster.... Here's a guy who murdered his three children.... Person after person has stood up and testified to the facts in this case."

In April 2011 the TFSC issued its final report on the Willingham case and an arson case from the 1980s involving the defendant Ernest Ray Willis. In *Report of the Texas Forensic Science Commission: Willingham/Willis Investigation* (http://www.fsc.state.tx.us/documents/FINAL.pdf),

the TFSC makes no direct findings about the guilt or innocence of Willingham, but it does review testimony given by the chief arson investigator during the trial about specific clues that led him to believe the fire was deliberately set. The commission critiques these statements and finds fault with them in light of the improvements made in fire science since that time. The TFSC notes that "there was no uniform standard of practice for state or local fire investigators in the early 1990's in Texas or elsewhere in the United States." The commission also presents an August 2010 letter it received from the Texas State Fire Marshal's Office in which the latter stated that "in reviewing documents and standards in place then and now, we stand by the original investigator's report and conclusions." The commission complains, "This appears to be an untenable [incapable of being defended] position in light of advances in fire science." However, the TFSC does not directly criticize the original investigator, noting that "in light of the jurisdictional issues discussed above and related litigation concerns, the Commission declines to issue any finding regarding negligence or professional misconduct."

Death penalty opponents hailed the TFSC report as proof that improper arson science was used to convict and execute Willingham. However, critics disputed this interpretation. In July 2011 the Texas attorney general Greg Wayne Abbott (1957–; http://www.fsc.state.tx.us/documents/11.pdf) issued an opinion stating that the commission could not consider evidence "that was tested or offered into evidence" prior to September 1, 2005, the date the TFSC was created. He also limited the TFSC's authority to investigate testing facilities and certain fields of forensic analysis. Abbott's opinion was seen by death penalty opponents as a political ploy to stifle any further investigation into the Willingham case. In the editorial "Forensic Science Commission Still Has Work to Do" (*Houston Chronicle*, August 14, 2011), Barry Scheck, the codirector of the Innocence Project, accuses Abbott and the state's fire marshal of "protecting themselves and shielding Gov. Rick Perry from potential criticism and political backlash stemming from the fact that a man was allowed to be executed even though his conviction was based on flawed and outdated science."

TROY DAVIS. In 1991 Troy Davis was convicted in Georgia for the 1989 murder of Mark MacPhail, an off-duty police officer. The case was unusual in that there was essentially no physical evidence tying Davis to the crime and the murder weapon was never found. Instead, his conviction was based almost entirely on the testimony of seven witnesses to the crime and two people who said Davis confessed to them after the murder. In the years following his conviction, Davis's lawyers obtained affidavits (sworn statements) from five of the witnesses and the two people alleging that Davis confessed to them, in which they recanted (withdrew) parts or all of their original testimony. The lawyers argued unsuccessfully during the appeals process that these recantations offered evidence of Davis's innocence. Publicity about Davis's case garnered him many supporters including human rights organizations, such as the National Association for the Advancement of Colored People and Amnesty International, and prominent public figures, such as former president Jimmy Carter (1924–) and former U.S. representative Bob Barr (1948–; R-GA). All advocated for a new hearing to consider Davis's postconviction innocence claims.

In "Davis Ruling Raises New Death-Penalty Questions" (*Time*, August 18, 2009), David Von Drehle reports that Davis's case was complicated by the 1996 passage of the Antiterrorism and Effective Death Penalty Act, which placed new restrictions on federal habeas corpus appeals for state and federal death row inmates. As noted in Chapter 5, a death row inmate who has exhausted all state appeals can file a petition for a federal habeas corpus review on grounds of violation of his or her constitutional rights. According to Von Drehle, the new law essentially limits inmates to one set of appeals at the federal level. Because Davis had already had a federal appeal, his subsequent attempts to obtain a rehearing in federal courts were denied.

In 2007 Davis was scheduled to be executed when he received a temporary stay of execution from the Georgia State Board of Pardons and Paroles. Von Drehle notes that the board "conducted a detailed examination of the new evidence," but was not convinced of his innocence. Davis's lawyers appealed to the Georgia Supreme Court and a federal court, but were again rebuffed. It should be noted that recantations are treated suspiciously by courts because they indicate witnesses have likely lied under oath. As Von Drehle explains, "The Davis case became a morass of contradictory statements from addled witnesses, many of whom were either lying then or are lying now—or maybe both." In 2008 Davis's lawyers petitioned the U.S. Supreme Court to force a federal court to hear the innocence claims. In 2009 the U.S. Supreme Court agreed. In *In Re Troy Anthony Davis* (555 U.S. ___), a federal court was ordered to "receive testimony and make findings of fact as to whether evidence that could not have been obtained at the time of trial clearly establishes petitioner's innocence."

Von Drehle states that the decision was highly controversial because it basically undermined the intent of the 1996 law. Ordinarily, nine Supreme Court justices take part in the court's decisions. In the Davis ruling, only three justices concurred in the decision, while two dissented. Another three justices mysteriously neither concurred nor dissented. A ninth justice had recently been installed on the court and took no part in the proceedings. The concurring justices stated that "the substantial risk of putting an innocent man to death clearly provides an adequate justification for holding an evidentiary hearing." The dissenting justices

complained that "the allegedly new evidence we shunt off to be examined by the District Court has already been considered (and rejected) multiple times. Davis's postconviction 'actual-innocence' claim is not new. Most of the evidence on which it is based is almost a decade old. A State Supreme Court, a State Board of Pardons and Paroles, and a Federal Court of Appeals have all considered the evidence Davis now presents and found it lacking."

In 2010 Davis received his long-sought hearing in federal court. However, the U.S. District Court for the Southern District of Georgia rejected Davis's "actual-innocence" claim. In *In Re Troy Anthony Davis* (No. CV409-130), Judge William Moore (1940–) recounted the testimony that was presented during the original trial and examined in detail the recanted statements. He noted that "Mr. Davis's new evidence does not change the balance of proof from trial. Of his seven 'recantations,' only one is a meaningful, credible recantation.... The value of that recantation is diminished because it only confirms that which was obvious at trial—that its author was testifying falsely.... Four of the remaining six recantations are either not credible or not true recantations and would be disregarded.... The remaining two recantations were presented under the most suspicious of circumstances, with Mr. Davis intentionally preventing the validity of the recantation from being challenged in open court through cross-examination." Some of the recanting witnesses claimed the police had coerced or pressured them during the original trial to identify Davis as the killer. Moore disputed these claims, noting that none of the recanting witnesses were absolute in their original identification of Davis as the killer. For example, Antoine Williams originally testified that he was 60% certain in his identification. Moore noted that "Mr. Williams's statements were far from ideal and if the State was to coerce testimony, it surely would have coerced testimony more favorable [to its case] than that actually provided by Mr. Williams."

The judge also criticized Davis's lawyers for not requesting a subpoena (a formal notice to appear before a court) to force the state's key witness during the original trial—Sylvester "Red" Coles—to testify at the hearing. Coles was standing near Davis when the murder occurred and has subsequently been claimed by some recanting witnesses and new witnesses to have been the actual killer. Moore discounted this "hearsay" testimony because Coles was not present for cross-examination. Likewise, Davis's lawyers did not call two of the recanting witnesses to testify at the hearing, but merely presented their written affidavits to the court. Thus, these two witnesses could not be cross-examined. Moore noted that "affidavit evidence is viewed with great suspicion and has diminished value." The judge concluded, "Ultimately, while Mr. Davis's new evidence casts some additional, minimal doubt on his conviction, it is largely smoke and mirrors. The vast majority of the evidence at trial remains intact, and the new evidence is largely not credible or lacking in probative [proof-supplying] value." The court rejected Davis's innocence claims.

The court's decision spurred the state of Georgia to set a September 2011 execution date for Davis. The U.S. Supreme Court refused to hear additional motions filed by his lawyers, and the Georgia State Board of Pardons and Paroles denied him clemency. As described earlier, Davis garnered much public support during his long fight against his death sentence. As his execution neared, his case received widespread media attention. Hundreds of thousands of supporters, including many celebrities and well-known public figures, signed petitions on his behalf and called for Davis to be pardoned. Nevertheless, he was executed on September 21, 2011. In his last words, Davis reportedly reiterated his innocence. The execution was widely condemned in the press. Former President Carter (September 22, 2011, http://www.cartercenter.org/news/pr/davis-092211.html) remarked, "If one of our fellow citizens can be executed with so much doubt surrounding his guilt, then the death penalty system in our country is unjust and outdated." However, according to the article "Ex DA: Doubt, Recantations 'Manufactured' in Troy Davis Case" (September 21, 2011, http://www.11alive.com/news/article/206167/40/Ex-DA-Doubt-recantations-manufactured-in-Troy-Davis-case), Spencer Lawton, the original prosecutor, argues that the public doubts about Davis's guilt were "manufactured" by death penalty opponents via the much-publicized recantations, which he says were coaxed out of the witnesses years after the murder by Davis's defense team and by supporters from Amnesty International.

MORATORIUMS

Since the turn of the 21st century a number of measures have been put in place in death penalty states to remedy perceived problems in their capital punishment systems. These measures include moratoriums (suspensions) in executions. Moratoriums fall into two types: de jure and de facto. The term *de jure* means "by right." A de jure moratorium is a moratorium imposed by law. The term *de facto* means "in reality" or "actually." A de facto moratorium on executions means that some other factor besides a law has caused executions not to take place.

States with de Jure Moratoriums

As of September 2011, 15 states had no capital offenses in their statutes: Alaska, Hawaii, Illinois, Iowa, Maine, Massachusetts, Michigan, Minnesota, New Jersey, New Mexico, North Dakota, Rhode Island, Vermont, West Virginia, and Wisconsin. The District of Columbia also did not have the death penalty. As described in Chapter 1, most of these states and the District of Columbia outlawed capital punishment many years ago:

- 1853—Wisconsin
- 1887—Maine
- 1911—Minnesota
- 1957—Alaska and Hawaii (both then territories)
- 1963—Michigan
- 1965—Iowa, Vermont, and West Virginia
- 1975—North Dakota
- 1984—Massachusetts and Rhode Island
- 2007—New Jersey
- 2009—New Mexico
- 2011—Illinois

In reality, some of these states had not executed anyone for decades before capital punishment was officially ended; for example, Alaska, Hawaii, Maine, Michigan, Minnesota, North Dakota, Rhode Island, and Wisconsin had not executed anyone since 1930. (See Table 8.2.) The District of Columbia and eight states—Iowa, Kansas, Massachusetts, New Hampshire, New Jersey, New York, Vermont, and West Virginia—had not executed anyone since 1977. Kansas, New Hampshire, and New York ceased executions due to de facto moratoriums, which will be discussed later in this chapter.

ILLINOIS. On January 31, 2000, Illinois became the first state in the modern death penalty era to declare a moratorium on the death penalty. Governor George Ryan (1934–), a death penalty supporter, suspended all executions because he believed the state's death penalty system was "fraught

TABLE 8.2

States with no executions, 1930–2009 and 1977–2009

	No executions since 1930	No executions since 1977
District of Columbia		X
Iowa		X
Kansas		X
Massachusetts		X
New Hampshire		X
New Jersey		X
New York		X
Vermont		X
West Virginia		X
Alaska	X	X
Hawaii	X	X
Maine	X	X
Michigan	X	X
Minnesota	X	X
North Dakota	X	X
Rhode Island	X	X
Wisconsin	X	X

SOURCE: Adapted from Tracy L. Snell, "Table 17. Number of Persons Executed, by Jurisdiction, 1930–2009," in *Capital Punishment, 2009—Statistical Tables*, U.S. Department of Justice, Office of Justice Programs, Bureau of Justice Statistics, December 2010, http://bjs.ojp.usdoj.gov/content/pub/pdf/cp09st.pdf (accessed July 5, 2011)

with errors." The *Chicago Tribune* had issued a report showing that 13 inmates in Illinois had been released from death row since 1976. The reasons for the exoneration of these inmates ranged from DNA evidence showing innocence, to false testimonies by jailhouse informants, to coercion of so-called witnesses by the prosecution and police.

Ryan then established the Governor's Commission on Capital Punishment to investigate the 13 cases, as well as all capital cases in Illinois. In April 2002 the commission published *Report of the Governor's Commission on Capital Punishment* (http://www.idoc.state.il.us/ccp/ccp/reports/commission_report/summary_recommendations.pdf). The commission issued 85 recommendations it thought would help reform the state's death penalty process. The recommended reforms included videotaping of capital suspects during interrogation at police facilities, banning the death penalty in cases where the conviction is based on a single eyewitness testimony, and thorough examination of jailhouse-informant testimonies at pretrial hearings to determine whether to use those testimonies during trial.

On January 10, 2003, the day before leaving office, Governor Ryan pardoned four inmates who had been on death row in Illinois for at least 12 years. The governor claimed the men were innocent of the murders for which they had been convicted. He found that the police had tortured the men into making false confessions. Three of the men had been released. The fourth inmate remained in prison because of a separate conviction. The following day Governor Ryan commuted 167 death sentences to life imprisonment without the possibility of parole, emptying death row.

In March 2011 Governor Pat Quinn (1948–) signed a bill that eliminated the death penalty in Illinois. He also commuted the sentences of the state's 15 death row inmates to life in prison without the possibility of parole.

NEW JERSEY. In 2006 the New Jersey legislature created the New Jersey Death Penalty Study Commission to assess the administration of capital punishment in the state. All death sentences were put on hold until at least 60 days after completion of the commission's report, *New Jersey Death Penalty Study Commission Report* (January 2007, http://www.njleg.state.nj.us/committees/dpsc_final.pdf). The report included eight major findings and recommendations:

- "No compelling evidence" was found to support the idea that the death penalty "serves a legitimate penological" purpose.

- The costs of capital punishment were found to be higher than the costs of life in prison without parole.

- Evidence indicated that the death penalty is "inconsistent with evolving standards of decency."

- Data did not support the idea that racial biases affect the application of capital punishment in New Jersey.

- The abolishment of the death penalty would eliminate the "risk of disproportionality in capital sentencing."

- The penological benefit of capital punishment was deemed not worth the risk of possibly making an "irreversible mistake."

- Life sentences with no chance of parole were declared sufficient to ensure public safety and address other social and penological concerns.

- State funds should be allocated to provide needed services to the families of murder victims.

In December 2007 New Jersey officially abolished the death penalty. According to Keith B. Richburg, in "N.J. Approves Abolition of Death Penalty; Corzine to Sign" (*Washington Post*, December 14, 2007), the New Jersey law replaced the death penalty with a sentence of life in prison without the possibility of parole. Tracy L. Snell of the Bureau of Justice Statistics indicates in *Capital Punishment, 2007—Statistical Tables* (December 1, 2008, http://bjs.ojp.usdoj.gov/content/pub/html/cp/2007/cp07st.pdf) that there were no inmates on New Jersey's death row at the time.

NEW MEXICO. In March 2009 the New Mexico governor Bill Richardson (1957–) signed into law a bill that repealed the state's death penalty and replaced it with a sentence of life in prison with no chance for parole. The article "New Mexico Governor Repeals Death Penalty in State" (CNN.com, March 18, 2009) reports that Richardson described himself as a "firm believer in the death penalty as a just punishment—in very rare instances, and only for the most heinous crimes." Regardless, he expressed serious reservations about capital punishment, particularly noting the number of cases in which death row prisoners had been exonerated. He was also concerned that minorities are "overrepresented" in the nation's death row population. However, the law change does not affect New Mexico's existing death row population. In *Death Row U.S.A.: Winter 2011* (August 24, 2011, http://naacpldf.org/files/publications/DRUSA_Winter_2011.pdf), Deborah Fins lists two inmates under sentence of death in the state as of January 1, 2011. The article "Two Remain on New Mexico's Death Row" (January 20, 2011, http://www.krqe.com/dpp/news/local/central/two-remain-on-new-mexico%27s-death-row) reports that as of January 2011 the two were still engaged in the appeals process, which could take at least another decade. The last execution in New Mexico was in 2001.

Death Penalty States with Long-Standing de Facto Moratoriums

As of September 2011, 34 states had death penalty statutes. However, three of these states—Kansas, New Hampshire, and New York—had not executed anyone since 1977.

KANSAS. The last executions in Kansas were in June 1965. It was not until 1994 that the state reinstated the death penalty following the nationwide moratorium triggered by the U.S. Supreme Court's decision in *Furman v. Georgia*. However, no inmate has been executed in Kansas under the new statute. For more than a decade the state's new death penalty law was subject to court challenges regarding its constitutionality. The issue was settled by the U.S. Supreme Court in 2006 in *Kansas v. Marsh* (548 U.S. 163) in which the new law was upheld. In *Death Row U.S.A.: Winter 2011*, Fins notes that Kansas had nine inmates on death row as of January 1, 2011.

NEW HAMPSHIRE. New Hampshire has not executed anyone since July 1939. Two death sentences handed out during the 1950s were later overturned by courts. In December 2008 a New Hampshire jury sentenced Michael Addison (1980–) to death for killing a police officer. According to Fins, in *Death Row U.S.A.: Winter 2011*, Addison was the sole inmate on death row as of January 1, 2011. New Hampshire law limits the crimes for which a death sentence can be imposed to the following: murder for hire, murdering a police officer, and murder during the course of a kidnapping. However, another man convicted of capital murder during 2009 received life in prison from a jury. John J. Brooks was found guilty of paying three men to kill a man he believed had cheated him. Katie Zezima reports in "Jury Issues First Death Sentence in New Hampshire since the 1950s" (*New York Times*, December 18, 2008) that the disparity in sentences between the two cases aroused controversy because Addison is African-American and not wealthy, whereas Brooks is white and a millionaire.

In July 2009 the New Hampshire governor John Lynch (1952–) established a commission to study the scope of the state's death penalty system, along with its strengths and weaknesses, associated costs, and issues such as discrimination and how best to serve the interests of crime victims. The commission included legislators as well as appointees representing prosecuting attorneys, defense lawyers, law enforcement officers, family members of murder victims, mental health professionals, and special interest organizations with objectives related to the capital punishment debate. In December 2010 the commission published *Final Report on HB 520, Chapter 284, Laws of 2009* (http://gencourt.state.nh.us/statstudcomm/reports/2009.pdf). The commission recommends that New Hampshire maintain the death penalty, noting that it "serves several important and legitimate social interests" and "is consistent with evolving standards of societal decency." In addition, the commission concludes that the application of capital punishment in New Hampshire is fair and is not plagued by racial bias or other discrimination.

NEW YORK. Until 1998 New York's death penalty statute prohibited the imposition of a death sentence when a defendant entered a guilty plea. The maximum penalty in such a case would be life imprisonment without parole. However, a defendant who pleaded not guilty would have to stand trial and face the possibility of a death sentence. The law provided two levels of penalty for the same offense, imposing the death penalty only on those who claimed innocence.

Defendants in two capital cases challenged the plea provisions of New York's death penalty statute, claiming these provisions violated their Fifth Amendment right against self-incrimination and Sixth Amendment right to a jury trial. This was the first major constitutional challenge to New York's death penalty law. In December 1998 the New York Court of Appeals (New York's highest court), in *Hynes v. Tomei* (including *Relin v. Mateo*, 92 N.Y. 2d. 613, 706 N.E. 2d. 1201, 684 N.Y.S. 2d. 177), unanimously agreed, thereby striking down these plea-bargaining provisions as unconstitutional. The court, relying on the U.S. Supreme Court decision in *United States v. Jackson* (390 U.S. 570 [1968]), observed that "the Supreme Court in *Jackson* prohibited statutes that 'needlessly' encourage guilty pleas, which are not constitutionally protected, by impermissibly burdening constitutional rights." The ruling left the death penalty intact, but the court could no longer give preference to those who entered a guilty plea.

JURY DEADLOCK INSTRUCTIONS. In 2004 the New York Court of Appeals agreed to hear another challenge to the constitutionality of New York's death penalty. Stephen LaValle (1967–) was sentenced to death in 1999 by a New York jury for the rape and murder of Cynthia Quinn. Under New York law, a jury can sentence a defendant convicted of murder to life in prison without parole or to death. All jurors must vote unanimously. In the event of a hung jury (a jury that cannot reach a verdict after a reasonable amount of time deliberating), the court sentences a guilty defendant to life imprisonment with parole eligibility after serving a minimum of 20 to 25 years, leaving room for the convict to be released.

LaValle claimed that this "jury deadlock instruction" violated his constitutional rights because it could encourage members of the jury who do not favor the death penalty to vote for the death penalty if they are in the minority. LaValle even presented a study showing that most jurors would choose the death penalty if given the choice of the death penalty or imprisonment with a chance of parole. In *People v. LaValle* (783 N.Y.S. 2d, 485 [2004]), the New York Court of Appeals agreed with LaValle and vacated his sentence. The state high court indicated that this jury instruction was a cruel and unusual punishment in violation of the Eighth and 14th Amendments, citing the U.S. Supreme Court's decision in *Woodson v. North Carolina* (428 U.S. 280 [1976]). The Supreme Court held in *Woodson* that a mandatory death sentence for a capital offense was unconstitutional and forced jurors to sentence the defendant with a lesser charge if they did not want to see the defendant sentenced to death.

This decision by the New York court in 2004 effectively put a de facto moratorium on the New York death penalty until the New York state legislature could change the death penalty statutes. About a year later the New York State Assembly Codes Committee (the state legislative committee in charge of changing death penalty statutes) defeated a bill to reinstate the death penalty, claiming that the system was riddled with flaws. In 2007 the state's last death row inmate was resentenced to life in prison without the chance of parole. As of September 2011, the de facto moratorium on the death penalty remained in effect in New York.

Death Penalty States with Recent de Facto Moratoriums

Since 2000 many death penalty states have put into place de facto moratoriums on executions for a number of reasons. As described in Chapter 3, the U.S. Supreme Court's decision in September 2007 to hear a case concerning the constitutionality of Kentucky's lethal injection protocol triggered a de facto moratorium on executions around the country. In *Baze v. Rees* (553 U.S. ___ [2008]), the nation's highest court upheld that protocol. Some states resumed executions immediately; however, other states continued to reexamine and sometimes adjust their lethal injection protocols to ensure their constitutionality.

CALIFORNIA. In 2004 the California Commission on the Fair Administration of Justice (CCFAJ) was created by the state legislature to examine California's criminal justice system and make recommendations to remedy any problems. The CCFAJ (http://www.ccfaj.org/reports.html) released 10 reports containing its findings and recommendations:

- *Report and Recommendations Regarding Eye Witness Identification Procedures* (April 13, 2006)

- *Report and Recommendations Regarding False Confessions* (July 25, 2006)

- *Report and Recommendations Regarding Informant Testimony* (November 20, 2006)

- *Report and Recommendations Regarding Forensic Science Evidence* (May 8, 2007)

- *Emergency Report and Recommendations Regarding DNA Testing Backlogs* (February 20, 2007)

- *Report and Recommendations on Funding of Defense Services in California* (April 14, 2008)

- *Report and Recommendations on Compliance with the Prosecutorial Duty to Disclose Exculpatory Evidence* (March 6, 2008)

- *Report and Recommendations on Reporting Misconduct* (October 18, 2007)

- *Report and Recommendations on the Administration of the Death Penalty in California* (June 30, 2008)

- *Final Report* (August 4, 2008)

California legislators acted on the recommendations provided in the early reports by passing bills that reformed the state's eyewitness identification procedures and required audio recording of suspect interrogations. In 2006 Governor Arnold Schwarzenegger (1947–) vetoed both bills by citing procedural problems with them. Revamped versions of the bills passed the legislature in 2007 but were again vetoed by the governor.

In December 2006 a federal judge in California ruled in *Morales v. Tilton* (No. C 06 219 JF RS) that the state's lethal injection protocol was unconstitutional after hearing arguments from the lawyers for the death row inmate Michael Morales (1959–). The judge complained that the protocol "lacks both reliability and transparency" and results in "undue and unnecessary risk of an Eighth Amendment violation." The state began construction of a new execution chamber and the development of new lethal injection protocols. Fins notes in *Death Row U.S.A.: Winter 2011* that as of January 1, 2011, California's death row contained 721 inmates, the largest number of any state. As of September 2011, a de facto moratorium remained in effect in California.

PHYSICIAN INVOLVEMENT. One issue that has triggered or prolonged temporary execution moratoriums in California, Missouri, and North Carolina has been the role of physicians in the execution process. Kevin O'Reilly reports on this issue on behalf of the American Medical Association (AMA) in "Controversial California Ruling Focuses on Physician Role in Execution" (March 13, 2006, http://www.ama-assn.org/amednews/2006/03/13/prl20313.htm). He notes that in February 2006 a federal judge ordered the state of California to have an anesthesiologist present during executions to ensure that the lethal injection procedure rendered the prisoner fully unconscious. California, like most other death penalty states, uses a three-part lethal injection protocol in which the first drug renders the prisoner unconscious, a second drug paralyzes the prisoner, and a third drug stops the heart beating. Questions have arisen about the effectiveness of the first drug at keeping prisoners fully unconscious during the remaining procedures.

The AMA and some state medical associations have warned doctors that actively participating in an execution would violate their ethical responsibilities. O'Reilly notes in "Physicians Resist Push for Execution Involvement"

(May 14, 2007, http://www.ama-assn.org/amednews/ 2007/05/14/prl20514.htm) that AMA policy prohibits doctors from being present at executions "in a professional capacity," taking any part in the execution process, or offering "technical advice" regarding execution. The only role the organization allows is for doctors to certify that a prisoner is dead. However, recent court rulings in California, Missouri, and North Carolina have forced corrections officials in those states to use doctors actively in the execution process. O'Reilly reports that doctors have been reluctant to participate for fear of losing their medical licenses. In March 2007 corrections officials in North Carolina sued that state's medical board after the board threatened disciplinary action against any doctor who actively participated in an execution. According to O'Reilly, in "North Carolina Medical Board Can't Discipline Doctors for Execution Work" (October 22, 2007, http://www.ama-assn.org/amednews/2007/10/22/prsc1022 .htm), in September 2007 a state court judge ruled that the medical board had "overstepped its authority" in making the threat. The medical board appealed, but in 2009 the North Carolina Supreme Court upheld the lower court's ruling.

In April 2010 the American Board of Anesthesiology (ABA; http://www.theaba.org/pdf/CapitalPunishmentCom mentary.pdf) announced that anesthesiologists who are candidates for membership or diplomates (certified specialists) in the organization "may not participate in capital punishment if they wish to be certified by the ABA." The ABA acknowledges that its members have differing opinions on the appropriateness of the death penalty, but insists "physicians should not be expected to act in ways that violate the ethics of medical practice, even if these acts are legal."

Death Penalty States That Rarely Impose the Death Penalty

As shown in Table 8.3, 16 states that had the death penalty in 2009 had executed 10 or fewer inmates between 1977 and 2009:

- Colorado (1)

- Connecticut (1)

- Idaho (1)

- Kentucky (3)

- Maryland (5)

- Mississippi (10)

- Montana (3)

- Nebraska (3)

- New Mexico (1)

- Oregon (2)

TABLE 8.3

Number of persons executed, by jurisdiction, 1977–2009

Jurisdiction	Since 1977
U.S. total	**1,188**
Texas	447
Virginia	105
Oklahoma	91
Florida	68
Missouri	67
Georgia	46
Alabama	44
North Carolina	43
South Carolina	42
Ohio	33
Louisiana	27
Arkansas	27
Arizona	23
Indiana	20
Delaware	14
California	13
Illinois	12
Nevada	12
Mississippi	10
Tennessee	6
Utah	6
Maryland	5
Washington	4
Pennsylvania	3
Kentucky	3
Federal system	3
Montana	3
Nebraska	3
Oregon	2
Colorado	1
Connecticut	1
New Mexico	1
Wyoming	1
Idaho	1
South Dakota	1

SOURCE: Adapted from Tracy L. Snell, "Table 17. Number of Persons Executed, by Jurisdiction, 1930–2009," in *Capital Punishment, 2009—Statistical Tables*, U.S. Department of Justice, Office of Justice Programs, Bureau of Justice Statistics, December 2010, http://bjs.ojp.usdoj.gov/content/ pub/pdf/cp09st.pdf (accessed July 5, 2011)

- Pennsylvania (3)

- South Dakota (1)

- Tennessee (6)

- Utah (6)

- Washington (4)

- Wyoming (1)

According to Fins, in *Death Row U.S.A.: Winter 2011*, 11 states had between one and 10 inmates on death row as of January 1, 2011:

- Colorado (4)

- Connecticut (10)

- Kansas (9)

- Maryland (5)

- Montana (2)

- New Hampshire (1)

- New Mexico (2)
- South Dakota (3)
- Utah (9)
- Washington (9)
- Wyoming (1)

With the exception of Connecticut, Maryland, and New Hampshire, all of these states are in the West. New Mexico abolished capital punishment in 2009; the new law, however, was not retroactive in commuting existing death sentences. As of September 2011, no laws had been passed that abolished the death penalty in the remaining 10 states.

CHAPTER 9
PUBLIC ATTITUDES TOWARD CAPITAL PUNISHMENT

Like all statistics, those contained in public opinion polls should be viewed cautiously. The way a question is phrased can influence the respondents' answers. Many other factors may also influence a response in ways that are often difficult to determine. Respondents might never have thought of the issue until asked, or they might be giving the pollster the answer they think the pollster wants to hear. Organizations that survey opinions do not claim absolute accuracy. Their findings are approximate snapshots of the attitudes of the nation at a given time.

THE MORALITY OF CAPITAL PUNISHMENT

The Gallup Organization conducts an annual values and beliefs poll in which it measures Americans' views about various moral issues. In May 2011 respondents were asked about 17 particular issues that were deemed important to society. As shown in Table 9.1, nearly two-thirds (65%) of those asked rated the death penalty as morally acceptable. It was the second-most morally acceptable issue to Americans, after divorce, for which 69% expressed moral acceptance. Capital punishment was considered more morally acceptable than many other controversial issues, including sex between an unmarried man and woman, having a baby outside of marriage, doctor-assisted suicide, and abortion.

Table 9.2 shows that the moral acceptability of capital punishment was virtually unchanged in Gallup's May 2011 poll compared with polls dating back to May 2001. Over this period 62% to 71% of respondents rated the death penalty to be morally acceptable, whereas 22% to 31% deemed it to be morally wrong. Small percentages (4% to 7%) said the moral acceptability of the death penalty depends on the situation.

In Table 9.3 the Gallup Organization provides a breakdown by age group of the moral acceptability ratings obtained in its May 2011 poll. The moral issues are ranked by the difference between the percentage of respondents

aged 18 to 34 years rating an issue morally acceptable and those aged 55 years and older giving the same opinion. Overall, the largest difference between the two age groups was on the subject of pornography. Whereas 42% of those aged 18 to 34 years deemed it to be morally acceptable, only 19% of those aged 55 years and older agreed, for a difference of 23 percentage points. Other issues that the younger age group deemed to be more morally acceptable than did the oldest age group include gay/lesbian relations (19 percentage points), premarital sex (18 percentage points), and out-of-wedlock births (16 percentage points). At the other end of the spectrum lie issues that people aged 55 years and older deemed to be more morally acceptable than did people aged 18 to 34 years. The death penalty and medical testing on animals fell into this category. In both cases, there was a 14 percentage point difference. Seventy percent of the respondents in the oldest age group said the death penalty is morally acceptable, compared with 56% of respondents in the youngest age group. Thus, the data indicate that capital punishment enjoys less moral support among younger Americans than it does among older Americans.

SUPPORT FOR THE DEATH PENALTY
Gallup Poll

According to Gallup poll results from 1937, about three out of five (59%) respondents favored the death penalty at that time for a person convicted of murder. (See Figure 9.1.) This was the first time the Gallup Organization polled Americans regarding their attitudes toward the death penalty for murder. For the next three decades support for capital punishment fluctuated, dropping to its lowest point in 1966 (42%). This was a period of civil rights and anti–Vietnam War (1954–1975) marches and the peace movement. It was also the only time in the period of record that those who opposed capital punishment (47%) outnumbered those who favored it. Starting in early 1972 support for capital punishment steadily increased, peaking at 80% in

1994. Between 1999 and 2010 support hovered from 64% to 70%. In 2010 Gallup found that 64% of Americans favored the death penalty for people convicted of murder.

TABLE 9.1

Public opinion on the moral acceptability of various issues, May 2011

["Sorted by morally acceptable"]

NEXT, I'M GOING TO READ YOU A LIST OF ISSUES. REGARDLESS OF WHETHER OR NOT YOU THINK IT SHOULD BE LEGAL, FOR EACH ONE, PLEASE TELL ME WHETHER YOU PERSONALLY BELIEVE THAT IN GENERAL IT IS MORALLY ACCEPTABLE OR MORALLY WRONG. HOW ABOUT—[RANDOM ORDER]?

	Morally acceptable	Morally wrong
Divorce	69	23
The death penalty	65	28
Gambling	64	31
Medical research using stem cells obtained from human embryos	62	30
Sex between an unmarried man and woman	60	36
Buying and wearing clothing made of animal fur	56	39
Gay or lesbian relations	56	39
Medical testing on animals	55	38
Having a baby outside of marriage	54	41
Doctor assisted suicide	45	48
Abortion	39	51
Cloning animals	32	62
Pornography	30	66
Suicide	15	80
Cloning humans	12	84
Polygamy, when one husband has more than one wife at the same time	11	86
Married men and women having an affair	7	91

SOURCE: Jeff Jones and Lydia Saad, "Next, I'm going to read you a list of issues. Regardless of whether or not you think it should be legal, for each one, please tell me whether you personally believe that in general it is morally acceptable or morally wrong. How about—[RANDOM ORDER]?" in *Gallup Poll Social Series: Values and Beliefs—Final Topline*, The Gallup Organization, May 5–8, 2011, http://www.gallup.com/poll/File/147845/Moral_Acceptability_110531.pdf (accessed July 4, 2011). Copyright © 2011 by the Gallup Organization. Reproduced by permission of The Gallup Organization.

The results for October 2010 are broken down by gender, race, and political party affiliation in Table 9.4. Support was higher among men (71% approval) than it was among women (58% approval). There were similar divides between white and nonwhite respondents. Whereas 69% of white respondents approved of the death penalty for a person convicted of murder, only 55% of nonwhite respondents shared this view. Overall, 78% of Republicans (or people who said they lean Republican) supported the death penalty, whereas 16% opposed it. Only a slim majority (55%) of Democrats expressed support for the death penalty; by contrast, 42% were opposed to it.

In previous Gallup surveys, pollsters asked respondents to choose between the death penalty and life imprisonment with "absolutely no possibility of parole" as the "better penalty for murder." This question was last asked in 2010. At that time the breakdown was nearly equal, with 49% choosing the death penalty option and 46% choosing the life imprisonment option. (See Figure 9.2.) Over the years the breakdown between the two choices varied somewhat. Preference for the death penalty was highest in 1997, when 61% of respondents chose it over the life imprisonment option. Preference for life imprisonment with absolutely no chance of parole was highest in the 2006 poll, when 48% of respondents preferred this option.

In *Racial Disagreement over Death Penalty Has Varied Historically* (July 30, 2007, http://www.gallup.com/poll/28243/Racial-Disagreement-Over-Death-Penalty-Has-Varied-Historically.aspx), Lydia Saad of the Gallup Organization discusses the results of a June 2007 poll that included a question about capital punishment. The results indicated that support for the death penalty for convicted murderers was voiced by 70% of whites, but by only 40% of

TABLE 9.2

Public opinion on the moral acceptability of the death penalty, May 2001–11

	Morally acceptable	Morally wrong	Depends on situation (vol.)	Not a moral issue (vol.)	No opinion
2011 May 5–8	65	28	5	*	2
2010 May 3–6	65	26	7	—	2
2009 May 7–10	62	30	6	*	2
2008 May 8–11	62	30	5	*	3
2007 May 10–13	66	27	5	*	2
2006 May 8–11	71	22	5	*	2
2005 May 2–5	70	25	4		1
2004 May 2–4	65	28	4	1	2
2003 May 5–7	64	31	4	—	1
2002 May 6–9	65	28	5	*	2
2001 May 10–14	63	27	7	1	2

* = Less than 1%.
— = None.

SOURCE: Jeff Jones and Lydia Saad, "Next, I'm going to read you a list of issues. Regardless of whether or not you think it should be legal, for each one, please tell me whether you personally believe that in general it is morally acceptable or morally wrong. How about the Death Penalty?" in *Gallup Poll Social Series: Values and Beliefs—Final Topline*, The Gallup Organization, May 5–8, 2011, http://www.gallup.com/poll/File/147845/Moral_Acceptability_110531.pdf (accessed July 4, 2011). Copyright © 2011 by the Gallup Organization. Reproduced by permission of The Gallup Organization.

TABLE 9.3

Public opinion on the moral acceptability of various issues, by age group, May 2011

[Percent morally acceptable, ranked by "difference"]

	18 to 34 years	35 to 54 years	55 and older	Difference, 18 to 34 minus 55 and older
	%	%	%	pct. pts
Pornography	42	29	19	+23
Gay/Lesbian relations	66	56	47	+19
Premarital sex	71	58	53	+18
Out-of-wedlock births	62	56	46	+16
Gambling	71	65	59	+12
Polygamy	19	8	8	+11
Abortion	44	42	34	+10
Cloning humans	18	10	9	+9
Cloning animals	36	32	28	+8
Embryonic stem cell research	66	59	62	+4
Doctor-assisted suicide	46	45	43	+3
Divorce	72	66	70	+2
Extramarital affairs.	8	7	7	+1
Use of animal fur for clothing	55	57	56	−1
Suicide	14	13	19	−5
Death penalty	56	67	70	−14
Medical testing on animals	47	57	61	−14

SOURCE: Lydia Saad, "U.S. Perceived Moral Acceptability of Behaviors and Social Policies—by Age," in *Doctor-Assisted Suicide Is Moral Issue Dividing Americans Most*, The Gallup Organization, May 31, 2011, http://www.gallup.com/poll/147842/Doctor-Assisted-Suicide-Moral-Issue-Dividing-Americans.aspx (accessed July 4, 2011). Copyright © 2011 by the Gallup Organization. Reproduced by permission of The Gallup Organization.

FIGURE 9.1

Public opinion poll on the death penalty, 1937–2010

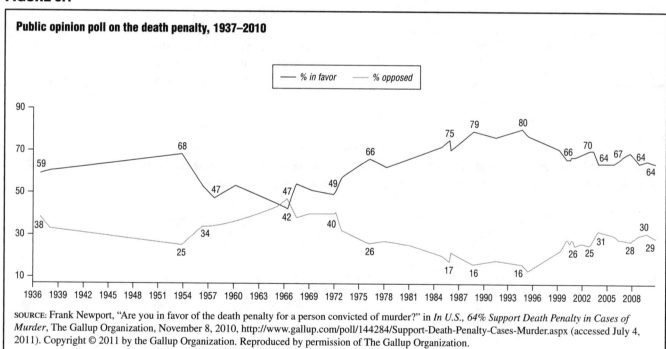

SOURCE: Frank Newport, "Are you in favor of the death penalty for a person convicted of murder?" in *In U.S., 64% Support Death Penalty in Cases of Murder*, The Gallup Organization, November 8, 2010, http://www.gallup.com/poll/144284/Support-Death-Penalty-Cases-Murder.aspx (accessed July 4, 2011). Copyright © 2011 by the Gallup Organization. Reproduced by permission of The Gallup Organization.

African-Americans. In fact, a majority (56%) of African-Americans were opposed to capital punishment. Saad notes that the difference of opinion between African-Americans and whites on this issue is evident in Gallup polls dating back to 1972. Historically, African-American respondents have expressed less support for the death penalty than have white respondents.

Rasmussen Reports Poll

Rasmussen Reports provides in the press release "63% Favor Death Penalty, 47% Say It Deters Crime" (June 29, 2011, http://www.rasmussenreports.com/public_content/politics/general_politics/june_2011/63_favor_death_penalty_47_say_it_deters_crime) the results from a poll conducted in June 2011 in which it found that 63% of respondents favored the death penalty, 25% opposed it, and 12% were undecided. The survey results were almost identical to those obtained by Rasmussen in June 2010. In the press release "62% Favor Death Penalty" (http://www.rasmussenreports.com/public_content/politics/general_politics/june_2010/62_favor_death_penalty), Rasmussen notes that at that time 62% of respondents indicated their support for capital punishment and roughly half said they believe the death penalty helps deter crime.

TABLE 9.4

Public opinion poll on the death penalty, by gender, race, and political affiliation, October 2010

ARE YOU IN FAVOR OF THE DEATH PENALTY FOR A PERSON CONVICTED OF MURDER?

	% approve	% disapprove	% no opinion
National adults	64	29	6
Men	71	24	6
Women	58	35	7
White	69	26	5
Nonwhite	55	37	8
Republicans/Leaners	78	16	5
Democrats/Leaners	55	42	3

SOURCE: Frank Newport, "Are you in favor of the death penalty for a person convicted of murder?" in *In U.S., 64% Support Death Penalty in Cases of Murder*, The Gallup Organization, November 8, 2010, http://www.gallup.com/poll/144284/Support-Death-Penalty-Cases-Murder.aspx (accessed July 4, 2011). Copyright © 2011 by the Gallup Organization. Reproduced by permission of The Gallup Organization.

Pew Research Center Poll

A poll performed between July and August 2010 by the Pew Research Center (2011, http://people-press.org/question-search/?qid=1770415&pid=51&ccid=51) revealed that 62% of Americans supported the death penalty for people convicted of murder, whereas 30% were opposed and 8% did not know or refused to answer. Among those who supported capital punishment, 30% said they "strongly favor" the death penalty and 32% said they "favor" it. Opposition to the death penalty was split between 10% of respondents who said they "strongly oppose" it and 20% who said they "oppose" it.

Angus Reid Public Opinion Poll

Angus Reid Public Opinion reports in "Americans Support Punishing Murder with the Death Penalty" (November 9, 2010, http://www.angus-reid.com/wp-content/uploads/2010/11/2010.11.09_Death_USA.pdf) the results of an online poll conducted in October 2010 in which 83% of respondents supported "punishing" murder with the death penalty. Thirteen percent of respondents were opposed and 4% were not sure. Support for capital punishment was highest in the Midwest (86% support) and among Republicans (88% support).

A DETERRING EFFECT?

In Rasmussen Reports's June 2011 poll, 47% of those asked believed the death penalty helps deter crime, whereas 39% believed it does not have a deterring effect on crime. Another 14% were unsure. Angus Reid pollsters found in

FIGURE 9.2

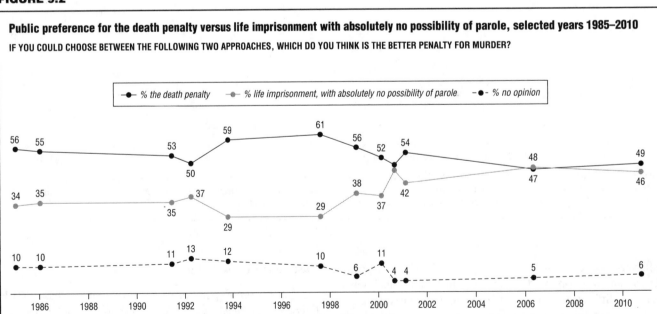

Public preference for the death penalty versus life imprisonment with absolutely no possibility of parole, selected years 1985–2010

IF YOU COULD CHOOSE BETWEEN THE FOLLOWING TWO APPROACHES, WHICH DO YOU THINK IS THE BETTER PENALTY FOR MURDER?

SOURCE: Frank Newport, "If you could choose between the following two approaches, which do you think is the better penalty for murder," in *In U.S., 64% Support Death Penalty in Cases of Murder*, The Gallup Organization, November 8, 2010, http://www.gallup.com/poll/144284/Support-Death-Penalty-Cases-Murder.aspx (accessed July 4, 2011). Copyright © 2011 by the Gallup Organization. Reproduced by permission of The Gallup Organization.

October 2010 that respondents were split about the deterrence effect of capital punishment, with 39% believing it does act as a deterrent, 35% saying it does not act as a deterrent, and 25% not sure.

Occasional Gallup polls dating back to 1985 have quizzed Americans about the deterrent effect of the death penalty. According to Gallop, in *Death Penalty* (2011, http://www.gallup.com/poll/1606/Death-Penalty.aspx), the most recent poll was conducted in 2006. At that time just over one-third (34%) of those asked thought that capital punishment "acts as a deterrent to the commitment of murder." Nearly two-thirds (64%) believed that it was not a deterrent. Another 2% had no opinion on the matter. Belief in the deterrent value of the death penalty has declined dramatically since 1985, when 62% of respondents said capital punishment deterred others from committing murder, 31% thought it was not a deterrent, and 7% expressed no opinion.

REASONS FOR SUPPORTING OR OPPOSING THE DEATH PENALTY

In *Death Penalty*, Gallup notes that in May 2003 (the most recent poll in which this question was asked) respondents were asked to give their reasons for supporting or opposing the death penalty. At that time, 64% of respondents believed that the death penalty was the appropriate punishment for murder. These capital punishment supporters were asked why they favor the death penalty for convicted murderers. Most of the responses reflect a philosophical, moral, or religious basis of reasoning. Thirty-seven percent gave their reason as "an eye for an eye/they took a life/fits the crime." Another 13% said "they deserve it," whereas 5% cited biblical beliefs. Four percent stated that the death penalty would "serve justice," and 3% considered it a "fair punishment." Together, these morality-based responses accounted for 62% of all responses.

A minority of people who supported capital punishment in May 2003 did so because of practical considerations. Eleven percent said the death penalty saves taxpayers' money. Another 11% thought that putting a murderer to death would set an example so that others would not commit similar crimes; 7% responded that the death penalty prevents murderers from killing again; 2% each said that capital punishment helps the victims' families or believed that prisoners could not be rehabilitated. One percent each noted that prisoners given life sentences do not always spend life in prison or said that capital punishment relieves prison overcrowding. In total, just over a third (35%) of the reasons given for supporting the death penalty appear to be based on issues of practicality, rather than on morality.

Interestingly enough, death penalty opponents also rely heavily on moral reasoning to support their position. In May 2003, 32% of respondents in the Gallup poll expressed opposition to capital punishment. Nearly half (46%) of opponents said it is "wrong to take a life." A quarter feared that some innocent suspects may be "wrongly convicted." Another 13% cited their religious beliefs or noted that "punishment should be left to God," and 5% said that murderers "need to pay/suffer longer/think about their crime" (presumably by serving long prison sentences). By contrast, 5% said that there is a possibility of rehabilitation, and 4% opposed the death penalty because of "unfair application."

Recent State Polls

The Quinnipiac University Polling Institute (http://www.quinnipiac.edu/x1296.xml?ReleaseID=1517) conducted a poll in October 2010 regarding Connecticut residents' opinions about the death penalty. The polling results revealed that 65% of respondents favored the death penalty for people convicted of murder, whereas 23% opposed it. Quinnipiac polls dating back to 1998 show that support for capital punishment has remained relatively stable at 59% to 67%. In the 2010 poll support was higher among Republicans (80%) than among Independents (68%) or Democrats (52%). Sixty-nine percent of men favored the death penalty, compared with 62% of women. However, when pollsters gave respondents a choice between the death penalty or life in prison with no chance of parole for people convicted of murder, the results were more evenly split. Whereas 46% preferred capital punishment, 41% preferred life in prison with no chance of parole.

In the press release "Seven in Ten Californians Continue to Support Capital Punishment" (July 22, 2010, http://field.com/fieldpollonline/subscribers/Rls2351.pdf), the Field Poll discusses the results of polling performed between June and July 2010 of registered voters in California. The pollsters found that 70% of those asked favored keeping the death penalty, compared with 24% who would abandon the sentence. Support was higher among Republicans (82%) than among Democrats (63%). There was little difference between age groups. Support was highest at 73% among those aged 18 to 20 years and lowest at 66% among those aged 65 years and older. Male respondents (72%) were slightly more likely than female respondents (69%) to support keeping capital punishment. In a breakdown by race and ethnic group the pollsters found support for the death penalty highest among Chinese-American respondents (76%), followed by non-Hispanic whites (71%), Latinos (69%), African-Americans (63%), Vietnamese-Americans (55%), and Korean-Americans (54%). When given a choice of punishments for first-degree murder, 42% of respondents chose life in prison with no chance of parole and 41% chose the death penalty. Another 13% said it would depend on the circumstances and 4% had no opinion on the matter.

IS THE DEATH PENALTY IMPOSED TOO OFTEN?

In May 2011 Gallup pollsters asked people whether they believed the death penalty is imposed "too often," "about the right amount," or "not often enough." As shown in Figure 9.3, only 18% of respondents thought capital punishment is imposed too often. Just over a quarter (26%) believed the death penalty is imposed about the right amount. Nearly half (49%) said the death penalty is not imposed enough. This breakdown differs little from results that were obtained in previous Gallup polls between 2001 and 2009.

FAIRNESS OF THE DEATH PENALTY

Figure 9.4 shows public opinion gauged by Gallup regarding the fairness of the death penalty. In 2010 a majority

FIGURE 9.3

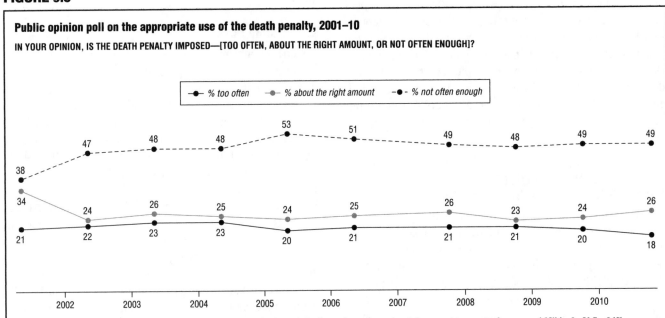

Public opinion poll on the appropriate use of the death penalty, 2001–10

IN YOUR OPINION, IS THE DEATH PENALTY IMPOSED—[TOO OFTEN, ABOUT THE RIGHT AMOUNT, OR NOT OFTEN ENOUGH]?

SOURCE: Frank Newport, "In your opinion, is the death penalty imposed—[too often, about the right amount, or not often enough]?" in *In U.S., 64% Support Death Penalty in Cases of Murder*, The Gallup Organization, November 8, 2010, http://www.gallup.com/poll/144284/Support-Death-Penalty-Cases-Murder.aspx (accessed July 4, 2011). Copyright © 2011 by the Gallup Organization. Reproduced by permission of The Gallup Organization.

FIGURE 9.4

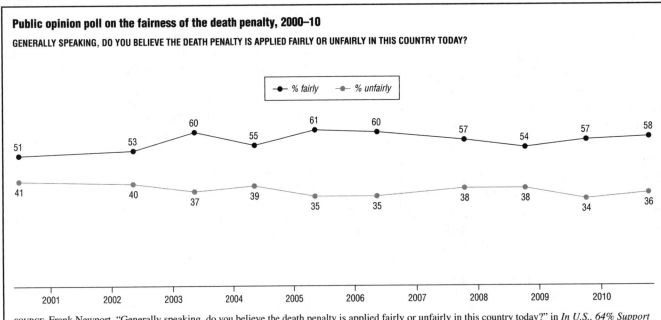

Public opinion poll on the fairness of the death penalty, 2000–10

GENERALLY SPEAKING, DO YOU BELIEVE THE DEATH PENALTY IS APPLIED FAIRLY OR UNFAIRLY IN THIS COUNTRY TODAY?

SOURCE: Frank Newport, "Generally speaking, do you believe the death penalty is applied fairly or unfairly in this country today?" in *In U.S., 64% Support Death Penalty in Cases of Murder*, The Gallup Organization, November 8, 2010, http://www.gallup.com/poll/144284/Support-Death-Penalty-Cases-Murder.aspx (accessed July 4, 2011). Copyright © 2011 by the Gallup Organization. Reproduced by permission of The Gallup Organization.

(58%) of those asked said the death penalty is applied fairly in the United States. More than a third (36%) said it is not applied fairly. These percentages are very similar to those found by Gallup in polls dating back to 2000.

THE DEATH PENALTY AND INNOCENCE

Despite the strong support for the death penalty demonstrated in Angus Reid's October 2010 poll, a large majority (81%) of those asked said they believe that "innocent people have been executed in the United States." Only 6% said they do not believe that this has occurred and 13% were unsure. The poll results reveal that respondents in the South (84%) and those with a Democratic political allegiance (85%) were the most likely to believe that innocent people have been executed.

The Gallup Organization notes in *Death Penalty* that in 2003, 2005, 2006, and 2009 pollsters found that a majority of people believed that an innocent person had been executed within the previous five years. In 2003 nearly three-quarters (73%) of those asked said that this had likely happened. In the later polls 59% to 63% of respondents shared this view.

In "Over Three in Five Americans Believe in Death Penalty" (March 18, 2008, http://www.harrisinteractive .com/vault/Harris-Interactive-Poll-Research-Over-Three-in-Five-Americans-Believe-in-Death-Penalty-2008-03.pdf), Harris Interactive notes that its February 2008 poll revealed that nearly all Americans (95%) believed that innocent people are "sometimes" convicted of murder. When asked if they would still support the death penalty if a "substantial" number of innocent people were convicted of murder, only 35% said they would still support the death penalty. Over half (58%) would oppose it under these conditions.

CHAPTER 10
CAPITAL PUNISHMENT AROUND THE WORLD

Capital punishment is practiced by only a few dozen countries around the world. As a result, the United States receives fierce criticism from many nations for its continued persistence in utilizing the death penalty. In addition, the United States increasingly faces legal challenges in its attempt to prosecute and execute foreign nationals for capital offenses.

UNITED NATIONS RESOLUTIONS

The United Nations' (UN) position on capital punishment is a compromise among those countries that want it completely abolished, those that want it limited to serious offenses, and those that want it left up to each country to decide. In 1946, just after the end of World War II (1939–1945), the UN General Assembly gathered to draft a bill of human rights for all UN member nations to follow. From the beginning, the death penalty was a topic of contention, and in 1948, when the assembly released the International Bill of Human Rights, there was no mention of the death penalty. After nine years of debate, the General Assembly included a statement on the death penalty in the International Covenant on Civil and Political Rights, which was later added to the International Bill of Human Rights. On December 16, 1966, the General Assembly adopted the covenant in Resolution 2200 (http://www.un-documents.net/iccpr.htm). Article 6 of the covenant states:

1. Every human being has the inherent right to life. This right shall be protected by law. No one shall be arbitrarily deprived of his life.

2. In countries which have not abolished the death penalty, sentence of death may be imposed only for the most serious crimes in accordance with the law in force at the time of the commission of the crime and not contrary to the provisions of the present Covenant and to the Convention on the Prevention and Punishment of the Crime of Genocide [systematic killing of a racial, political, or cultural group]. This penalty can only be carried out pursuant to a final judgement rendered by a competent court.

3. When deprivation of life constitutes the crime of genocide, it is understood that nothing in this article shall authorize any State Party to the present Covenant to derogate [turn away] in any way from any obligation assumed under the provisions of the Convention on the Prevention and Punishment of the Crime of Genocide.

4. Anyone sentenced to death shall have the right to seek pardon or commutation of the sentence [replacement of the death sentence with a lesser sentence]. Amnesty, pardon or commutation of the sentence of death may be granted in all cases.

5. Sentence of death shall not be imposed for crimes committed by persons below eighteen years of age and shall not be carried out on pregnant women.

6. Nothing in this article shall be invoked to delay or to prevent the abolition of capital punishment by any State Party to the present Covenant.

The General Assembly has dealt with the death penalty in several other documents and meetings. Among them is Resolution 2393 (November 26, 1968, http://untreaty.un.org/cod/UNJuridicalYearbook/pdfs/english/ByChapter/chpIII/1968/chpIII.pdf), which specifies the following legal safeguards that should be offered to condemned prisoners by countries with capital punishment:

1. A person condemned to death shall not be deprived of the right to appeal to a higher judicial authority or, as the case may be, to petition for pardon or reprieve;

2. A death sentence shall not be carried out until the procedures of appeal or, as the case may be, of petition for pardon or reprieve have been terminated;

3. Special attention be given in the case of indigent [poor] persons by the provision of adequate legal assistance at all stages of the proceedings.

Since that time the General Assembly has more explicitly appealed for an end to capital punishment throughout the world. For example, Resolution 2857 (December 20, 1971, http://www.un.org/documents/ga/res/26/ares26.htm) observes that "in order fully to guarantee the right to life, provided for in article 3 of the Universal Declaration of Human Rights [a section of the International Bill of Human Rights], the main objective to be pursued is that of progressively restricting the number of offences for which capital punishment may be imposed, with a view to the desirability of abolishing this punishment in all countries."

The UN Economic and Social Council Resolution 1574 of May 20, 1971, made a similar declaration. In 1984 the Economic and Social Council then adopted the Safeguards Guaranteeing Protection of the Rights of Those Facing the Death Penalty (http://www1.umn.edu/humanrts/instree/i8sgpr.htm), which included people who were younger than the age of 18 years at the time the crime was committed. Over the succeeding years, resolutions emanating from the General Assembly and the Economic and Social Council continued to call for the abolition of the death penalty.

On December 15, 1989, the General Assembly, under Resolution 44/128 (http://www.un.org/Depts/dhl/resguide/r44.htm), adopted the Second Optional Protocol to the International Covenant on Civil and Political Rights, aiming at the Abolition of the Death Penalty. This international treaty allows countries to retain the death penalty in wartime as long as they reserve the right to do so at the time they become party to the treaty. As of September 2011, 35 countries had signed the treaty (http://treaties.un.org/Pages/ViewDetails.aspx?src=TREATY&mtdsg_no=IV-12&chapter=4&lang=en), which indicated their intention to become parties to it at a later date. Signatories are not legally bound by the treaty but are obliged to avoid acts that would go against the treaty. Seventy-three countries had become parties to the protocol by ratification or accession, which means that they are legally bound by the terms of the treaty. Accession is similar to ratification, except that it occurs after the treaty has entered into force. In 1992 the United States ratified the International Covenant on Civil and Political Rights, but as of September 2011, it had not signed the Second Optional Protocol to this treaty.

Push for a Moratorium

On December 18, 2000, the UN secretary general Kofi Annan (1938–; http://www.unhchr.ch/huricane/huricane.nsf/view01/0CFC538C82EBB17FC12569BA002BE9A6?opendocument) announced that he received a petition signed by more than 3 million people from 130 countries appealing for an end to executions. Subsequently, the secretary general called for a worldwide moratorium on the death penalty, noting that the taking of life as punishment for crime is "too absolute, too irreversible, for one human

being to inflict it on another, even when backed by legal process."

Since April 1997 the UN Human Rights Council (formerly the UN Commission on Human Rights) has adopted resolutions calling for a moratorium on executions and an eventual abolition of the death penalty. The United States has consistently voted against these resolutions. During its 2002 session the Human Rights Council, in Resolution 2002/77 (http://www.unhchr.ch/Huridocda/Huridoca.nsf/0/e93443efabf7a6c4c1256bab00500ef6?Opendocument), asked countries with the death penalty "to ensure that . . . the death penalty is not imposed for non-violent acts such as financial crimes, non-violent religious practice or expression of conscience and sexual relations between consenting adults." The part of the resolution referring to sexual relations between consenting adults resulted from the potential execution of a Nigerian woman who became pregnant while divorced. She was convicted of adultery and, in 2002, was sentenced to die by stoning. The man who fathered the child claimed innocence, brought in three men to corroborate his claim as required by law, and was released. The woman was acquitted in 2003.

The Human Rights Council adopted Resolution 2003/67 on April 24, 2003. For the first time, the council asked countries that retained capital punishment not to extend the application of the death penalty to offenses to which it does not currently apply. It also admonished those countries to inform the public of any scheduled execution and to abstain from holding public executions and inhumane forms of executions, such as stoning. The UN also called on death penalty countries not to impose the death sentence on mothers with dependent children.

On December 18, 2007, the UN General Assembly (http://www.un.org/News/Press/docs/2007/ga10678.doc.htm) adopted Resolution 62/149 by a vote of 104 to 54 with 29 abstentions calling for a worldwide moratorium on the use of the death penalty. The United States was among the nations that voted against the resolution. On December 18, 2008, the General Assembly (http://www.un.org/News/Press/docs/2008/ga10801.doc.htm) reaffirmed its call for the moratorium through passage of Resolution 63/168 by a vote of 106 to 46 with 34 abstentions. The United States also voted against this resolution. In December 2010 the General Assembly (http://daccess-ods.un.org/access.nsf/Get?Open&DS=A/65/PV.71&Lang=E) again affirmed the moratorium via passage of Resolution 65/206 with a vote of 108 in favor, 41 not in favor (including the United States), and 36 abstentions. All of the resolutions are nonbinding, that is, they are not issuances of international law.

THE INTERNATIONAL STATUS OF CAPITAL PUNISHMENT

Amnesty International (2011, http://www.amnesty.org/en/death-penalty) is a private human rights organization that calls the death penalty "the ultimate denial of human rights." Amnesty International maintains information on capital punishment throughout the world. The organization refers to countries that retain and use the death penalty as retentionist countries; those that no longer use the death penalty are called abolitionist countries.

Retentionist Countries

As of 2011, 58 countries and territories retained and used the death penalty as a possible punishment for ordinary crimes. (See Table 10.1.) Ordinary crimes are crimes that are committed during peacetime. Ordinary crimes that can lead to the death penalty include murder, rape, and, in some countries, robbery or embezzlement of large sums of money. Exceptional crimes are military crimes that are committed during exceptional times, mainly wartime. Examples are treason, spying, or desertion (leaving the armed services without permission).

Amnesty International notes in *Death Sentences and Executions, 2010* (March 2011, http://www.amnesty.org/en/library/asset/ACT50/001/2011/en/ea1b6b25-a62a-4074-927d-ba51e88df2e9/act500012011en.pdf) that only 23 of the retentionist countries were known to have carried out executions in 2010. The organization estimates that at least 527 people (excluding China) were executed in 2010. Thousands more are believed to have been executed in

China; the exact figure is not divulged by the Chinese government. Amnesty International estimates that excluding China, the 10 countries with the most executions in 2010 were Iran (252+), North Korea (60+), Yemen (53+), the United States (46), Saudi Arabia (27+), Libya (18+), Syria (17+), Bangladesh (9+), Somalia (8+), and Sudan (6+). The organization also reports that 67 countries imposed a total of at least 2,024 death sentences in 2010.

Table 10.2 is a list of the 34 countries that Amnesty International considered to be abolitionist in practice in 2011. These countries had death penalty laws for crimes such as murder but had not carried out an execution for several years. Some of these nations had not executed anyone for the past 50 years or more. Others had made

TABLE 10.1

Countries and territories that retain the death penalty for ordinary crimes, 2011

Afghanistan	Lebanon
Antigua and Barbuda	Lesotho
Bahamas	Libya
Bahrain	Malaysia
Bangladesh	Mongolia
Barbados	Nigeria
Belarus	North Korea
Belize	Oman
Botswana	Pakistan
Chad	Palestinian Authority
China	Qatar
Comoros	Saint Kitts and Nevis
Democratic Republic of Congo	Saint Lucia
Cuba	Saint Vincent and the Grenadines
Dominica	Saudi Arabia
Egypt	Sierra Leone
Equatorial Guinea	Singapore
Ethiopia	Somalia
Guatemala	Sudan
Guinea	Syria
Guyana	Taiwan
India	Thailand
Indonesia	Trinidad and Tobago
Iran	Uganda
Iraq	United Arab Emirates
Jamaica	United States of America
Japan	Viet Nam
Jordan	Yemen
Kuwait	Zimbabwe

SOURCE: "Countries and Territories That Retain the Death Penalty for Ordinary Crimes," in *Abolitionist and Retentionist Countries*, Amnesty International, 2011, http://www.amnesty.org/en/death-penalty/abolitionist-and-retentionist-countries#ordinary (accessed July 27, 2011)

TABLE 10.2

Countries that are abolitionist in practice, 2011

Countries that retain the death penalty for ordinary crimes such as murder but can be considered abolitionist in practice in that they have not executed anyone during the past 10 years and are believed to have a policy or established practice of not carrying out executions. The list also includes countries which have made an international commitment not to use the death penalty.

The Russian Federation introduced a moratorium on executions in August 1996. However, executions were carried out between 1996 and 1999 in the Chechen Republic.

Country	Date (last ex.)
Algeria	1993
Benin	1987
Brunei	1957(K)
Burkina Faso	1988
Cameroon	1997
Central African Republic	1981
Congo (Republic of)	1982
Eritrea	1989
Gambia	1981
Ghana	1993
Grenada	1978
Kenya	1987
Laos	1989
Liberia	2000
Madagascar	1958(K)
Malawi	1992
Maldives	1952(K)
Mali	1980
Mauritania	1987
Morocco	1993
Myanmar	1980s
Nauru	Ind.
Niger	1976(K)
Papua New Guinea	1950
Russian Federation	1999
South Korea	1997
Sri Lanka	1976
Suriname	1982
Swaziland	1983
Tajikistan	2004
Tanzania	1995
Tonga	1982
Tunisia	1991
Zambia	1997

Date (last ex.) = Date of last execution. K = Date of last known execution.
Ind. = No executions since independence.

SOURCE: "Death Penalty: Countries Abolitionist in Practice," in *Abolitionist and Retentionist Countries*, Amnesty International, 2011, http://www.amnesty.org/en/death-penalty/countries-abolitionist-in-practice (accessed July 27, 2011)

an international commitment not to impose the death sentence.

Abolitionist Countries

Amnesty International reports that in 2011, 96 countries around the world were abolitionist for all crimes. (See Table 10.3.) Since 1976, when the United States reinstated the death penalty after a nine-year moratorium, many countries have stopped imposing capital punishment. Belgium, the United Kingdom, and Greece, the last three west European democracies to have the death sentence, abolished it for all crimes in 1996, 1998, and 2004, respectively. In reality, Belgium has not executed any prisoner since 1950. The last two executions in the United Kingdom occurred in 1964. In 2002 Yugoslavia (now Serbia and Montenegro) and Cyprus abolished the death penalty for all crimes. Armenia shut down its death penalty system in 2003. Bhutan, Greece, Samoa, Senegal, and Turkey abolished the death penalty for all crimes in 2004, and Mexico abolished the death penalty for all crimes in 2005. They were followed by the Philippines in 2006, Albania, Kyrgyzstan, and Rwanda in 2007, Argentina and Uzbekistan in 2008, Burundi and Togo in 2009, and Gabon in 2010.

ABOLITIONIST COUNTRIES FOR ORDINARY CRIMES ONLY. Amnesty International indicates that in 2011, nine countries did not impose the death penalty for ordinary crimes committed during peacetime, although they may impose it for exceptional crimes. (See Table 10.4.) Since 2000 two countries—Chile (2001) and Kazakhstan (2007)—have joined this group.

A list of all countries that have abolished the death penalty for ordinary crimes or for all crimes since 1976 is provided by year in Table 10.5.

FOCUS ON CHINA

As noted earlier, Amnesty International estimates that China executed at least 1,000 people in 2010. Human rights groups claim that China executes more people each year than all the other death penalty nations combined. The Chinese government does not publish statistics on death sentences or executions. In "China: Human Rights in People's Republic of China" (2011, http://www.amnesty.org/en/region/china/report-2009), Amnesty International estimates that at least 1,700 executions took place in China in 2008 and approximately 7,000 death sentences were handed out. The organization notes that these numbers could be higher.

Tania Branigan reports in "China to Restrict Death Penalty and Cut Executions" (*Guardian* [London, England], July 29, 2009) that a member of the Chinese supreme people's court announced in July 2009 that restrictions will be tightened on the use of capital punishment so that fewer people will be executed. The announcement was greeted with cautious optimism by human rights activists.

TABLE 10.3

Countries that are abolitionist for all crimes, 2011

Countries whose laws do not provide for the death penalty for any crime

Country	Date (A)	Date (AO)	Date (last ex.)
Albania	2007	2000	
Andorra	1990		1943
Angola	1992		
Argentina	2008	1984	
Armenia	2003		
Australia	1985	1984	1967
Austria	1968	1950	1950
Azerbaijan	1998		1993
Belgium	1996		1950
Bhutan	2004		1964K
Bosnia-Herzegovina	2001	1997	
Bulgaria	1998		1989
Burundi	2009		
Cambodia	1989		
Canada	1998	1976	1962
Cape Verde	1981		1835
Colombia	1910		1909
Cook Islands	2007		
Costa Rica	1877		
Cote D'Ivoire	2000		
Croatia	1990		1987
Cyprus	2002	1983	1962
Czech Republic	1990		
Denmark	1978	1933	1950
Djibouti	1995		Ind.
Dominican Republic	1966		
Ecuador	1906		
Estonia	1998		1991
Finland	1972	1949	1944
France	1981		1977
Gabon	2010		1985
Georgia	1997		1994K
Germany	1987		
Greece	2004	1993	1972
Guinea-Bissau	1993		1986K
Haiti	1987		1972K
Honduras	1956		1940
Hungary	1990		1988
Iceland	1928		1830
Ireland	1990		1954
Italy	1994	1947	1947
Kyrgyzstan	2007		
Kiribati			Ind.
Liechtenstein	1987		1785
Lithuania	1998		1995
Luxembourg	1979		1949
Macedonia	1991		
Malta	2000	1971	1943
Marshall Islands			Ind.
Mauritius	1995		1987
Mexico	2005		1961
Micronesia			Ind.
Moldova	1995		
Monaco	1962		1847
Montenegro	2002		
Mozambique	1990		1986
Namibia	1990		1988K
Nepal	1997	1990	1979
Netherlands	1982	1870	1952
New Zealand	1989	1961	1957
Nicaragua	1979		1930
Niue			
Norway	1979	1905	1948
Palau			
Panama	1922		1903K
Paraguay	1992		1928
Philippines	2006 (1987)		2000
Poland	1997		1988
Portugal	1976	1867	1849K

TABLE 10.3

Countries that are abolitionist for all crimes, 2011 [CONTINUED]

Countries whose laws do not provide for the death penalty for any crime

Country	Date (A)	Date (AO)	Date (last ex.)
Romania	1989		1989
Rwanda	2007		1998
Samoa	2004		Ind.
San Marino	1865	1848	1468K
Sao Tome And Principe	1990		Ind.
Senegal	2004		1967
Serbia (including Kosovo)	2002		1992
Seychelles	1993		Ind.
Slovakia	1990		
Slovenia	1989		
Solomon Islands		1966	Ind.
South Africa	1997	1995	1991
Spain	1995	1978	1975
Sweden	1972	1921	1910
Switzerland	1992	1942	1944
Togo	2009		1978
Timor-Leste	1999		
Turkey	2004	2002	1984
Turkmenistan	1999		
Tuvalu			Ind.
Ukraine	1999		
United Kingdom	1998	1973	1964
Uruguay	1907		
Uzbekistan	2008		2005
Vanuatu			Ind.
Holy See	1969		
Venezuela	1863		

Date (A) = Date of abolition for all crimes. Date (AO) = Date of abolition for ordinary crimes. Date (last ex.) = Date of last execution. K = Date of last known execution. Ind. = No executions since independence.

SOURCE: "Death Penalty: Countries Abolitionist for All Crimes," in *Abolitionist and Retentionist Countries*, Amnesty International, 2011, http://www.amnesty.org/en/death-penalty/countries-abolitionist-for-all-crimes (accessed July 27, 2011)

TABLE 10.4

Countries that are abolitionist for ordinary crimes only, 2011

Countries whose laws provide for the death penalty only for exceptional crimes such as crimes under military law or crimes committed in exceptional circumstances, such as wartime crimes.

Country	Date (AO)	Date (last ex.)
Bolivia	1997	1974
Brazil	1979	1855
Chile	2001	1985
El Salvador	1983	1973K
Fiji	1979	1964
Israel	1954	1962
Kazakstan	2007	
Latvia	1999	1996
Peru	1979	1979

Date (AO) = Date of abolition for ordinary crimes. Date (last ex.) = Date of last execution. K = Date of last known execution. Ind. = No executions since independence.

SOURCE: "Death Penalty: Countries Abolitionist for Ordinary Crimes Only," in *Abolitionist and Retentionist Countries*, Amnesty International, 2011, http://www.amnesty.org/en/death-penalty/countries-abolitionist-for-ordinary-crimes-only (accessed July 27, 2011)

However, the Amnesty International spokesperson Si-si Liu told Branigan that it will be difficult for outside observers to track any decrease, because the number of executions conducted each year is a "state secret." According to Branigan, more than 60 crimes are punishable by the death penalty in China, including nonviolent offenses and economic crimes.

In "China Quick to Execute Drug Official" (*New York Times*, July 11, 2007), Joseph Kahn indicates that in July 2007 Zheng Xiaoyu (1944–2007), the nation's former head of food and drug safety, was executed for taking bribes to approve medicines that had not been properly tested. He was sentenced in May 2007 and lost a subsequent appeal to China's Supreme Court. Zheng's execution was believed by many observers to be a political move to bolster international confidence in the quality of Chinese food and drugs after well-publicized problems surfaced with some products, including pet foods and toothpaste sold in the United States.

According to Amnesty International, in "China's Latest Use of the Death Penalty for Drug Offences Condemned" (March 29, 2011, http://www.amnesty.org/en/library/asset/ASA17/016/2011/en/2cb0cdd8-b8a0-4e94-9aea-eaf8cea722ae/asa170162011en.html), three Filipinos convicted of nonviolent drug crimes were to be executed in China in March 2011. The organization complains that capital punishment in this case "falls short of the legal threshold of the 'most serious' crimes as set in the International Covenant on Civil and Political Rights." In early 2011 China reportedly abolished the death penalty for 13 crimes (mostly nonviolent offenses), but expanded the punishment for use in at least two other nonviolent crimes. Amnesty International claims that "people sentenced to death in China do not receive fair trials. The accused are not presumed innocent, but must prove it, and police often extract confessions through torture or other ill treatment."

THE UNITED STATES CONFLICTS WITH THE INTERNATIONAL COMMUNITY

The Death Penalty Information Center indicates in "Facts about the Death Penalty" (September 14, 2011, http://www.deathpenaltyinfo.org/documents/FactSheet.pdf) that as of September 2011 the laws of 34 U.S. states allowed the death penalty. The vast majority of other countries in the world have abolished capital punishment. As a result, the United States often faces intense criticism and complicated legal challenges from other nations over its continued use of the death penalty.

A Human Rights Issue

The UN Human Rights Council conducts periodic reviews of the human rights records of all 192 member states of the UN. In November 2010 the United States underwent its first-ever review. The results are detailed in *Working Group on the Universal Periodic Review: United*

TABLE 10.5

Countries that have abolished the death penalty since 1976

1976: **Portugal** abolished the death penalty for all crimes.
1978: **Denmark** abolished the death penalty for all crimes.
1979: **Luxembourg, Nicaragua** and **Norway** abolished the death penalty for all crimes. **Brazil, Fiji** and **Peru** abolished the death penalty for ordinary crimes.
1981: **France** and **Cape Verde** abolished the death penalty for all crimes.
1982: The **Netherlands** abolished the death penalty for all crimes.
1983: **Cyprus** and **El Salvador** abolished the death penalty for ordinary crimes.
1984: **Argentina** abolished the death penalty for ordinary crimes.
1985: **Australia** abolished the death penalty for all crimes.
1987: **Haiti, Liechtenstein** and the **German Democratic Republic**[a] abolished the death penalty for all crimes.
1989: **Cambodia, New Zealand, Romania** and **Slovenia**[b] abolished the death penalty for all crimes.
1990: **Andorra, Croatia (2),** the **Czech and Slovak Federal Republic**[c], **Hungary, Ireland, Mozambique, Namibia** and **Sao Tomé** and **Príncipe** abolished the death penalty for all crimes.
1992: **Angola, Paraguay** and **Switzerland** abolished the death penalty for all crimes.
1993: **Guninea-Bissau, Hong Kong**[d] and **Seychelles** abolished the death penalty for all crimes.
1994: **Italy** abolished the death penalty for all crimes.
1995: **Djibouti, Mauritius, Moldova** and **Spain** abolished the death penalty for all crimes.
1996: **Belgium** abolished the death penalty for all crimes.
1997: **Georgia, Nepal, Poland** and **South Africa** abolished the death penalty for all crimes. **Bolivia** abolished the death penalty for ordinary crimes.
1998: **Azerbaijan, Bulgaria, Canada, Estonia, Lithuania** and the **United Kingdom** abolished the death penalty for all crimes.
1999: **East Timor, Turkmenistan** and **Ukraine** abolished the death penalty for all crimes. **Latvia**[e] abolished the death penalty for ordinary crimes.
2000: **Cote D'Ivoire** and **Malta** abolished the death penalty for all crimes. **Albania**[f] abolished the death penalty for ordinary crimes.
2001: **Bosnia-Herzegovina**[a] abolished the death penalty for all crimes. **Chile** abolished the death penalty for ordinary crimes.
2002: **Cyprus** and **Yugoslavia** (now two states **Serbia** and **Montenegro**[i]) abolished the death penalty for all crimes.
2003: **Armenia** abolished the death penalty for all crimes.
2004: **Bhutan, Greece, Samoa, Senegal** and **Turkey** abolished the death penalty for all crimes.
2005: **Liberia**[h] and **Mexico** abolished the death penalty for all crimes.
2006: **Philippines** abolished the death penalty for all crimes.
2007: **Albania**[f], **Cook Islands, Kyrgyzstan** and **Rwanda** abolished the death penalty for all crimes. **Kazakhstan** abolished the death penalty for ordinary crimes.
2008: **Uzbekistan** and **Argentina** abolished the death penalty for all crimes.
2009: **Burundi** and **Togo** abolished the death penalty for all crimes.
2010: **Gabon** abolished the death penalty for all crimes.

Notes:
[a]In 1990 the German Democratic Republic became unified with the Federal Republic of Germany, where the death penalty had been abolished in 1949.
[b]Slovenia and Croatia abolished the death penalty while they were still republics of the Socialist Federal Republic of Yugoslavia. The two republics became independent in 1991.
[c]In 1993 the Czech and Slovak Federal Republic divided into two states, the Czech Republic and Slovakia.
[d]In 1997 Hong Kong was returned to Chinese rule as a special administrative region of China. Since then Hong Kong has remained abolitionist.
[e]In 1999 the Latvian parliament voted to ratify Protocol No. 6 to the European Convention on Human Rights, abolishing the death penalty for peacetime offences.
[f]In 2007 Albania ratified Protocol No. 13 to the European Convention on Human Rights, abolishing the death penalty in all circumstances. In 2000 it had ratified Protocol No. 6 to the European Convention on Human Rights, abolishing the death penalty for peacetime offences.
[g]In 2001 Bosnia-Herzegovina ratified the Second Optional Protocol to the International Covenant on Civil and Political Rights, abolishing the death penalty for all crimes.
[h]In 2005 Liberia ratified the Second Optional Protocol to the International Covenant on Civil and Political Rights, abolishing the death penalty for all crimes.
[i]Montenegro had already abolished the death penalty in 2002 when it was part of a state union with Serbia. It became an independent member state of the United Nations on 28 June 2006. Its ratification of Protocol No. 13 to the European Convention on Human Rights, abolishing the death penalty in all circumstances, came into effect on 6 June 2006.

SOURCE: "Countries That Have Abolished the Death Penalty since 1976," in *Abolitionist and Retentionist Countries*, Amnesty International, 2011, http://www.amnesty.org/en/death-penalty/abolitionist-and-retentionist-countries#ordinary (accessed July 27, 2011)

States of America (January 4, 2011, http://daccess-ods.un.org/access.nsf/Get?Open&DS=A/HRC/16/11&Lang=E). The representatives of more than 80 nations provided input about the United States' human rights record. Hundreds of statements and recommendations involving the death penalty were made by countries from around the world, including some of the United States' closest allies. For example, the United Kingdom representative expressed concern "that the death penalty could sometimes be administered in a discriminatory manner and encouraged the United States to address those systemic issues." Other nations also expressed concern about the United States' use of capital punishment, including Australia, Belgium, Cyprus, Denmark, Ireland, Italy, the Netherlands, New Zealand, and Sweden. The review resulted in 228 recommendations to the United States to improve its human rights practices. More than 20 of the recommendations involved the death penalty; many nations called for the United States to issue a moratorium on executions or to restrict the number of crimes that are subject to the death penalty as a first step toward abolishing capital punish-

ment. France recommended that the United States "undertake studies to determine the factors of racial disparity in the application of the death penalty [and] to prepare effective strategies aimed at ending possible discriminatory practices." The council notes in the report that the United States' responses to the recommendations will be published by the council during its 16th session, which was scheduled to take place in 2013.

Executing Foreign Nationals

The Death Penalty Information Center reports that as of July 11, 2011, 133 foreign nationals were on death row in the United States. (See Table 10.6.) Approximately 44% (58) were Mexican. As shown in Table 10.7, the vast majority of foreign nationals under the sentence of death were in California (56), Texas (24), and Florida (22).

Under Article 36 of the Vienna Convention on Consular Relations (VCCR) local U.S. law enforcement officials are required to notify detained foreigners "without

TABLE 10.6

Reported foreign nationals under sentence of death in the United States, by foreign nationality, July 11, 2011

[Total: 133. Total nationalities: 34.]

Active death sentences

Mexico	58	Spain	1
Cuba	10	Tonga	1
Jamaica	3	Trinidad	1
El Salvador	10	Costa Rica	1
Colombia	4	Nicaragua	1
Cambodia	5	Laos	1
Viet Nam	8	Estonia	1
Honduras	5	Egypt	1
Germany	1	Bangladesh	1
Philippines	1	Haiti	1
Lithuania	1	Lebanon	1
Serbia	1	Jordan	1
Iran	2	Russia	1
Peru	1	Guatemala	1
Canada	2	France	1
St. Kitts and Nevis	1	Argentina	1
Bahamas	3	China	1

Inactive death sentences

Mexico (reversed on appeal)	1

Note: Inmates with Immigration & Naturalization Services (INS) or United States Citizenship and Immigration Services (USCIS) registration numbers (indicating foreign nationality), but for whom no specific nationality information is currently available.

SOURCE: Adapted from "Reported Foreign Nationals under Sentence of Death in the U.S.," in *Foreign Nationals and the Death Penalty in the US*, Death Penalty Information Center, July 11, 2011, http://www.deathpenaltyinfo.org/foreign-nationals-and-death-penalty-us#jurisdiction (accessed July 27, 2011). Data from Mark Warren, Human Rights Research.

TABLE 10.7

Reported foreign nationals under sentence of death in the United States, by state of confinement, July 11, 2011

California	56
Texas	24
Florida	22
Arizona	2
Ohio	3
Nevada	4
Pennsylvania	5
Louisiana	3
Alabama	2
Virginia	1
Oregon	2
Montana	1
Georgia	1
Mississippi	1
Nebraska	1
Arkansas	1
Federal	5

Notes: Totals include all reported foreign nationals under sentence of death, including those awaiting new sentencing hearings and cases where the individual's immigration status is uncertain or their nationality is disputed. Confirmed cases of dual citizenship (individuals possessing both U.S. citizenship and that of another country) are not listed.

SOURCE: "Reported Foreign Nationals under Sentence of Death in the U.S. by State of Confinement," in *Foreign Nationals and the Death Penalty in the US*, Death Penalty Information Center, July 11, 2011, http://www.deathpenaltyinfo.org/foreign-nationals-and-death-penalty-us#jurisdiction (accessed July 27, 2011). Data from Mark Warren, Human Rights Research.

delay" of their right to consult with the consulate of their home country. The United States ratified (formally approved and sanctioned) this international agreement and an Optional Protocol to the VCCR in 1969. The Optional Protocol provided that the International Court of Justice (ICJ; the UN's highest court) would have the authority to decide when VCCR rights have been violated. Capital punishment opponents claim that the United States has a poor record of informing foreign nationals under arrest of their rights under the VCCR.

During the 1990s Paraguay and Germany brought suits against the United States before the ICJ regarding pending executions in Virginia and Arizona, respectively. In both cases the ICJ ruled that the executions should be stayed (postponed) pending further analysis. However, both condemned men—Angel Francisco Breard (1966–1998) of Paraguay and Walter LaGrand (1962–1999) of Germany—were executed for murder. The U.S. Supreme Court refused to intervene in Breard's case, noting in *Breard v. Greene* (523 U.S. 371 [1998]) that because he had failed to exercise his VCCR rights at the state level, he could not raise a claim of violation on federal habeas review.

MEXICO SUES THE UNITED STATES. In 2003 the ICJ was asked to settle another case involving the United States and consular notification. Mexico sued the United States for allegedly violating the VCCR with respect to 54 Mexican nationals on death row in U.S. prisons. The ICJ ordered that the pending executions of three of the inmates be stayed until it could make a final ruling in the case. In 2004 the ICJ (http://www.icj-cij.org/docket/files/128/8188.pdf) found that the United States had violated sections of the VCCR by not informing the 54 Mexicans on death row of their right to notify their government about their detention. The court did not annul the convictions and sentences as Mexico had requested, but it did rule that the United States must review and reconsider the Mexican nationals' convictions and sentences.

José E. Medellin (1975–2008) was one of the 54 Mexicans on death row. Texas jurors sentenced him to death for participating in the rape and murder of two teenage girls in 1993. The Mexican consular did not learn of or have the opportunity to help Medellin with his legal defense until 1997, after Medellin had exhausted most of his appeals. When the ICJ decision regarding Mexican nationals was handed down, Medellin appealed once again to the U.S. Court of Appeals for the Fifth Circuit, claiming that he did not receive adequate counsel and that he was not allowed to contact the Mexican consulate after his indictment. The federal appellate court ruled against Medellin. The court cited *Breard v. Greene*, which stated that the issues addressed by the VCCR had to be considered in the state courts before they could be addressed in federal court. Because Medellin had already gone through his appeals on the state level, he had no recourse. Medellin appealed to the U.S. Supreme Court, and in December 2004 the court agreed to hear his case and to reassess its position on the VCCR and ICJ rulings.

Just before the oral arguments in the Medellin case, President George W. Bush (1946–) signed an executive order in February 2005 demanding that the appropriate U.S. state courts review the sentences and convictions of the 54 Mexicans on death row without applying the procedural default rule discussed in *Breard v. Greene*. By issuing this order, the president in essence tried to force the courts to comply with the ICJ ruling regarding the Mexicans. In light of the executive order, the U.S. Supreme Court dismissed Medellin's case, and it was sent back to the state courts for review.

According to Linda Greenhouse, in "Supreme Court to Hear Appeal of Mexican Death Row Inmate" (*New York Times*, May 1, 2007), the Texas Court of Criminal Appeals subsequently accused Bush of "intrusive" meddling in the state's court system and refused to comply with the president's order. In response, the Bush administration urged the U.S. Supreme Court to overturn the Texas court's decision. In March 2008 the U.S. Supreme Court ruled in *Medellin v. Texas* (No. 06-984) that the VCCR was not binding on state courts because it had not been enacted into law by Congress. In August 2008 Medellin was executed by the state of Texas.

THE U.S. WITHDRAWS FROM THE OPTIONAL PROTOCOL TO THE VCCR. In March 2005 President Bush pulled the United States out of the Optional Protocol to the VCCR, which had been in place for 30 years. Charles Lane indicates in "U.S. Quits Pact Used in Capital Cases" (*Washington Post*, March 10, 2005) that the administration no longer wanted the U.S. court system to be influenced by the ICJ with regard to executing foreign nationals. It should be noted, however, that this action did not affect U.S. obligations under the VCCR to inform foreign arrestees about their consular rights.

ANOTHER EXECUTION. In 2011 the VCCR debate arose again after the state of Texas set an execution date of July 7, 2011, for another Mexican citizen involved in the original lawsuit against the United States. Humberto Leal Garcia Jr. (1973–2011) was sentenced to death for murdering a 16-year-old girl in 1994. The administration of Barack Obama (1961–) petitioned the U.S. Supreme Court to delay the execution while Congress considered VCCR-related legislation that had been proposed earlier in the year by Senator Patrick Leahy (1940–; D-VT). According to the press release "Leahy Renews Effort to Bring U.S. into Compliance with International Consular Notification Treaty" (http://leahy .senate.gov/press/press_releases/release/?id=5f4b8b0e-d975-4aa7-94d5-8860de1a6bc0), the Consular Notification Compliance Act would allow federal courts to review the cases of all foreign nationals currently on death row who were not granted their consular rights under the VCCR at the time of their arrests. It would also "clarify for future cases that courts must ensure that all foreign nationals charged with a capital offense are informed of their right to contact their consulate." The press release notes that U.S. noncompliance with the VCCR has repercussions to Americans traveling abroad, stating that "it would also be completely unacceptable to us if our citizens were treated in this manner."

In a 5–4 opinion issued on July 7, 2011, the U.S. Supreme Court declined to stay Leal's execution, and he was executed hours later. In *Humberto Leal v. Texas* (564 U. S. ___), the court stated, "We are doubtful that it is ever appropriate to stay a lower court judgment in light of unenacted legislation. Our task is to rule on what the law is, not what it might eventually be." As of September 2011, the Consular Notification Compliance Act had not been passed by Congress.

Extradition Complications

An increasing number of countries refuse to extradite (surrender for trial) criminals to the United States who might face the death penalty. In 2005 the German government refused to extradite Mohammed Ali Hamadi (1964–) to the United States out of fear that Hamadi would face the death penalty for his role in killing a U.S. Navy diver during a 1985 airplane hijacking. Hamadi served 19 years of a life sentence in Germany for the hijacking before being paroled in 2005 and deported to his native Lebanon. The Lebanese government has refused to turn him over to U.S. authorities. As of September 2011, Hamadi was on the Federal Bureau of Investigation's "Most Wanted Terrorists" list (http://www.fbi.gov/wanted/wanted_terrorists/ mohammed-ali-hamadei), and a $5 million reward was offered for information leading to his capture.

In 2007 U.S. authorities filed an extradition request for the accused drug-cartel leader Benjamin Arellano-Félix (1952–), who had been in custody in Mexico since 2002. His brother Francisco Javier Arellano-Félix (1969–) was captured by the U.S. Coast Guard while in international waters in 2006. Both men are accused of operating a violent drug smuggling ring and committing multiple capital crimes that are subject to the death penalty under U.S. law. In November 2007 Francisco Javier received a life sentence without parole after a plea bargain deal was reached that eliminated the death penalty as an option in exchange for his guilty plea. In April 2011 Mexico extradited Benjamin to the United States. Adriana Gomez Licon and Elliot Spagat note in "Mexico Extradites Reputed Drug Lord Arellano Felix" (Associated Press, April 30, 2011) that Benjamin was indicted in 1986 in the United States for engaging in "widespread violence" along the U.S.-Mexican border. However, in 2008 he was charged with racketeering, a noncapital crime. According to Licon and Spagat, this was done by U.S. officials "in an effort to increase their chances of winning extradition from Mexico, which opposes the death penalty."

CHAPTER 11
THE DEBATE: CAPITAL PUNISHMENT SHOULD BE MAINTAINED

THE TESTIMONY OF ANNE ROSSI BEFORE THE JOINT COMMITTEE ON JUDICIARY, CONNECTICUT GENERAL ASSEMBLY, REGARDING SENATE BILL 1035, AN ACT REVISING THE PENALTY FOR CAPITAL FELONIES TO REPEAL THE DEATH PENALTY AND SUBSTITUTE LIFE IMPRISONMENT WITHOUT THE POSSIBILITY OF RELEASE AS THE AUTHORIZED SENTENCE FOR PERSONS CONVICTED OF CERTAIN MURDERS, MARCH 7, 2011

Thank you for allowing me to be here today. I am here as a supporter of the death penalty.

In 2003, my husband Barry Rossi, his business partner and friend Robert Stears and their employee Lorne Stevens were murdered. All three of them were asked to lie on the dirty garage floor where they worked, they were asked to put their hands over their heads before they were all shot multiple times. All of them killed in a premeditated execution spurred by a murder for hire plot. Forethought and conscience [*sic*] decisions were made to take their lives and to kill them. You must unfortunately experience the pure evil that penetrates every aspect of your life when this happens to comprehend the importance and purpose of the death penalty. I am one of those individuals that can now understand after being forced into a forever changed world. A world not for the better. My assumption is that most of you have not personally experienced an event of this nature. I ask you to considerer that before you make any decisions in regards to the death penalty.

There must be accountability for actions so unjust as this. It crushes you into a million jagged pieces. The pieces cannot be put back together the same as they were before. I will never be the same.

Prosecutors in our case were able to use the death penalty to secure the convictions of the shooter and mastermind of Barry's, Robert's and Lorne's murders. The shooter agreed to testify, saving the state the cost of his trial, saving the state the cost of his appeals, all while securing the conviction of the mastermind. He would not have testified had he not been facing the death penalty.

The people that commit these crimes DO NOT want to sit on death row in isolation. They want to be in general population. Death isn't what scares them, the isolation does. Facing death row is a motivator for them to cooperate which in turn helps bring others to justice.

What I've seen is that the death penalty is a necessary and valuable tool for prosecution. It provides our prosecutors with a resource, a tool in prosecuting the types of cases that warrant it. I see them using the death penalty only in the most heinous of crimes. It frightens and concerns me that this tool would even be considered to be taken away. We need to provide our prosecutors with the tools they need to perform their jobs to the best of their ability.

While the process right now is not perfect, it IS fixable without abolishing it. Abolishing the death penalty now will only lead to lesser punishments for criminals in the future. It is in existence because it is an apt punishment for certain crimes, it is justified. Finding justice is so very important to us living victims and must be served to balance the injustice served on the lives so unnecessarily taken.

Cost should not be a factor in abolishing the death penalty when something so immoral and evil has occurred. Costs can be controlled. My husband's life held value. Losing him was costly. Changing the laws to place time limits on the unending appeals would certainly be a good start.

Some will argue that the process re-victimizes you. Personally I do not feel that way. The judicial system is there to do what is right, to protect us, to serve justice. It is not about the living victim more than it is to see justice served upon the evil. Yes the court proceedings are painful, but they are necessary. Lengthy court proceedings will occur with these types of crimes regardless of if it is a death penalty case or not. The living victims, or survivors, have a choice. I know for me, there was no question in my mind that I would be sitting at every court proceeding no matter what, no matter how long.

Polls have showed that 65% of Connecticut's residents are in favor of the death penalty. To me that means 65% of our legislative body should be in favor of it. You have the responsibility of respecting and supporting the wishes of the people of this state. The jurors in the Steven Hayes trial spoke loud and clear of how our state citizens feel in regards to the death penalty when they delivered their sentence. A death sentence was appropriate in that case. It should speak volumes to you when you are considering abolishing the death penalty. There are certain crimes and certain people that warrant punishment by death. These people can never be in society again. Your responsibility is to secure that they never are in society again.

I believe in capital punishment. You may think you know how you feel about it, but until something like what happened to me, happens to you, you don't really know. My husband was [a] good man, he was viciously killed for no reason. I've been given the reason to really contemplate, to think, and debate with myself how I really feel about [capital punishment]. Recently the person who planned and paid for the murders of Barry, Robert and Lorne was attacked by his cellmate. He was in critical condition in the hospital and the word I received was that he wasn't going to make it through the night. I have to tell you I felt relief. I was good with it if he died. That would have been justice. It is important for the living victims to find justice. It is needed to heal. Our society must have rules, parameters and punishment appropriate for each type of crime.

I am asking you today to maintain the death penalty as a tool for our prosecutors and to work together to fix what is broken such as the lengthy appeals process. Consider long and hard before abolishing something that holds a place in our society and has a purpose. For my husband Barry, for Robert Stears, for Lorne Stevens, and for everyone who was so unnecessarily taken from us before their time, and for those to come, you must maintain the death penalty to maintain justice in our world for the unspeakable evil that does exist. (http://www.cga.ct.gov/2011/JUDdata/Tmy/2011SB-01035-R000307-Anne%20Rossi-TMY.PDF)

FROM THE TESTIMONY OF REPRESENTATIVE STEVEN T. MIKUTEL, 45TH ASSEMBLY DISTRICT, STATE OF CONNECTICUT, HOUSE OF REPRESENTATIVES, BEFORE THE JOINT COMMITTEE ON JUDICIARY, CONNECTICUT GENERAL ASSEMBLY, REGARDING SENATE BILL 1035, AN ACT REVISING THE PENALTY FOR CAPITAL FELONIES TO REPEAL THE DEATH PENALTY AND SUBSTITUTE LIFE IMPRISONMENT WITHOUT THE POSSIBILITY OF RELEASE AS THE AUTHORIZED SENTENCE FOR PERSONS CONVICTED OF CERTAIN MURDERS, MARCH 7, 2011

This latest attempt to abolish capital punishment subverts the will of the people, thereby further eroding their faith in this democratic institution. It makes a strong case for a constitutional amendment to allow direct initiative petitions by citizens.

Nearly 70% of Connecticut residents support capital punishment because the arguments in its favor are far stronger than those that advocate abolishment. Unfortunately, the arguments for abolishing capital punishment in our state have been dominated by misinformation coming out of [the] anti-death penalty movement. Their main argument—that the death penalty is not a deterrent—is contradicted by the research. And their other main arguments—such as an innocent person may be executed—have no validity in Connecticut.

The Chief State's Attorney, in testimony before this committee in 2009, said and I quote, "There are numerous studies published in peer-reviewed journals establishing that executions do deter the crime of murder." A series of academic studies over the last 6 years concluded that between 3 and 18 lives would be saved by the execution of each convicted killer.

Executions save lives! Period. Our choice is to spare the lives of those who have committed the most horrendous crimes and to, thereby, sacrifice the lives of the innocent or to execute them and to, thereby, spare the lives of the innocent.

But for me and many citizens of Connecticut, the case for the death penalty doesn't rest on the concept of deterrence, but on the moral grounds of justice. This penalty is the just and appropriate societal response for specific crimes, the most brutal and horrible and premeditated of murders, such as those committed by serial killer Michael Ross and Cheshire home invasion murderer Steven Hayes.

For justice to exist, the punishment must fit the crime. If human life is the ultimate value in our society, then murder must rank as the most heinous of crimes and those that commit it should receive the ultimate penalty. To quote Dr. Petit when he testified before this committee in 2009, "My family gets the death penalty and you want to give murderers life. That is not justice."

When debating the death penalty, it is important to focus attention on Connecticut, not states where problems existed. Connecticut administers capital punishment fairly, with restraint and with every possible safeguard to assure that the innocent is protected while the guilty are held accountable. No reasonable person disputes the guilt of any of the persons currently on death row in Connecticut. Death sentences are rare in our state and limited to those who commit unspeakable horrors.

What the people of our state cannot understand is why it takes 15 years to execute a serial killer like Michael Ross. Instead of taking Connecticut citizens down a road they would rather not go, this committee should give the people what they really want—a workable death penalty—one that results in the timely execution of society's worst human rights violators. To this end, I urge the Committee to support HB's 6427 and 6439. Passage of these bills into law will serve to speed up the post-conviction process in death penalty cases by requiring a state habeas corpus petition be filed within a specific period of time.

Speeding up the post conviction process will serve two worthy goals—it would enhance the deterrent value of capital punishment (and thus save even more innocent lives) and it would serve the interests of justice because justice delayed is justice denied.

When the death penalty becomes more real, murderers and would be murderers will fear it even more. Although you will never deter all murderers, the effect of deterrence will rise as the probability of executions rise, because, as the probability of execution rises, the fear of the punishment will also rise.

As for LWOP [life without parole], it desecrates life merely to deprive someone of liberty for murder. Prison is no moral substitute for capital punishment for the likes of those who reside on Connecticut's death row. They live better than many homeless people.

There are other problems with LWOP. With no death penalty and only life, there is no deterrent for LWOP inmates killing or seriously injuring others while in prison, which is not a rare event. They would in effect have a free pass to kill and maim again and again.

But the most fundamental problem with LWOP is that the same activists who don't like the death penalty don't really like long prison sentences either. (If the death penalty is abolished, this will quickly become obvious.) Many believe this will become the next rallying cry of the anti-death penalty movement. Some of them have already laid the groundwork for this. Abolishing LWOP would, in their eyes, be justified from the point of view that murderers deserve to be re-educated and re-habilitated and the LWOP

constitutes "cruel and unusual" punishment. (http://www.cga.ct.gov/2011/JUDdata/Tmy/2011SB-01035-R000307-Representative%20Steven%20T.%20Mikutel-TMY.PDF)

FROM THE TESTIMONY OF ROBERT BLECKER, PROFESSOR OF LAW, NEW YORK LAW SCHOOL, BEFORE THE JOINT COMMITTEE ON JUDICIARY, CONNECTICUT GENERAL ASSEMBLY, REGARDING SENATE BILL 1035, AN ACT REVISING THE PENALTY FOR CAPITAL FELONIES TO REPEAL THE DEATH PENALTY AND SUBSTITUTE LIFE IMPRISONMENT WITHOUT THE POSSIBILITY OF RELEASE AS THE AUTHORIZED SENTENCE FOR PERSONS CONVICTED OF CERTAIN MURDERS, MARCH 7, 2011

Killing Killers: A Like Kind Response

Early witnesses disparaged retributive support for the death penalty as vestigial hypocrisy. We debase and degrade ourselves by resorting to the same conduct that we condemn for those who kill. Killing because someone else has killed was not consistent with the mores of a civilized society. We cannot teach respect for life by taking life. Or as former Warden Mary Wolff testified to this committee, by killing the heinous killer, we "follow in the footsteps of the criminal." But this well-worn argument—that we debase life by taking life—if it proves anything, proves too much. When we imprison kidnappers, do we thereby debase liberty? When we impose fines on thieves, do we debase property? Punishment acts as a like kind response—inflicting justified pain upon a person who earlier inflicted unjustified pain (so, too, of course celebration—returning pleasure for past pleasure). Thus the basic retributive measure—like for like—"as he has done, so shall it be done to him"; "giving a person a taste of her own medicine"; "fighting fire with fire"—satisfies at a primal level. Reciprocity is not hypocrisy.

Two years ago, in your earlier hearings, witnesses disparaged retribution as a synonym for vengeance. Those who insist on equating retribution with revenge must recognize deterrence for what it is. Because if retribution is pure revenge, then deterrence is pure terrorism, as Hobbes—the first and greatest modern utilitarian—said in disparaging retribution and proposing deterrence: "The ayme of punishment is not revenge but terror." Now, we've come to appreciate that deterrence is not pure terror. You should also appreciate that retribution is not pure revenge.

Although they stem from a common desire to inflict pain on the source of pain, revenge may be limitless and misdirected at the undeserving, as with collective punishment. Retribution, however, must be limited and proportional—no more (or less) than what's deserved.

Retribution provides the basis for limiting punishment as well as for affirming it. We retributive advocates of the death penalty are as concerned that those who do not deserve it do not get it, as we are that those who do, do.

Abolitionists who reject retribution—who do not feel the urge to punish, or do feel it but suppress that feeling of righteous indignation as irrational and shameful—cannot really grasp what moves us retributivists. Most retributive death penalty supporters, then, define the "worst of the worst" as deserving to die for the extreme harms they cause (rape-murder, mass-murder, child-murder, torture-murder) along with the attitude with which they cause it—sadistically or with a depraved callousness.

According to Immanuel Kant's classic retributivism, we impose punishment as an abstract duty without any emotion. By punishing, we dignify the transgressor, acknowledging the free will that produced the crime. More persistent and popular than Kant's retributivism from an abstract sense of duty, emotive/intuitive retributivism has deeper roots.

Abolitionist critics of retribution insist that emotion may never properly move us individually or collectively. They sympathize with the anger of the victims' friends or family, but insist that no humane person would want to act out of that anger. Emotive retributivists' urge to punish, however, stems directly from a projected empathy with the victim's suffering. "Our heart, as it adopts and beats time to his grief," declared Adam Smith in *A Theory of Moral Sentiments*, the first great work of modern retributive psychology. Haunted by the victim's suffering, retributive death penalty supporters cannot forget or forgive the victim's fate: "We feel that resentment which we imagine he ought to feel, and which he would feel if in his cold and lifeless body there remained any consciousness of what passes upon earth," Smith further explained. "His blood . . . calls aloud."

Jennifer Hawke-Petit's blood calls aloud. Hayley Petit's blood calls aloud. Michaela's too.

Embracing human dignity as our primary value, emotive retributivists since Adam Smith emphasize "a humanity that is more generous and comprehensive," "opposing to the emotions of compassion which we feel for a particular" criminal, "a more enlarged compassion which we feel for mankind."

Financial Costs of the Death Penalty

The death penalty enhances costs from investigation to appeal. Public Defender's offices estimate that abolishing capital punishment would save money. Departments of Corrections estimate that eliminating the death penalty would save $1 million per death row prisoner over each inmate's lifetime.

The vast majority of criminal cases result in plea bargains which not only save time, effort, and costs of trial and appeal, but also protect against an unpredictable

and errant jury ignoring the evidence and acquitting a sympathetic accused. In return for pleading guilty, criminals almost always receive lesser charges or lighter sentences.

Without a death penalty as a threat, what would move an aggravated murderer to waive trial and appeal, and accept life without parole? Perhaps, in a rare case, remorse. Overwhelmingly, however, first degree murderers plead guilty and accept life without parole only to avoid the death penalty. Each such guilty plea saves the people hundreds of thousands of dollars.

Emotional and Psychological Costs of the Death Penalty

Before committee and commission such as this, family members of murder victims testify about the devastating emotional costs of the death penalty. Survivors testify to the pain of being forced to relive the trauma of their loved ones' murders during prolonged appeals. Victims' families talk of the frustration of wanting and waiting for their loved ones' killers to die. Much of the victims' family bitterness and frustration came from the false promise of justice. The system would never deliver on its promise—endless stays and reversals.

Psychologists can testify to the adverse effects of executions on judges, jurors, correctional staff, journalists, clergy and spiritual advisors, as well as the families of the condemned. These intangible emotional and psychological costs must also be taken into consideration in weighing the costs of the death penalty, abolitionists insist.

But if non-quantifiable emotional costs *do* count, then how about the cost of not doing justice? In some cases, abolishing the death penalty—retributively, the only proportional punishment—abolishes justice. If you abolish the death penalty, how about the cost to parents who realize their child's rapist murderer now lives in prison playing basketball or watching the Huskies play on a color TV? What does it cost to contemplate the person who tortured your child to death now in art class or lying on a prison bed, lost in a good book? (http://www.cga.ct.gov/2011/JUDdata/Tmy/2011SB-01035-R000307-Professor%20Robert%20Blecker-TMY.PDF)

THE STATEMENT OF JOHN C. KISSINGER JR., ATTORNEY, FORMERLY A HOMICIDE PROSECUTOR WITH THE ASSISTANT ATTORNEY GENERAL AT THE NEW HAMPSHIRE ATTORNEY GENERAL'S OFFICE, TO THE COMMISSION TO STUDY THE DEATH PENALTY IN NEW HAMPSHIRE, DECEMBER 1, 2010

I am not in favor of abolishing the death penalty. It is my belief that in very limited circumstances the death penalty represents appropriate punishment. Although I join in the majority report, my reasons for supporting capital punishment differ in certain respects from aspects of the majority report. Like many of those who spoke eloquently before the Commission, I share a personal belief in the sanctity of life. This belief must be balanced against the sincere and legitimate societal interest in "justice."

In reaching my opinion, I draw upon my experience as a prosecutor working in the Attorney General's office. In particular, I recall the pain and anguish suffered by family members of murder victims. I recognize that the family members of murder victims who testified before the Commission do not have a single unified view on the acceptability of capital punishment. The views of people of good faith can be found on both sides of this issue. As I listened to the moving testimony from the many family members of murder victims, I was reminded of the ongoing struggles faced by the survivors with whom I worked. The devastating consequences caused by the heinous act of murder cannot be overstated.

Reserving the death penalty for the few who society concludes to be the perpetrators of the most heinous forms of murder is measured and appropriate. It is important to point out the extremely narrow circumstances in which the death penalty statute has been applied in New Hampshire over the past 70 years. It is hard not to conclude from this experience that the death penalty has not been over utilized or abused by prosecutors. This limited application strikes a balance between the demands of society for just punishment for the perpetrators of the most serious offenses with a respect for the sanctity of human life.

I am not persuaded by the use of economic models to find a measurable correlation between the presence of a capital murder statute and avoidance of specific numbers of murders. That is not to say that I reject the notion of deterrence as a justification generally. Rather, I am not persuaded that a statistically sound correlation has been established. I do not believe that the perpetrators of such crimes weigh the consequences of their actions in ways even remotely similar to how most of us go through life.

The reality in New Hampshire is that recent efforts to try to eliminate the death penalty have been unsuccessful. I believe the reason it has survived these challenges lies in the depths to which many people of this state sincerely believe it represents a just punishment. While some proponents of the death penalty may want to see a significant expansion in its application, I do not believe that would be consistent with societal standards of decency. In my opinion, limiting the situations in which the death penalty applies is essential to meeting the evolving societal standard.

Because imposition of the death penalty is irreversible, we must remain committed as a state to conducting complete and thorough investigations in cases which might involve application of the death penalty. That commitment eliminates to the extent possible the risk that any innocent person is convicted of capital murder. To make sure the application of the statute is as fair as possible, the state must also continue to provide the resources necessary to ensure that all defendants faced with a capital crime are provided highly competent and trained defense counsel. This representation must include the ability to retain the necessary experts for both the guilt/innocence and sentencing phases of proceedings. These protections for people accused of capital murder should not be viewed as roadblocks. They are important safeguards to make sure justice is served. (http://www.nhbar.org/uploads/pdf/BJ-Summer2011-Vol52-No2-Pg24.pdf)

FROM THE STATEMENT OF JUSTICE CLARENCE THOMAS, CONCURRING, IN *THOMPSON V. MCNEIL* (556 U.S. ___), U.S. SUPREME COURT, MARCH 9, 2009

I also disagree with JUSTICE STEVENS that other aspects of the criminal justice system in this country require the fresh examination of the costs and benefits of retaining the death penalty that he seeks.... For example, JUSTICE STEVENS criticizes the "dehumanizing effects" of the manner in which petitioner has been confined,... but he never pauses to consider whether there is a legitimate penological reason for keeping certain inmates in restrictive confinement.... Indeed, the disastrous consequences of this Court's recent foray into prison management,... should have suppressed any urge to second-guess these difficult institutional decisions....

JUSTICE STEVENS also points to the 129 death row inmates that have been "exonerated" since 1973.... These inmates may have been freed from prison, but that does not necessarily mean that they were declared innocent of the crime for which they were convicted.... Many were merely the beneficiaries of "this Court's Byzantine death penalty jurisprudence."... Moreover, by citing these statistics, JUSTICE STEVENS implies "that the death penalty can only be just in a system that does not permit error."... But no criminal justice system operates without error. There is no constitutional basis for prohibiting Florida "from authorizing the death penalty, even in our imperfect system."...

Finally, JUSTICE STEVENS altogether refuses to take into consideration the gruesome nature of the crimes that legitimately lead States to authorize the death penalty and juries to impose it.

The facts of this case illustrate the point. On March 30, 1976, petitioner and his codefendant were in a motel room with the victim and another woman. They instructed the women to contact their families to obtain money. The victim made the mistake of promising that she could obtain

$200 to $300; she was able to secure only $25. Enraged, petitioner's codefendant ordered her into the bedroom, removed his chain belt, forced her to undress, and began hitting her in the face while petitioner beat her with the belt. They then rammed a chair leg into her vagina, tearing its inner wall and causing internal bleeding; they repeated the process with a nightstick. Petitioner and his codefendant then tortured her with lit cigarettes and lighters and forced her to eat her sanitary napkin and to lick spilt beer off the floor. All the while, they continued to beat her with the chain belt, the club, and the chair leg. They stopped the attack once to force the victim to again call her mother to ask for money. After the call, petitioner and his codefendant resumed the torture until the victim died.... Three juries recommended that petitioner receive the death penalty for this heinous murder, and petitioner has received judicial review of his sentence on at least 17 occasions. The decision to sentence petitioner to death is not "'the product of habit and inattention rather than an acceptable deliberative process.'"...It represents the considered judgment of the people of Florida that a death sentence, which is expressly contemplated by the Constitution,...is warranted in this case. It is the crime—and not the punishment imposed by the jury or the delay in petitioner's execution—that was "unacceptably cruel." (http://www.supremecourt.gov/opinions/08pdf/08-7369Thomas.pdf)

CHAPTER 12
THE DEBATE: CAPITAL PUNISHMENT SHOULD BE ABOLISHED

THE TESTIMONY OF RAY KRONE BEFORE THE JOINT COMMITTEE ON JUDICIARY, CONNECTICUT GENERAL ASSEMBLY, REGARDING SENATE BILL 1035, AN ACT REVISING THE PENALTY FOR CAPITAL FELONIES TO REPEAL THE DEATH PENALTY AND SUBSTITUTE LIFE IMPRISONMENT WITHOUT THE POSSIBILITY OF RELEASE AS THE AUTHORIZED SENTENCE FOR PERSONS CONVICTED OF CERTAIN MURDERS, MARCH 7, 2011

My name is Ray Krone, I am the 100th death row inmate in America freed due to my innocence. Today I'm the Director of Training and Communications for a group called Witness to Innocence, which is consisted solely of death row survivors, people that were sentenced to death for something they didn't do.

I'm from a small agriculture town in southern Pennsylvania. I was in a church choir, was an acolyte, I played Little League baseball, Pee Wee football, did good in high school, graduated, enlisted for six years in the U.S. Air Force. When I got out of the Air Force in Phoenix, Arizona, I got a job at the U.S. Post Office, bought my own home, living the American dream, if you will. I've been an honest citizen, no record, not even traffic violations.

One day I was questioned about a murder of a local bar maid at a bar that I played darts at, that I played on their volleyball team for. Within two days I was arrested for that murder based on testimony from the local medical examiner who said a mark on the body matched my teeth. Just seven months after that murder I was sitting trial with the court-appointed attorney that was granted $5,000 to defend me. Of course, I had nothing to worry about. I didn't do anything. I was sure. I believed in the system. I actually supported the death penalty.

After the three and a half day trial, I was convicted and sentenced to death because I didn't show remorse. How do you show remorse for a crime you didn't commit? And so I went to death row and was there for three years.

My case was overturned because the prosecutor withheld evidence. I got a new trial. By the second trial my family realized this was serious, and they mortgaged their home, cashed in their retirement funds. Friends of my high school took up donations, and churches took up donations. My second cousin spent more than $100,000 on legal fees. I had a luxury few on death row have: I was able to hire my own attorney. My second trial lasted six and a half weeks. Over 30 experts testified, 500 exhibits were introduced. And after that six and a half weeks I was again found guilty because the jury said it was too hard for them to understand the DNA, and they believed the bite mark expert by the prosecutor. However, this time the judge ruled that there was a residual doubt in my guilt. He sat there for six and a half weeks and listened to all the testimony; he wasn't sure I did it. He said this case will haunt him for the rest of his life. And so he sentenced me to 25 to life instead sending me back to death row.

As horrible as death row was, I tell you—prison is worse. When I was on death row I saw people taken off and executed. There was nobody kicking and screaming saying I want to live. I don't want to die. You make peace with dying. It was easier to die than to live in prison. It was easier to be killed because you no longer have to think about your consequences of what you've done. The ultimate punishment is sitting everyday in prison knowing you're never going to get out. It's your fault. You deserved it.

Thankfully, in 2001, the legislature in Arizona passed legislation allowing inmates to request DNA testing on the evidence that had not previously been tested if it might have bearing on their innocence. I was one of the first cases that filed for post-conviction relief—to have testing done on the victim's pants and underwear that had never been tested. It was always available and stored in a police evidence locker in that courtroom, but had never been tested.

DNA testing was done from the victims' pants and from her underwear. That DNA matched on both those sources and it was not mine and it was not the victim's. So that DNA was taken and plugged into the nationwide DNA data bank and it did come back with a match to a man who had a history of sexual assault against women and children, a man who was on parole at the time of this murder and lived right behind the bar where the murder took place.

I was lucky to have this DNA evidence. DNA evidence is available in only about 15% of murders. Even after DNA showed this man was the offender and I was innocent, I still had to fight to be released. Once a man is convicted of a crime, it is tremendously difficult to exonerate him. But eventually, after 10 years, three months, and eight days, I was released to reunite with my family and my friends, start my life all over again at the age of 45 and wondering why did this happen? What was the point? I was perfectly happy being a mailman. I certainly expected to retire in my mid-fifties after 30 years of serving in our government. Instead, now I find myself sometimes having to testify and relive that nightmare for me, and not just for me, but for what my family went through.

But for those innocent people like me, and there's a multitude of them. We still had a chance at life, a chance to be released, a chance to be reunited with our family. I know that Connecticut has a fine criminal justice system. But mistakes happen for all sorts of reasons. It happened to me, I assure you, wrongful convictions can happen to anyone. Thank you. (http://www.cga.ct.gov/2011/JUDdata/Tmy/2011SB-01035-R000307-Ray%20Krone-TMY.PDF)

THE TESTIMONY OF SENATOR MARTIN M. LOONEY, 11TH DISTRICT, STATE OF CONNECTICUT, SENATE, BEFORE THE JOINT COMMITTEE ON JUDICIARY, CONNECTICUT GENERAL ASSEMBLY, REGARDING SENATE BILL 1035, AN ACT REVISING THE PENALTY FOR CAPITAL FELONIES TO REPEAL THE DEATH PENALTY AND SUBSTITUTE LIFE IMPRISONMENT WITHOUT THE POSSIBILITY OF RELEASE AS THE AUTHORIZED SENTENCE FOR PERSONS CONVICTED OF CERTAIN MURDERS, MARCH 7, 2011

In 1994 Justice Harry Blackmun, who at one time had been a proponent of the death penalty, wrote in dissent in *Callins v. Collins*, "From this day forward, I no longer shall tinker with the machinery of death." After many years on the United States Supreme Court, Justice Blackmun recognized the reality that the death penalty cannot be applied in a fair and impartial manner and there can be no guarantee against error. The State, as a fallible human institution, should not have the power to take a human life and to act with hubris and arrogance when humility and restraint should prevail.

In Connecticut, this is a difficult moment to oppose the death penalty. The unimaginable and horrific crimes in Cheshire have understandably increased some public support for this ultimate penalty. At times, however, it is important to clearly separate objective reality from understandable human emotion and this is one of those times.

Executing criminals who have committed the worst crimes does not bring the victims back to life, it does not make our state safer, and it does not save our state money. More importantly though, our criminal justice system is simply not accurate enough to entrust with the ultimate penalty. We know that the system has convicted innocent people; the death penalty will eventually execute an innocent person here. This is not a risk that we can accept.

To date, since 1973, 138 people throughout the United States have been released from death row due to improper prosecution or outright innocence. During the same period, more than 1,242 people have been put to death. This ratio of 1 release from death row for every 9 executions is deeply troubling. It demonstrates what we all know: the government is not infallible. It makes errors and this kind of deadly error cannot be undone. Former U.S. Supreme Court Justice John Paul Stevens called his vote to reinstate the death penalty as "the one vote I would change."

Not only does the government make errors and put innocent people on death row, but as Justice Blackmun explained, the death penalty is not meted out fairly. Application of the death penalty has been shown to be racially biased. Furthermore, a person is much more likely to receive a death sentence if he or she murders a white victim. The death penalty is often unevenly applied. Differences in prosecutorial discretion have led to a disproportionate number of people being sentenced to death in certain judicial districts. Such disparities are indicative of an arbitrary and capricious system. There is no consistent standard for the application of the death penalty. Our own statute in allowing the weighing and balancing of mitigating vs. aggravating factors introduces the possibility of dangerous subjectivity producing different results in cases where the circumstances are virtually identical. What if the prosecutor is more eloquent and persuasive than the defense counsel? Should life or death hang in the balance? What if the conviction is achieved by perjured or simply mistaken testimony? What if there is an undiscovered bias held by one or more jurors? The choice between life and death should not depend on the quality of legal representation and the vagaries of the trial process.

Some argue that in cases of the most heinous crimes, the death penalty saves resources. This argument does not square with reality: the costs of capital felony cases are significantly higher than the costs of non-capital felony cases. Others argue that the death penalty will be a deterrent. The death penalty is not a deterrent to violent crime. The south has the highest execution rate and the highest homicide rate—a rate that has risen as the rates of executions have risen, while in the northeast, the homicide rate is the lowest in the country and there have been no executions in the last decade other than Michael Ross. The 15 states without the death penalty have a significantly lower (35%) homicide rate than the 35 states that have it. The death penalty is simply retribution and retribution solves nothing and is not a rational part of our criminal justice system. We must not as a state and nation take lives for the sake of vengeance. Killing human beings is wrong whether done by the state or by a criminal. Certainly there are criminals who should never be at large in society; that is why we must have the option of life in prison without parole.

I again cite Justice Blackmun: "It is virtually self evident to me now that no combination of procedural rules or substantive regulations ever can save the death penalty from its inherent constitutional deficiencies. The basic question—does the system accurately and consistently determine which defendants 'deserve' to die?—cannot be answered in the affirmative. It is not simply that this Court has allowed vague aggravating circumstances to be employed, relevant mitigating evidence to be disregarded, and vital judicial review to be blocked. The problem is that the inevitability of factual, legal, and moral error gives us a system that we know must wrongly kill some defendants, a system that fails to deliver the fair, consistent, and reliable sentences of death required by the Constitution."

The death penalty offers no constructive contribution to society's efforts to defeat violent crime, and in fact diverts resources and energies from such efforts. Finally, the death penalty undermines a civilized society by perpetuating the idea that life is disposable at the hands of our fellow human beings. (http://www.cga.ct.gov/2011/JUD data/Tmy/2011SB-01035-R000307-Senator%20Martin%20M.%20Looney,%20Majority%20Leader-TMY.PDF)

THE STATEMENT OF THE YALE UNIVERSITY CHAPTER OF AMNESTY INTERNATIONAL BEFORE THE JOINT COMMITTEE ON JUDICIARY, CONNECTICUT GENERAL ASSEMBLY, REGARDING SENATE BILL 1035, AN ACT REVISING THE PENALTY FOR CAPITAL FELONIES TO REPEAL THE DEATH PENALTY AND SUBSTITUTE LIFE IMPRISONMENT WITHOUT THE POSSIBILITY OF RELEASE AS THE AUTHORIZED SENTENCE FOR PERSONS CONVICTED OF CERTAIN MURDERS, MARCH 7, 2011

Amnesty International campaigns against the death penalty worldwide because the death penalty is a fundamental, irreversible denial of human rights. It is an affront to human dignity and perpetuates a cycle of violence that constitutes state affirmation of the expendability of human life. It is also an affront to American values. This country was founded on soaring aspirations, on the inherent truth that we are all created equal and endowed with inalienable rights. One of these is the right to life, and as a *right*, it cannot be abridged, it cannot be undermined, it cannot be revoked. Our founding documents exist to affirm our individual rights and to protect us from abuse by the state. The death penalty is in undeniable tension with these documents, with the right to life and the basic tenets of our system of government.

Two years ago the Connecticut state legislature voted to abolish the death penalty, but could not override then-Governor [M. Jodi] Rell's veto. In her veto message, Governor Rell described the death penalty as being reserved for those who "committed crimes that are revolting to our humanity and civilized society." What she failed to realize is that the death penalty—a system of state execution reserved for, yes, only the most heinous and despicable criminals—is also revolting to our humanity.

The belief that the death penalty ultimately and unequivocally violates human rights is not only a deeply held passion, as Governor Rell acknowledged. The death penalty is an attack on our foundational and universal human dignity—our common humanity. Governor Rell steadfastly rebuked those who "killed for the sake of killing," highlighting intent as the greater contributor to the egregiousness of such crimes. The effect, though—the elimination of a human life—is not to be diminished. The death penalty also has this cruel and inhuman result.

This is not to say that those who engage easily or frivolously in capital offenses, in acts that shock the conscience of humankind, should be given any reprieve. Our justice system has valid alternatives to the death penalty, such as life imprisonment without parole, that constitute adequate punishment even for the most repugnant crimes. Moreover, it is dangerous to engage in ethical equivalencies and hierarchically rank human beings; the point should not be to judge whose life is more worthwhile, but rather to affirm that all human life must be valued. A systemic process that ends a human existence cannot stand in a righteous and just society.

Supporters of the death penalty have argued that it serves as a valid deterrent for potential criminals, and that it is an application of firm but due justice. Yet our justice system is supposed to provide remedy to victims, not vengeance. Moreover, this view fails to give due credence to the reality that the death penalty system has not been and cannot be proven to be a successful deterrent, is more expensive than relevant alternatives because of the appellate process, is subject to human error, and is often riddled with economic and racial bias in its application, as Governor Rell briefly alluded to in her veto message. The risk of executing innocents is simply too high. The irrevocable nature of the death penalty renders it an unsustainable and indefensible remedy in an imperfect justice system.

FROM THE STATEMENT OF RENNY CUSHING TO THE COMMISSION TO STUDY THE DEATH PENALTY IN NEW HAMPSHIRE, DECEMBER 1, 2010

My father, Robert Cushing, Sr., was shotgunned to death in front of my mother in our family home two decades ago. For me, thinking about what should be done after a murder happens is not just an intellectual exercise; it's part of my life. The pain that is difficult to give words to, the emptiness and trauma, are part of my personal reality that I brought to the work of the Commission. . . .

The death penalty can divide and damage families. Because "death is different," and because individuals have deeply held beliefs about the morality and utility of executions, unlike any other punishment the death penalty sometimes creates irreconcilable conflict amongst the surviving family members of murder victims. At a time when mutual support to weather a shared loss is so important, disagreement over the death penalty, instead of helping bring families together, creates fissures and compounds the tragedy of murder.

The death penalty fosters a hierarchy of victims. Depending upon one's perspective, family members of murder victims are often judged by others on their position on the death penalty, and get divided into categories of "good victims" and "bad victims." Sometimes family members of murder victims who oppose the death penalty have their love for their murdered family member challenged—opposition to the death penalty is taken as a sign that that they really didn't love [their] parent/sibling/child. Or, opposition the death penalty is taken as an implication that somehow the victim must be responsible for his or her own murder. Or, opponents of the death penalty are dismissed as either psychos or saints—crazy for not wanting to see the person who killed their loved one executed, or uncommonly holy for this earth. In some instances opposition to the death penalty results in denial of status and rights under victims' rights laws. Fortunately New Hampshire recently amended its Victims Bill of Rights to guarantee equality of treatment for all victims irrespective of their position on the death penalty, but subtle prejudices against some victims based upon either their support or opposition to the death penalty remain.

The death penalty puts the media spotlight on murderers and makes rock stars out of killers. Efforts to seek and carry out the death penalty draw attention to the person facing execution. In the process, the life and good work of the victim can be ignored or impugned. In the minds of the public, executions turn offenders into victims, and they gain celebrity in their death. Everyone knows the name of Tim McVeigh, but far fewer people know the name of Julie Welch or any of the other 167 victims of his crime.

The death penalty creates additional victims. When a prisoner is executed, that person is often someone's parent, someone's child. The Commission gave no consideration to the impact the death penalty has upon the family of the condemned, but when the state carries out an execution, his or her surviving family members become the family of a homicide victim. The faces of that family are hidden by silence and shame, but we cannot ignore the reality that the innocent children of killers put to death are impacted in ways society, as a whole, has never examined.

The death penalty is a false promise to victims. Proponents of the death penalty put forth the notion that an execution can be a solution to the pain experienced by a survivor of a murder victim. Offering up this promise of a ritual event represents a fundamental misunderstanding of a victim's journey. Healing is a process, not an event. When public employees take a killer from a prison cell, strap him on a gurney, put a needle in his vein, and pump him full of poison to kill him, that is not, as my retentionist colleagues on the Commission assert, an act consistent with a standard of decency, it is an act of despair. Executions do not accomplish the thing that victims want above all else—they do not bring back their murdered loved one.

The hardest thing for a victim to do is accept that they cannot change the past. But what they can do, what they need to do, is make decisions about the future, about how they live their lives in the future. Sometimes victims get so fixated on how their loved one died that they almost forget how their loved one lived. Our broken death penalty system, with its years of delays and other problems, holds a victim's focus, and society's focus, on the killer, anticipating and expecting an event, the event, the killer's execution. If and when an execution occurs, another coffin is filled and another family grieves a killing, but, sadly, very little changes for the victim. Their loved one is still dead. What sometimes ends up happening is the murder claims two victims: the person killed by the murderer, and the person who is the survivor of that person who was killed, whose life gets claimed by a system that is a set up for failure.

At the end of the day the death penalty is not about those who kill, it is about us. We, as a society, become what we say we abhor, killers. I don't want the state killing in my name. (http://www.deathpenaltyinfo.org/new-hampshire-death-penalty-study-commission)

FROM THE STATEMENT OF JUSTICE JOHN PAUL STEVENS IN *THOMPSON V. MCNEIL* (556 U.S. ___), U.S. SUPREME COURT, MARCH 9, 2009

Last term, in my opinion in *Baze v. Rees*, 553 U. S. ___ (2008), I suggested that the "time for a dispassionate, impartial comparison of the enormous costs that death penalty litigation imposes on society with the benefits that it produces has surely arrived." ... This petition for certiorari describes costs that merit consideration in any such study.

In June 1976, having been advised by counsel that he would not receive the death penalty if he accepted responsibility for his crime, petitioner pleaded guilty to a capital offense. The advice was erroneous, and he was sentenced to death. Since that time, two state-court judgments have set aside his death sentence.... At a third penalty hearing—after petitioner presented mitigation evidence about his limited mental capacity and dysfunctional childhood that had previously been barred—five members of the advisory jury voted against a death sentence, but the court again imposed a sentence of death.

Thirty-two years have passed since petitioner was first sentenced to death. In prior cases, both JUSTICE BREYER and I have noted that substantially delayed executions arguably violate the Eighth Amendment's prohibition against cruel and unusual punishment.... Petitioner's case involves a longer delay than any of those earlier cases.

As he awaits execution, petitioner has endured especially severe conditions of confinement, spending up to 23 hours per day in isolation in a 6- by 9-foot cell. Two death warrants have been signed against him and stayed only shortly before he was scheduled to be put to death. The dehumanizing effects of such treatment are undeniable. See *People v. Anderson*, 6 Cal. 3d 628, 649, 493 P. 2d 880, 894 (1972) ("[T]he process of carrying out a verdict of death is often so degrading and brutalizing to the human spirit as to constitute psychological torture"); *Furman v. Georgia*, 408 U. S. 238, 288 (1972) ... ("[T]he prospect of pending execution exacts a frightful toll during the inevitable long wait between the imposition of sentence and the actual infliction of death"). Moreover, as I explained in *Lackey* [*Lackey v. Texas*, 514 U.S. 1045 (1995)], delaying an execution does not further public purposes of retribution and deterrence but only dimin-

ishes whatever possible benefit society might receive from petitioner's death. It would therefore be appropriate to conclude that a punishment of death after significant delay is "so totally without penological justification that it results in the gratuitous infliction of suffering." ...

While the length of petitioner's confinement under sentence of death is extraordinary, the concerns his case raises are not unique. Clarence Allen Lackey had spent 17 years on death row when this Court reviewed his petition for certiorari. Today, condemned inmates await execution for an average of nearly 13 years.... To my mind, this figure underscores the fundamental inhumanity and unworkability of the death penalty as it is administered in the United States.

Some respond that delays in carrying out executions are the result of this Court's insistence on excessive process. But delays have multiple causes, including "the States' failure to apply constitutionally sufficient procedures at the time of initial [conviction or] sentencing." ... The reversible error rate in capital trials is staggering. More than 30 percent of death verdicts imposed between 1973 and 2000 have been overturned, and 129 inmates sentenced to death during that time have been exonerated, often more than a decade after they were convicted. Judicial process takes time, but the error rate in capital cases illustrates its necessity. We are duty bound to "insure that every safeguard is observed" when "a defendant's life is at stake." ...

In sum, our experience during the past three decades has demonstrated that delays in state-sponsored killings are inescapable and that executing defendants after such delays is unacceptably cruel. This inevitable cruelty, coupled with the diminished justification for carrying out an execution after the lapse of so much time, reinforces my opinion that contemporary decisions "to retain the death penalty as a part of our law are the product of habit and inattention rather than an acceptable deliberative process." (http://www.supremecourt.gov/opinions/08pdf/08-7369Stevens.pdf)

IMPORTANT NAMES
AND ADDRESSES

American Bar Association
Criminal Justice Section
740 15th St. NW, 10th Floor
Washington, DC 20005-1009
(202) 662-1500
FAX: (202) 662-1501
E-mail: crimjustice@americanbar.org
URL: http://www.abanet.org/crimjust/
home.html/

American Civil Liberties Union
125 Broad St., 18th Floor
New York, NY 10004
(212) 549-2500
URL: http://www.aclu.org/

Amnesty International U.S.A.
Five Penn Plaza
New York, NY 10001
(212) 807-8400
FAX: (212) 627-1451
E-mail: aimember@aiusa.org
URL: http://www.amnestyusa.org/

Bureau of Justice Statistics
U.S. Department of Justice
810 Seventh St. NW
Washington, DC 20531
(202) 307-0765
E-mail: askbjs@usdoj.gov
URL: http://www.ojp.usdoj.gov/bjs

Center on Wrongful Convictions
Bluhm Legal Clinic
Northwestern University School of Law
375 E. Chicago Ave.
Chicago, IL 60611
(312) 503-2391
FAX: (312) 503-8977
E-mail: cwc@law.northwestern.edu
URL: http://www.law.northwestern.edu/cwc/

Constitution Project
1200 18th St. NW, Ste. 1000
Washington, DC 20036
(202) 580-6920

FAX: (202) 580-6929
E-mail: info@constitutionproject.org
URL: http://www.constitutionproject.org/

Criminal Justice Legal Foundation
PO Box 1199
Sacramento, CA 95812
(916) 446-0345
URL: http://www.cjlf.org/

Death Penalty Information Center
1015 18th St. NW, Ste. 704
Washington, DC 20036
(202) 289-2275
FAX: (202) 289-7336
E-mail: dpic@deathpenaltyinfo.org
URL: http://www.deathpenaltyinfo.org/

Equal Justice Initiative
122 Commerce St.
Montgomery, AL 36104
(334) 269-1803
FAX: (334) 269-1806
E-mail: contact_us@eji.org
URL: http://eji.org/eji/

Federal Bureau of Investigation
J. Edgar Hoover Bldg.
935 Pennsylvania Ave. NW
Washington, DC 20535-0001
(202) 324-3000
URL: http://www.fbi.gov/

Federal Bureau of Prisons
320 First St. NW
Washington, DC 20534
(202) 307-3198
URL: http://www.bop.gov/

Innocence Project
40 Worth St., Ste. 701
New York, NY 10013
(212) 364-5340
E-mail: info@innocenceproject.org
URL: http://www.innocenceproject.org/

Innocence Project Clinic
University of Virginia School of Law
580 Massie Rd.
Charlottesville, VA 22903
(434) 924-7354
E-mail: lawcomm@virginia.edu
URL: http://www.law.virginia.edu/html/
academics/practical/innocenceclinic.htm

JURIST
c/o Professor Bernard Hibbitts
University of Pittsburgh School of Law
Pittsburgh, PA 15260
(412) 648-1400
E-mail: JURIST@pitt.edu
URL: http://jurist.law.pitt.edu/

Justice for All
(713) 935-9300
E-mail: info@jfa.net
URL: http://www.jfa.net/

Justice Research and Statistics Association
777 N. Capitol St. NE, Ste. 801
Washington, DC 20002
(202) 842-9330
FAX: (202) 842-9329
E-mail: cjinfo@jrsa.org
URL: http://www.jrsa.org/

Moratorium Campaign
586 Harding Blvd.
Baton Rouge, LA 70807
URL: http://www.moratoriumcampaign.org/

Murder Victims' Families for Reconciliation
2100 M St. NW, Ste. 170-296
Washington, DC 20037
(877) 896-4702
E-mail: info@mvfr.org
URL: http://www.mvfr.org/

NAACP Legal Defense and Educational
Fund
99 Hudson St., Ste. 1600
New York, NY 10013

(212) 965-2200
URL: http://www.naacpldf.org/

National Association of Criminal Defense Lawyers
1660 L St. NW, 12th Floor
Washington, DC 20036
(202) 872-8600
FAX: (202) 872-8690
E-mail: assist@nacdl.com
URL: http://www.nacdl.org/

National Center for Victims of Crime
2000 M St. NW, Ste. 480
Washington, DC 20036
(202) 467-8700
FAX: (202) 467-8701
URL: http://www.ncvc.org/

National Coalition to Abolish the Death Penalty
1705 DeSales St. NW, Fifth Floor
Washington, DC 20036
(202) 331-4090
E-mail: info@ncadp.org
URL: http://www.ncadp.org/

National District Attorneys Association
44 Canal Center Plaza, Ste. 110
Alexandria, VA 22314
(703) 549-9222

FAX: (703) 836-3195
URL: http://www.ndaa.org/

Office of the United Nations High Commissioner for Human Rights
Palais des Nations, CH-1211
Geneva 10 Switzerland
(011-41) 22-917-9220
E-mail: InfoDesk@ohchr.org
URL: http://www.ohchr.org/EN/Pages/WelcomePage.aspx/

Sentencing Project
1705 DeSales St., Eighth Floor
Washington, DC 20036
(202) 628-0871
FAX: (202) 628-1091
E-mail: staff@sentencingproject.org
URL: http://www.sentencingproject.org/

U.S. Commission on Civil Rights
624 Ninth St. NW
Washington, DC 20425
(202) 376-7700
URL: http://www.usccr.gov/

U.S. Department of Justice
950 Pennsylvania Ave. NW
Washington, DC 20530-0001
(202) 514-2000
E-mail: askdoj@usdoj.gov
URL: http://www.usdoj.gov/

U.S. Government Accountability Office
441 G St. NW
Washington, DC 20548
(202) 512-3000
E-mail: contact@gao.gov
URL: http://www.gao.gov/

U.S. House Committee on the Judiciary
2138 Rayburn House Office Bldg.
Washington, DC 20515
(202) 225-3951
URL: http://judiciary.house.gov/

U.S. Senate Committee on the Judiciary
224 Dirksen Senate Office Bldg.
Washington, DC 20510
(202) 224-7703
FAX: (202) 224-9516
URL: http://judiciary.senate.gov/

U.S. Sentencing Commission Office of Public Affairs
One Columbus Circle NE, Ste. 2-500
Washington, DC 20002-8002
(202) 502-4500
E-mail: pubaffairs@ussc.gov
URL: http://www.ussc.gov/

U.S. Supreme Court
1 First St. NE
Washington, DC 20543
(202) 479-3000
URL: http://www.supremecourtus.gov/

RESOURCES

Numerous federal and state agencies, courts, legislative bodies, committees, and commissions served as resources for this book. The Bureau of Justice Statistics (BJS) within the U.S. Department of Justice collects statistics on death row inmates as part of its National Prisoner Statistics. Since 1993 the BJS has prepared the annual bulletin *Capital Punishment*, which provides an overview of capital punishment in the United States. Bulletins published through 2006 include much historical data. The BJS also maintains the website Capital Punishment Facts at a Glance that includes some historical data on the death penalty and the nation's death rows. The Federal Bureau of Investigation collects and publishes crime data through its annual *Uniform Crime Report* and *Crime in the United States*.

Information about the current status of death row inmates was obtained from the websites of state departments of corrections and the federal Bureau of Prisons. Legal opinions from state courts, federal district courts, and the U.S. Supreme Court were an invaluable resource in preparation of this book. In addition, public hearings held by state legislatures provided records of testimony given by many stakeholders—both for and against capital punishment. Other government sources included the reports of committees and commissions that were tasked by various states and the federal government to examine contentious issues related to the death penalty, such as costs, the appeals process, and racial discrimination and other fairness issues. Offices established and/or funded by the government to provide legal assistance to inmates charged in capital cases also provided useful information.

Prominent law schools around the country publish journal articles and news releases concerning death penalty cases and the legal issues involved in them. Several schools host or sponsor organizations or student clinics that are dedicated to clearing wrongfully convicted death row inmates. Examples include the Center on Wrongful Convictions at the Northwestern University School of Law, the Innocence Project at the Benjamin N. Cardozo School of Law at Yeshiva University, and the Innocence Project Clinic at Virginia Law School. All of these sources were consulted.

The Death Penalty Information Center (DPIC) is a nonprofit organization that provides the media and the general public with information and analysis regarding capital punishment. The DPIC, which is against the death penalty, serves as a resource for those working on this issue. Its reports and graphics on capital punishment were used in preparing this book. The National Coalition to Abolish the Death Penalty maintains an up-to-date list of news stories from the media regarding death penalty.

The National Association for the Advancement of Colored People's Legal Defense and Educational Fund (LDF) maintains statistics on capital punishment and is strongly opposed to the death penalty. The LDF publishes *Death Row U.S.A.*, a periodic compilation of capital punishment statistics and information, including the names, gender, and race of all those who have been executed or are currently on death row. Gender and racial information on the victims of those executed is also provided. Data from this publication were helpful in preparing this book.

Other private organizations consulted for this book include the American Bar Association, the American Board of Anesthesiology, the American Civil Liberties Union, the American Constitution Society for Law and Policy, the American Medical Association, Amnesty International, the Criminal Justice Legal Foundation, the Equal Justice Initiative, Murder Victims' Families for Reconciliation, the National Center of Victims of Crime, Pro-Death Penalty .com, and the Urban Institute.

Major media sources consulted for this book include ABC News, the Associated Press, the BBC, CBS News, CNN, Fox

News, NBC News, Reuters News Service, *Austin Chronicle, Boston Globe, Chicago Tribune, Houston Chronicle, Los Angeles Times, National Review, New York Times, Philadelphia Inquirer, Providence Journal, Sacramento Bee, San Francisco Chronicle, Times* (London, England), *Wall Street Journal,* and *Washington Post.* Polls taken by Angus Reid Public Opinion, the Field Research Corporation, the Gallup Organization, the Pew Research Center, the Quinnipiac University Polling Institute, and Rasmussen Reports were also used in preparing this book.

INDEX

Page references in italics refer to photographs. References with the letter t following them indicate the presence of a table. The letter f indicates a figure. If more than one table or figure appears on a particular page, the exact item number for the table or figure being referenced is provided.

A

I

ICJ (International Court of Justice), 131, 132
Idaho, executions in, 114
Idaho, Lankford v., 22–23
"Illegal Racial Discrimination in Jury Selection: A Continuing Legacy" (EJI), 98
Illinois
    de jure moratorium, 110–111
    exonerations in, 101
    Governor's Commission on Capital Punishment, 111
Illinois, Witherspoon v., 16
"The Impact of Legally Inappropriate Factors on Death Sentencing for California Homicides, 1990–99" (Pierce & Radelet), 93
"In Pursuit of the Public Good: Lawyers Who Care" (Supreme Court), 99–100
In Re Troy Anthony Davis, 109
Indigent capital defense, 98–99
"Information on Defendants Who Were Executed since 1976 and Designated as 'Volunteers'" (DPIC), 57
Innocence
    arguments for capital punishment and, 136
    death penalty, reasons for supporting/opposing, 121
    dispute of Innocence List, 104–105
    Innocence List, 101
    Krone, Ray, innocence of, 139–140
    number of exonerations of innocent people on death row, 140
    postconviction DNA testing, 106
    public opinion on death penalty and, 123
    See also Exonerations
Innocence List, 101, 104–105
"Innocence: List of Those Freed from Death Row" (DPIC), 101
Innocence Project
    Graves, Anthony, exoneration of, and, 103
    Willingham case, 108
Innocence Project Clinic, Virginia Law School, 104
"Innocence Project Clinic Seeks to Overturn Death Sentence" (Virginia Law School), 104
Innocence Protection Act
    description of, 10
    federal grants to states, 100
    postconviction DNA testing, 106
Insanity
    execution of insane, 7, 44–45
    psychiatrist's testimony, validity of, 42–44
International Bill of Human Rights, statement on death penalty in, 125
International community
    China, 128–129
    countries that are abolitionist for all crimes, 128*t*–129*t*

countries that are abolitionist for ordinary crimes only, 129(*t*10.4)
countries that are abolitionist in practice, 127(*t*10.2)
countries that have abolished death penalty since 1976, 130*t*
countries/territories that retain death penalty for ordinary crimes, 127(*t*10.1)
foreign nationals under sentence of death in U.S., by foreign nationality, 131(*t*10.6)
foreign nationals under sentence of death in U.S., by state of confinement, 131(*t*10.7)
international status of capital punishment, 126–128
United Nations resolutions, 125–126
U.S. conflicts with, 129–132
International Court of Justice (ICJ), 131, 132
International Covenant on Civil and Political Rights
    statement on death penalty in, 125
    U.S. ratification of, 126
Iowa, de jure moratorium, 110
Iran, executions in, 127
Ivester, Sally, 37

J

Jackson, United States v., 112
Jackson v. Georgia, 13
Jensen, Max, 6
Jindal, Bobby, 26
John Paul II, Pope, 10
Johnson, Cory, 64
Johnson, Dorsie Lee, Jr., 41–42
Johnson, Penry v., 46
Johnson, Terrell, 100
Jolly, David, 62
Jones, Louis, Jr., 63–64
Judges
    death penalty cases, guidelines for, 15
    delayed executions via habeas corpus reviews, 29
    sentencing by, 18–19
Judicial districts, 89
Judicial override, description of, 55
Jurek v. Texas, 14, 15, 42–43
Juries
    anti–death penalty jurors, exclusion of, 16–17
    death penalty cases, guidelines for, 15
    "death-qualified," 17
    jury selection, racial bias and, 97–98
    lesser charge by, 15–16
    parole information, withholding from, 18
    role of in death penalty decisions, 17–18
    selection, racial bias and, 97–98
    selection, racially based peremptory challenges, 50–51
Jurisdictions
    capital offenses under state law, 53
    differences in states, 87

executions in, 70
Hispanics under death sentence by, 79(*t*6.18)
lengths of time on death row and, 70
number of persons executed, by jurisdiction, 1977–2009, 83*f*
number of persons executed, by jurisdiction, 2010, 83*t*
prisoners on death row, by jurisdiction/region/race, 88(*t*7.2)
prisoners removed from sentence of death by, 70*t*
prisoners under sentence of death by, 69*t*
racial bias in, 89
women under death sentence by, 79(*t*6.17)
See also Fairness
Jury deadlock, 112–113
"Jury Issues First Death Sentence in New Hampshire since the 1950s" (Zezima), 112
Jury sentencing, Supreme Court rulings on, 19–21
Justice, miscarriage of, 32–33
"Justin Wolfe Could Soon Be Released from Prison" (Associated Press), 104
The Juvenile Death Penalty Today: Death Sentences and Executions for Juvenile Crimes (Streib), 8–9
Juveniles
    executed in the modern era, 9*t*
    execution of, 8–9
    rape of, 25
    See also Minors

K

Kahn, Joseph, 129
Kansas, de facto moratorium in, 111, 112
Kansas v. Marsh, 112
Kant, Immanuel, 136
Kazakhstan, 128
Keaton, David, 101–103
Keil, Thomas J., 91
Keller, Morris, Jr., 34
Kemp, McCleskey v., 49–50, 90, 94
Kendall, George, 1
Kennedy, Anthony M.
    on child rape, 25–26
    on death sentence for minors, 40, 42
Kennedy, Patrick, 25
Kennedy v. Louisiana, 25
Kentucky
    executions in, 114
    study on racial bias, 91
Kentucky, Batson v., 51, 97–98
Kentucky, Stanford v., 40
Kentucky Racial Justice Act, 91
Kersey, Thomas, 26
Kidd, Daniel, 66
Kidnapping, 25
Kilgore, Tony, 100

countries that are abolitionist for ordinary crimes only, 129(*t*10.4)

countries that are abolitionist in practice, 127(*t*10.2)

countries/territories that retain death penalty for ordinary crimes, 127(*t*10.1)

criminal history of prisoners under sentence of death, by race/Hispanic origin, 74(*t*6.13)

death row exonerations by race, 102*t*

death row exonerations by state, 102(*f*8.2)

death row exonerations by year, 102(*f*8.1)

death row locations, by state, 68(*t*6.1)

death sentences, national/Texas, 11*f*

defendant/victim racial combinations in execution cases, breakdown of, 96(*t*7.5)

educational level of prisoners under sentence of death, 71(*t*6.6)

executions, by jurisdiction/method, 85(*t*6.21)

executions, by year/race/Hispanic origin, 95*t*

executions, cumulative number of, 82(*f*6.5)

executions, number executed per year, 82(*f*6.4)

executions, number executed per year, 1930–2010, 7*f*

executions, number of persons executed, by jurisdiction, 114*t*

executions, numbers executed, by year, 1977–2010, 6*t*

executions, states with no, 110*t*

executions by state, 61*f*

executions/dispositions of inmates sentenced to death, by race/Hispanic origin, 96(*t*7.4)

foreign nationals under sentence of death in U.S., by foreign nationality, 131(*t*10.6)

foreign nationals under sentence of death in U.S., by state of confinement, 131(*t*10.7)

geographic boundaries, Courts of Appeals/District Courts, 57*f*

Hispanics under death sentence, by jurisdiction, 79(*t*6.18)

homicide rate/number of executions, 8*f*

juveniles executed in the modern era, 9*t*

marital status, prisoners under sentence of death, 71(*t*6.7)

method of execution by state, 60*t*

number of death row inmates, as reported by NAACP, 78*t*

number of death sentences commuted, 58(*t*5.3)

number of persons executed, by jurisdiction, 81*t*

number of persons executed, by jurisdiction, 1977–2009, 83*f*

number of persons executed, by jurisdiction, 2010, 83*t*

number of persons executed, by race/Hispanic origin, method, 85(*t*6.22)

number of prisoners under sentence of death, 78*f*

number sentenced to death/removals, by jurisdiction/reason for removal, 77*t*

numbers under death sentence, 2(*f*1.1)

numbers under death sentence/number of executions, 1953–2009, 7*f*

prisoners on death row, by race, 95*f*

prisoners on death row, by jurisdiction/region/race, 88(*t*7.2)

prisoners removed from sentence of death, by jurisdiction/method of removal, 70*t*

prisoners sentenced to death, by year/jurisdiction, 73*t*

prisoners sentenced to death each year, 79*f*

prisoners sentenced to death/number of removals, 76*f*

prisoners sentenced to death/outcome of sentence, 75*t*

prisoners under sentence of death, by jurisdiction, region, race, 69*t*

prisoners under sentence of death, by race, 68(*t*6.2)

public opinion on moral acceptability of death penalty, 118(*t*9.2)

public opinion on moral acceptability of various issues, 118(*t*9.1)

public opinion on moral acceptability of various issues, by age group, 119*t*

public opinion poll on appropriate use of death penalty, 122(*f*9.3)

public opinion poll on death penalty, 119*f*, 2(*f*1.2)

public opinion poll on death penalty, by gender, race, political affiliation, 120*t*

public opinion poll on fairness of death penalty, 122(*f*9.4)

public preference for death penalty *vs.* life imprisonment with absolutely no possibility of parole, 120*f*

race of persons executed, 84*f*

race/homicide statistics, 97

sex, race, Hispanic origin of prisoners under sentence of death, 71(*t*6.5)

states with death penalty, 2*t*

states without death penalty, 3*t*

Supreme Court decisions involving death penalty, 5*t*

time since sentencing, inmates under sentence of death, 71(*t*6.8)

time under sentence of death, 74(*t*6.11)

total number sentenced to death, by jurisdiction, 88(*t*7.1)

women under death sentence by race/jurisdiction, 79(*t*6.17)

years under sentence of death, average number of, 72*t*

Stavinsky, Robin, 57

Stay of Execution: Saving the Death Penalty (Lane), 94

Stears, Robert, 133–134

Stevens, John Paul
  argument against capital punishment, 142–143

  on double jeopardy, 21

  due process/advance notice of death penalty imposition, 22–23

  on execution of mentally retarded people, 47

  on extended stays on death row, 37

  on judge sentencing in death cases, 19

  opinion of death sentence for minors, 40, 42

  on right to effective counsel, 28–29

  in statement of Justice Clarence Thomas, 136–137

  on victim impact statements, 48

  on vote to reinstate death penalty, 140

Stevens, Lorne, 133–134

Stewart, Potter J.
  on bifurcated trial system, 14–15

  Furman v. Georgia, opinion on, 13–14

  on predictability of future criminal behavior, 15

Stewart, Summerlin v., 20

"The Stigma Is Always There" (Freedberg), 102–103

Streib, Victor L., 8–9, 83

Strengthening Forensic Science in the United States: A Path Forward (Forensic Science Committee), 107

Strickland, Ted, 59

Strickland v. Washington, 33–34, 98

Strikes. *See* Peremptory challenges

Sudan, executions in, 127

Summerlin, Schriro v., 20–21

Summerlin, Warren, 20

Summerlin v. Stewart, 20

"Supreme Court to Hear Appeal of Mexican Death Row Inmate" (Greenhouse), 132

Swain v. Alabama, 50–51

Syria, executions in, 127

T

"Tarnish on the 'Gold Standard': Recent Problems in Forensic DNA Testing" (Thompson), 107

Taylor, Marisa, 66

Taylor, Stephen, 37

Taylor, Williams v., 33–35, 65

Tennessee, executions in, 114

Tennessee, Payne v., 48

Terre Haute, Indiana, 64

Terrorism, changes in state laws and, 55

Terrorist Bombings Convention Implementation Act, 62

Tessmer, John, 41